ACKNOWLEDGEMENTS

Editor - Colin McAlpin
Sub Editors - Orla Wilkinson and Elizabeth Stewa
Commercial Consultant - Catherine O'Hara.
Image Scanning - Vincent Agnew, Gregory McToal, and Adam Byrne of Scan Images Services, Craigavon.

Ladbrokes

GRATEFUL thanks to

Jim Gracey - Group Sports Editor, *Belfast Telegraph/Sunday Life.*
Paul Ferguson - Acting Sports Editor, *Sunday Life.*
Deric Henderson - Head of *Press Association* Ireland
Steven Beacom - Sports Editor, *Belfast Telegraph.*
Thomas Hawkins - Sports Editor, *Irish News.*
Paul Tweed, Senior Partner, Johnsons Solicitors, Belfast.
Holly Reid - USA National Archives and Records Administration.
Jim Parker 11 - Double Delta Industries Archival Research International & Pike Military Research at Woodbine, Maryland. USA.
Tommy McDonald, Peter McCaughan and Fred Bottomley of Impact Printing, Ballycastle.
Research included the Web sites of *Boxrec.com* and *Google.co.uk.*
Newspapers and magazines used during historical research were *Irish Independent, Belfast Telegraph, News Letter, Irish Press, Northern Whig, Irish News* and *The Ring Magazine.*
Grateful appreciation to the Newspaper Library staff, especially Brian Girvin and ex-fighter Sean McCafferty at Central Library, Belfast.
Thank you very much Mr Eastwood, for the frank interviews.
This book would also not be possible but for the willing co-operation of all the interviewees.

PHOTOGRAPHS in this publication are mainly from the Eastwood family Collection, mostly commissioned through Allan J McCullough, late of Twaddell Avenue, Belfast.
Also pictures by kind permission of . . .
Press Association Photos - Suzy Harrison.
Associated Press Images, via PA - Kezia Storr.
Irish News, Belfast - through Ann McManus, Hugh Russell, Brendan Murphy and Librarian Kathleen Bell.
Belfast Telegraph Newspapers Limited - through Group Sports Editor Jim Gracey, Steven Beacom, *Belfast Telegraph* Sports Editor, and Librarian Paul Carson.
Sunday Life through Paul Ferguson, Acting Sports Editor.
Tracy O'Toole, King's Hall, Belfast.
US National Archives Photographs (No. 236).
Some pictures also sourced to the late Belfast press photographers Eddie Dineen, George Craig and Trevor Dickson.
Copyright holders of some photographs could not be established, despite a widespread search.
Every effort was made to source all pictures.
We apologise if, by being unable to trace other photograph source, we have failed to acknowledge copyright material.
* Cover design by Impact, Ballycastle.

Front cover photograph by kind permission of *Sunday Life, Belfast Telegraph* Newspapers Limited. Picture by Stephen Wilson.
Back cover photograph of King's Hall, Belfast, by kind permission Tracy O'Toole.

Printed by Impact Design, Print and Publishing, Ballycastle, in association with Glendun Publishing (denisjohn@utvinternet.com).

DENIS O'HARA is a highly respected Irish journalist, who has majored in boxing, soccer, golf, Gaelic football and hurling. Born in the Glens of Antrim, his career began in the *Irish News* in October 1959, and he also went on to be a staff reporter with the Belfast *News Letter.*

He had varied Freelance contract work with the *Sunday News, Independent Newspapers. News Letter, Sunday Life, Press Association Teletext, Downtown Radio, Ulster Television,* and for a period of 17 years with the *Sunday Express* - using the pseudonym of Bill Parke.

His interest in boxing began at Juvenile level. He was a member of clubs at Larne, Queen's University and Immaculata - where, for a short period, he was the Belfast club's President. A winner of two Ulster Colleges' hurling titles, with St MacNissi's College (Garron Tower), and one Ulster minor hurling title with Antrim, he is a founder member and past Chairman of the Northern Ireland Football Writers' Association and the Irish Golf Writers' Association. He is also an original member of the GAA All-Star Selection Committee, a founder member and past Captain of the Belfast Press Golf Society, and a past Captain of Cushendall Golf Club (1983).

CONTENTS

INTRODUCTION

BERNARD JOSEPH EASTWOOD, born on March 26, 1932, in Cookstown, County Tyrone, became a self made success on a massive scale, both in business and as a global influence in boxing. From the moment he signed a young Barry McGuigan on professional forms the world looked on in awe, transfixed by the amazingly meteoric rise of BJ's prospect to prize-fight fame and fortune.

That was at the start of 1981. Four years later, Eastwood was to achieve his dream of steering a home-bred Irish boxer to world title honours. On a uniquely emotional and balmy summer's night at Shepherd's Bush, in west London, 'Clones Cyclone' McGuigan, then moulded into a magnificently aggressive fighting machine, won the WBA Featherweight belt.

Tragically, the Eastwood-McGuigan stairway to stardom disintegrated twelve months after the epic beating of Panamanian legend Eusebio Pedroza. The alliance imploded, after McGuigan lost his title to Texan Steve Cruz at Las Vegas, in mid-summer 1986. Ever since the subsequent bust-up, leading to acrimonious and enormously expensive court cases, the man who worked 24/7 to not only mastermind McGuigan's charge to universal acclaim but also produce five other World champions, retained an almost reclusive vice-like grip on his innermost thoughts of the unsavoury side of the saga. Until now, that is.

He revealed how the sickening split between manager and fighter might well have been avoided, or at least delayed. Eastwood insisted McGuigan would have become a two-weight World champion had the fighter listened to his advice, and made a temporary move up a weight category. I have seen a contract once worth $775,000 that was signed and sealed near the end of 1985 by Eastwood and ring legend Wilfredo Gomez. The Puerto Rican agreed to defend his WBA Junior Lightweight title against McGuigan, and with Eastwood Promotions in charge of selecting the venue.

Sadly, a glamour fight, and one that would not have affected McGuigan's status as Featherweight king, was spurned. Instead, the champion, after a mandatory defence against American Bernard Taylor in the King's Hall, Belfast, made a second voluntary Championship outing in a million-dollar match in Las Vegas that led to the end of dream time.

The once great and virtually unbeatable partnership that brought so much joy to a people heavily burdened by the violence and tragedy of 'The Troubles' in Northern Ireland was already beginning to fracture, more hostile than happy. The rancour that emanated from the rift between Eastwood and McGuigan will, unsurprisingly, remain forever one of the great tragedies of world boxing. I found this a difficult part of the story to portray in the remarkable adventures of B. J. Eastwood.

The hurt remains at 'The Hill', the Eastwood mansion that rests in the Craigavad stockbroker belt east of Belfast, in Holywood, County Down. Despite the many successes of BJ and wife Frances, during a fairytale life that secured millionaire status from a stupendously lucrative bookmaking empire, there is that one serious blot in the memory bank. Even though Eastwood came out on top from the ugliness of the closing High Court case of 1992, I could sense the serious angst still lingered in the air when it came down to amplifying that high-profile part of the family's history. I suspect the Eastwoods will never forgive, nor forget.

BJ emphasised he did not seek the odious ending to his fabulously exciting adventure with McGuigan. It remains a deep mental scar in the history of Eastwood's vibrant progress in business, from the day he left the family home in Cookstown to branch out as a modest small-time publican in Carrickfergus, County Antrim.

Always with the steadying influence of childhood sweetheart Frances, the teenage Eastwood progressed from being a 'mine host' in a modest ale house to adding a humble small-change illegal bookmaking enterprise in the historic harbour town on the shores of Belfast Lough, and also further up the Antrim coast at nearby Larne, before creating an empire of 55 bookmaker shops throughout Northern Ireland.

Headquarters of the enterprise were in Chapel Lane, Belfast, and just a few strides around the corner was the setting for his famous Castle Street gym, where Eastwood, a man with a Midas Touch and not afraid to take gambles, abdicated his high status in world boxing in 1992. Also referred to as Barney Eastwood, and once a leading figure in greyhound and horse racing, he pulled down the curtain on the staggeringly successful family bookmaking business in February 2008.

Fifty-five years after BJ and Frances decided to take a huge risk by selling the pub in Carrickfergus, and really dipping into the fiercely competitive, almost cut-throat, bookmaking business, they sold the chain of shops in a deal worth £135 million to the Ladbrokes Irish section of

North West Bookmakers Limited. There was obvious nostalgia in the Eastwood family once the deal was done. The offer from the UK gambling giants was one too good to refuse. So, with the shutters down on both his boxing and bookmaking interests, I felt it a fitting time to reflect on the B.J. Eastwood phenomenon as a top bookmaker in Ireland and a leading maker and shaker in World professional boxing during a good chunk of four decades.

The two enterprises went hand in glove. The gambling game allowed Eastwood the financial clout to follow his dream as a fight promoter, and more importantly as a boxing manager. He attended major shows in Belfast, then became a professional promoter, and later progressed to be a manager of global acclaim. His careful cultivation of McGuigan to World Featherweight Championship laurels, during the first half of the 1980's, was one of the most exhilarating eras of Irish boxing. His name is synonymous with McGuigan in that rip-roaring rise to glory.

Initially, Eastwood had one target in mind, to charter a path of thrilling progress and spectacular success for McGuigan. The spin-off from the Cyclone's swift march to universal supremacy was to guide other boxers to World titles, and also a host of fighters to lower level Championships. His other chief credits as a kingmaker supreme were Larne's Dave 'Boy' McAuley, Venezuela's Crisanto 'Claws' Espana, Liverpool's Paul 'Hoko' Hodkinson, Luxembourg-based Fabrice Benichou, and Panamanian Victor 'Toby' Cordoba.

It is a subjective exercise when trying to precisely quantify Eastwood's contribution to world boxing, but he richly deserves a lofty place in the pantheon of Irish sport. In 1991, he was recognised as the World's top fight manager by the World Boxing Association, the first Irishman to reach such heady heights. He reigned as one of the Tsars of world boxing until June 1992, when Dave McAuley packed it in, after the IBF Flyweight champion lost his title to Colombian Rodolfo Blanco in Bilbao. This then, is the colourful story of a true Irish sporting icon - B. J. Eastwood.

(Denis O'Hara - March, 2010)

1
GUARD DOGS

GERMAN shepherd dogs kept a watchful eye on the master. They prowled outside the doors and windows at The Hill on the outskirts of Holywood, County Down, noting every move of the folks involved in animated conversion inside Eastwood's favourite meeting room. I knew it would be unwise to make sudden moves.

One foolish wave of a hand, to press home a viewpoint, and suddenly a guard dog would be growling outside a window or menacingly trying to smash down the glass-panelled door. Fittingly, former fighter Danny Juma and also Ray Boyd, the man who drove the World champions for Eastwood Promotions during the hey-day times, kept the canines quiet. Eastwood seemed to relate to the power such devoted dogs can command, and conversely how he had their total respect and attention. The point wasn't lost on me. This was my first day to try and scratch below the surface of an astonishingly successful business and sporting career. My objective was to formulate a balanced and objective narrative.

It may appear Eastwood enjoyed a favoured life, massive dollops of loot just dropping on his lap. That was far from reality. You don't have to be high in the Mensa charts to accept Eastwood did not get to the top, both in the ruthlessly competitive world of bookmaking, boxer management, boxing promoting, and property tycoonery, without being a really hard-nosed gent. He knew he had to be up early in the morning to stay with the moves of the big boys of World boxing, such as Don King, Bob Arum, Louis Spada, and WBA acolyte Jose 'Pepe' Cordero. With a knowing grin he conceded a little bit of chicanery helped along the way. Then he set out the ground rules for the trip down memory lane.

"There are things I am prepared to tell you, and other deals I cannot reveal, even to this day. It was certainly an eye opener for me when the time came in boxing that I had to make contact with the top people. Now, let's get down to business. Tell me what you want to know," Eastwood said as he faced a cluttered desk, and looked out towards Belfast Lough as he carefully pondered my questions. In the middle of the large room, a place you had the feeling was the hub of the empire, sat a full-sized snooker table that once belonged to the McAlinden family of Belfast Celtic Football Club and Celtic Park greyhound stadium fame.

It supported pile upon pile of business folders, family photographs, and old boxing paraphernalia. It was as if there was a strong link with most of Eastwood's amazing life strewn throughout this room. My efforts in trying to delve into the good and the bad memories cast an early changing mixture of joy and sombre reflection on the face of the great man. He's cute, though. Always the quick thinker on his feet, he could suddenly change the subject by pointing out the window to the heavy set figure of Juma working on the front lawn. "There's the man who drew with World champion Robin Reid, when nobody gave him a hope. Danny Juma was a really tough guy, a very strong super-middleweight." Juma, born in Accra, was the visible link to the boxing past. He was the gardener in charge of maintaining the twelve acres at The Hill.

After viewing the glittering gallery of fight memorabilia it was down other avenues of the punching past to the obvious end game, when the Irish boxing world of Eastwood and McGuigan was irrevocably shredded in the Nevada desert during mid summer 1986. The core ingredient in the B. J. Eastwood success story in boxing was his nurturing of McGuigan to a World belt in 1985. I pondered the thought, if there had been no Clones Cyclone connection there might well have been no fame game, and conversely no ultimate heartbreak.

I suspected the sores created by one of the biggest manager-boxer bust-ups in the history of world prize-fighting were as fresh over a quarter-century after of the ill-fated 1986 McGuigan-Steve Cruz World Championship contest in Las Vegas. It was a sad saga, never to be air-brushed out of either camp. The do's and don'ts, and where-to-fors of the depressing legal battles were garishly illustrated by the searching glare of the print, radio and television media. Not unlike the often unremittingly ugliness of a high-profile divorce case, there is no denying this was a bitter and protracted feud. The cruel ending was light years way from Eastwood's origins in County Tyrone.

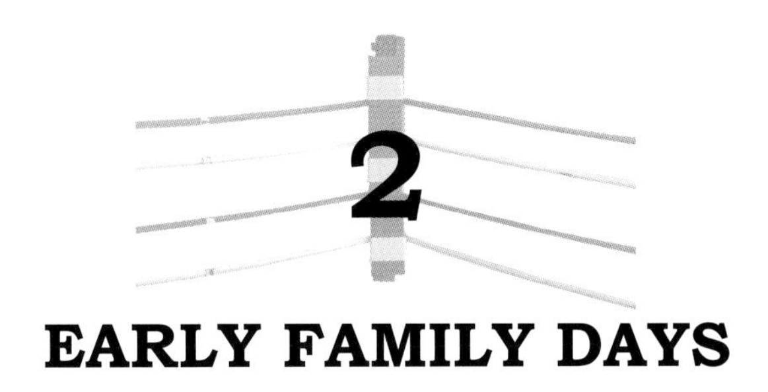

2

EARLY FAMILY DAYS

EASTWOOD was the youngest of eight children. He was nine years of age when rocked by the sudden death of his father John, in 1941. His mother Mary, I suspect, was the main inspiration and influence in the overall Eastwood family success story, one that meandered through varied business enterprises.

Many forces helped to mould the sharp mind of a young Eastwood, and none more than his mother - a resolute and enterprising lady of substance. She became the firm guiding light for the family. Her maiden name was Mary Gertrude Campbell, from nearby Ballinderry. She was 25 when she married 33-year-old John Eastwood.

BJ, whose father died at 58 and his mother when 59 years of age, reflected with warmth on his childhood days: "My mother was a great woman. We had a hardware shop in Cookstown. Her father went to the United States as a barman, and ended up owning a pub in Philadelphia. He did well in America. There was that adventurous spirit to go into business, and there was a good work ethic." His father John Charles Eastwood, died of a heart problem. BJ's grandfather was in the R.I.C. (Royal Irish Constabulary), and he contended if his dad had been half-an-inch taller, the requirement then was six feet, it is highly likely he too would have been in the police force. Where did the Eastwoods originally hail from, I asked.

He replied: "I heard it said that way back in the mists of time the Eastwoods were English people. Our family history reveals my ancestors came originally to Ireland from the Nottingham area. I suppose they were

Planters. I imagine somewhere down the line they took up with Irish girls, married, and became Roman Catholics. On my mother's side, her mother was a Lavery and came from the country area of Ardboe, County Tyrone. John Lavery, the painter, was from that family circle."

Incidentally, the late Sir John Lavery is regarded as one of Ireland's most accomplished portrait painters. Born in Belfast, in March 1856, he died in January 1941, at the house of his step-daughter Mrs John McEnery at Kilmoganny, County Kilkenny. He was 84. Lavery studied in the Glasgow School of Art, and at Haldane Julian in Paris, before being commissioned in 1888 to paint the State visit of Queen Victoria to the Glasgow International Exhibition. He moved from Glasgow to London, and became an associate of James Mitchell Whistler. He was appointed an official artist for World War One, but couldn't travel to the Western Front because of illness and an injury sustained in a car crash.

At the age of 34 he married Kathleen MacDermott, who sadly died a year later - after the birth of a daughter who became the wife of Lord Sempill. In 1910 he re-married to Irish-American Hazel Martin of Chicago, who was also an artist and her husband's favourite model. She was to become the model of the Irish colleen depicted on the Irish Free State currency notes, designed by Lavery (in 1928).

After the Great War he was knighted, in 1918. Lavery, known as a leading social painter, was elected to the Royal Academy in 1921. He became interested in his Irish roots, and what was happening during the Irish War of Independence and the Irish Civil War. Sir John's noted portraits include one of Michael Collins. In 1929, he made a significant contribution of his paintings to the Ulster Museum and Art Gallery at Stranmillis, and in the 1930's moved from London to live in Ireland. He received Honorary Degrees from both Queen's University, Belfast, and University College, Dublin. Lavery was also made a freeman of Belfast and Dublin.

No wonder Eastwood developed an acute interest in the works of world-renowned artists. He also inherited a high devotion to hard work from the same family strain, and said: "My mother was a good business women, and many customers came into the shop in what was essentially a market town. They were regulars, who came from Ardboe, Ballinderry, and all around the Cookstown vicinity. My mother attended the shop, and looked after the house as well. She worked morning, noon and night, a 16 hour-a-day woman. Anyway, if you were in our shop when she closed it for half-an-hour or so, at one o'clock every day, you were offered a cup of tea and a biscuit, maybe a wee bit of dinner - a spud or two."

There was obvious admiration in Eastwood's tone for his mother, a lady of single-minded determination who knew how to handle trade. She commanded enormous respect in the Cookstown area, and reared a family of four boys and four girls. BJ was the baby. Next was Elizabeth - a Mrs Lynch living in Dublin; then it was Margaret Cooke, married to a chemist near Holywood, County Down. Billy and wife Pauline lived at Lisburn. Gertie married Michael Bodenham, a former British Army officer during World War Two and part of a perfume-producing family in England. Another sister, Johanna died in 2007. She was married to the late Dr Foncie McLynn in Cookstown. Eastwood's brother Jack ran the old family hardware shop in Cookstown. He died aged 69. He was married into the Begley family of Pomeroy, to an aunt of fabled country and western singer Philomena Begley. The oldest Eastwood boy, Tommy Joe, who had the shoe shops and various other business enterprises in Cookstown and Dublin, died aged 55 in 1974.

American Armed Forces forged a character-building link for a wide-eyed Eastwood during the early years of World War Two. At first, the sport of boxing was the common denominator, but then he saw other outlets to expand his own mini black market enterprise around the Cookstown area. The American soldiers arrived during the early 1940's. Theodore Delano Roosevelt, President of the United States, sent his troops to the theatre of war after the Japanese attacked Pearl Harbour on December 7, 1941. World War Two records reveal the Americans sent reinforcements to Iceland and Northern Ireland in early 1942.

The first soldiers from the American Expeditionary Force to move into the European war zone went through the Northern Ireland launching pad. Under the code name of MAGNET, the Yanks were billeted in specially selected bases throughout Northern Ireland, including County Tyrone camps at Cookstown and in Clontoe, near Ardboe. The first US contingent of 4,058 left New York on January 14, 1942, and arrived at Dufferin Quay, Belfast, on January 26. A second batch of some 7.000 in a 21-ship convoy arrived on March 2. By June of that year the troop total was 41,205.

History reveals the first recorded American to step ashore in Northern Ireland was Milburn Henke from Huchinson, Minnesota. He was a member of Company B, 133rd Infantry of the 34th Red Bull Division. The

Americans became an influence once they were stationed around Cookstown. Eastwood was still a student at the Public Elementary School in the town when the Americans hit town. "I suppose I was not fully aware of exactly why they were there. I knew there was a war going on in Europe, that Belfast had been attacked by German bombers. It seemed unreal at the time. We appeared to be so far away from it all, until the American base camps were set up."

He looked back at a time that proved horrendous in terms of world peace. The cruel loss of life in World War One was described in somewhat contradictory terms as the 'Great War'. It was to be the last conflict of nations on planet earth. How wrong the predictions of politicians and statesmen proved to be.

In 1942, World Heavyweight champion Joe Louis Barrow joined the US Forces. For a short spell the famous 'Brown Bomber' was stationed in the American maintenance depot at Langford Lodge, outside Antrim town. He also made a few appearances on Balmoral's parkland golf course in south Belfast. The base that housed Louis opened for the Americans in July 1942, near the village of Crumlin, was on the opposite shoreline of Lough Neagh to the camps in and around Cookstown. In 1943, Americans were also training in the Sperrins and Mourne Mountains.

On November 23, 1943, a subordinate Quartermaster base was set up at Moneymore, a few miles north of Cookstown. The unexpected invasion of American troops, also armed to the teeth with chewing gum, cigarettes and money to burn during a difficult time of severe rationing in Northern Ireland, provided an unexpected outlet to a very resourceful B. J. Eastwood. Before a rewarding passage of profound influence, that helped shape the fertile mind of the youngster, he progressed through the school system. His first brush with education was in the Convent of Mercy school run by nuns. He moved from there to the Boys' Public Elementary School, which was a Catholic school.

His boxing interest started early, at primary school. After a Miss Kelly taught him in preps, the beginner's section, he moved into the next class where the Master was a Mr Finbarr Leyden. This was to provide the basic step in boxing for the youngster. Mr Leyden came originally from Cork. He was a follower of boxing, just a general interest yet he was always talking about the sport. This fascinated Eastwood, who described Mr Leyden as "a tough old boy who would give you a slap with a stick."

Through all the talk about the noble art of self-defence, Eastwood became extremely interested in the sport. During that period he made a first trip to Dublin, on a family outing, and came back with a spanking new set of boxing gloves. He went with his mother and a couple of his brothers on an exciting train journey, and saw a set of boxing gloves for sale in the shop window of Clery's store on Dublin's main thoroughfare, O'Connell Street.

"That was what I wanted," he said, "I whinged at my mother and big brothers so much I managed to get the gloves. But we were in for a scare when going home on the train. There was the Customs & Excise stop in those days at Goraghwood, outside Newry. That was where you were searched, at the Border, to make sure you were not smuggling contraband from the Republic of Ireland into Northern Ireland. The Customs Officers took us all off the train. The bits and pieces we had with us - - they took the whole lot, boxing gloves and all. A brother of mine chirped up: 'Ah jeez, the wee lad has been waiting to get those gloves for years. He is just interested in boxing. Surely you are not going to take them away from the kid?' “The brothers kept at this Customs Officer, who eventually weakened, saying: 'All the rest stays, but he can have the gloves.' That was all we salvaged from the smuggling trip."

Here was the true beginning of the Eastwood link to the fight game. Delighted to have the boxing gloves, he began beating up an old canvas bag stuffed with hay. There was also some sparring against his brothers in the family shed. Word leaked out about BJ's new interest, and what was going down behind the out-house door. Master Leyden suggested he bring the gloves to the school. Eastwood obliged, and the schoolteacher began instructing the willing kids in the class how to put up a defence, how to throw a jab. Youngsters began taking a fighting posture, not unlike the way James J. Corbett posed for pictures.

Eastwood added: "The next thing was he started pairing us for boxing, all the boys from my class. We had boxing three times a week, and always after he lit a cigarette - which was exactly at three o'clock every day to signal the end of classes." Master Leyden used to smoke Gold Flake cigarettes, according to Eastwood, and when he lit up his cigarette at the end of school it was also the signal to begin the boxing. A few of his pals from downtown, people he socialised with, were allowed to see the fisticuffs. As the boxing improved, and the talent became better, more people wanted to see Master Leyden's kids in ring action.

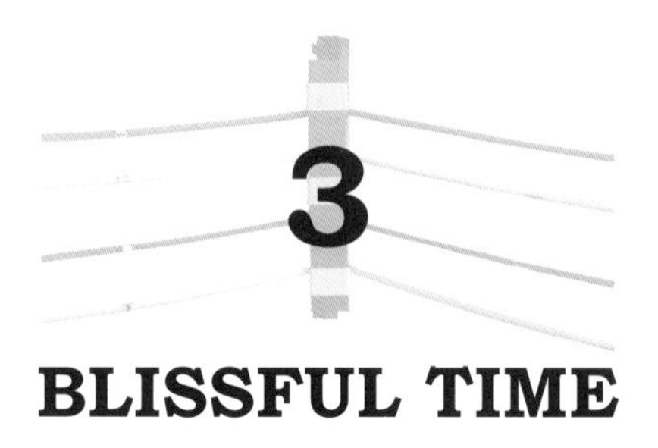

BLISSFUL TIME

EASTWOOD recalled with relish those happy days: "It was magic. The better we became the Master matched us with boys from two classes higher than us, boys who were two to three years older. Still, we were always able to beat the bigger boys. We had the advantage of some tutoring from Mr Leyden. So, we were then matched with the senior boys. It was like a bantamweight fighting a middleweight."

He also remembered the dramatic change after the American soldiers arrived to settle in various camps in and around Cookstown. There was the Parish Hall, which the Americans used for boxing tournaments. The Yanks had a boxing ring, and all the rest of high quality equipment for training. Fascinated, Eastwood never saw the likes before. "The Americans had everything needed for boxing," he added, "The other soldiers stationed in the area, mainly from England, had nothing. The Americans sparred every day. It was a fabulous time."

Cookstown's mile-long main thoroughfare sometimes turned to bedlam when the Americans came to town at weekends. Young wide-eyed Eastwood soaked it all up: "It was like a scene from an old-time Wild West frontier town. You had the madness and mayhem of Friday and Saturday nights, and especially if it was a pay night for the soldiers." He explained the local police had no control over the members of the American forces. That dubious duty fell to the Military Police: "The MPs patrolled the streets, English MPs, American MPs. There were MPs for the soldiers, and MPs for the sailors, the airmen, all in charge of their own people. Apparently there was occasional fighting among themselves."

According to BJ it was like Western film scene of namesake Clint Eastwood riding into town. After a feed of Guinness, the protagonists could be American army guys against the sailors, or Americans against the British. "About the town of Cookstown, at that time, were a few local boys who were reputed to be handy with their fists," added Eastwood, "One fellow named Farmer McKenna, even though he wasn't a farmer, could chin everybody. I also had a brother Billy, who was also very useful operator in the cobbles, too - in a street scrap, but the Americans were in a different class when it came down to fighting.

"However, the professional boxers among them very seldom got into trouble. If they were being pestered they always said: 'Have a bit of sense' or, 'Take him away, please'. Sometimes a fellow wouldn't take heed, and when coming in to take a swing would be chinned by a short, quick punch. Just one shot, and bing - and the American would turn his back and walk away. The professional boxer obviously could not be caught hitting anyone, and especially an American professional fighter hitting a civilian."

Once the general mayhem started the MPs would arrive to try and stop the street brawling. They would wade into everybody, and take no prisoners. As a result of all that, eager Eastwood became more curious to learn that clinical, snappy way to fire a punch. One punching problem facing the young adventurer was that he was a southpaw who did not have a clue how to cope with a fellow portsider. The punching puzzle came to light when Master Leyden matched him against a class colleague Freddie Murphy.

The kids were arguably among the best boxers in the class, yet Eastwood always seemed to experience terrible trouble against Freddie. That was before the Americans came to Cookstown. The schoolboys really had no proper schooling in boxing then, on what you should do or should not do in certain situations. "I remember saying to myself: how can I work this out. I was strong and athletic. Why can I not get through to this guy? There were bigger and tougher fellows in the class, yet I could sail around them nicely. Anyway, the Americans came. They had me in the ring this day against a guy from another school, and I had the same problem.

"It was then I was told my difficulty was that I was a southpaw. What made things awkward for me was that the lad I was boxing was also a southpaw. I just did not know how to handle another southpaw. Simple as that. One of the Yanks, a former boxer from New York, nicknamed Scotty, tried to turn me round, to orthodox. I couldn't. He then told me how to fight a southpaw. He showed me what I was doing wrong."

Those free lessons way back in the early 1940's stuck by Eastwood, proving that with patience, when preparing a fighter, there is a way around a problem in the ring. He was also left-handed, and used to lift the pen and write with his left hand. Master Leyden would make him put his left hand behind his back, and force him try to write with his right hand. Eventually a weary and aching Eastwood couldn't keep the left hand up his back no longer.

He would bring it down, return to writing with his left, and then he'd be smacked on the back of the knuckles by the master's cane. It is no surprise to find the pupil has since been right-handed with a pen, and does all his writing with his right hand. He was also left-sided when kicking a football, as he proved to great reward as a teenager. Eastwood had other things to do before then. He used his head to great effect after the Yanks arrived. He could sniff out financial openings. Even at that young age he had an automatic aptitude to turn a fast dollar. He was born with a quick-thinking approach of never missing the opportunity to make a shilling. A black market business was there for the taking, he reckoned.

As a kid in short trousers he enjoyed the excitement and the adrenaline rush of the chase as much as the reward. The arrival of American soldiers was just the perfect playing field to test and hone his skills at buying and selling. He used to hang about the different US Army bases, where there was money to be made. There was one camp base at Molesworth Street that housed a few hundred soldiers. There were bases at outlying districts, including at Springhill, Moneymore, five miles away. At Magherafelt there were also English soldiers based. There were sailors, paratroopers, all kinds of guys camped there. His first encounter in making money then was when he used to run messages for the Yanks.

"I would have done anything for them, for money - which was very tight in those days. Everybody was skint. I wasn't the only one at this, as other boys were doing it. I had my own men, my American clients as it were." He knew all the different boxers in the American camp. All this intrigued him. There is that indefinable attraction of boxing, and also being around boxers. If anybody in the American camp was involved in the boxing, they were on his team. He was getting them whatever they wanted. They would seek all sorts of things, but goods were scarce in those days.

"Don't forget," explained Eastwood, "We were well into the War years. You needed coupons to purchase goods. Whiskey was one of the things the Yanks wanted. Generally, you could not get whiskey for love nor money, but I had a source. I had an uncle, Tom Eastwood, who was a veterinarian surgeon and also owned a pub. I used to go into the country with him, when he was attending to sick farming stock: calves, horses with colic, and so forth. He let me drive his Austin 10. That was my perk. I was around nine or ten years of age then. Two cushions were placed under my backside - so that I was propped up behind the steering wheel.

"At his pub he would have had two or three hogsheads of this full-proof DWD Whiskey that was bought in bulk by pub owners. It was 'unreduced' at that stage. Then it was made legal. It was reduced in strength, by putting water and colouring into it. It was clear and colourless when he got it first. It would then be taken out of casks and bottled. You were some performer if you could get a bottle of whiskey. I would get a bottle off him for the Americans, and to be able to get two bottles was something special. I had to give him the black market price, and then I had to get a turn out of the transaction. My bottles of whiskey were the best, okay for the Yanks. There was also a load of hooch, if you wanted it - mountain dew from the Tyrone hills. Obviously, there were bottles of moonshine the Americans loved to get their hands on."

He ran messages for bases in the town, and the soldiers always gave him a tip. If he didn't arrive home with money in his pockets he came back with a packet of Lucky Strike, Camel, Chesterfield, or one of the other brands of American cigarettes. He was starting to smoke on the sly then, too. "There was also always plenty of chewing gum. The Americans would unexpectedly give you things. If you said to them: 'That's a lovely thing you are wearing' they would say: 'Here, have it'. My mother loved me to associate with them, a link from the past because her father had been in America. She was also in the USA for a time, as a young girl working in her father's pub.

"She used to say: 'Isn't it an awful pity of those young men - so far away from home, going to war.' The Americans were always very good to me. I was hoping then it would never end, but all of a sudden it did. I thought those days would never stop. I was never off the batter. Those were exceptional times for me, and I was also really hooked on the boxing bit. I didn't know until later in life the great Joe Louis had been stationed close by, just across Lough Neagh."

Eastwood's ring education and flourishing personal enterprises suddenly came to a halt. The idyllic time ended when the Yanks upped stakes, and left town to begin combat in the serious business of war. "I remember the Americans leaving, all the battalions departing, all the sadness. They had a parade up the big main street at Cookstown. There were thousands of them in the farewell. They all stood to attention, and played their anthems before taking off. Everybody was crying, because they were going away to the war in Europe. Many of the Americans at Cookstown were paratroopers, and some were never to go home again. The paratroopers had special boots they nicked with a knife. They marked notches, which I believe was to indicate how many parachute jumps they made."

4

CARDINAL SIN

CARDINAL John Francis Dalton, the former Catholic Archbishop of Armagh and Primate of All-Ireland, unwittingly contributed to the expulsion of a 14-year-old Eastwood from St Patrick's College, Armagh. The incident ironically pointed the young firebrand in the direction of world fame and an immense fortune.

Born in Claremorris, County Mayo, on October 11, 1882, Cardinal Dalton took over from Cardinal Joseph MacRory, who died on October 13, 1945. Dalton was listed the 100th successor to St Patrick, and became Archbishop of Armagh in 1946. He was promoted to Cardinal by Pope Pius X11 in November, 1952. This latter date resulted in a special occasion at St Patrick's College, and ironically and dramatically changed the course of Eastwood's career. Destiny took a hand, and he maintained Cardinal Dalton's visit did him a favour.

"I went to St Patrick's College as a boarder, at 12 years of age. At the age of 14 things changed as I got involved in a bit of a fracas. A couple of senior students were also involved. It may now seem a relatively harmless incident. At school there was little to eat, and boys became very hungry. It was a time after Cardinal MacRory died, and we were expecting Cardinal Dalton, who was to take over as Primate of Ireland. There was a big welcoming party for him. They were cooking in the College kitchen over a period of seven or eight days beforehand.

"It was a massive affair, the luminaries of the Catholic hierarchy about to look on and join in the great occasion. Anyway, a couple of days before Cardinal Dalton was about to arrive in Armagh the smell of this grub was putting everybody mad in St Pat's. There was a bit of a night raid, you could call it, on the kitchen - and a lot of grub went missing. A few boys were accused. I was also accused, and told not to come back to the College. It may now seem not such a big deal, but there you are. It was exactly what I wanted, because I hated school. By then, I was a kid who was street-wise. I had no interest in school. I wasn't made for school. The only thing I liked about being in the Armagh college was that I played in Gaelic football teams. I was in the Rannafast Cup squad, although only a beginner there.

"I smoked too, then, and you were not allowed to, obviously. If you were caught, you went to the Dean's room. He beat you on the rear end with a cane, until you were red and blue. I was relieved to be out of there, back on the streets at Cookstown. I went to work for my older brother, Tommy Joe, who had the boot and shoe shop in Cookstown. I was happier on the streets than boarding at College.

"I don't know if it was the earlier influence of meeting the American troops, but I was free again. I enjoyed the wheeler dealing. I hated having to study at school. I was interested in other things, getting involved in the action. I also used to kick up a storm in our house, to get to football matches and boxing shows with my brother. My mother would say to Tommy Joe: 'If Bernard is not going, you are not going.' I usually managed to get to some of the big fight shows in Belfast."

Tommy Joe maintained the family's boot and shoe interests in Cookstown. Incidentally, BJ's father could make a first class pair of boots. From that, his brother, Charles Eastwood, opened a boot shop in Cookstown. He had a very good shop, and was doing well. Nonetheless, Tommy Joe decided he was going to do something similar. He fancied starting in opposition to his uncle, rented an empty shop, and started in the shoe business. The progressive Tommy Joe, once the chairman of the Fr Rock's GAC, Cookstown, also ran a small bookmaking enterprise in Cookstown, after winning part of the shop when the bookmaker couldn't pay him on a bet. He took over a half-share of the book, and used to send BJ to check on what was going on. That was a significant introduction to the requirements of the betting world.

The Eastwood family also had uncles and cousins who owned pubs, so it was no surprise when Tommy Joe spread his wings to move into that business. He purchased a pub at 29, Patrick Street, The Coomb, Dublin. BJ used to go down there with him, and help out. Apart from that, young Eastwood really didn't have much experience of running a public house, but soon came to know every aspect of that business when he bought a pub in Carrickfergus.

GAELIC GLEE

SHORTLY after the Americans left Cookstown life took on a fresh challenge when the young eagle-eyed Eastwood was encouraged to concentrate on honing his skills in Gaelic football. He started playing the game at ten years of age. He was backed by Tommy Joe, an ardent Gaelic football supporter. After the two years spent in St Patrick's College, Eastwood started to participate in street League football.

He lived in William Street, which was the main shopping area: "On one occasion Tommy Joe brought me to Dublin to see my first big Gaelic football game, at Croke Park. That was a wonderful experience. Tommy Joe always called our Tyrone county team the 'Lily Whites' - not Kildare. It was the name he had for the Tyrone team that featured some outstanding footballers. Iggy Jones was a great player. He was one of the stars at the Armagh college. He was small, devastating, and was at St Patrick's College when I went there."

The iconic Iggy was a Senior player at the College, and also a great all-round athlete. Eastwood knew him well, and also the versatile Eddie Devlin from Coalisland, who became a dentist, and was another exceptional footballer. Devlin played Minor County football during BJ's time in the underage team colours. A couple of years older than Eastwood, he amazingly featured for five years in the Tyrone Minor team. That was an unbelievable feat, starting in Minor county football when he was 13. He was special. After Eastwood began playing for the Cookstown club team, he was picked for the Tyrone Minor '15'. He remained two years in the side, and won one All-Ireland Minor medal in 1948, when the Ulster champions beat a good Dublin team in the final at Croke Park.

That was a wonderful occasion. The report of that final reveals two Cookstown kids did most of the scoring: Eastwood with four points, and Malachy Dargan hitting three scores from a total of ten points against the Dubs. Eddie Devlin was the main man, and the inspirational team captain and the remaining marksman. Eastwood, who didn't progress from Minor to Senior county duty, was eligible to compete for the Minor team of 1949, but Tyrone lost the Ulster and All-Ireland titles when going out of the Provincial Championship after a couple of matches. He played for the Fr Rocks club adult team, but soon walked away from the game.

"Perhaps had I stayed single for a few more years, it is possible I may have played Senior football regularly for Tyrone. But, I have no regrets about that," he insisted, "I enjoy bumping into a few of my Tyrone Minor team colleagues, and chin wagging over old times. When I was playing in the Minor county team, and also for the Fr Rock's club side, the other players generally called me Barney Joe. I meet up from time to time, mostly at Gaelic functions in County Tyrone, with one of the 1948 team members, my good friend John Joe O'Hagan of Coalisland. Not too long ago, in late 2009, I attended his 50th wedding anniversary celebration."

Talented footballer O'Hagan went on to play for the Tyrone's adult team, and with a fair degree of success. Also, two of his sons followed the family tradition to play for the county Senior team. Eastwood said: "At one meeting with John Joe, the young men at the function did not know I played for Tyrone, and that I won a national Under-18 medal. They linked my name to boxing and bookmaking only, not to Gaelic football. I remember John Joe remarking: 'Guess who scored the first point in the 1948 All-Ireland Minor final? It was this man, Barney Joe Eastwood.' They all knew John Joe, but nobody in the room connected me to playing football. I was pleased and very proud when John Joe cleared up the confusion."

O'Hagan, incidentally, was a winner of back-to-back All-Ireland Minor Championship medals, in 1947 and '48. His son Damien, an U-18 ace in 1975, made the county Senior team in 1979. John Joe, 79 years of age in late 2007, said: "Barney Joe was in and out of football very quickly. He is younger than me, while Eddie Devlin and me are the same age. Eastwood was left corner-forward, a good player, a first-class Minor footballer. He was merely 16 in that 1948 team.

"I was playing full-forward, and I remember having bad luck in not scoring a goal - when a shot hit their goalman's knee. We were well over

Dublin. I also recall kicking a ball that broke their full-back's finger. Eastwood, a great lad to solo the ball, would go on terrific runs. He had a superb left boot. In 1948 we were sort of in full-time training. Before the All-Ireland semi final we went to Pomeroy, and stayed in the Parish Hall, with 24 of us in the squad, and the team trainer. We slept in a row of beds up each side of the Hall, stayed there for the fortnight, and trained every day. After beating Galway in the semi-final, at Castlebar, we went back to Pomeroy for another fortnight of full-time training before the final. Gerry Browne of Down was the team coach, taking over from Peter O'Reilly of Dublin, who trained the team in '47. College players made up most of the Tyrone squad.

"I was working in a garage by then. The wages were not big. I looked for compensation for my loss of wages while away with the team. I asked Tyrone officials, and they agreed. It was 50 shillings, or two pounds and a ten bob note in old money. Desperate not to lose the wages was my biggest problem. Anyhow, Barney Joe heard about this, and he said to the officials: 'I am working in a bookmaker's shop in Cookstown, and would also need to be paid.' Barney Joe and me were the two players in the squad to be paid. He was after the bob, the same as myself. We were nearly professional then!"

Tyrone lost the Ulster Championship, going out to Donegal. The referee disallowed a goal in the last kick of the game, in Donegal. Armagh marched on to win the All-Ireland Minor title of 1949. "Eastwood dropped out early from football," stated O'Hagan, "I continued on, but we kept in touch. I also played in a Tyrone club hurling final for Clonoe, but lost to Cappagh. I played Minor football, illegally, for Ballinderry in the Derry county final. Ballinderry lost the game on a protest - not on account of me, but because the team names were not written out on Irish watermark paper."

Incidentally, an interesting point about the 1947 Minor final, against Mayo, is that it featured in a double bill alongside a Junior football final at Croke Park. That was because the All-Ireland Senior final was staged outside Ireland for a first time, in the Polo Grounds, New York, where Cavan beat Kerry in the historic decider. Despite not being involved in the traditional curtain-raiser to the big boys, Tyrone attracted a huge following in Dublin.

O'Hagan remembered: "It was a big occasion for us, yet the wettest day that ever fell. In '48 the Senior final was Cavan against Mayo at Croke

Park, and that was another very big day for us in Dublin. Eddie Devlin was the team captain, along with Harry Hartop in the midfield. Malachy Dargan from Cookstown was centre half-forward, and was a class footballer. He later took ill, and that was the big loss to Tyrone football at that time. When he was a Minor for Tyrone he was also in the Senior county team. He disappeared out of football then. Of the two Minor teams of 1947 and '48 only five players went on to win Ulster Senior title medals, in 1956 and '57. The players were Eddie Devlin, Donal Donnelly, Mick Cushanan, Sean Donnelly and me. Sean was a printer with the old 'Irish Press' newspaper in Dublin."

Eastwood never forgot those early experiences as a player, and kept a close interest in Gaelic games: "I always thought the Antrim team of 1946 was great, with players such as Sean Gibson, Paddy O'Hara, Harry O'Neill, Harry Vernon, George Watterson. My family connection with Gaelic football went back before the formation of the Fr Rocks Club. I had a cousin, Eddie Eastwood, who was a good goalkeeper for the Brian Og team in Cookstown. A number of the Eastwood clan also played rugby for Rainey Endowed College teams at Magherafelt."

6

DYNASTY STARTS

BJ and Frances Brigid Monaghan were teenagers when they married in June 1951, and went straight into relatively unknown territory by purchasing a public house in Carrickfergus. They hardly knew what road to take from Cookstown to the Antrim Coast town on the shores of Belfast Lough. Eastwood was determined to give the vintners' trade a chance. After all, he had a little bit of knowledge about how pubs were run when he occasionally helped his older brother Tommy Joe in Dublin.

Indeed, the Eastwood story might well have taken a different route had Frances and BJ been able to rustle up sufficient cash to buy a pub in Dublin's dockland. "I had this notion I would buy a pub in Dublin. I was close to purchasing one, but there was one big problem. I couldn't dig up enough money to pay for it. £7,000 was the asking price for the business, one that was situated on the North Wall. That was big dough then. It was a lunch-time drinking place, Dockers, Stevedores, and so forth."

He turned his attention to the north end of the island when a pub came up for sale in Carrickfergus, County Antrim. In 1951 the Eastwoods purchased 'The Corner House Bar' for £2,000. The business came on the market at a time when it was nine o'clock evening closing. They lived over the pub. The remarkable achievement in building a bookmaking dynasty had to wait, as they concentrated on pulling pints of porter in a strange town, and raising a family. The determination to succeed in this enterprise epitomises the couple's high work rate mixed with a willingness to take a risk.

Love's young dream first met in the workplace in Cookstown. Frances came to work for Tommy Joe. She was from the village of Loup, outside Moneymore, and rode a bicycle four miles to the main bus station, and then on by bus to Cookstown. "Frances often recalls how her mother used to give her two old pence for a cup of tea," recalled Eastwood, "She had her sandwiches with her. Her weekly wage was one pound (£1), and she was the top paid operator in the shop. Frances was the office secretary, and really good at what she did. I started off at ten shillings a week, and having to do all sorts of hours. I was also driving, delivering stuff. Tommy Joe had branches all over Northern Ireland. You would be on the road early, maybe from seven o'clock in the morning, and not back until eight or nine o'clock in the evening."

Sometimes he'd track down Tommy Joe in Heaney's Public House, where politician Bernadette Devlin's mother was born. "She was a walking Bible, the historian of all that happened in Ireland. That is where Bernadette got it all from, all the knowledge. I remember going to the pub, and waiting outside for Tommy Joe until nine o'clock closing. I was after a Christmas bonus." He secured some successful plea bargaining with big brother, suggesting he should have something extra in his wage packet. He mentioned all the hours he was working.

Other staff members were also talking about the long hours, and asking what was their hours of work. Tommy Joe's reply was: 'Your hours are early and late.' Still, the boss weakened, and handed young brother another half-quid: "I was delighted, and later I met up with Frances. I don't know how long I was going with her, courting, maybe a year when I said to Frances, what about getting married? At that time, I rode a bicycle down to where Frances lived."

BJ and Frances just turned 19 years of age when they married. It was a big undertaking. They were hitched at The Loup, and held the wedding reception in Hall's Hotel, Antrim. Eastwood disclosed: "We went to Dublin for our honeymoon, and stayed for a week in the Wicklow Hotel. Frances still has the bill for the whole show. It cost £10. 12 shillings and 11 pence. That was a big go then, a lot of money. Following my mother's death, in 1950, I had a few bob, but not all that much. She left me a few hundred pounds, and I told Tommy Joe I was going to try and buy a pub in Dublin. Before then, I spent a little bit of time in his public house in Dublin. I remember it was tough pub. Upstairs there was a piano, a singing place."

After the honeymoon, Frances and BJ took the plunge and went straight into the pub business at Carrickfergus. It was a whole strange new world for them, real greenhorns handling a pub among complete strangers. "Frances had never been involved in the workings of a pub. There was a stairway at the side of the bar that led to our living quarters. Another thing I distinctly recall about my first time to live there. I was used to living inland, never at the seaside. The smell of the sea, off Belfast Lough and Irish Sea, made me sick at first, and I hardly went outside the door for three months."

The nearby Courtaulds factory was the big industry employment outlet in the area, and the Eastwoods had a lot of customers coming from there. "We met all types of people," he recalled, "Later on, we built a house, 200 yards out the Belfast Road. A man named Bannon from Larne built it for us, and we didn't leave there until 1972."

The Eastwoods raised a family of seven. By early 2008, they were proud grandparents of 23. The growing dynasty also included one great grandchild. The eldest of the immediate family is Bernard Jnr, better known as Brian or Bruno. Next is Peter, and then Adrian. Fiona is the lone girl, and lives with her own family in London. She is married to Kevin Gardiner from Wales, but holds her own name. Fiona's husband, a banker in London, coined the phrase 'The Celtic Tiger'. Stephen was the fifth born, and then Fintan, who tragically died at 30. The youngest is Fearghal, a shrewd judge of boxing talent and heavily involved in the Eastwood property portfolio. During the vibrant boxing era, Fergal was also a faithful assistant to his father, Eddie Shaw and Paddy Byrne in the corner during most of the big fights.

While the Eastwoods were emerging in Carrickfergus, some of the boys went to study at St Malachy's College, Belfast. In the early Sixties, the kids also became interested in boxing, when their father sponsored amateur shows in Carrickfergus: "Two of my sons, Brian and Peter, boxed on the shows, as five and six stoners. Billy Corbett trained them in the Carrick Club. In 1972, we moved to Craigavad, first living on the shore side of the road outside Holywood, at Gortnagreenan. In 1985 Frances and me then moved to The Hill, a property originally owned by the people who ran the Belfast Shipping Company. They sold it in 1934 to a Mrs

Betty Duffin. She spoke four different languages, was the daughter of the then Belfast Lord Mayor, and lived a good part of her life in France."

He offered an interesting observation on the family progress. The trappings of affluence are there at The Hill, the quality cars a giveaway. He confessed he learned a valuable early personal lesson on how to fly low and fall soft. He lost, as they say, the run of himself during the formative family rise at Carrickfergus. "My first car, when coming up to Carrickfergus from Cookstown, was an old second-hand Austin Ten, but then I went over the top, money-wise, with my next car purchase. It was a brand new Vanguard, and I put Frances and myself in bad debt. I paid £1,200, and borrowed from a bank. Very soon I knew I made a mistake, taking a jump too far, too quickly.

"Then I went back down to a second-hand car, which was a Morris. It was a heap, costing about £150. This third car of ours was really clapped out. It needed a new engine, and used a lot of oil. We were still in the pub business then, and I had to stick with the Morris for a while. There was no other way. Money was very tight. I learned a lesson from that purchase of the new car, when going over my head. I just went too big too fast. Eventually we moved to a new Ford Zodiac." The progression is perhaps best marked by those sleek limousines at Craigavad. He added: "The kids bought me a black (Mercedes Benz), and it is registered BE. J. The Rolls Royce has a County Tyrone number plate, BJI 1. I also have another car, with the number, OKI 111, that belonged to my late son Fintan. The plates came off his Mercedes."

7 BOOKMAKING

GAMBLING instincts were well grounded into a young Eastwood before he began to seriously dabble in the bookmaking business, illegally. BJ and Frances started taking under-the-counter bets in the bar. Workmen came up from the Quay at Carrickfergus, some from anchored coal boats. They had money to spend. The punters normally came into the Eastwood bar around lunchtime, after laying bets with the local bookmaker. They left after a quick pint to go back to work.

In Carrickfergus at that time Bob Gardiner was the 'legal' bookmaker, and was a member of the Turf Guardians' Association. He was better known as the colourful professional boxing promoter who staged major shows in Belfast during the late 1940's, big fight nights generally headlined by World Flyweight champion John 'Rinty' Monaghan. The occasional early closing of Gardiner's bookmaking shop unwittingly and ironically, led to Eastwood taking off on the great adventure to build a bookmaking and boxing empire. He understood the needs of the workmen who returned to his pub around five o'clock, looking for the race results, and then frustratingly finding the bookie's shop was sometimes shut.

The punters couldn't collect on the successful bets laid, and this often created a financial problem. The workmen had no extra money to spend on drink. This inspired a move to eventually make millions for the adventurous Eastwood couple, to start dabbling in the shady side of Northern Ireland's already uncertain and generally unlawful bookmaking trade. Eastwood remembered the first sortie into the gambling business. The razor-sharp mind of the young entrepreneur could see a new avenue developing, solving the problem of punters having winning dockets yet empty pockets.

"Our bar was packed with people standing around with dockets in their pockets, and no dough. So, Frances and I decided to pay out on a few of the dockets, collecting the money the next day from the bookmaker. We moved to getting the race results, working on that side of things. I was never personally into gambling then. I never had a horse or a greyhound in those early days. I had no interest, yet it was not my first experience of gambling, as I helped out my brother Tommy Joe in the bookmaker's shop in Cookstown.

"I remember on a couple of occasions he would send me down to see how it was doing, to look things over. Tommy Joe was into everything. I picked up a few tips from him. He was the eldest in the family, away ahead of me then. Picking up business ideas from him helped Frances and me at Carrickfergus, when we started to pay out on a few dockets. We would then have a pile of dockets, and later on get the money off the local bookmaker. We fiddled at that for a while, and then decided to open a small pitch of our own, in an old store at the back of the pub. At that time nobody was licensed. No legal licences were available for people to run bookmaker offices. If you were in the Turf Guardians' Association you were all right.

"They did a lot of work for the establishment, like sending out cars to take the electorate to the polls, but the Turf Guardians wouldn't let us in. There were people outside the system - like Jimmy Nelson, Johnny Magennis, George Clarke, me . . . over forty of us in all, and we were called 'The Pirates'. The police clamped down on us, and along with the punters, we were fined every two weeks or so. The local Turf Guardian bookmaker would merely be fined about once a year. That all changed, however. There were trial cases. It was put up to certain judges asking why we were being consistently fined. It was ridiculous. Things began to change then. A new Bill was introduced in the late 1950's, to licence bookmakers in Northern Ireland. Again, it had a sting in the tail, a dirty trick. The Act was back-dated. It was cruel.

"Unless you had been in the business before a certain date, two to three years earlier, you could not apply. You were out. What the Bill really meant was if you were a member of the Turf Guardians, and in the business for years and years, you were OK. You had been breaking the law all that time, it seemed to me, yet the more you broke the law the more you were entitled to a licence. That's the way it looked. 'The Pirates', who were just on the bookmaking scene at a late stage, and only in business two or three years, were goners. It was very difficult to get around it."

Never one to back off from a battle, he knew there had to be an answer to the great irony. There was. It was to splash out and purchase legitimate betting shops. So, the pirate bookmakers soon began to buy out some of the Turf Guardian-affiliated shops. "Gradually, 'Pirates' like myself got into the business on a better footing, and into a more solid system," added BJ, "Frances and I were never legit in the bookmaking business at Carrickfergus, not at any time during twenty years there. We opened an office in Larne, and had an interest in a place in Cookstown. Our first legal bookmaking shop in Belfast was on the Ormeau Road. We managed to get our foot in the door there during the early 1960's. It was the first big shop. The Chapel Lane headquarters came much later."

Pub life in Carrickfergus was the initial sortie into the business world, yet no member of his offspring was interested in carrying on in the licensed vintner trade. "We decided not to expand the pub business," explained Eastwood, "It is very hard work, with long and late hours. Running a pub, I always thought, would do OK, but always providing you gave it your personal attention. We decided back then the bookmaking business was the path to take. I had some idea of running a bookmaker shop while in Cookstown. Then, the chance came to buy the place on the Ormeau Road. This is it, I felt. It was a big move, into the city, in 1962. It was a gamble to make all the moves. Yes, we took chances, and they eventually paid off." The Eastwood bookmaking empire remarkably mushroomed to 55 shops throughout Northern Ireland.

UP THE CREEK

EASTWOOD was well known on the other side of the betting slips. At a time he was a prominent punter during a period when he owned greyhounds and race horses. Perhaps the biggest betting coup, in a double act with fellow Northern Ireland bookmaker Alfie McLean, was at Doncaster race track in England where his horse, Sandy Creek, an outsider, was involved.

"Sandy Creek won there in the 1970's," he said, "The trainer then, the late Con Collins, wanted to have a bet on our horse. He felt it had a chance. It was trained at The Curragh. We had half-a-dozen horses in training there at that time. Sandy Creek was a good two-year-old. It was returned, I think, at 12-1 at Doncaster. We backed the horse at 16-1. I put money on him, but in the confusion we ended up with double bets on the horse, through fellow bookmaker Alfie (McLean) of Ballymena. We also backed it before we went over to Doncaster, and then a few quid bet at the track. We also won big money from the main event at Ascot on a Con Collins-owned horse. At the time I tipped it to Welsh boxing referee Jimmy Brimmell. Alfie and I had a good bet. We put money on it, long odds. Christy Roche was the jockey."

There was a follow-on episode to the Sandy Creek saga, as Eastwood explained: "The following year he was not working that well at home, so we pulled him out two or three times from racing. Con Collins told us, from Cunningham Lodge at The Curragh, he couldn't get the horse to work well enough. He also told us Sandy Creek was a valuable horse for stud. In 1978 a guy named Barney Curley from County Fermanagh, rang us, and said he was interested in buying the horse. He was a noted gambler and horse racing man, and we arranged to meet him in a cafe in Irvinestown.

"Alfie and I sold the horse for £625,000. He made out two cheques for £312,500 each. That was the deal. Later, it was announced in the media that Barney Curley purchased the horse on behalf of noted breeder John Magnier. That was fine. Magnier put the horse to stud. He rang me to say he had taken over the horse, and told me he was going to syndicate Sandy Creek. He asked me if I would like a share in the deal, in for forty shares. I said I didn't mind. It was to cost £40,000. From time to time I would get receipts of stud fees, and of the cost of keeping the horse taken out of that. My fortieth of the syndicate share of Sandy Creek wasn't looking too hot two years afterwards. The horse had to prove to be good, to breed good stuff. That didn't happen.

"Sandy Creek never ran again, of course. In the first year at stud it wasn't good news, and in the second year it proved to be worse. I was saying to myself the money invested was away, going down the drain. One evening I had a surprise telephone call from John Magnier to say the horse didn't turn out too well, but at that stage I would have taken buttons for my share. Magnier said Japanese people were coming in to Ireland to buy horses. He wanted to know if I would be a seller of my fortieth. He said what about price, and what would I be expecting. I told him I was expecting nothing once I heard he was on the phone asking to speak with me.

"Things, in the end of the episode, turned out better than I anticipated. I just got out of trouble, came close to getting my money back, nearly washed my face on the deal. I thought that was very good of Magnier, who saved everyone's share investment through the sale of Sandy Creek. I also had a horse named Red Russell, called after Hugh Russell. The horse was OK. I also other horses, including Vanavechhia and one named Fintan J, called after my late son Fintan. It won the Balrothery Stakes."

The wily Eastwood and the equally shrewd McLean formed a formidable alliance in those days. McLean and his sons also joined Eastwood on the fringes of boxing, taking a special interest in Belfast southpaw Sam Storey. Some of Storey's contests were announced from a McLean bookmaking office on Belfast's Lisburn Road. The earlier enterprises in horse racing ended in the mid-1990's: "I got out of horse racing then. So did my wife Frances, who owned a horse that won the Galway Hurdle in

1968. It was named Annalong, was trained by Bunny Cox, and ridden by Pat Black."

He also spent a profitable period in greyhound racing, and was closely involved with famed trainer 'Noble' Artie McGookin. The McGookin dog strain all had the word 'Noble' as part of the name. Artie McGookin as also President of Carrickfergus Golf Club. A great greyhound man he bred high-pedigree greyhounds and had many winners. Eastwood took a big interest in 'the dogs' for a spell, when he was living in Carrickfergus, and first became involved with noted trainer Mick Horan from Craigavad. He also worked with Paddy Turbridy. There were successes with winners of the McAlevey Gold Cup, the Guinness National Sprint, and a jet black dog named Black Ball that won 1956 Ulster Belsize and Connacht Cups.

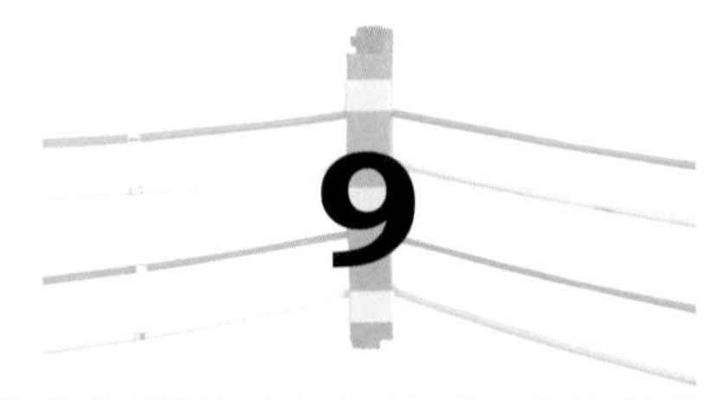

9

FIRST BLOODINGS

MEMORIES of major fight nights in Belfast for Eastwood stretch back to the late 1940's. It is a faded recollection of a time when he was first taken to the Ulster Hall. The Bedford Street venue moulded many great champions - including iconic Belfast flyweight John Joseph Monaghan.

A fascinated Eastwood was taken to what proved the breakthrough bout for Rinty Monaghan, when the 'Singing Slugger' beat his Belfast-born cousin and another world-class scrapper, Eddie 'Bunty' Doran. Monaghan won the Northern Ireland Flyweight title on a fourth-round knock-out. It was a significant result, on Tuesday November 6, 1945, and one that eventually led to the charismatic Sailorstown fighter to achieving world title fame.

Strangely though, the misty memory of that show for an impressionable and curious 13-year-old Eastwood is the clearer recollection of a big puncher from overseas who was boxing on the undercard. During the 1940's, Fijian Ben Valentine was a hard-punching heavyweight who left a trail of destruction throughout the British Isles. On that Rinty show, he beat Chris Cole of Mullingar in seven tough rounds. Eastwood was also back a month later, when Valentine stopped Alex Woods of Randalstown.

"When Tommy Joe brought me for a first time to a big boxing show it was a wonderful experience. After that bill in the Ulster Hall we mostly went to the King's Hall. I remember him going to see Tommy Armour, a very good southpaw. I recall Tommy Joe saying: 'Let's go, head for the car, because as soon as Armour hit this guy the opponent will be out like a light.' That's the way it happened. My brother said when the great Armour hits them like that they don't get up again. I always loved the boxing. I listened to the big international contests on the radio - Rinty singing after his fights. On the really big occasions, I would nag at Tommy Joe: Why can we not go to the King's Hall?'"

He was taken to three or four fight shows a year, either in the King's Hall or the Ulster Hall. Eastwood was at boxing bills between the ages of 13 and 19, starting back to the days of promoter Bob Gardiner. George Connell came after that. He loved the shows, especially those staged in the King's Hall, a venue with a fabulous fight history. Probably one of more bizarre incidents there was the night the lights went out during a Jimmy Warnock contest.

Eastwood said: "The old-time boxing fans still recall that show when the great Belfast flyweight was knocked down, and the lights went out. I was far too young then to be at that one. My big memory is of Rinty (Monaghan) bringing the house down with a win, and then singing 'When Irish eyes are Smiling'." Later on, he saw Billy 'Spider' Kelly unfortunately being knocked out by Hogan 'Kid' Bassey. He also witnessed Belfast southpaw John Kelly losing the European Bantamweight title to French-Algerian Robert Cohen, and afterwards, through Mike Callahan, becoming friendly with Cohen's mentor, Bobby Diamond, a manager/agent once also associated with Dick Tiger.

Cohen, born on November 15, 1930, in the Algerian port of Bone, took Kelly's belt through a devastating third-round knock-out in the King's Hall on February 27, 1954. Four fights later Cohen won the World title from Thailand's Chamron Songiktrat, a 15-round decision in Bangkok. In his first defence he drew over 15 rounds in Johannesburg against South Africa's Willie Toweel, and then lost the title on June 29, 1956, to Italian Mario D'Agata in Rome's Olympic Stadium at Lazio. England referee Teddy Waltham stopped the bout near mid-point. Gaston Charles-Raymond was the officially listed manager of Cohen.

Raymond was a former French lightweight who boxed mainly in the United States. Diamond, born in 1896, was a familiar fight figure on the UK scene. As an agent he regularly imported overseas boxers, mainly from Europe and the African continent, to Belfast. He died in 1972, and was buried at Kensal Green, London. "Diamond was one of the most knowledgeable guys I ever met in boxing," claimed Eastwood, "He was also noted for his appetite, eating huge meals. Often he'd bring me a couple of bottles of high quality wines when he came to Belfast. Bobby placed a bet on Cohen, his own fighter, and I think the late Jim Rice laid the wager of a couple of grand. That was big cash then. During those super shows I went to I saw great fighters such as Armour, the Warnock brothers, Gerry

Smyth, Tommy Meli and Jim Keery. I also recall Tommy Meli bringing John Kelly down from Belfast to our pub in Carrickfergus. They were at the top of their game in those days."

Soon, he was to meet Mike Callahan, one of the most extravagantly flamboyant promoters, matchmakers and managers ever to grace Irish professional boxing. Once the pilot of British Featherweight Championship finalist Jimmy Brown, a Belfast native, the always sartorially elegant Callahan brought audacious flair to the local fight game. Mercurial Mike had a nose for sniffing out the right pairings to fill the Ulster Hall. He served his apprenticeship under legendary King's Hall promoter George Connell.

When he went out on his own in the early 1960's, to try and resurrect boxing in Belfast, colourful Callahan needed some financial clout. He successfully secured the backing of fight fanatic Eastwood. Lured into the tricky and sometimes treacherous world of professional boxing promoting, Eastwood could not resist the challenge. After all, boxing was in his blood. Bitten by the boxing bug, Eastwood enjoyed moving closer to the coalface. He helped out, and, as they say, the rest is history. It was interesting, the first significant step into the running of professional fighting. This period proved a crucial part of Eastwood's education.

Boxing eras in Ireland seem to come in cycles. In the old days you could pick out some fighters such as Jim 'Spider' Kelly, Armour, Warnock, and the world success of Rinty. Then it moved on to the unrelated Kellys, John and Billy. After that superb spell of exciting fights it was into the injection of the inimitable Gilroy and Caldwell era. Irish prize-fighting then passed into another period of relative quiet, a time when Eastwood started to earn his spurs as a promoter.

He said he first became involved when there was some interesting domestic action that featured boxers such as Jim McCann against Seanie McCaffrey and Peter Sharpe colliding with Henry Turkington. They boxed on very entertaining small-hall shows, and then the Irish fight game moved on to the vibrant and magical McGuigan era. Eastwood's first big involvement was obviously through Callahan, and he secured a promoter's licence in the mid-1960's. Callahan was the matchmaker. BJ said: "Mike was a good showman. I learned a lot from him, about the ins and outs of promoting boxing. Anybody who couldn't learn from the legendary Callahan just couldn't learn."

The remarkable Callahan, who in later life guided Belfast southpaw Eamonn Magee to the WBU and Commonwealth Light-welterweight titles, was a matchmaker for Jack Solomons, often featuring Irish fighters such as Danny McAlinden and Charlie Nash. He was father-in-law of former Belfast middleweight and top trainer/manager John Breen, the man behind the very successful Breen's Gym for professional fighters. Callahan died aged 83 on May 8, 2009.

Eastwood Promotions was up and running strongly in the Sixties. It was an exciting sideline for BJ, who recalled when the entrance fee to an Ulster Hall bill cost was 7 shillings and 6 pence for a seat in the balcony. There were some crackerjack bills, good fights. It was a very interesting period, headed really by the very exciting Sharpe-Turkington contests. One of the early attractions was the mid-city Belfast bantamweight rivalry of McCafferty, a former top amateur from Donegall Street's Bosco gym, and Markets' box-fighter McCann.

Born on December 17, 1944, McCafferty finished on a 12-6 tally. His ability was much better than that. The Irish amateur Flyweight champion of 1963 and '64 took the paid plunge on October 12, 1965, in the Ulster Hall. He stopped Coalisland's Johnjo Donaghy in the third round. McCafferty ran up eight straight wins, including results against Tommy Connor (Glasgow), Tommy Burgoyne (Hamilton), Kid Hassan (Nigeria), Ron Elliott (Hackney), Norman Coles (Swansea), Nigerian Orfui Obilaso, and Ceylon born Winston Van Guylenburg. High honour was predicted, but his first defeat, over 12 rounds to McCann on December 13,1966, in the Ulster Hall, for the vacant Northern Ireland Bantamweight belt proved a severe spanner in the works.

Seanie recovered with three facile wins - against Dagenham's Reg Gullefel, Llanelli southpaw Glynne Davies, and Londoner Carl Taylor. However, his first sample of London nightlife proved frustrating. On Grand National Day - Saturday April 13, 1967 - he topped the bill on a special Jack Solomons bowtie-dinner-boxing show in the World Sporting Club, Grosvenor House, at Mayfair, London. The posh-nosh punch-up ended in a disputed points loss over ten rounds to Tunisian-born Jewish ace Felix Said Brami. Referee Bill White made the tally 49.5 to 49.25 in favour of the Paris-based Brami, who once reached Number 6 in the World Bantamweight ratings. Also on the show were Belfast fighters Terry McTigue and Davy Rainey, and Dubliner Gussie Farrell.

"That was a unique occasion for me, my first time to fight on a dinner-jacket show," recalled McCafferty, "It was a great occasion, apart from my result. The bill was for jockeys. At the show were big name jockeys such as Terry Biddlecombe, Josh Gifford, and the man who rode the famous 100 to 1 outsider, Foinavon, to victory earlier that day at Aintree - Johnny Buckingham. I met them after my fight. Buckingham came especially to see me, to congratulate me. He felt I was the winner."

A rematch was instantly agreed, yet McCafferty did not come out well in another bow-tie affair, on a mid-summer Sean Graham show arranged by Al McMurray in the Fiesta Ballroom, near Belfast Markets area. Brami took the eight-rounder on Belfast referee Billy Duncan's 40-39.5 summary. McCafferty recovered with a points win, over eight rounds in the Ulster Hall, against Brindisi, Italy-born French citizen Giancarlo Centa. But, his next outing, on December 7, 1967, and in Rome against a more formidable Italian, European Bantamweight champion Franco Zurlo, was a 10th-round stoppage loss. His penultimate bout, on October 30, 1968, was a losing one over eight rounds, against Wishaw-born featherweight Bobby Fisher in Hamilton Town Hall.

On February 10, 1970, after a 16-month gap, McCafferty moved up to super-featherweight, but lost on a fourth-round disqualification to Lisburn southpaw Sammy Lockhart for the vacant Northern Ireland title. Incidentally, hard-hooking Lockhart, born on July 20, 1946, lost on a second-round stoppage to up and coming Scottish southpaw lightweight and future World champion Jim Watt in the Ulster Hall on October 20, 1970. Sammy bowed out after 19 contests, including ten wins and one draw.

McCafferty highlighted the fight-game famine in Northern Ireland immediately after the iconic Gilroy-Caldwell war in the King's Hall, 1962. Then it was salvation offered through the emergence of enterprising Eastwood. The in-between years, after the glittering Gilroy-Caldwell showdown and the beginnings of McGuigan, marked Eastwood's vigorous incursion into serious contact with professional boxing.

"Barney Eastwood's contribution to Irish professional boxing was very significant," insisted McCafferty, "He was the best thing that happened to boxing here, first of all after the lull that followed the Gilroy-Caldwell era. He revived boxing. He put the injection back into professional boxing, starting it again around 1965. That was when and why I turned professional, because Eastwood came in as a promoter. I was boxing for him. Jim McCann was there, and so too was Peter Sharpe. I fought on the Sharpe-Turkington bills at the Ulster Hall. During that era the venue was always packed.

"Barney (Eastwood) gave boxing a big leg-up on two occasions. Don't forget, he revived it for a second time when he started the career of Barry McGuigan. He moved to be a manager then, and brought his son Stephen in to promote. He was definitely good for boxing, and for boxers at that time." McCafferty's first interest in fighting was when reading about Ma Copley's promotions at Chapel Fields. As a kid in juvenile boxing he used to sneak through the turnstiles without paying to attend some of George Connell's shows. Connell had a big office at the Ulster Sports Club, in High Street, Belfast. Later on, Mike Callahan was also there. When Freddie Gilroy came up the ranks, with Jimmy McAree as his manager, it was Jack Solomons who promoted many of his contests. We had the famous Gilroy fight with John Caldwell, who started out in the Immaculata under former fighter Jack McCusker.

"After that big scrap at the King's Hall, we had the local game confined mainly to the Ulster Hall - until Eastwood introduced McGuigan. The great revival of boxing in the North during the 'Troubles' was on. Eastwood was able to get the crowds back, the peace banner, and so on. He did a good job. There was no King's Hall in my day, unfortunately, because we didn't have the drawing power to fill the place. Eastwood and McGuigan changed all that."

Eastwood's formative years as a promoter laid a firm foundation in making contacts with various managers and promoters in the UK and Europe. It was an eye-opener to be involved. He was quick to learn in the jungle, ready to appreciate help and guidance but also a person with a long memory when on the receiving end of a mischief.

He enjoyed the Swinging Sixties: "In that era we had Dublin-born Young McCormack in from London, with his manager Paddy Byrne. I remember Barney Wilson Jnr boxing Jim Monaghan, the 'Gentle Giant', for the vacant Northern Ireland Heavyweight Championship. It was on the same Ulster Hall show that Young McCormack beat Belgium's Lion Ven in the top-of-the-bill contest. One of the hilarious incidents that night, on November 22, 1966, was when Wilson's pants split during the fight. We had to rush to the dressing rooms and borrow a pair that would fit, from Lion Ven, I think. Barney (Wilson) was a good puncher, winning the title inside the distance. We also promoted 'Big' Jim in a few fights, and after the shows we used to go to Mooney's hostelry at Cornmarket. It was great craic."

He had a lot of time for the enormously popular Monaghan. The happy heavyweight tragically died in September, 2002. Jim began in amateur boxing with the St Eugene's Boys Club. Coached by the late Patsy Haveron, he was Ulster Senior amateur Heavyweight champion from 1960 to 1963. In amateur international bouts the towering figure of Monaghan beat name fighters such as Carl Gizzi, Jack McVicker, Len Hobbs and Rocky James, but lost to England's blond bombshell Billy Walker. He turned professional in October 1963. Jack Solomons promoted a number of Monaghan's bouts in England, including a special Heavyweight competition.

10

SHARPE OPERATOR

PETER Sharpe was one of Belfast's last classic throw-back fighter, a wonderful technician who could turn a left jab into a hook at lightening speed. He came into the game towards the end of an old-fashioned era, when it seemed the right thing was to always be ready to accept the offer of ring work at a moment's notice, and no matter where it was. He was a quiet, unassuming 'have-gloves-will-travel' guy, who sometimes boxed two and three times in the same month. Perhaps with more careful and selective planning he might have achieved British and European title honours.

Born on January 29, 1934, he was reared in Garnett Street, Belfast. He moved to Slate Street, also in the lower Falls, and later reared his own family in Belfast's Twinbrook, Andersonstown. Sharpe's day job was in the Northern Ireland Railways' yard at the Belfast York Street terminal. Registered as 'Al' Sharpe, he boxed 122 times, starting in the Ulster Hall on February 13, 1952, and ending in the Ellis Park Tennis Stadium, Johannesburg, on July 23, 1968.

He operated behind a peek-a-boo high guard, and snaking left jab, before setting about opponents with slick combinations. Peter bowed out on a points loss to South African hard-man Pierre Fourie, who lost over the distance in four World Light-heavyweight title fights - two against Victor Galindez, and two against the merciless punching Bob Foster.

Sharpe, whose brother Joe was also a professional boxer, reinvented his career a couple of times. The former Northern Ireland Lightweight, Welterweight and Middleweight champion once lost in an All-Ireland

Welterweight title 12-rounder to 1956 Olympic silver medallist Freddie Teidt, in an outdoor show at Tolka Park, Dublin, on July 28, 1961. He had the dapper Dubliner on the deck in the final round, and after Teidt's hand was raised disillusioned Sharpe announced his retirement.

Thirty fights later he finally hung up the gloves! Nine months after the loss to Teidt, he was tempted back to meet Killough-born Paddy Graham for the Northern Ireland Welterweight belt, but narrowly lost the 10-rounder in the King's Hall. Trained by the enigmatic Ned McCormick, who was also a highly astute corner and premier cuts man, he was about to really pack it in after losing on points over eight rounds to Nat Jacobs in Manchester on April 13, 1964.

Eastwood said: "First Jim McCann and then Peter Sharpe played special roles. Sharpe was almost finished with fighting when I felt it was an obvious contest for him against Henry Turkington. I suppose Sharpe had seen Turkington fight, and wanted to be involved in what would be a good local match. Peter's long-time trainer Ned McCormick believed his fighter would have too much experience and craft for the Turk. Money talks, and I said a match could be made between the two. That is how it all started. Sharpe was a lovely fellow. He was a good professional, a nice guy, very clever boxer. The Sharpe-Turkington fights were great, Henry had great heart."

Every time Sharpe and the Turk collided it proved a terrific and tingling occasion, an unbelievable attraction with the Ulster Hall packed to the gunnels, the fans virtually swinging from the rafters. "I recall over 500 people queuing on the footpath outside the Hall and around the sidestreets off Bedford Street," added Eastwood, "They were patiently waiting to get inside, and go upstairs where that area didn't hold much more than a couple of hundred spectators. During the two Sharpe-Turkington bouts in the Ulster Hall we must have somehow squeezed in 2,000 folk. The fans were standing in the corridors. They were in back rooms. They were everywhere in the building.

"It was bedlam, amazing. I remember going up the aisle where the fighters emerged from the dressing rooms to the ring, only to find there was no aisle-room remaining between the seats. It was packed with people - some standing, some on their hunkers at the front, and also up in the Ulster Hall's Orchestra area. In the four aisles leading to the ring you could hardly get your boxer to the steps and his stool. You could barely get room to swing a cat, get near your boxer to do your cornerwork. I remember the famous Belfast street-fighter Patrick 'Silver' McKee kneeling in one of the isles, almost at ringside. The wisest thing was to leave 'Silver' alone, try an ease around him when attempting to get your boxer into the ring."

Ageing expert Sharpe's performances proved an unexpectedly big draw for the young promoter. He was a very popular fighter with the local fans, and especially boxing followers from his Falls Road stronghold. They loved him. Turkington was equally as popular, in other parts of Northern Ireland. From his amateur exploits to signing professional for manager Coe McConnell, Henry carried a huge following from the Doagh, Ballyclare, and throughout all of the east Antrim area. He was blessed with awesome punching power. Turkington versus Sharpe made for an outstanding clash of styles.

After Sharpe was invited by Eastwood to meet the rising hit-man, an offer he couldn't refuse, the 31-year-old went into strict training, including lively rota sparring programme in the old gym that housed the Immaculata Youth club in Devonshire Street. Master-craftsman Sharpe, now beefed-up to Middleweight, believed he held the antidote to withstand the Turk's anticipated heavy bombs. It was a fascinating scenario, the appetite of the pleasantly surprised fans whetted in what became an intriguing parochial trilogy. Sharpe, with a large edge in boxing's 'street smarts', won all three contests, the first in the Ulster Hall on February 9, 1965, with referee Jim McCreanor doing the sums. The second showdown, again in the packed Ulster Hall, had the Northern Ireland Middleweight title up for grabs, and the same outcome, this time a ninth-round technical stoppage on October 10, 1965. Referee was Billy Duncan of Belfast.

All of a sudden, after one of the most accomplished performances of his career, Sharpe was big news. He was on the march up the British rankings. He had to do things the hard way. In November 1965, Sharpe was listed British 14th in the ratings when he was handed a re-match against the Number 2 - black fighter Nat Jacobs, the Central Area Middleweight champion from Manchester. They met in the Ulster Hall, with Peter the Great blazing to the tape from four strong late rounds to take referee Andy Smyth's decision. In the supporting cast were Belfast's Jim McCann, Davie Rainey, Sean McCafferty, and a draw outcome for debut middleweight Billy Turkington of Doagh against flashy Larne fighter Chris 'Cassius' McAuley.

Sharpe's rise continued with wins against the Manchester based and Dublin-connected Jim Swords and West Ham's Johnny Kramer to shoot into British Middleweight title contention. He secured a Championship eliminator against another wily veteran, Nottingham's hard-nosed Wally Swift. Eastwood won the purse offer to stage the 12-rounder in the Ulster Hall. Unfortunately, an eyebrow gash sustained during a sparring session with fellow Belfast professional Oliver Lyttle, in the old Immaculata gym, forced a delay. Perhaps the momentum was dented because, on May 5, 1966, Sharpe went down to a points loss against Swift.

After that, it was back on the journeyman road for a spell, to fight and lose distance tests against rising class acts such as Bo Hogberg in Malmo, Tom Bogs in Copenhagen, and Bo Petterson in Stockholm. Back home, the 'rubber' meeting between Sharpe and Turkington was set for the A.E.I. Factory Canteen, Larne, on January 26, 1967. A disputed points decision in favour of Sharpe was not convincing. The old half point winning margin seemed extremely unfair to the harder working Turkington. Fans of Hammerin' Henry were furious. I recall Sharpe, Ned McCormick and Eddie Shaw hastily slipping out the back door of the County Antrim seaport arena, and scampering back to Belfast. A month later, Sharpe out-scored fellow Belfast fighter Terry McTigue over 12 rounds in the Ulster Hall for the Irish and Northern Ireland Middleweight titles. It was to prove his last win. He dropped three points decisions - to Bunny Sterling, Les McAteer and Pierre Fourie before putting away the gloves for good.

Eastwood said: "Peter (Sharpe) was always one of my favourites. He held a special memory for me, a boxer who made fair fighters look foolish. Decades after his career ended I met him again, during the funeral of Barney Wilson in Belfast in November, 2009. I hadn't see him in years, yet he looked as fit as ever, not changed a bit - almost ready to box at a moments notice, yet 74-years-of-age. Goodwill from the old days with Belfast boxing people was still there. Indeed, it reminded me of the many, many boxing people who supported me along the way.

"As well as Sharpe, Turkington, McCafferty, McCann and Wilson I hold great memories of fight folk such as Young McCormack, Jim Monaghan, Paddy Fitzsimons, Rocky McGran, Harry Enright, Fra McCullagh, Sean Canavan, Terry Christle, Davy Larmour, Mickey Duddy, Jim Jordan, Hugh Russell, Young Patsy Quinn, David Irving, Roy Webb, Terry McTigue, Kevin Hyland, Sam Storey, Hugh Gilhooley, Gerry Storey, John Breen, Noel Magee, Seamus McGuinness, Damian Fryer, Gerry and Bobby McAllister, and Gerry Hassett - who was both boxer and Chief Whip on occasions for my shows in the Ulster Hall. I could go on and on. There were loads more from up and down the country.

"During the Wilson funeral, Peter (Sharpe) came over to me and declared it was a pleasure to box for me back in the 1960's. He took fights all over the world then, and at short notice. I told him it was a pity he wasn't with me in the latter period when I was a manager, in the 1980's. In Sharpie's day there was no TV backing. In the 1980's he would have been class, would have been lifted and laid - and, in my opinion, could have gone a long, long way."

BJ also helped to bring fighters to England, once taking Turkington to the Empire Pool, Wembley, in March 1964. "It was Henry's third fight, and against a future British and Commonwealth Light-heavyweight champion Eddie Avoth. He outboxed the Welshman, in my opinion, until losing on a technical stoppage in the fourth round. We also used to go to the Free Trade Hall in Manchester, taking over several fighters from Belfast to box for promoter Selwyn Demmy."

For one of those shows he brought Barney Wilson Jnr to the Manchester Free Trade Hall, in January 1965, in what was believed to be a path to a British Heavyweight eliminator. Born on August 8, 1942, Wilson weighed in marginally above the old Light-heavyweight limit when he met Jack Grant, who came off a loss before that yet the match still stood. This was Wilson's fifth fight. Managed by Jack Burns of London, he connected with thundering shots, had Grant down three times, but the trend dramatically changed in the fourth round. Grant retaliated, and after six rounds Barney went down. Referee Harry Humphries stopped it in the seventh, and that setback about ended big British Championship plans for Wilson. Also on that bill was Chris McAuley.

Ginger-haired Wilson, of course, became a leading referee before suffering serious illness. He died on November 17, 2009, following a lengthy battle against Parkinson's Disease. He was 67. From Lincoln Street, off Belfast's Falls Road, he was an Ulster amateur Middleweight champion and Irish international who boxed out of the Immaculata club. He had a professional record of six wins and five defeats. On January 26, 1968, he bowed out after an eight-round points loss to Ron Redrup of England, in the Bedfordshire Sporting Club.

A bricklayer to trade, he was also a noted greyhound owner, breeder and trainer, with his dogs competing on track and also in coursing events throughout Ireland. He stayed close to professional boxing and became a regular middleman in many Ulster Hall and King's Hall tournaments. Early in his career he headed a security operation for top Irish Showband impresario Jim Aiken. The Wilson security squad also included former Belfast lightweight Billy Smyth, generally working out of the once famous Orpheus Ballroom on Belfast's York Street. Eastwood was close to Barney (Wilson), and added: "I remember the first time I met him. He was just married to Teresa, and living in Distillery Street. Teresa was a very good singer. Barney's father Barney Snr was also a useful fighter, and for a time a bouncer for Mike Callahan."

Late in the 1960's a disillusioned Eastwood decided to pull the plug on his promotion venture, and explained why: "After all that happened, good small-hall shows featuring Sharpe, Turkington, McCann, McCafferty, Wilson, Walter McGowan, Young McCormick and so forth, things changed. We made money on those shows, because they were not the hardest to set up. I am not saying I got rich on them. You would have managed a spell when you had two or three winning shows, but then a couple of bad results thrown in that did your money. Still, I got enough encouragement in those times to keep trying, and was always hoping some day we would hit for something big."

He stepped down from promoting when the British Boxing Board of Control, through the local Area Council members, decided to grant a licence to Bob McCalmont of Ballyclare. Eastwood insisted he had nothing personal against the new man, but told the Area officials there was not enough room for two promoters. He claimed he felt one would smother the other. There were not enough local boxers to go around, to service two promoters in Northern Ireland, so he told the Board there would be a clash of interests.

The British Boxing Board of Control officials wouldn't listen to him, he said. Eastwood then told them he was getting out of promoting further shows. He felt he used up too much effort, and too much hard work to continue. He also made a clean break with Mike Callahan and all concerned, because he believed there was nothing more to be gained by way of promoting boxing shows at that time. He, nevertheless, retained glowing recollection of that period. "Obviously I have great fights to recall, yet my happiest memories of the shows in Belfast was in chatting to some wonderful people. We had regular faithful ringside clients such as the great soccer star Jimmy McAlinden, of Portsmouth and Northern Ireland fame. He was a nice fellow, and a tremendous fan of boxing."

.Tyrone's Ulster and All-Ireland Minor Championship winning squad of 1948.
B.J Eastwood is kneeling third right.

Eastwood (right) in action during Tyrone's 1948 All-Ireland Minor championship final win against Dublin at Croke Park.

World Heavyweight champion Joe Louis Barrow fixes up his US Army uniform. The Brown Bomber served a spell in Northen Ireland during World War Two.

Belfast's undefeated World Flyweight champion Rinty Monaghan.

Frances Eastwood seen receiving the McAlevey Gold Cup from Noelle Nicholl (Mrs Brendan Macaulay) at Celtic Park, Belfast. Holding the successful greyhound is Artie McGookin.

Belfast lightweight Jim Jordan, left, against Scotland's Olympic champion Dick McTaggart in the 1958 Empire Games final at Cardiff.

- Belfast bantamweight Jim McCann headlined the infamous 'Mob-night' 1966 Eastwood bill in Belfast's Ulster Hall.

A young B.J. Eastwood during his boxing promotion days of the 1960's

Dublin's 'Young' John McCormack, the British Light-heavyweight champion, about to enter the Ulster Hall ring.

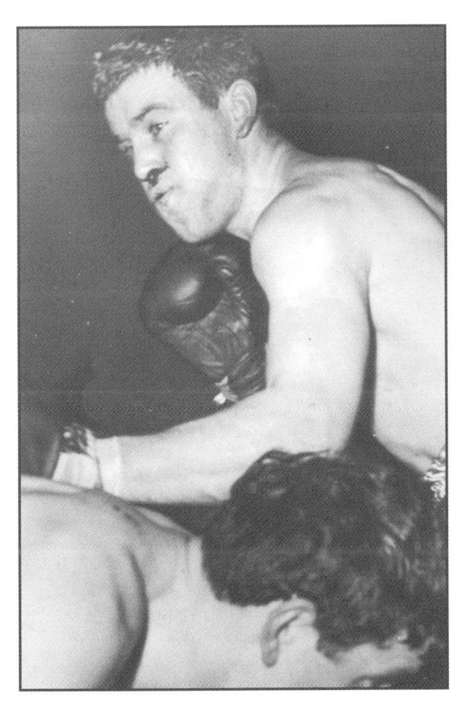

Irish Middleweight Henry Turkingtion

Belfast's Peter 'Al' Sharpe, a British Middleweight title contender of the late 1960's, and one of Eastwood's favourite Irish fighters.

Flamboyant Belfast promoter/matchmaker Mike Callahan.

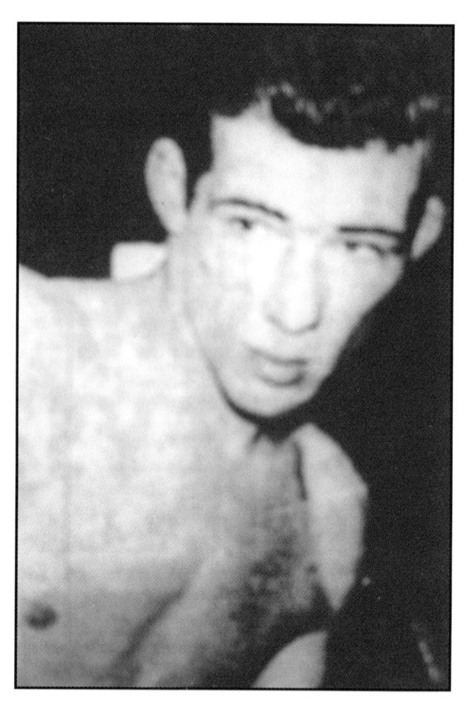

Belfast featherweight Sean McCafferty

England middleweight Wally Swift, left, and Belfast opponent Peter Sharpe check out Eastwood greyhounds before their British Championship eliminator, won by Swift in the Ulster Hall, Belfast.

Chirpy Larne bantamweight Roy Webb

Belfast warriors Davy Larmour and Hugh Russell in a blood-letting British Bantamweight Championship battle.

Iconic London referee Harry Gibbs (2nd left) celebrating in Belfast's Europa Hotel after a fight show with British Boxing Board of Control officer Deryk Monteith (left), Frances Eastwood, Belfast News Letter *Sports Editor George Ace, B J Eastwood, and Derry-born Dublin promoter Philip McLaughlin. Eastwood later remarked: "Those were great days. We thought they would go on forever."*

MOBBED UP

THE RICHARDSON brothers, heading up London's fearsome street frighteners of the mid-1960's, decided to take time out from their manor to pay a flying visit to Belfast's Ulster Hall in 1966. The heavy mob arrived in numbers to support Pat Dwyer, a new middleweight prospect from Bootle, England. Burgeoning boxing promoter Eastwood was not prepared for the unexpected invasion of such high-powered hoods.

The awesome reputation of Charlie, Eddie and William Richardson, monarchs of muscle and arguably second only in England to their bitter rivals the Kray brothers, was well known world-wide in the 1960's. The gang allegedly dominated the mobster world of south London, and included that master of menace of the Metropolitan gangster scene, the unpredictable 'Mad' Frankie Fraser.

The Richardsons became involved in an infamous 'Turf War' with the Krays, one that led to some horrific happenings near the end of 1965. Reputed leader Charlie Richardson, born in 1934, was officially in the scrap metal business, while Eddie apparently operated a thriving fruit-machine franchise. The Richardson outfit, said to also include ice-cold hardman Jimmy Moody, became known as the 'Torture Gang' during the high-profile Old Bailey court case of 1967.

The much-publicised feud with the Kray brothers is suspected to have started during Christmas, 1965. Former Kray tough nut George Cornell, then with the Richardsons, allegedly bad-mouthed Ronnie Kray. Later, it emerged a brawl erupted in a club at Catford. It seems the club had 'protectors' in Eddie Richardson, and with 'Mad' Frankie allegedly telling Kray gang members such as one reportedly named Peter Hennessey to leave the premises. A Kray associate was shot, and following that incident came the killing of Cornell in the 'Blind Beggar' pub. It was claimed

Cornell was shot through the head at point-blank range. London police connected Ronnie Kray to the incident. Into the public domain came extensive reporting of some Richardson victims of torture turning Queen's Evidence. Mob members were rounded up to face a massive trial that started in April 1967 at the Old Bailey.

It was described as the first 'Supergrass' trial to be held in London. The so-termed 'show trial' began not that long after the boxing programme featuring Dwyer in Belfast. Charlie Richardson, who was arrested on Wembley World Cup Final day, July 30, 1966, was later 'put away' on a 25-year sentence. He served 18 years. Eddie was initially sent to prison for five years, and along with younger brother William had an additional 10 years added. Incidentally, Charlie escaped from open prison in 1980, but gave himself up a year later. In 1990, Eddie was sentenced to 25 years in prison for alleged drug trafficking.

It was such scary company Eastwood had to facilitate in the Ulster Hall. Many times in his long and eventful business and sporting life he had to deal with tough guys, but nothing came close to this spooky sequence when the Richardson entourage took time out from nefarious activities in London to breeze into Belfast. The date was February 8, 1966. Dwyer's opponent was Belfast's Terry McTigue, later to become the Northern Ireland Light-heavyweight champion. The Richardsons had a business interest in new sensation Dwyer, through the fighter's manager Bert McCarthy. The gang bosses decided a night out in Belfast would do 'the soldiers' a power of good. Eastwood used Dwyer a month earlier in the Bedford Street arena, where the former England amateur international halted Belfast fighter Hugh Gilhooley in two rounds.

Born on May 2, 1946, Dwyer looked the real deal, but became a talent of unfulfilled promise in world terms. His career seemed to stall after losing in the eighth round to Charles Ramon in Melbourne, on October, 1972, for the vacant Commonwealth Light-middleweight crown. He finished with a 38-11-2 professional record, winning his last bout against Brendan Ingle for the Central Area middleweight title. Dwyer tangled with many top middleweights such as Alan Minter, Les McAteer and Mark Rowe. Incidentally, he drew over eight rounds with 'Doagh Destroyer' Henry Turkington in the National Sporting Club, London, a few weeks after his fight with McTigue. Dwyer was keen to again impress in a second successive appearance in a Belfast ring.

It is unlikely he expected such a crew of heavy hitters in his corner that night. Many of London's leading hard cases booked seats and arrived by private 'plane. Everything went swimmingly for the Richardson entourage, until the fight result. Eastwood was on eggs. There was no repeat big win for Dwyer. The Richardsons were not amused when Dwyer had to share a points decision with McTigue, who was a former top Ulster amateur (Terry Montague) from Akkie Kelly's Star Club in north Belfast. No wonder Eastwood felt uneasy when the decision was announced. He knew of the Richardsons' reputations - racketeers at the height of their powers when they decided to pop over to Belfast for a night of fun at the fights.

He also appreciated one wrong move could light a fuse. The after-fight tension, when Dwyer did not get the decision, was palpable, but quickly washed away during a good old booze-up and knees-up in Dobbin's Hotel, Carrickfergus. Eastwood still suffered goosepimples on the nape of his neck when he recalled that unexpected invasion by some of the world's most intimidating racketeers of that era. London fight manager McCarthy, later to be known as Burt, also had Belfast southpaw featherweight Sammy Vernon on his books.

Eastwood said: "As far as I could tell McCarthy was a right-hand man for the Richardsons. George Ace, the colourful Sports Editor of the Belfast *News Letter* at that time, and a very knowledgeable boxing and rugby authority, was friendly with McCarthy, who was a small guy, a sharp dresser. The Richardson brothers backed McCarthy. They sent over a very good boxer in Dwyer. The kid was nicknamed 'E I Adio'. He was a great fighter, and had been a terrific amateur before turning professional.

"When Dwyer came to Belfast for a second contest, a 'plane load of supporters arrived from London, all Richardson-connected folk. You can guess how they felt after the draw decision. Mind you, I was a bit uneasy, because I was one of the few people who knew so many mob guys were in the Ulster Hall. The Richardsons rang in advance of the show, telling me they were coming over to Belfast in a private 'plane. Then, one of the Richardsons approached me to enquire if I could fix up a room in some quiet hotel after the fight. They asked me to make the necessary booking on their behalf. They wanted a small place out of town, to hold a nice quiet party - not to attract any attention, and have bit of peace on their own."

The normal after-fight watering holes in those days included The Elsinore Hotel, on Belfast's Antrim Road, and Mooney's in the city centre Cornmarket area, but the Richardsons wanted complete privacy. "They also told me to invite all my friends to the party," said BJ, "I was living in Carrickfergus then, so I booked them into Dobbin's. Cash money was no problem. I asked Eddie Richardson how many people did they want facilitated by the hotel, for snacks and stuff. He asked could the hotel cater for anything from 60 to 70 people, including my guests. Dobbin's did a good job for them. I knew it was going to be big stuff, because I was asked to tell the management of the hotel to order up at least a dozen cases of the best vintage champagne.

"I don't know if it was true, but I was later told some of the London guys were 'carrying rods' - as they say in the gangster movies. I recall one of the London boys becoming a bit boisterous. A regular follower of our fight shows, Dermot O'Hara from Belfast, was one of the locals I invited to join the party. He happened to remark in front of me and one of the Richardson's that the unruly guy should be asked to behave. He was firmly and politely told it would be wiser not to interfere, as the guy, apparently one of the toughest members of the gang, was 'carrying'. Anyway, everything turned out OK. We didn't leave the Hotel until about three in the morning.

"On the way out home, as Frances and I jumped off at our gate on the Belfast Road, one of the Richardson people left a couple of cases of champagne at our front door. There were two coach loads of them. Jackie Mahood, an outside man for us at that time who worked in the field betting, and another guy who worked for Eastwoods, drove the Richardsons to Belfast where they had booked and paid for rooms in the Grand Central Hotel. They went to the hotel for a short while, yet never used their rooms, didn't go to bed.

"From there, the Richardsons were driven to their private 'plane at Aldergrove, and as they were boarding for take-off to London they 'parted' Jackie Mahood and the other driver with a very large tip. I believe it was £500 between the two. That was huge money then. There were some famous tough guys in that party, and it certainly was a night to remember. The ironic thing about the Richardson story was that the detective who arrested them, Nipper Read, later became the Chairman of the British Boxing Board of Control. I got to know him too, because he came to Belfast as a Boxing Board representative at some of our shows."

Once that sweaty-palm saga of '66 faded, Eastwood could take time to seriously concentrate on the continuing progress of Belfast bantamweight Jim McCann Jnr. The prospect headlined that famous 'Richardson gang' show. Northern Ireland champion McCann met Spaniard Angel Chinea, from Santa Cruz in the Canary Islands. It was the local lad's debut as a top-of- the-bill boxer, unbeaten in six starts. It was a meteoric start for tenacious box-fighter, who was trained by his father of the same name and was then ranked fourth in the British list behind Alan Rudkin.

'Wee' Jim, fresh from a third-round cuts stoppage win against Terry Gale, beat Barcelona-based Chinea, a so-so fighter with a spotty record that included contests against Jose Legra, Kamara Diop and Salvatore Burruni. Born on March 1, 1944, McCann had a short and spectacular paid career of a dozen bouts. In his third outing he participated in a 12-rounder in the Ulster Hall, on December 13, 1966. It was a rousing all-Belfast battle with Seanie McCafferty for the Northern Ireland Area

Bantamweight belt. His previous outing was an interesting test against much-travelled Mexican Ernesto Mirando at the Empire Pool, on June 14, 1966. Mirando came to London with a record of 76-9-10. It seemed overly ambitious for the Irish rookie, yet McCann scored an eye-catching points victory over eight rounds.

Earlier in his ring crusade, he took the Northern Ireland Area title on a ninth-round stoppage against fellow Belfast fighter Alex O'Neill, at the Ulster Hall on October 12, 1965. One month later he suffered the first of two defeats. McCann was disqualified against a veteran 'name' box-fighter nine years his elder - Jackie Brown, Edinburgh's former British and Commonwealth Flyweight champion of 1962. When John Caldwell vacated the British Flyweight Championship, Brown out-pointed Brian Cartwright in Birmingham for the crown, in February 1962. Also the Scottish Bantamweight champion, he was stopped in the 12th round by fellow Scot Walter McGowan in a British and European Flyweight showdown in 1963.

Before that, he out-jabbed a rookie McGowan (having his third contest) over eight rounds in Paisley Ice Rink. Brown also tangled with name bantamweights of that era such as Freddie Gilroy, Mario D'Agata, Pierro Rollo and in November 1964 drew over ten rounds with Caldwell in Paisley Ice Rink. I mention Brown's impressive ring CV to illustrate how rapidly McCann zipped up the British ladder. It was ironic another Scot, rope-muscled Evan Armstrong, should end the Irish fighter's career. Eastwood had high hopes of major titles coming McCann's way. Jim's upward surge continued with a ten-round points win against the very useful Tommaso Galli of Italy in the Ulster Hall on January 17, 1967.

This result catapulted Jim into the British title frame. He agreed to a final eliminator against craggy Caledonian Armstrong, but had to travel into the Ayrshire fighter's backyard on May 11, 1967. English referee Roland Dakin halted the battle in the fifth round. McCann packed away the gloves for good, to concentrate on a flourishing bookmaking enterprise.

Incidentally, the programme for the memorable 'Night of the Mob' in the Ulster Hall, lists J.F.Conroy as matchmaker, Jimmy Allen the M.C, Timekeeper-P.G. Burns, Chief whip-Gerry Hassett, Chief Steward-Jimmy George, Press Steward-Harry O'Neill. Tournament medic-Dr Pat McHugh. Steward in Charge-Andrew Smyth. Referees-Jim McCreanor and William Duncan. The programme cost One Shilling. Ringside seats sold at 40/-, Outer ringside at 20/-, and then Balcony and Orchestra areas at 15/- and 10/- respectively.

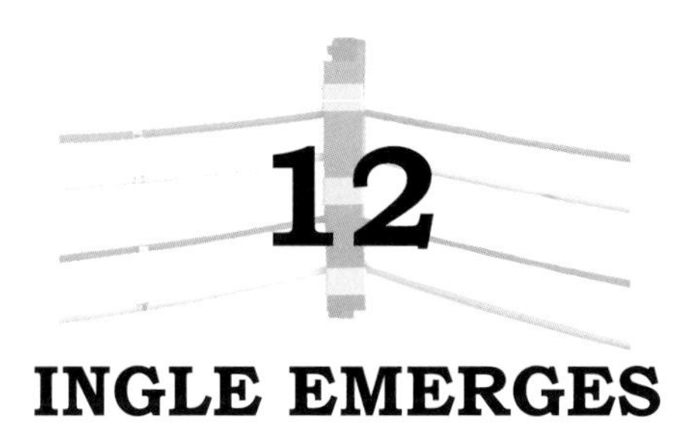

12

INGLE EMERGES

BRENDAN Ingle, also on the show, later became one of the truly familiar faces of world boxing, and particularly through his association with a young Prince Naseem. Ingle, in the first of two trips to Belfast as a fighter, met heavy- hitting Doagh middleweight Billy Turkington. The 'Young Turk' put an end to Ingle's unbeaten four-fight run.

In later years, during Ingle's coaching and management career, he ran into a little bit of strife with Eastwood over the contract of middleweight Herol 'Bomber' Graham. "Let me tell you, I had my ups and downs with Barney. Bomber Graham was with Eastwood for a spell, and later Graham returned to me," he recalled, "Barney did a great job for boxing in Ireland. Look at his record, as a promoter and as a manager. It is excellent. The kids he turned out from there were tremendous, eventually including six world champions. You cannot beat or argue with results like that.

"Loftus Road was a high point for Barney, with Barry McGuigan's world title win. The time Barney put in then was six to seven days a week, and he put his money where his mouth was. He fetched in the best of sparring partners, and promoted the shows from the Ulster Hall to the King's Hall. The development of boxers from the small Ulster Hall to the big King's Hall resulted in the major venue being packed out."

Ingle, who was born in Dublin on June 19, 1941, spent his early days as part of a special family contribution to Irish boxing. John, Jimmy and Brendan embarked on professional boxing careers. Other brothers, Bernie, Peter, Nago (Ignatius) and Eddie, also boxed, as amateurs. Jimmy, the 1939 European amateur Flyweight gold medallist, first boxed for the St Andrew's Club off Stephen's Green, in the centre of Dublin. The other club he represented was Mount Street. Brendan boxed for the Corinthians

Club. The other brothers moved in there, when the club was based in Lower Gardiner Street. Jimmy later went to England, and worked for Vauxhall Motors in Luton. During his professional boxing adventure he muscled up to middleweight, and had a 16-16-2 record.

He made his paid debut in Belfast on March 20, 1943, losing a 10-rounder to the great Tommy Armour. He met Armour five times, winning three times and drawing in another. He also drew with England's Ernie Roderick in Tolka Park, Dublin, and boxed against other quality opponents such as Randy Turpin and Albert Finch. On June 13, 1939, he retired after losing to Alex Buxton in Watford. A year earlier, he joined brother John on a show in Douglas, Isle of Man, beating Billy Stevens. John Ingle was the Irish professional Lightweight champion, and had a 9-7-1 career. He hung up the gloves after that trip to Douglas, where he won over eight rounds against Ted Ansell. During his time he also tangled with such Irish notables as Gerry Smyth, Dave Warnock, Dan McAllister, Jim McCann Snr, and Dublin's 'Spike' McCormick. John emigrated to New Zealand, and later returned home to spend the last ten years of his life in Dublin.

Brendan, a member of a family of 15 from the south Dublin dockland area of Ringsend, had four sisters. In 1958, after 20 amateur contests, he emigrated to Sheffield at 18-years-of-age, and turned professional in Manchester on October 4, 1965, when winning a six-round decision against Dick Griffiths. He reached seventh in the British Middleweight ratings. After losing on a seventh-round cuts stoppage to Chris Finnegan in August 1969, in Manchester, he fittingly secured his closing career victory while in his native Dublin, where he halted England's Joe Gregory in the third round of a bow-tie show in the European Sporting Club on July 3, 1973. Next time out, his penultimate bout, he lost on points to Pat Dwyer in Southend, with the Central Area Middleweight title on the line. He bowed out after losing in the third round to Poul Knudsen of Randers in Copenhagen, on November 1, 1973.

Ingle said: "I remember boxing for Barney Eastwood in Belfast. The younger brother of Henry Turkington was a great prospect then. Billy was a talent who should have gone to the top. On February 27, 1968, I returned to Belfast, and out-pointed Chris McAuley in a bit of a brawl over six rounds in the Fiesta Ballroom. Johnny Campbell was my manager. For most of the time I trained myself, as there was no boxing trainer in Sheffield at that time. Also, I used to go over to Liverpool, about 80 miles away, twice a week to train. It was very inconvenient and difficult.

“Because I was training myself, I gradually helped to coach some kids in my area. Youngsters were coming in off the streets. It was a bit rough and ready. Because the kids had no experience of boxing I started body sparring with them. The new phrase for that is technical sparring. Forty years ago we were doing body sparring, and some people used to say it was a waste of time, but we got terrific results. Eventually, we had some great boxers coming out of the gym, including Junior Witter, Johnny Nelson, Naseem Hamed, Herol Graham and Brian Anderson - who became Governor of Doncaster Prison. Brian was a good middleweight from Sheffield, boxing around the same time as Herol Graham."

Anderson also held a significant link with Belfast, making one appearance there in his penultimate outing of a 27-9-3 career. On October 29, 1986, by some quirk of fate he met and stopped fellow English fighter Tony Burke for the vacant British Middleweight title. Referee Larry O'Connell called a halt after 45 seconds of the eighth round. That was the same Tony Burke who was later to lose to Sam Storey in the first-ever title scrap for the British Super-middleweight Championship. Anderson's next and final fight, eleven months later, was a stoppage loss in the seventh round to Tony Sibson, in the Royal Albert Hall, for the British and Commonwealth Middleweight belts.

When Brendan Ingle decided to put away the gloves he had a professional fight record of 19-12. He was awarded an MBE in 1998 for his unstinting work for boxing and helping young people in the Wincobank area of Sheffield. He was in charge of the St Thomas's Boys' and Girls' Club, and in January, 2008 was given the highest honour in his adopted city when inducted into the Sheffield 'Hall of Fame'. Also there is a bronze plaque placed at the front of City Hall to mark the award.

Following Ingle's last visit to box in Belfast, I met up with him again on September 24, 1993, in Dublin, at the National Basketball Arena, Tallaght. He introduced a new button-bright featherweight prospect named Naseem Hamed to Irish fight fans. Hamed, already an audaciously cocky young boxer who spring-heeled over the top rope, did mesmeric somersaults inside the ring, and then proceeded to showboat and clobber Chris Clarkson of Hull into second-round submission. It was the then 18-year-old extrovert Naseem's ninth straight win. It was also a proud night for the loquacious Ingle, back in his home city for a first official boxing occasion since his own ring days.

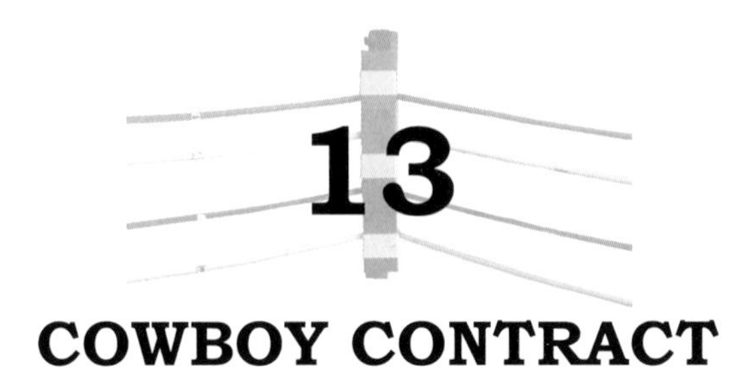

13
COWBOY CONTRACT

EASTWOOD had ambitious designs to bring major international boxing back to the King's Hall in the mid 1960's, put the place back on the map, but the dream would have to remain on hold until twenty years later. Still, he came close. He knew he needed world renowned boxers on board to take the gamble. He made a daring and successful bid to win the purse offer to stage a mouth-watering match between rival Glasgow fighters Chic Calderwood and John 'Cowboy' McCormick.

He intended to stage the Caledonian clash in Belfast: "We were trying to stage a big show in Belfast, maybe an outdoor promotion or go to the King's Hall. We had never been out of the Ulster Hall then, and we had a few good fighters. I felt if we could get this fight it would be a good attraction in Belfast. Maybe we could fill the King's Hall with such a contest at the head of the bill. It was both sides of the house. Belfast boxing fans knew all about the two Scottish boxers.

"Calderwood was a strong football follower of Glasgow Rangers, and McCormick was a big fan of Glasgow Celtic. It was my thinking at the time that such a huge fight would be a draw. We had nobody of our own near ready to head a King's Hall show. If I was going to get any television at that time the only chance was to have the right top of the bill. Unfortunately one of the boxers pulled out. I was messed about. Then there was a further postponement from the other boxer. And so it went on. I became fed up after all the delays. I eventually said bye-bye to the contract to stage the fight."

On June 10, 1965, the fighters eventually met in their native Scotland. McCormick beat Calderwood on a second-round knock-out in Paisley Ice

Rink. Referee was George Smith. This was a scheduled 10-rounder, no titles around at the time. Calderwood, born on January 9, 1937, tragically died at 29-years-of-age in an automobile accident on November 12, 1966. From Craigneuk, he made a brave but futile bid for the WBC and WBA Light-heavyweight belts, stopped in the second round by Jose Torres. The fight was in San Juan on October 15, 1961.

Big Chic, winner of the British title after Randy Turpin vacated, gained World recognition when he clearly outscored American ace Willie Pastrano over ten rounds in Glasgow's Kelvin Hall on September 16, 1960. Referee was Ike Powell. Calderwood (44-9-1) also won the Commonwealth Championship. Colourful southpaw McCormick, from Glasgow's Maryhill district, won a bronze medal at the 1956 Olympic Games in Melbourne. He lost to the USA's Jose Torres of Puerto Rico in the semi-finals. Born on January 9, 1935, he was the Scottish and ABA Light-middleweight champion for 1956. He started out as a professional middleweight, and in late 1959 he won and lost to Terry Downes for the British and Empire Middleweight titles.

On September 9, 1959, McCormick, a close pal of Eddie Shaw, took the titles on an eighth-round disqualification. In an instant rematch, on November 3, 1959, at the Empire Pool, Wembley, former US Marine Downes gained revenge through an eighth-round knock-out. The Cowboy's career also included a win over American tough-guy Henry Hank, a stoppage loss to George Aldridge for the British Middleweight title (vacated by Downes), and a win against Dutch fighter Harko Kokmeijer of Amsterdam for the European Middleweight crown, vacated by Gustav Scholtz. Another milestone victory was against American legend George Benton of Philadelphia, who had wins over Joey Giardello, Holly Mims and Jimmy Ellis before becoming one of the world's most respected coaches - starting under Eddie Futch. Benton was inducted to the International Boxing 'Hall of Fame' for his successes as a trainer of such notables as Joe Frazier, Leon Spinks, Randall 'Tex' Cobb, Mike McCallum, Meldrick Taylor, Pernell Whitaker, Benny Briscoe, Jimmy Young, Evander Holyfield and Rocky Lockridge.

The Cowboy's farewell fight, on June 28, 1966, was ironic in that he lost to Dublin's 'Young' John McCormack in a British Light-heavyweight eliminator in the Royal Albert Hall. Incidentally, the Scot's second fight ended the career of Dundalk's Irish Middleweight champion Cliff Garvey, on March 1957, in the National Sporting Club, Edinburgh, with an early stoppage. Garvey won the vacant Irish crown in Dublin by beating Belfast's Joe Quinn on July 22, 1955. Nine months later, on February 28.1956, he was involved in a third-round 'no-contest' outcome with one of my old trainers George Lavery of Belfast. Garvey quit with a 21-26-1 record.

Eastwood said: "Winning the purse offer bid for the McCormick-Calderwood contest was a one-off by me. I won purse offers for other fights, including one for Herol Graham when he was with me, but I stuck to making purse bids only for fighters attached to our gym." His extra curriculum activities, as he sent out fight feelers beyond Belfast, included one venture into a new American boxing phenomenon of the late 1960's, pay-per-view screening of major fights from the States and into world-wide cinemas. He organised the showing of Muhammad Ali's WBA Heavyweight title defence against Ernie Terrell, screened from the Houston Astrodome.

He added: "I was out of promoting then. At that period Jarvis Astaire of London was occasionally in contact with me about news of how we ran our betting shops in Northern Ireland. He was involved in betting shops with Terry Downes and Downes' manager Sam Burns. He had been on to me a few times, because we in Northern Ireland were the first to have betting shops in the whole of Europe and probably in the whole of the world. At one time if you wanted to have a bet in London, Glasgow or wherever in England, Scotland or Wales, you had to go to a street corner and place your bet with runners.

"In Northern Ireland you could go into a betting shop, albeit maybe it was not much of a betting shop in some cases, perhaps just a run-down shed up a back alleyway. Or it may have been an old bottling store, that type of thing. I had three shops then, and through that connection Jarvis Astaire offered me the chance to screen that Ali fight in Belfast. Astaire was also the Mr X of boxing in England in those days. Nobody knew him really. He was not referred to as Mr Astaire, but as Mr X. He ran the professional boxing." Astaire, once a power behind a few thrones in prize-fighting, had an association with former British Featherweight champion Sammy McCarthy. He became a joint-manager, along with McCarthy, when London's baby-faced 1956 Melbourne Olympic Games 'Golden Boy' Terry Spinks turned professional as a Flyweight in April 1957.

Eastwood added: "The people Astaire employed to run the boxing business were Mike Barrett and Mickey Duff. Barrett did the office work.

Duff was the matchmaker. You rarely heard the name of Astaire mentioned in those days. It wasn't until much later he came to the forefront. Before that, Harry Levene ran the boxing. One day, Jarvis Astaire rang to offer me the opportunity to stage a fight that was to be screened direct from the United States into cinemas in the UK.

"He told me had the pay-per-view rights of this Ali title fight against Ernie Terrell. Says Astaire:'Barney, would you like to get the rights for Belfast?. It will cost so much up front, and depending on how you do I want a percentage after that. By the way, Barney, the money up front is non-returnable.' We played to a full house in Belfast's Ritz ABC Cinema. Mike Callahan was there that night with the dickie bow on, and so forth, organising things. He was great." Ali, born January 17, 1942, and the Rome Olympics Light-heavyweight gold medallist, retained the WBA Heavyweight belt against lanky Terrell, on a points decision over 15 rounds.

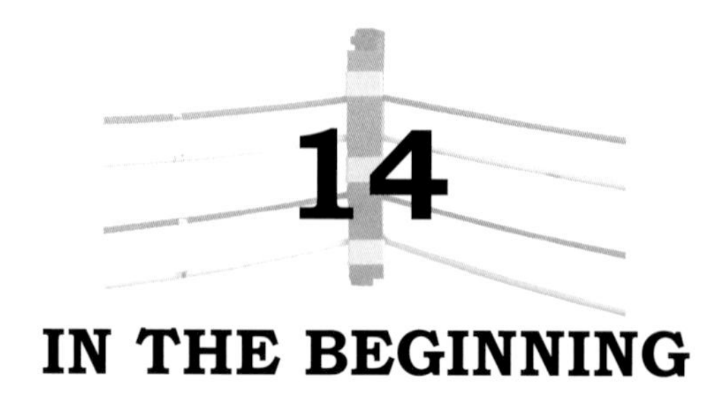

14

IN THE BEGINNING

TAKING a back seat from boxing wasn't easy, even then. Eastwood, however, placed his ingrained interest in the business end of professional boxing on a long finger in the late 1960's. Despite a sense of disillusionment at the time he never turned his back on boxing. He regularly turned up as a spectator at local shows. As always, he would be asked for an opinion on such and such a fighter's ability and prospects - and was never short of a viewpoint.

Neither would he shirk a wager on the outcome of a contest. I remember bumping into BJ at many fight shows where he was usually accompanied by his faithful shadow, Davy 'The Hat' Donnelly. One occasion that springs to mind was the 15 rounder on October 11, 1978, in Maysfield Leisure Centre. Up for grabs was the vacant British Light-welterweight crown. Local southpaw Jim Montague's hopes of winning the title ended in tenth-round heartbreak against London's Clinton McKenzie.

Eastwood would materialise at the back of the arenas, to watch fights that included Jim Watt beating Lisburn's Sammy Lockhart in the Ulster Hall, or rising heavyweight Gordon Ferris boxing in the Lakeland Forum, Enniskillen, or Ferris beating Tommy Kiely in the Ulster Hall for the Irish and Northern Ireland titles. He also kept an eye on the progress of Derry southpaw Charlie Nash, winning British and European Lightweight belts in the Templemore Sports Complex. Eastwood joined a strong Irish contingent, one that included ex-World Flyweight champion Rinty Monaghan, to support Nash in his quest for world honours in Glasgow on March 14, 1980. Watt stopped brave Nash in the fourth round of their WBC Lightweight title clash in the Kelvin Hall arena.

At the start of the 1980's he was truly hooked again. On this occasion he set his sights on the highest honour possible, to guide an Irish fighter to a world title. So, he became a manager for a first time, after witnessing a screen gem in the form of a young all-action amateur named Barry McGuigan. He couldn't resist the temptation to return to an active interest in the fight game. His natural boxing know-how and instincts were stimulated when images on a TV screen featured two amateur boxers slugging it out during an international match. The move to manifest the dream of a world champion in the making happened by accident. When he first turned his back on boxing involvement Eastwood insisted he'd stay away. But, the lure to mould a special fighter capable of winning a universal crown proved irresistible.

He was fascinated by that fight show on television, captivated from the moment he saw McGuigan in a Kuttner Shield match against Scotland's Ian MacLeod. He saw immense potential in the dynamic prospect from Clones. The seeds were firmly planted. Perhaps fate took a hand, because Eastwood insisted he held no serious ambition of coming back in as a main player in the Irish professional boxing scene. However, the magnetic attraction of guiding McGuigan to world fame proved too great to turn down. He made the decision after consultation with wife Frances, and then set about doing all in his power to sign the youngster.

Eastwood now had his vision: "I suppose it was not unlike training a thoroughbred to win the Derby. Perhaps I achieved my Derby success at Loftus Road in 1985. Quite by chance, in 1980, I saw Ian MacLeod fight McGuigan. I spotted something special, and I said to myself - that boy McGuigan has promise. Frances was there too, and we started talking about McGuigan – saying: 'There is a strong gutsy kid.' I thought he was just beginning to get going into the contest when it was over. I managed to get a video recording of that contest, and then carefully studied the boxer."

There was a long road to travel to achieve the ultimate target. First of all, he had to try and sign the fighter, and then get down to setting out a programme of specialist training and astute matchmaking. He conceded he was secretly tempted to look for a good Irish heavyweight prospect to manage, but conceded finding such a broth of bhoy was as rare as hen's teeth. He moved down the weights to unearth a featherweight nugget, finding a fighter sufficiently talented and dedicated and likely to fulfil the ultimate target. He felt the young tearaway from Clones might have a chance. I remember Frances saying: 'You are surely not going to again get involved in boxing, are you?' But, I was so interested I took another look at the fight on tape. You could tell then McGuigan was not a three-round fighter, but with a lot more to come. So, I believed something could be done, but nothing more happened at the time."

He was not to be deflected. In his own inimitable off-hand pincer-style manner he held a curiosity chat with prominent Belfast amateur coach Gerry Storey, who was the Northern Ireland boxing team trainer when McGuigan won Bantamweight gold in the 1978 Edmonton Commonwealth Games. Storey, from the Holy Family club in north Belfast,. knew the boy, and informed Eastwood the kid was a good fighter, was very dedicated, and was a teetotaller.

Eastwood recalled how he sealed the deal, and by accident: "Some time after that discussion with Gerry Storey I was in Dundalk to attend a function in the Imperial Hotel. It was sheer coincidence I bumped briefly into McGuigan. I think he had been involved in some boxing. I introduced myself, and told him about my previous experience as a boxing promoter. As a result of that I met him at the Ballymascanlon Hotel. I told him I thought he might have a chance as a professional boxer. Along with his father, Pat McGuigan - a very nice man - he came to see me at my then house at Gortnagreenan. We had a bit of a talk. I told his father we would do whatever was necessary to try and improve his son's ability. That was the beginning of an era."

The wheels were quickly set in motion to begin one of the most exciting adventures ever in Irish boxing. A training programme was formed, with Ned McCormick coaching in the Immaculata gym on the Lower Falls. Ned, who traversed the globe with Belfast prize-fighters Peter 'Al' Sharpe and Jim 'Spike' McCormick, was McGuigan's first professional coach. 'Young Barry' trained in a relatively new and well-equipped gym beside Divis Flats. Although, at times, getting in and out of the area was a problem. Eddie Shaw was also there, in the Immaculata gym alongside Ned at the beginning of McGuigan's career. It was the starting point to an exceptional time in Irish sport, and remained that way for the fanatical faithful fans, a great odyssey for everybody. The excitement was unique, uplifting for everyone. McGuigan's magical progress became almost like a runaway train of fabulously entertaining events.

During a dark, troubled time in Northern Ireland the exhilarating action lifted the hearts of the mixed masses, the Catholic and Protestant population. It was a tremendous period in Irish boxing. McGuigan lived up to all expectations. His 'search and destroy' mission accomplished the pinnacle of success, the winning of the World Featherweight Championship. Eastwood, who became an expert at forward planning to manoeuvre McGuigan into line for a shot at Eusebio Pedroza, agreed it became a case of following the treasure trail to the rainbow's end. Obviously the brightest point was achieving the WBA crown.

"Oh sure," Eastwood said, "It was a train of exciting events that just kept going. Then it got sour. Remember this. The success in winning the WBA title didn't happen on its own. It had to be made to happen. Various things were completed at certain times. Nothing just happened by accident. Many important things clicked into place, such as Eddie Shaw taking over the coaching, such as the bringing in of Ken Buchanan, the bringing in of Bobby McQuillar from the United States, sparring partners from Panama and the United States - and so on. It probably was a dream to try and win a world title. At first, McGuigan was at his family home in Clones, coming up and down to Belfast to train. If he was to really prepare properly for each fight, we felt he had to be in Belfast."

The room that became the gym at Castle Street was part of a big old building Eastwood purchased. It was next door to the Head Office of the Eastwood bookmaking enterprise. There was an empty area that was eventually fitted out with everything needed, including a shower. It became a very functional gym, and also a great focal point for boxing. It was central, right in the heart of the city. Everybody, especially the members of the Belfast media - written, radio and television, or otherwise - could nip in to see what was going on. Of course, if the mood took you, you could also pop into the Hercules Bar, or go around the corner to Chapel Lane and say a few prayers at the nearby St Mary's Church Grotto.

After the first managerial signing of McGuigan the second was Hugh 'Little Red' Russell, also a good prospect. Then it was the arrival of Dave McAuley, and a lot of very entertaining undercard fighters. Belfast light-heavyweight Frank 'Fra' McCullagh boxed on Ulster Hall bills. There were other good young fighters, including Roy Webb from Larne. Eastwood always took an interest in backing local boxers. He did so as a promoter during the 1960's, and then as a manager in the Eighties, and on into the early Nineties.

"There were other young boxers in our gym from time to time, who had the talent to make it to the top, but lacked real ambition, I fear. Very good prospects such as Damien Friars and Patsy Quinn came in for a while. I was their manager. Friars used to spar with McGuigan, and at first I felt he could have gone a long way. In my opinion he had nearly as good a chance of making it as McGuigan. He was very strong. Unfortunately, he could put on a stone in weight, from 9st 4lbs, over one weekend. Quinn, whose real name was Danny McAllister, was the same. Quinn and Friars were 'chinas', great pals then. They were boxers of good potential, but perhaps short on dedication."

The 'Cyclone-to-be', of course, was the prime focus to reshape Eastwood's interest in professional boxing. Born on February 28, 1961,

Finbar Patrick McGuigan broke into the Senior amateur ranks at 17 – years-of-age. Boxing out of the Smithboro club, County Monaghan, he upset the odds by beating defending Ulster Bantamweight champion and Belfast postman Sean Russell of the Holy Family Club for the 1978 provincial title.

That night in the Ulster Hall unwrapped this exiting prospect. Barry was really illegal at the time. He was under the age limit for Senior competition, yet made the Belfast fight fans sit up and take notice. Here was a live one, a high energy, super-fit young fighter. Before his dramatic debut in the Senior amateur grade, he created havoc and mayhem throughout the Juvenile, Junior and Intermediate ranks. Already the boy with the big fists, big heart, and ferocious tenacity was parading special qualities. He proved too strong in the Ulster final for a then very experienced Russell, older brother of Hugh Russell. Sean, who later became a professional boxing referee, was seeking a third successive win of the Ulster Bantamweight title.

I recall an after-show vehicle transport problem for the jubilant McGuigan entourage that poured out of the venue into Bedford Street, only to discover the family car had a flat tyre. I believe there may also have been no spare wheel. I vaguely remember coming across the mechanical crisis, and negotiating some help. Ironically, the incident was to become a first meeting of the McGuigans with some of my colleagues in the Belfast Immaculata Club. Inimitable trainer McCormick, Shaw and also another ex-professional fighter Jim Jordan rustled up assistance from the Falls Road area. Eventually they helped to send the McGuigan clan safely back home to County Monaghan.

Not that many miles down the trail, in boxing terms, there was to be a close, if short-lived, alliance between McGuigan and the quiet cornerman with the calm and reassuring words, Eddie Shaw. In 1978, Barry, after winning the Irish amateur Bantamweight crown, and Belfast Holy Family club's lightweight Gerry 'Ducksy' Hamill were the golden boys of the Commonwealth Games at Edmonton. Ballymena-based Hamill was expected to turn professional, but declined.

15

STEPHEN'S SHINER

THE HAPPY early days of the Eastwood-McGuigan alliance are the times best remembered. Once an accommodation was reached to launch a professional partnership, other cogs in the wheel were set in motion. Stephen Eastwood, third youngest of the family, was installed as promoter for the new era while his father concentrated on his baptism as a boxing manager. But, it proved a painful introduction during the early fight nights in the Ulster Hall.

On one occasion Stephen had good reason to ask himself: 'What am I doing here?' as he lay on the flat of his back, seeing stars out of a damaged left eye. He sported the perfect 'shiner' from an altercation with fight fans on a foggy night at the tradesman's entrance to the famed Bedford Street emporium. There was a problem at the back door in a dimly lit Linenhall Street, near the rear of Belfast's City Hall. It was October 5, 1982. "So this is what being a boxing promoter is all about, I thought. I didn't have time to duck. I was slugged, nailed by a Judas punch," recalled Stephen, who had the 'House Full' signs up early at the front door on Bedford Street.

Close on 2,000 fans were already shoe-horned into the small arena, "I was told of crowd bother outside the back door. The interest in Barry McGuigan was gaining pace. The show had him topping the bill against 'Jumping' Jimmy Duncan." McGuigan forced a fourth-round retirement stoppage win that led to a British Championship final eliminator a month later, against Paul Huggins. The match-up against Duncan was the Cyclone's 13th contest, but the occasion was a slightly unlucky one for the rookie promoter. The heaving, unruly mob of frustrated punters was in no mood to be turned back.

"It was an ugly situation," recalled Stephen, "It was a bit of a shock to the system, when I was beaten up. I tried to stop a crowd from gatecrashing, but the guys broke down the door. Then they stampeded, kicking and punching all over me. They got into the Hall. We started looking for them, but they hid, and I never found out who thumped me. I was at ringside immediately after the incident, and wearing borrowed sun glasses. I can still feel the glasses being pushed out second by second as my face continued to swell."

Qualified out of Queen's University, Belfast, in Economics and Accountancy, Stephen had no initial intention of becoming involved in the boxing end of the family business. Later he would shift, following the Loftus Road monumental, to help head up the bookmaking empire. Fight fame was thrust upon him, as his dad concentrated on overseeing the training programme and plotting the path to world honours for of his prized possession.

"Becoming a boxing Promoter? I often think about all that, and why," he added, "It just happened at the time. I came out of University, and into the family business. I suppose my dad trusted me to organise things, to get things done. I just fell into the position, and did it. It was exciting. I have many happy memories. Generally things went like clockwork, clicked into place, including the use of a wonderful bell for the fights. Little things like that proved very important. We still have the bell. It was once Jack Solomon's bell, and was given to us by our matchmaker Paddy Byrne. He first brought it over from Brighton for the McGuigan fight against Jean Marc Renard at the Ulster Hall. In those days, the man to ring it was ex-Belfast boxer 'Nipper' Dan McAllister, who was the officially appointed timekeeper."

Stephen was press-ganged into promoting. His father initially held a boxing promoter's licence, but in those times could not retain that position and also be a manager of fighters. This was the rule, so Stephen stepped in. The cruelly demanding yet intriguing sport of boxing was not foreign to him, nor any members of the family. It was in the genes, all part of a boxing legacy. "I remember selling fight programmes outside Carrickfergus Town Hall when my brother Bruno (Brian) was boxing on an amateur bill there. I rushed into the Hall in time to see Bruno pretending to be Muhammad Ali, doing an imitation of the Ali shuffle. He reminded me of a baby in the ring; he was so small, so skinny and bony. He was about four stone in weight."

Topping that bill was the big-hitting Doagh amateur welterweight Billy Turkington against Belfast's Hughie McGavock. The furious fighting didn't last a round. Turkington had to quit because of eyebrow damage. Stocky McGavock, who lost a year later to the 'Wee' Turk in the 1965 Ulster amateur final, said: "I remember being involved in very well run shows at Carrickfergus. I beat Billy (Turkington) in March, 1964, but amateur officials later took the decision off me. The fight only lasted about a minute, and they said Billy was ahead on points. I split his eyebrow, yet we were never in a clinch. I was on the ropes when I fired about three or four punches. He went back, and with blood spurting from a gash in an eyebrow. Ulster Council officials strangely reversed the stoppage decision, and awarded the fight to Billy on points. I represented Queen's University then, and was trained by former Northern Ireland professional Middleweight champion George Lavery."

Stephen added: "That fight created a lot of interest in the area. The Turkington brothers, Henry and Billy, were so popular then. I was probably six or seven-years-of-age, and going to the Carrickfergus Boxing Club two or three times a week. We had the smell of boxing in our nostrils from very early primary school days. Dad sponsored those amateur shows in Carrick. The local club had ex-professional Billy Anthony as the coach. He married my mum's sister Kathleen from the Loup, near Ballyronan. Billy was a good boxer. Dad took him on board during the Sixties. He was a handy one, turned pro as Billy Corbett, and was from Carrickfergus. I recall Billy and my dad bringing us to the Carrickfergus Boxing Club. It was upstairs. We went there to train - Bruno, Peter, Adrian and me.

"Before that, my father would stock the bar in the pub on a Sunday and bring us down. There was a fellow called Stevie who ran the bar. He would come in to do the stock, and my dad would get the boxing gloves out. He would show us how to box. He would clear the tables to make space. The bar, of course, was shut on Sundays then. He would have Adrian, Peter, Brian and me boxing each other. I remember Adrian, who was bigger than me, getting the better of things so I 'Dirty Joe'd' him one time. He was furious, chasing me around the place.

"My father got us to go and train in the Carrickfergus gym, which was then in Minorca Place. I was training there for a while when a young boy came into the club who was a year older than me in school. He got in to do a couple of sessions with me. I said I would take him around, and I'd place one hand behind my back. I was cheeky, but I learned my lesson.

He knocked the duff out of me. I started to cry, felt bad at letting myself down so much in front of everybody, and after being so cocky. The one thing I was proud of, nonetheless, was I never took the one hand from behind my back. However, to come from so high to fall so low in such a short space of time taught me a very valuable lesson in life."

Stephen's vague memory, and it is just that, includes his father's move to promote shows in Belfast during the 1960's: "I recall my dad getting dressed up, dickie bow and all, putting on a penguin suit during the Sixties, to go and do the professional boxing shows in the Ulster Hall. I remember the names of Turkington and Sharpe being involved in great middleweight fights. I never saw any of those contests, because I was too young - and never taken to the Ulster Hall in those days. But, we were always kept well informed of what was happening, and especially in world boxing affairs such as the rise then of Cassius Clay. I recall the second Ali World Heavyweight title fight with Sonny Liston at Lewiston, Maine. That town, I believe, sponsored the contest in a venue probably smaller than the Ulster Hall.

"The fight was on the radio. My father also had this huge tape recording thing, the size of a suitcase with one reel of tape on one side of the machine. The tape then moved into another reel on the other side. He taped the world title bout off the radio, so that he could relay the fight next morning. I got up in the middle of the night, when half asleep, to listen to a big fight from America. As you can see, the boxing theme ran through our family from we were tiny tots." With shrewd Stephen in place as the promoter, and the coaching team sorted out for the start of the exhilarating climb to stardom for McGuigan, the next significant thing to happen was to lure Brighton-based Paddy Byrne, the best cutsman in the business, into the Eastwood camp.

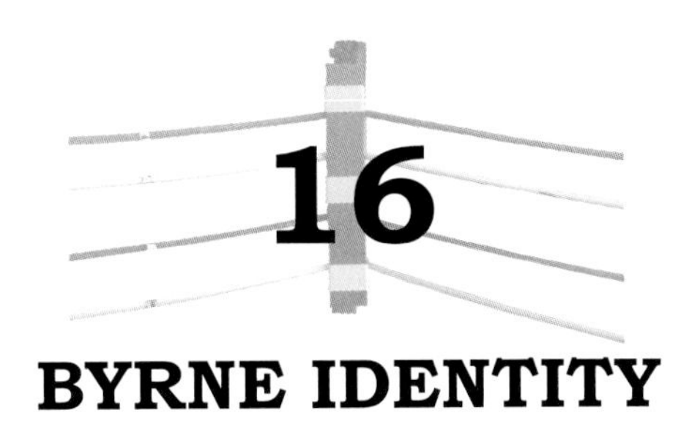

BYRNE IDENTITY

FIGHT agent, manager and matchmaker extraordinaire for over half-a-century, Paddy Byrne also held a world-wide reputationand respect as one of professional boxing's most accomplished cuts expert. The November 2007 WBO Super-middleweight title fight in Wales, where champion Joe Calzaghe beat Denmark's Mikkel Kessler, marked the retirement of Byrne. He was in Kessler's corner, and about to celebrate his 80th birthday.

He decided the Cardiff show would be his last big occasion. It was time to call it a day. He was with Kessler on and off during the previous four years, including a jaunt to Australia for a crucial win against Anthony Mundine in Sydney. Byrne was also in the corner for Kessler's defence of the WBA and WBC belts, a great fight to defeat the previously unbeaten Librado Andrare of Mexico on a unanimous decision. Andrade was a very good kid, claimed Byrne. Kessler won in front of 15,000 fans in what was a Pay-Per-View sensation on Scandinavian television.

Byrne, tagged the 'Peter Pan of Punch', became something of a cult figure in Nordic boxing circles. On September 14, 1968, he first made serious contact with Danish fight mogul Mogens Palle, who later looked after the affairs of Kessler. The meeting was during the last big show in Sweden, a first world title promotion by Edvin Ahlquist that attracted 18,792 fans. It was an all-American WBA Heavyweight title fight. Louisville's Jimmy Ellis was an earlier winner of the vacant title, on a close decision over Jerry Quarry in Oakland, California. A big-bucks offer from Ahlquist brought Ellis to Sweden, to make a unique and successful first defence by outpointing former champion Floyd Patterson in the Solna Fotballstadum, Stockholm. Referee was Harold Valan. The decision was 9-6.

Palle and Byrne began a working relationship that survived through the decades. Byrne was associated with most of the Palle shows, working as cutsman and also bringing in opponents for the local Danish fighters. "I have travelled a lot down the years," said Byrne, who did the exacting corner 'cut' work for over half-a-century. He moved all over the globe to do cuts, including in Zimbabwe, and very often in Copenhagen. He worked with Ken Buchanan during the Scot's closing contests. Paddy also set up a show in Dubai for Chris Eubank, and was down in South Africa to work the corner for 'Baby' Jake Matlala and for Harry Simon, when the latter boxed Winky Wright for the world title.

Byrne's background as an ace cornerman began through a chance meeting with a Canadian in London, following World War Two. He first learned the cuts business from a very good boxing agent who worked in Jack Solomon's office. He was Dave Egger, who helped to import great American fighters to England, including Joe Baksi, Gus Lesnevich, Ike Williams, Sandy Saddler and Roy Harris, a heavyweight from Cut and Shoot, Texas. Incidentally, the man who brought Harris to London was the son of the legendary Jack 'Doc' Kearns, once the manager of Jack Dempsey. "I met a lot of important boxing people and boxers in my time," added Byrne, "I got to know Dave Egger very well. He was a great cornerman, very clever. I picked up all the tips from him, on how to cope with facial injuries during fights. You have to first clean the cut before you put any adrenaline in. You have to get rid of the blood first of all.

"You have merely the sixty seconds to work on the cut between rounds, so you are in trouble if you panic in there, even though it is always a race against the clock. You must not panic, although other people might be doing just that around you in the same corner. You have to be very cool, and try to transmit that calm to the fighter. I've been all over the world to do cuts, helping out in a crisis, including with fighters such as Billy Hardy when he boxed for the European title three times in San Remo."

He was, of course, heavily involved as cutsman and matchmaker throughout most of McGuigan's career. He worked in the corner during many of the World title fights. He first came in contact with Eastwood in the mid-1960's, when he brought 'Young' John McCormick of Dublin over from Brixton to fight Leon Ven and Derek Nicholson in the Ulster Hall. In the 1980's Byrne provided a varied and specialist service to the Eastwood camp during the phenomenally exciting, hugely successful but sadly short-lived McGuigan era. The amenable boxing entrepreneur was a vital cog in the Eastwood machine. He imported fighters for contests, and also as sparring partners.

Adamant that Eastwood gave Irish sport a very special shot in the arm during that halcyon McGuigan period, he declared: "Barney definitely lifted the boxing game in Ireland. He made a great contribution. You had to have the will and the wealth to do it. He had to spend big money by bringing in foreign fighters. He had to spend money on fighters to make them the best. He had to spend money on the McGuigan thing, getting the young boxer into the new purpose-built gym, getting the best possible equipment, putting him up. Sparring partners from all over the world came in, and they had to be put up in accommodation and paid before you put on a show. I had to be paid.

"Of the key fights for McGuigan, on the way to beating Pedroza, I felt the toughest early bout for Barry was against Charm Chiteule. Then Juan LaPorte was the next big test, that right cross catching McGuigan. Barney spent a fortune on grooming McGuigan. I did the deal for Buchanan to come in. He stayed in a Belfast hotel for the best part of six weeks, and was well paid by Barney. During sparring sessions Ken showed Barry how to move, swing, swerve, roll. Buchanan was very clever," added Byrne, who took an early personal if painful interest in boxing at Lightweight when he went to England, started reading up about famous world fighters as a primary schoolboy in Dun Laoghaire, County Dublin:

"My dad, Patrick was a very good Gaelic footballer. He never had an argument in his life, yet they called him 'Boxer'. I started reading about boxing at a very early age. I was selling papers in Dun Laoghaire. I could read from about four-years-old, and loved scanning through the sports pages and looking mainly for news of boxing. Joe Louis was my first hero. He was brilliant. Later, it was Gus Lesnevich, Gene Fullmer, Roland LaStarza, Rocky Marciano. I just got into it, and suddenly there I was - involved in boxing, but never with an amateur club. My idol was Sugar Ray Robinson, but I didn't get to see him until he was nearing the end of his days, when he again came to the United Kingdom. That is mainly how it started for me. Also, and very importantly, I was friendly with John McCormick's father Spike, the old middleweight legend from Dublin."

Spike is worth a mention. He was one of Dublin's all-time tough guys. He made his debut against the formidable Tommy Armour in Belfast on December 12, 1943, and lost on points over ten rounds. At that time the ring-wise southpaw Armour had 95 contests under his belt, winning 82.

Such a match-up would not be allowed to happen nowadays. On July 14, 1944, McCormick had the return in his second outing, this time in Dublin, and the result was the same. Spike was stubborn. The determined Dubliner reversed the two setbacks in a third meeting with Armour on September 16, 1944, when winning on a seventh-round knockout in Dublin.

Overall, Spike, who contested ten contests, winning seven, included a ten-round decision against Belfast's Freddie Price in the Rotunda Cinema, Dublin, on March 9, 1945. Incidentally, the unheralded Price, who finished his ring career with six contests in the United States, was also involved in running battles with 'Shankill Thunderbolt' Armour, winning two of four meetings. Price also crossed gloves with notable English middleweights Dick Turpin, Albert Finch and the powerhouse Randolph Turpin. Spike out-pointed Jack Sean Clancy in his penultimate bout, in Waterford's Olympic Ballroom on May 25, 1945. On August 24, 1945, he had his final fight. It was a win against Paddy Lyons in Dublin's Theatre Royal.

Byrne added: "It was through Spike I really got my teeth into boxing management. I took his sons John and Pat to England. They became my first champions. I also managed Liam 'Ske' Mullan, when he beat fellow Dubliner Gussie Farrell for the Irish Welterweight title. I managed Pat Stapleton, who was the Irish Heavyweight champion." Born in 1935, Stapleton had 17 bouts, winning 13. He made his pro debut at the National Sporting Club, London, in January, 1959. He beat Cliff Purnell on points over six rounds. Pat also won three fights on the same night, in a Novice Heavyweight tournament at the Empire Pool, Wembley. In March, 1960, he beat Belfast-based Garnett Denny on a fifth-round technical stoppage in the King's Hall. It was Denny's last fight. On April 4, 1960, Stapleton then clinched the Irish Heavyweight title from Paddy Slavin, taking the crown on a sixth-round knock-out in the King's Hall, Belfast. Andy Smyth was the referee. Pat's last fight was on April 15, 1969, when he lost on a first-round stoppage to American Bill McMurray in Sacramento, California.

Enthusiastic Byrne gained valuable early experience through the handling of capable ring men such as Stapleton. It all helped in moulding the sons of Spike. The McCormick boys became British champions. Pat was a rough, tough kid, a really good fighter who finished with a 49-fight record, winning 30, and with 24 by the short route. Born on April 28,

1946, Pat was on the undercard of the Muhammad Ali 10-round contest against Al 'Blue' Lewis at Croke Park on July 19, 1972, when he halted French fighter David Pesanti in five rounds. On March 26, 1973, Pat won the British Light-welterweight title on an eleventh-round knock-out of Des Morrison in the Royal Albert Hall. In November 1974, he lost the title to Joey Singleton, on points over 15 rounds in Liverpool Stadium. He decided to quit after a 13th-round stoppage loss to Pat Thomas, in a bid to win the vacant British Welterweight Championship in December 1975.

John McCormick, later to coach in Dublin's St Gabriel's gym, fought Eddie Avoth when winning the British Light-heavyweight title. The Welshman suffered a cut. They had the return fight. John was apparently beating Eddie again, but was disqualified, and quit boxing after that. Byrne also had 'Wee' Joe Kelly of Scotland on his books, when the Glasgow fighter won the vacant British Bantamweight title over twelve rounds against Ronnie Carroll. In June 1992, he lost the title in a first defence against another Scot, Drew Docherty, and then retired. Before all that, Kelly lost to Dave McAuley for the vacant British Flyweight Championship. Byrne also took Joe to America, where he stopped Richard Brown in Richmond, Virginia, for the vacant IBF Inter-Continental Flyweight title.

"Roy Webb, a bantamweight from Larne, was another very useful fighter I kept an eye on," added Byrne, "At one time I was also keen to sign the great Irish amateur Jim McCourt, an Olympic bronze medallist and Commonwealth Games Light-welterweight champion from Belfast. I thought he would turn professional. I chased him, but he stayed amateur. Jim was a big name then, in the 1960's, a good strong southpaw with an ideal clean-cut image."

SOLOMON'S GIFTS

CIGAR-chomping London fight mogul Jack Solomons was a father figure to Paddy Byrne. The big man with the distinctive rounded face in the white suit made his mark on world boxing when he lured fashionable American fighters to Great Britain after World War Two. He staged-managed mega productions, mainly in London, and they included the landmark Turpin Robinson World Middleweight contest.

Solomons set the standard. He also held more than a passing interest in the careers of Irish fighters such as Billy Kelly, Freddie Gilroy, Danny McAlinden and Charlie Nash. Byrne was right at the ring apron with Solomons, quickly learning the moves. It proved a rewarding working relationship, with Solomons handing down in his Will some personal mementos to Byrne. Married in Brighton in 1947, Byrne lived most of the years with wife Madge in the Marina area of the English south coast town. However, he did his ducking and diving in the boxing business in London.

"The old car Jack Solomons left me was a snub-nosed Amazon Volvo, with a personalised registration number, JS 121. The car had an exceptional history. It was presented as a gift to Jack by the Israeli Government, then under Golda Maier. I think it was something to do with a charity occasion. The car was beautiful. One day a prominent cricketer, Jack Spooner, came down from London to Brighton with a case full of money to buy the car. I sold it. Jack Solomons also left me some money, and silver cufflinks that I later gave to Barney (Eastwood). The cufflinks had boxer logos on them. I also presented Jack's ringside bell to Barney.

That fight bell made the sounds to start and finish rounds during many historic contents such as Randy Turpin's win against Sugar Ray Robinson for the World Middleweight Championship. Just imagine the many other famous major international fights this particular bell tolled - involving noted ring men such as Bruce Woodcock, Freddie Mills, Eric Boon and Henry Cooper.

"There was also a second Solomon's bell, used for fights in the World Sporting Club in London, where many other big shows were held. Solomons left £20,000 in his Will to help needy former boxers. A few thousand quid was to aid old fighters in the Ex-Boxers' Association. Jack was generous. That gift from Jack came to the end by early 2008. I believe there was around five grand remaining that had to be distributed with the help of boxing commentator Reg Gutteridge."

The famous bell and Byrne arrived in Belfast for a first time as a part of the official backroom squad in the Eastwood enterprise when McGuigan had his fourth fight. Incidentally, Eastwood Promotions was also presented a bell by the Belfast Fire Authorities. There was widespread involvement, and a belief a new and special Irish boxing spell was under way. Paddy 'Leave-this-to-me' Byrne was not matchmaker for McGuigan's first fight, at Dalymount Park, Dublin. His opening assignment, as importer of opponents for shows in Belfast, was when he brought in the very useful Jean Marc Renard. The battling Belgian was a good tough fighter, a strong hitter, and, in hindsight, more dangerous than anticipated.

Eastwood agreed: "Renard proved a very difficult fight. I must say we were worried. He (McGuigan) went on the floor. He got all the advantages that night, in what was a very close fight. Referee was Harry Gibbs, an admirer of McGuigan." The thrilling contest was arguably the first rung successfully conquered by Barry, climbing off the boards to do so. Byrne was on-board the Eastwood boxing bandwagon when the Cyclone ruled the world. He rated the world title win in London as an extra-special occasion for Irish boxing. The other very dramatic night was Barry's last successful defence of the WBA Featherweight title, in Dublin.

Memorable moments, as Byrne recalled: "In the King's Hall ring we had some terrific fight nights. Battles staged there often seemed unreal. It was fabulous. It was as exciting as anything I ever experienced in major boxing shows throughout the world, and I attended some great nights at Madison Square Garden, Las Vegas, Copenhagen, Atlantic City, to name but a few. I went with Steve Collins to big fights in New York and Italy, but the King's Hall was special. It even tops a massive show I attended at Atlantic City in 2006, featuring the great Arturo Gatti. The atmosphere there, the support for Gatti was unbelievable, but I'd have to give it to the King's Hall. It was a very special place as far as premier boxing shows were concerned. There were some great promotions in Belfast."

Byrne was in the corner for Dave 'Boy' McAuley's famous battles against Colombian tough nuts Bassa and Blanco at the King's Hall. He enjoyed the spine-jingling excitement. "It didn't get much better than that, McAuley's fights. The fans were sitting open-mouthed on the edge of their seats when the Boy was in action. There was no knowing what might happen. I match-made quite a few contests for McAuley. I was also in Dave Boy's corner at Loftus Road where he broke a hand against Scotland's Bobby McDermott, yet sensationally won. McAuley could really fight. I didn't have too much to do as far as cuts were concerned for him, but it was different when I was in the corner for Hugh Russell. There was a lot of blood about."

SPOOKY SEVEN UP

DUBLIN doctor Terry Christle made a little bit of quirky fight history when boxing under the Eastwood banner in the Ulster Hall on February 22, 1982. The record books reveal the odd-ball battle of a seven-round contest, won by Christle against the then noted journeyman Winston Burnett. What the cold statistic does not illustrate is the fact former Irish amateur ace Christle, also an ex-French amateur Middleweight champion, not only cut up brave Burnett but also stitched his facially damaged opponent after the fight.

"What a weird night that was," said Stephen Eastwood, whose top-of-the-bill was Barry McGuigan in a ninth outing. Christle was involved in the only official seven-round professional fight ever recorded, as far as I can tell. He beat Burnett, after setting up the match in Dublin where the Eastwoods met his father in Wynn's Hotel on Boxing Day 1981. "My father, along with Paddy Byrne and me, met Terry's father, Joe, whose three sons fought in Irish amateur teams. The meeting in the hotel was more like Mr Christle interviewing dad, who wasn't going to manage his son Terry, or anything like that. It turned into one of the most amazing fights of all time, in my view. Terry's father insisted on a six-rounder.

"Terry was a very sharp middleweight, a good puncher. Winston was an old journeyman. Burnett stayed longer in the fight game than the in-laws, as the old joke goes. He was durable, could go the distance - eight, ten rounds, whatever." Christle, an Olympian, was up and coming as a professional. His match with Burnett was listed in the programme as an eight-rounder. He was gloved up when he informed Stephen Eastwood that his father insisted he was not ready for an eight rounder. Paddy Byrne did the matchmaking. and the Eastwoods believed the fight was to be an eight-rounder.

The Christles insisted it was to be a six rounder. Terry's brother Mel was there when the re-negotiating began to try and solve the impasse. Burnett insisted he wanted eight rounds, as he claimed he felt stronger as a fight progressed. Eventually, a compromise was reached for a contest over seven rounds. "Terry beat him, and also split Burnett's lower lip in the process. There was a lot of blood about. Winston had a real bad injury," said Stephen, "This led to another rare happening in boxing, a first probably. Terry, who was also a medical doctor, stitched up his opponent's badly gashed lip after the fight. Surely that fight ranks one of the most amazing and bizarre happenings in professional boxing!"

Mel Christle, Terry's barrister brother, agreed: "As far as I can ascertain, a seven-round professional fight never happened before, nor since. I certainly remember that fight. My recollection also is there was obviously a complete misunderstanding between the parties, which gave rise to the seven-rounder. My father Joe, who died in May 1998, told us Terry was going up to Belfast for a six-rounder. It came as a surprise to me when I went there to see posters for the show stating Terry was down to fight in an eight-rounder. I rang home, and my father said: 'No, it is a contest over six rounds'. Father added it was agreed a six, not Terry doing eight. I said: 'Is there no compromise here?' Father said: 'Sure, tell them we will agree to seven'. It was more a case that my father would not be bested. Barney Eastwood was delighted. He got more publicity for the unique seven-rounder, much more than he would have for an eight-rounder."

Incidentally, the Christle seven-round affair was part of a bill headlined by a burgeoning Barry McGuigan, who knocked out Angel Oliver in the third round. Hugh Russell won on points over six rounds against Jimmy Bott. Before coming to the Ulster Hall, Terry Christle won on points over the six-round distance against Burnett at Mayfair, London - on February 16, 1981. That was his second professional contest, and he wanted to stay in the six-round zone for the rematch in Belfast. Jamaica-born Burnett, who lived in Cardiff, arrived with a 6-10-2 record at the Ulster Hall, and finished his career with 121 bouts, winning 20 and losing 98. He became an active manager/trainer in Wales.

Christle moved to America, where he had a combined career as a surgeon and professional boxer. He came back from the United States in 2004, to live in Ireland with his family. When he was in the States he first settled on the east coast, andlater moved to America's west coast, to live in Santa Barbara. He returned to the eastern seaboard, and was based in Andover, Massachusetts. When he boxed he was managed by Goody and Pat Petronelli. He spent some time living in Brockton, Massachusetts, where he completed his ring career. His last seven fights, 6-1 from a 13-1-1 record, were in the United States. He put away the gloves after losing an eight-rounder to Dave Tiberi of Delaware in Atlantic City on August 1987. Tiberi later lost to James Toney on a split decision over 12 rounds in an IBF World Middleweight title bout.

Mel, President of the Boxing Union of Ireland since 1982, was the first of the Christle dynasty to win an Irish amateur Senior title, at Light-heavyweight in 1977. Three years later he clinched the Super-heavyweight crown, while brother Joe won the Irish amateur Heavyweight crown in 1979 and '80. Terry also distinguished himself on the Continent, where he won the French amateur Middleweight title. He made history by achieving a unique double. A week after he clinched the Irish Championship he won the French laurels at Agen, in the south of France.

The fighting Christle boys boxed out of the Crumlin Club, Dublin, with Terry taking a hat-trick of national Middleweight titles, in 1978, '79 and '80. The Christle's mother, Mimi was born in France. That made Terry eligible not only to contest the French Championships but also to represent France in an international match against the United States. "Joe and Terry were born in Dublin," added Mel, "I was born in France. Terry, as the French champion, boxed for France against an American selection in Paris to mark the anniversary of Marcel Cerdan's death. Terry hammered a Yank in the centrepiece pairing."

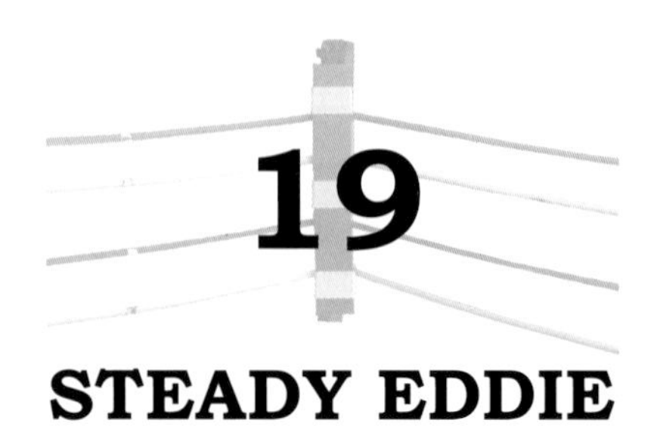

19

STEADY EDDIE

EDDIE Shaw, born on January 5, 1942, in west Belfast, patiently tried to find new ways of improving the boxers under hiswing. He firmly believed different methods suited the varying styles of his fighters, and being able to instantly adopt to a change of direction. Boxers needed the skills to handle certain situations, be prepared for the unexpected, make the most of their natural talent. He searched for ways to help fighters cope in unexpected situations. He repeatedly probed fresh possibilities. His first priority was to try and improve the progress of Barry McGuigan. Later on, his shrewd observations of life inside the ropes related to other Eastwood fighters such Hugh Russell, Dave McAuley, Paul Hodkinson and Crisanto Espana.

In a commissioned article of mine, published on September 28, 1985, the then 43-year-old former professional featherweight disclosed: 'You never stop learning in this game, trying to figure out opponents' styles, learning new methods of training that can be of benefit to Barry. I have learned a lot of tips since becoming Barry's coach, and I continue to search for new ideas.' The ex-Irish amateur international added: 'I've had some great experiences since I began working with McGuigan. I've learned quite a lot, especially meeting some of the world's top trainers such as Bobby McQuillar, picking the brains of the very experienced New Jersey fighter and coach Gerald Hayes, gaining tips from Ken Buchanan. While in Chicago and New York I also met a few of the best in the business.'

A fastidious fighter during his own short-lived ring days, he knew all about the pitfalls that can crop up in professional boxing. He was fairly well prepared for the challenge ahead, after he was approached by

Eastwood in February, 1981 to help train McGuigan. On his return from Italy, as coach of an Ulster amateur team, he was invited to join the Eastwood team, and the happy alliance took off from there. Lots of hard work had to be put into the shaping of McGuigan. It was a long and sometimes bumpy road that required sacrifices. McGuigan didn't reach the top by taking the easy options. Working the hard methods stood to the fighter.

Eddie added: "In the early days he was far too eager for his own good - a raw pro for the first year. Once he accepted the training methods, he settled down. I'm sure a lot of coaching tips I picked up along the way, from the first day I stepped into the Mac gym as a kid, helped me do my job in the McGuigan camp." Shaw was a protégé, just like former World Bantamweight champion Johnny Caldwell, of the late great Belfast trainer Jack McCusker, when based in the old Immaculata gym in Devonshire Street.

The boy from Baker Street joined 'The Mac' in 1953. He quickly won a variety of Juvenile titles, and then the Ulster Junior Flyweight crown from Jimmy Henry in the 1959-'60 season. He also completed the double, clinching the Irish Junior Flyweight Championship. He won the Ulster amateur Bantamweight crown in 1961. In November, 1960, Eddie made the first of twelve Irish international appearances, even though still a Junior, when losing a split decision to famed England Bantamweight Alan Rudkin in London. His last two international outings were in the Featherweight division.

He switched to the punch-for-pay ranks, and joined the growing Jimmy McAree stable headed by southpaw bantamweight Freddie Gilroy from Belfast's Ardoyne district. Included was classy Dublin-born welterweight Freddie Teidt, the 1956 Olympic Games silver medallist. Shaw made his professional debut at 19-years-of-age, had nine bouts, mainly at super-featherweight, and boxed on two occasions on the undercard of shows headlined by manager McAree's golden nugget Gilroy. He out-scored Bobby Mack over four rounds in London's Empire Pool, Wembley, on June 5, 1962, when Gilroy met and defeated the then French Flyweight champion Rene Libeer.

On October 20, 1962, he was also a bit player in the King's Hall, Belfast. He halted Sheffield lightweight Neil Shawcroft on the memorable all-Belfast bantamweight battle when Gilroy beat Caldwell in a British title fight. On Saturday September 14, 1963, Eddie's penultimate contest was an eight-round points win over Tommy Burgoyne during a special night in the Ulster Hall. The main attraction was the touring World Heavyweight champion Charles 'Sonny' Liston. Local fight fans had no idea the mean-looking Liston, fresh from icing Floyd Patterson, was allegedly 'mobbed-up' in the States. The ferocious puncher was then regarded the baddest man on the planet. Sonny was billed to take part in three rounds of exhibition sparring against fellow American professionals. That didn't materialise.

Before the Ulster Hall show, he was first introduced earlier in the day to the Belfast public in Bannon's city centre furniture showrooms. During the opening of the new Bannon enterprise, Paddy Toner, a leading sports writer in those days, welcomed Liston to Belfast. Toner, sporting a heavy bushy beard, was invited along by the late Frank Bannon, a boxing enthusiast who signed up Liston to officially open the family's newly acquired shop. Crowds flocked to see Liston. "I spoke on behalf of the local boxing media," said Toner, "Big Sonny replied: 'Thanks Castro', because I had a beard to match that of the Cuban President. Later, Liston went through a couple of rounds of his skipping routine in the Ulster Hall. That was about it." Liston, who stayed in the old Royal Avenue Hotel, stepped through the ring ropes in the Ulster Hall and performed his renowned skipping routine to the 'Night Train' tune.

Heading the competitive boxing side of that programme was Freddie Teidt. It was, like Shaw's, to be the stylist's penultimate contest. He decisioned Zimbabwe's Ernesto Musso over eight rounds. Belfast flyweight Alex O'Neill lost to Carl Taylor. Welterweight Mick Harvey beat local lad Harry Stamford. County Monaghan's Maurice Loughran, a former Irish amateur Light-middleweight champion, had his farewell outing when losing to Andy Barry. Ballyclare welterweight Bob Sempey lost to Liverpool's Dave Arnold. Incidentally, Musso, born in Bulawayo, was involved in a milestone contest three years later at Solihull, against Johnny Cooke of Bootle. On September 9, 1966, history was made. For the first time in a British ring the referee's score tally was made public. Referee Austin O'Connor totalled the action 40-39 in favour of Musso.

On October 22, 1963, Eddie Shaw called it a day, after suffering a fifth-round stoppage at the fists of Ghana lightweight Abe Francie in Derry's Guildhall. Eddie won six, with four knockouts, and lost three professional fights, mainly against super-featherweight opponents. He weighed between 120 and 123 lbs, and generally conceded up to half-a-stone in some contests. Eastwood, who recognised the cool temperament and vision of Shaw would be perfect for his plans to prod McGuigan to world stardom, holds a vague recollection of a young stylish boxer making his professional debut in 1962. It was in Carrickfergus Town Hall, and the promoter was the late Larry McMahon, who ran other shows, including one in the old Troxy Cinema on Belfast's Shore Road.

"Eddie told me he used to get five shillings or sometimes half-a-quid (10/-) a round to spar with his stablemate Freddie Gilroy," said BJ. Shaw, who began to pick up coaching knowledge in his old club, the Immaculata, where he helped Ned McCormick, once said: "Those were happy days. The Immaculata gym was filled with all sizes and shapes of quality boxers, both amateur and professional. There were great characters, including Spike McCormick, Peter Sharpe, Jim McCourt, Bernie Meli, Andrew McCormick, Terry and Sean Hanna, Paddy Graham, Alex McGavock, Jim McAuley, Hugh Gilhooley, Paddy Moore, Barney Wilson, Paddy Maguire, Toby Shannon and the Brady brothers."

Eastwood highlighted the importance of his faithful right arm in the Castle Street fight factory: "Eddie picked up bits and pieces of knowledge along the way from key people such as Ken Buchanan and Bobby McQuillar. He was very interested in all aspects of boxing, always eager to learn new coaching ideas. He started in the fight game under good trainers, when an amateur in the Immaculata Youth Club. As a professional boxer, he trained alongside Gilroy, yet knew there was still so much more to learn. He was able to decipher what he thought was rubbish, and what he considered was good. He retained all the good bits, and was a great advocate of the left hook to the body."

Eastwood added: "Eddie insisted that special shot to the body generally discouraged opponents. It was his favoured punch for an orthodox boxer. He used to say: 'Bend, bend, feint, and throw it' - dishing out instructions to the fighters in our gym . . . 'Move your head - and bump, get the shots in there below the ribcage'. That was one of his specialities. When we were in America for a first McGuigan fight there, in Chicago, Eddie studied the Mexican boys in training there. Also, he was on the lookout how top professionals were trained by top coaches in New York." Single-minded Shaw, a man who had a close ally in another former Belfast fighter Jim Jordan, brought all his ideas to the Eastwood gym. When the cosmopolitan centre was running at full pelt there was an influx of twenty world champions coming through the door, at one time or another. It was an amazing place.

20

JORDAN AIRS

JIM JORDAN, the 1958 Empire Games Lightweight silver medallist at Cardiff, was never far away from Shaw's ear during the halcyon days of the Eastwood stable. They were near-neighbours as kids in the 'Pound Loney' district, and went to the same Primary School at the lower end of Belfast's Falls Road. Living wasn't easy for all families in this breeding ground for boxers. It was prudent to learn how to fight. Jordan came from a very interesting boxing background. His father John boxed professionally in the olden time Ma Copley shows in Belfast.

A student of the game, just like Shaw, he added: "I viewed many old fight films to see if I could pick up some further knowledge about the game. Of all the world-class fighters I have come across and watched on tapes or read about I was especially fond of Muhammad Ali. I didn't see too much of Joe Louis on film clips, or of Sugar Ray Robinson, but I studied a lot of Ali's fights. He was different. The other fighter I admired was Roberto Duran. He was amazing, ruthless. Of my own era in Belfast, I thought John Kelly was the best. John Caldwell was an absolute cracker, yet I felt he should have stayed in the Flyweight division. Going to South America to fight Eder Jofre in a World Bantamweight title fight was tough ask for Caldwell."

He also highlighted the great Gilroy, his former stablemate: "You can't take it away from Freddie. He was very exciting to watch. His two fights with Billy Rafferty of Glasgow were superb." Also, Jordan selected Belfast's Terry Milligan as Ireland's all-time top amateur. He claimed the outstanding Milligan was set to turn professional, and about to receive a licence from the British Boxing Board of Control, when his trainer George Scott of the Short and Harland Club suddenly died. Terry then didn't go ahead with it. His outstanding amateur record not only included gold from the 1958 Empire Games, but also a bronze medal from the European Championships in Milan, 1951, and silver from the Europeans held in Warsaw, 1953. Milligan won six Irish titles, starting in the Featherweight division in 1950, and then on to three successive Light-welterweight titles from 1951, the Welterweight crown in 1954, and a year later the Light-middleweight Championship.

"Terry was a fabulous all-action fighter," insisted Jordan, "He picked up five Ulster titles, from Bantamweight in 1949, then two at Light-welterweight in 1952 and '53, Welterweight in '54, and finishing at Middleweight in 1958. I was on six representative team trips with Terry and never saw him lose. I was in the same Northern Ireland team when he took the Middleweight gold medal from the 1958 Empire Games in Cardiff. He was a better pro than some of the professionals in Belfast. Terry knew all the tricks of the trade. He had over 400 amateur fights, and it is estimated he won all but 21. Terry died aged 73."

Jordan added: "Boxing was in my blood. I literally grew up with boxing gloves on my hands. I came from a family of eight including four girls. John, Gerry and me took up boxing, Tony didn't. He emigrated to Australia." As a schoolboy he was in the Immaculata Club for a very short spell, after starting with St Mary's Youth Club in King Street. "I was out of boxing for a good while. My brother John worked in Belfast Shipyard, where he was friendly with a Jackie Gorman, trainer of a club in Lisburn. He coaxed John to join Lisburn, and when John went there so did I. John reached the finals of the Ulster Junior Championships, but my father wouldn't let him box in the final because of a damaged hand."

Jim secured his first of many boxing titles while at Lisburn, in the Ulster Youth Championships. In that same year Dickie Hanna, who won a Bantamweight bronze medal at the 1958 Empire Games, also took an Ulster title and that helped Lisburn clinch the Higginson Cup for the most successful club in Ulster Youth competition. It was the first time Lisburn managed to win the Cup. The club had other good boxers such as Leo McCutcheon and Joe 'Boy' Collins. The great Lisburn professional, Jim Keery, then retired, used to come in and out of the Lisburn club, do a bit of sparring and help out. Keery had a lengthy ring career, and was the only man in the UK willing to fight the legendary American Sandy Saddler in London. He was stopped by Saddler.

Jordan moved from the Lisburn club: "I used to work for a firm on the Shankill Road. The owner, Fred Paige, was also the President of the Lisburn club. When I told him it was becoming too difficult to travel to Lisburn for training he recommended I join the St George's Club in the Markets district." The switch saw him collect one Ulster Junior title, three successive Ulster Senior amateur Lightweight titles from 1956, and one All-Ireland, in 1957. When he first moved into the St George's gym he was trained by Jim McStravick. Mickey Mullan took over after McStravick retired, and fabled fight trainer Jimmy Clinton then came in. The club ended up the joint St George's and St Malachy's unit. It was known as the 'Cradle of Champions.'

The St George's boxers worked out of premises in Crown Entry, beside the city centre's Cornmarket. It was in the same building as the Crown Boxing Club, then run by Arthur Anderson. The next move was to Catherine Street North, in the Markets. The nomads had no set place to train in those days, and were housed in the Hollerith and Bosco Clubs before finding a place behind Trimbles clothes shop in Cromac Square. Jordan reached the old Empire Games Lightweight final in 1958, losing to Scotland's Dick McTaggart. There wasn't much in that fight. Some people thought skilful Irish fighter did enough to win the final, but others felt McTaggart deserved to get the decision. McTaggart was one of the world's most distinguished amateurs. Two years before he edged Jordan, the lanky southpaw won gold from the 1956 Olympic Games. Dick also clinched the 'Best Boxer' Val Barker trophy from the Melbourne finals. From Dundee, he boxed in three Olympics and took home a bronze medal from Rome in 1960. He also won the European amateur Lightweight title at Belgrade in 1961, and became the only British boxer to win all three gold medals from the Empire (since renamed Commonwealth), Olympic and European events.

Jordan, whose wife Bryl died in 2002, had a multitude of boxing tales. Sadly, younger brother Gerry, a former amateur bantamweight and featherweight, died of heart failure in Florida in 2006. Gerry emigrated to America in 1974, after boxing for Northern Ireland in the Commonwealth Games. "Gerry was a plumber to trade, and a proud fighter who never had any inclination to turn professional. I remember bringing him and other Bosco Club boxers Mickey Tohill, Paul Carson and Martin Quinn in my car to the 1968 Irish Senior Championships in Dublin's National Stadium. It was Gerry's first fight at that level, and when he was merely

8st 2lbs - very light for a bantamweight, and up against top Irish international Mick Dowling.

"In fact, for that meeting Dowling didn't make the weight at the first attempt, and had to go out and train to sweat off the extra. In the end Dowling beat Gerry, and did the same every year after that for about four seasons. Mick won eight Irish Bantamweight crowns from 1968. Once I brought Gerry up to Sligo town to fight Dowling on a club show. Gerry beat him with plenty to spare but could never get the better of Mick in the Dublin Stadium. Eventually, in 1972, Gerry moved up a grade and won the Irish Featherweight title."

After Cardiff, Jordan claimed he was informed he was going to represent Ireland in the European Championships at Lucerne in 1959. There was a shock to the system when the Irish champion was not picked to fight in a warm-up international against an Italian team in Dublin. He was listed for the reserve match against Italy in the Ulster Hall. "I was told if I won I was going to the Europeans. Along with brother Tony, I was locked out of the Ulster Hall by a prominent Belfast amateur official because we had no pass tickets. I was pretty upset. We turned to go home when I was called back, and then placed in the last bout on the show. I easily beat the Italian, but didn't get the decision. That finished me for good with amateur boxing, so I turned professional, in 1959."

John Kelly, the former British Bantamweight champion from Belfast's Ormeau Road, was Jordan's first manager, indeed the one and only fighter the then retired southpaw managed. Kelly was a former St George's amateur, and along with the Club's devoted official Johnny Black helped Jordan take the plunge. Jim reckoned quiet-man Kelly was one of the best boxers he ever saw. He once marvelled at the retired fighter during a sparring session, when Kelly helped out Freddie Gilroy, who was preparing for a European title fight.

"He gave Freddie an interesting time. John kept very fit, and trained me in the St George's gym, then back in Catherine Street North," added Jordan. Kelly was manager for his first four fights, until Jordan left to work in London, and was out of boxing for a year. His first defeat was that fourth fight, when stopped on cuts in the Ulster Hall by Paddy Loughran - formerly a Bosco club amateur and later trainer of a club in Carnlough, County Antrim. Loughran finished on an 8-7 pro record, and included contests against luminaries Maurice Cullen of England and Ghana's Floyd Robertson.

On May 9, 1960, Jordan resumed hostilities with another old amateur foe, Jimmy Gibson of Scotland, who was unbeaten in four contests before the meeting in Manchester's Free Trade Hall. Jordan won again. Gibson was disqualified in the seventh round after a head clash split the Belfast fighter's forehead. Scottish amateur and professional champion Gibson, from Dunfermline, first arrived in Ireland when he was one of the top UK amateurs. Jordan beat him on a club show run by the Belfast Hollerith club. That match was over five two-minute rounds. A few weeks before that Gibson beat the European amateur champion.

"His trainer started shouting I was too heavy for his boy. Two weeks later I boxed him in the Ireland v Scotland international Kuttner Shield match in Dublin, and beat him again," said Jordan, who joined his buddy Shaw in the vibrant Jimmy McAree stable for the latter part of his professional career, "Eddie was one of best fellows I ever met, a true friend. We were great pals for many, many years. Both of us were born at the bottom of the Falls Road. I came from Millford Street. He lived around the corner from me, in Baker Street. We went to St Comgall's Primary School, but were in different grades as I was a bit older than Eddie. He would have done anything for you, just a brilliant bloke. Like me, he came from a big family circle that was very close."

Shortly after his fourth paid fight Jordan married in London, and later joined the McAree camp. He went to Wembley to watch Gilroy beat Italy's Pierro Rollo for the European Bantamweight belt. He had a chat then with Gilroy's manager McAree, who said he'd look after things if Jordan returned to Belfast. So, Jim resumed training in the old Bosco gym in Donegall Street. He went to Manchester in April, 1960, when Gilroy was matched with Mexican Ignacio Pina. Freddie, who suffered his first defeat, was to be there 24 hours before that fight, but, along with Jordan, missed the flight. The pair then travelled via Glasgow, and on to Manchester. They were met at Manchester airport by worried promoter Harry Levene and matchmaker Mickey Duff. Jim's tiring trip was hardly worth the bother.

He revealed the alarmingly poor wages for his fight on the undercard against Harry Shaw was a measly five pounds sterling! On June 29, 1962, an outdoor contest on a Dublin football pitch against Cork's Sean Leahy was his last fight. He was stopped in the first round, after his left eyebrow sustained a severe gash. Manager McAree took him to the Mater Hospital in Dublin, where he received nine stitches in the wound. When his wife saw the state of his face, now badly swollen on the morning after, she started to cry. Jim decided then and there that was it. After he quit boxing he did a bit of amateur coaching, launching a club in Cypress Street off the Falls Road, but eased out after a year. He later revived his fight interest when working closely with Shaw - once the McGuigan era got under way. He insisted Eddie was always his own man, knew his boxing, and never let the success of helping fighters win an assortment of World titles go to his head. Also lending a hand was Sean 'Skull' Feeney.

Jordan added: "Eddie had important help from Buchanan, McQuillar, and later on Bernardo Checa. In total, Eddie trained six world champions for Eastwood. During that time we always talked things over, on how best to try and improve the boxers. Eddie worked tremendously hard to try and achieve perfection for his fighters. I felt McGuigan never really gave Eddie much credit, even though he put the finishing touches to all the World champions in the Eastwood stable. Those were marvellous times. McGuigan, of course, was the first world champion for Eastwood. Barry was good - very strong, and very fit. Getting past Juan LaPorte's big punches that night in the King's Hall was impressive. In my opinion, Eastwood looked after McGuigan very well, and got him the right fights at the right time - especially setting up the contest against Pedroza for the world title. Pedroza was on his way out.

"Then there was Dave 'Boy' McAuley. I never saw a fighter with guts like McAuley. His first World Championship fight with Fidel Bassa was amazing. He kept coming back off the deck to put the South American down, until Dave was stopped in the 13th round. Eddie just treated all those guys like schoolchildren, and they did everything he asked of them. They did what he told them. As a matter of fact, I recall one fighter, a local lad in the Eastwood stable, saying to Eddie he was not keen to train that day, and wanted a rest. Quick as a flash Eddie said: 'You train or you don't come back to this gym.' So, the guy changed into his gear, and started to do the training routine. Eddie took no nonsense in the gym.

"Crisanto (Espana) was a cracker, very powerful. I was in London to watch him beat Meldrick Taylor for the World Welterweight title. That was impressive. Also, Cordoba was a solid fighter. All those guys were great fellows, no big heads in the camp, including World Featherweight champion Hodkinson. He was excellent, very brave, a great heart. Unfortunately he cut quite a bit." He took a special interest in the local boys in the gym, such as Close and went to Glasgow with Ray for the first fight against Eubank, in a world WBO Super-middleweight title fight. Jim carried Ray's European Championship belt into the ring ahead of the boxer. He thought Ray won that fight, unlucky not to get the decision.

THE CANNY SCOT

FORMER World Lightweight champion Ken Buchanan provided some of the most significant help in the shaping of Barry McGuigan's ring career. Eastwood always maintained one of the important things to happen during the early days was getting Buchanan to assist with sparring and coaching. Born in Edinburgh in 1945, the Tartan tearaway was well schooled in the Noble Art. During the main part of his illustrious professional career he was guided by famous American trainer/manager Gil Clancy.

Welsh ace Eddie Thomas was also there when he achieved World Lightweight title honours. He brought a goldmine of boxing knowledge to the burgeoning career of McGuigan. It proved to be a smart move by far-sighted Eastwood. Buchanan was a revelation. "He was a sharp guy in the ring, good at explaining. He could give anybody a lesson," said BJ, "Ken had a treasure trove of boxing know-how. I brought him into Belfast during those formative McGuigan days because I felt we'd used up sparring partners from our own local area, and from England. There were boxers coming in from Liverpool, but we needed something different to help move to a higher level. Better opposition was needed to help the learning process. So, Buchanan spent up to ten weeks here, overall. It was nice and quiet in the Lisburn gym we used for a short while. It was good sparring. McGuigan, I felt, also didn't want a lot of press people there to see how he got on with the great Buchanan."

The slick Scot arrived in Belfast after McGuigan lost in his third outing, to Peter Eubank. Eastwood quickly decided something had to be done to inject a fresh direction into the operation. He had a chat with Byrne. They discussed what went wrong at Brighton. Both agreed the supremely strong McGuigan was getting to Eubank at the end of every round. BJ believed, with the benefit of hindsight, the defeat did no harm, taking away the pressure that can come with trying to maintain an unbeaten record. However, a new move was needed to usher along the masterplan. Byrne mentioned the use of Buchanan might be of help. He knew what was happening then with the ex-champion, who was persuaded to come to Belfast. It was felt the grooming of McGuigan needed somebody of the former world champion's calibre, stature and class to come in and help try to smooth the rough edges.

Eastwood added: "Paddy believed we could get him, but it would cost a lot of money. I said I would prefer to spend a fair bit of cash on bringing in someone really good who is going to help teach McGuigan things. At that time it was an outlay of a good lot of money. Ken was to come in on a Monday morning, and go home on a Friday night. He stayed in the world famous Europa Hotel. He was met at Belfast International Airport, with a car waiting to bring him into the City Centre. Buchanan was a part of the overall investment. He was good. Ken first stayed for five weeks, had a break, and then came back for a couple more weeks. It was a great move."

Byrne remarked: "Barney spent a fortune in the grooming of McGuigan. I was involved with Buchanan when he was at the end of his career. It proved a good move for McGuigan. Ken showed it all during sparring sessions with Barry . . . how to move, swing, swerve, roll. Buchanan was very clever. I took Ken to Zimbabwe to fight, and also had him over in Copenhagen to box Charlie Nash in what was a close European title fight."

Buchanan, elected to the International Boxing Hall of Fame and the 1970 'Boxer of the Year' Edward J. Neill Trophy winner, recalled a happy time spent in Northern Ireland: "I was retired from boxing when Barney Eastwood made contact with me. He asked if I would come across from Scotland and work with Barry. I went there on a few occasions to spar and work with Barry." Kenny enjoyed his trip as a tutor to the new kid on the U.K. boxing block: "I had a great time in Belfast. It was smashing. I will never forget the very first round when Barry and I started boxing, the first spar. I said: 'Work away Barry and if I see any mistakes I will pull you up, and so forth.' After about a minute of the first round he hit me right on the unmentionables - below the waistline. It brought water to my eyes. Christ, I says to myself, I had more than my share of hits south of the border when I fought Roberto Duran. I don't need anymore. I said to Barry I was hit a right few times in that area by Duran and he had no need to copy him. We had a laugh about it.

"Barry used to come up to the Europa Hotel. We would go running, do our roadwork. He used to go like a hare, pull away from me. I'd shout after Barry: 'Where the hell are you going?' I said to him: 'You don't need to run fast, you jog. All you need to do Barry, I said, is jog nice and lightly with the heavy boots on, and the tracksuit on. That builds the strength in your body, in your legs. That's the way you do your roadwork.' Years later, Barry was talking on television, and he said he remembered Ken Buchanan working with him over in Belfast, the sparring. He also recalled he went running with me, and then admitting he ran too fast. Barry said he liked to run fast. He then added it wasn't until he was in New York at one time when he was watching Duran and a couple of other top fighters doing their roadwork he noticed all they were doing was just jogging."

Ken added: "I have many great memories of being over in Belfast. The basic material was there, in Barry, and right away I saw the tremendous potential. I first sparred in the Lisburn gym. I could see World Championship potential at that early stage of his career. Every time I went into the ring with him I could see he had a very bright future in boxing. There were a couple of raw bits about him, and these needed to be ironed out. Once that was done I felt the guy was going to the top. I knew then he was going to go far, providing he kept his chin down and his hands up. I also said to Barry then to look after himself. If you miss that shot you cannot come back.

"I told him I came back, made a return, but it was no good. You only get one bite at the cherry, really, so go for it. I also advised Barry to watch his weight, and also not kill himself doing the weight. I told him he was to make sure he was a pound or two over the weight for three or four days before a fight as he would work off the extra poundage through nerves. I felt if he did that he would go into the ring strong. Barry developed the left hook to the body, and eventually started using that punch - because he was mostly straight left and right hand. The hook to the body was a good punch for Barry.

"I also advised him then to relax a bit more, when it was necessary, and not overtrain. I told him he could not train in the gym and also run all day. You have guys nowadays who train three times a day. These guys have probably got weight problems. Normally, nobody should train three times daily. All you really need to do is train once a day, either on the roads or in the gym. I used to train on Monday, Tuesday, Thursday and Friday in the gym, at night. Saturday, Sunday and also on a Wednesday I would do roadwork. That was my training schedule, and I became an undisputed world champion. It was good enough for me. I did not kill my body. I was a natural lightweight, and Barry was a pretty natural featherweight.

"Barney Eastwood was a good manager for Barry, and I was sorry when they fell out. When Barry went to America, to defend his title, Barney later said to me he was sorry he didn't bring me with them. This was wrong and that was wrong, and Barry was blaming the heat. I fought outdoors when I won the world title from Panama's Ismael Laguna. It was 125 degrees, the heat in Puerto Rico. It was two o'clock in the afternoon for the open-air show. I feel that was harder than Barry's fight in Las Vegas." The classy Caledonian revealed he revived his strong Irish roots during that visit to Belfast. He said he was 'half Irish' because his mother Kathleen, whose maiden name was McManus, was born in Ireland. His father, Thomas, was Scottish and born in Wick. Buchanan maintained the family clan arrived in Scotland from Ireland centuries ago, first settling on the east coast of Loch Lomond and from there spreading out all over Scotland.

Always willing to learn during his own formative years, Buchanan, a joiner to trade who began boxing as an amateur in the Edinburgh Sparta gym, declared the trickiest customer he met in the ring was Belfast's Jim 'Spike' McCormack. In late 1967, they met in a British Lightweight Championship eliminator at the Cafe Royal, Piccadilly. Legendary trainer Ned McCormick was in Spike's corner. "Spike gave me a hard fight. It was all part of my ring education. He was very elusive, shifty. Spike was so clever, so difficult to catch. It was a harder contest for me than when meeting Maurice Cullen for the title. Maurice later went up to light-welterweight. He was a nice fighter. I won in eleven rounds, knocking Maurice out."

Three years later, on September 26, 1970, the piercing left jab of the brilliant Buchanan helped to take a split decision over 15 rounds for the WBA world crown against Panamanian all-time boxing great Ismael Laguna in San Juan's Hiram Bithorn Stadium. He clinically defied the odds. Still, there was more than a touch of curiosity when the one points tally of 144-143 against him was by Puerto Rican referee Waldemar Schmidt. A professional since 19-years-of-age, Ken won 36 from 37 bouts before he became the first British lightweight to win the world title since Freddie Welsh in 1917. Apparently, because the British Board of Control did not give him backing nor recognise the WBA then, the main British boxing writers did not attend the fight. It was with a nice touch of irony when Buchanan was named the 'Fighter of the Year' for 1970 by the American Boxing Writers' Association.

One of his successful defences was against Laguna in September 13, 1971, in Madison Square Garden. Buchanan's crown was saved by the gruesome intervention of a razor bade. His cornerman and ex-British Welterweight champion Eddie Thomas of Merthyr Tydfil slit open severe swelling in the right eyebrow. Laguna (65-9-1) from Colon City retired after the contest. Buchanan, who topped five Garden bills, also put another ring legend into retirement. He beat classy Puerto Rican Carlos Ortiz, on the undercard to Muhammad Ali fighting Floyd Patterson. Again wearing his traditional tartan shorts, Buchanan lost the title in a gruelling battle with the rising Roberto Duran of Panama. He suffered a technical stoppage at the start of the 14th round in Madison Square Garden. The fight attracted a new record gate of almost $224,000 from a crowd of 18,820. Referee Johnny LoBianco was criticised for not ruling a low blow when Buchanan was floored, and apparently after the bell sounded at the end of the 13th round. The champion was unable to continue. Buchanan claimed Duran blatantly stepped outside the rules.

They met socially in later years in England. "The dirtiest fighter I ever met was Duran. I make no apology for stating that," he insisted, "I did a bit of after-dinner speaking and met up with Duran when he was on a tour in England. We joined up for five days during speaking gatherings in London, Exeter and Swindon. It was brilliant. Duran attracted 800 guests in London." Buchanan didn't have a rematch, after losing the title to Duran: "I came out of that world title fight without a visible mark of damage on me, apart from the undercarriage. He hit me there so often I was later detained ten days in hospital in Edinburgh. I could not stop the blood coming through me. Duran hit me illegally so hard below the belt he burst a vein in my right testicle. Even now, I still get pains. Sometimes when I run I get a shooting pain coming up from there."

Experts argued for some time after the world title thriller why Duran was allowed to take this painful sport outside the rules and allegedly brutalise Buchanan off the Lightweight throne. The proud Scot's excruciating pain scattered all other emotions, especially a desire to continue. The cruelly crippled ring mechanic had to concede his crown on the stool. Even the classiest of acts, Buchanan had to endure the darkest of corners against deadly Duran. After the agony in the Garden, he was back in the same ring on September 20, 1972, to force three-time World champion and Hall of Famer Ortiz to retire on the stool at the end of the sixth round. It was end of the road for Ortiz.

Buchanan also defeated fellow Scot Jim Watt to regain the British title, but lost in a bid to win the WBC title against Ishimatsu 'Guts' Suzuki in Tokyo, in 1975. Parallels could be made between Buchanan and his future pupil McGuigan. Both Celtic tigers suffered fearful setbacks in world title defences in the United States. On December 6, 1979, Buchanan also lost on points to Charlie Nash, when the Derry southpaw made a first defence of the European Lightweight belt in the Brondby Hallen, Copenhagen.

Ken recalled a close contest: "I came out of retirement, after three years away, and had a couple of fights before I met Charlie for the European title. The winner of that fight was going to meet Jim Watt for the WBC World title. I couldn't see Charlie beating me, even though he was not a bad fighter. I thought I won the contest in Copenhagen. I felt after ten rounds I was well ahead on points. I believed I won, even though the fight was close, but I had a feeling Charlie would get the decision. I managed myself at the time. I felt no way would I get a shot at the world title again. Anyway, Charlie got the crack at the World Championship. He fought Jim Watt in Glasgow. Charlie was never known as a heavy puncher. Still, he put Watt on the seat of his pants. Then Charlie's face was opened like a trout's mouth, with a very bad injury. I had 69 professional fights, and out of that I had merely four contests in my native Scotland. I am in the record books as one of the most travelled World champions in the history of boxing. Hilario Zapata was also like me. We went everywhere to box."

Ken retired from the ring in January 1982, and this master craftsman proved an invaluable help to the relentless rise of the Cyclone. Eastwood was a big admirer of the Scot: "Ken was class. I had long talks with him about his fight with Duran, and he revealed Duran hit him everywhere, including the Adam's Apple. Ken had to sip through a straw, and was also releasing blood for weeks. Duran was some performer. He was only small guy, but with great shoulders. If only he behaved himself nobody would ever have beaten him. Luis Spada would tell me about Duran, declaring Roberto was the greatest ever. Spada was the manager for a spell. Duran was urged to go on and win another and yet another title, yet Roberto was a lightweight, at most. Duran would be very high in my list of all-time boxing greats, but Sugar Ray Robinson was better than any of them. I feel Robinson was 100 years ahead of his time, uniquely gifted."

He studied many old grainy black and white films of Robinson in action. Born Walker Smith, the Sugarman was the ultimate showman, a slick tap dancer, film and TV actor, and also a trumpet and drums jazz player. The Prince of Punchers, the complete box-fighter, drove a light pink Cadillac while on tours in Europe. In his entourage the flashman had an impressive retinue that not only included sparring partners and manager George Gainsford but also a personal barber and a golf professional. During a second stylish junket, and after six wins on a whistle-stop tour throughout the Continent of Europe, the classiest act of them all famously lost his World Middleweight title to Randolph Turpin at Earls Court.

Eastwood added: "Some might argue Muhammad Ali the greatest ever. Obviously it all comes down to personal choice. For me, Robinson must come first. If Robinson had been around in the latter years he still would have been better than Ali, in my opinion. Muhammad Ali was great, don't get me wrong. A lot of his world success went down to publicity, showmanship, television. Sugar Ray generally did it without all that. He could be just as good a showman, but he didn't get the same exposure that was available to Ali."

22

McQUILLAR MEMORANDUM

LACONIC lightweight Bobby McQuillar was an unknown fight figure when he arrived in Belfast, but had a profound influence in the grooming of the Cyclone. His knowledge as a class coach was instantly recognised by Eastwood during an accidental meeting in Manhattan. There was a soft menace about the easy-going McQuillar, when he seamlessly slipped into the frenzied action of the Castle Street gym.

The accomplished and worldly Yank stalked along the gym ring ropes with the same cat-like grace he used in his active boxing days. You could tell McQuillar's home was a boxing gym. The training regime, supervised during that formative time for McGuigan by Eddie Shaw, gained momentum after settling into the new custom-built gym. The sometimes claustrophobic fight factory was then the sole professional boxing training unit in Ireland. Things moved quickly.

Eastwood, always striving for ways to improve his young tiger, said: "From the opening months, after McGuigan turned professional, the training programme was mainly in the Immaculata gym. It was so awkward without a home of our own - so many obstructions, distractions, and also a difficulty in getting in overseas sparring partners to the Immaculata." That resulted in Eastwood creating and developing his own gym by setting up a privately-owned purpose-built fight facility in Castle Street. After they settled into the specially furbished premises things moved at a pace. Eastwood looked for new ways to improve, which is where the excellent McQuillar came into the big picture.

Perhaps he was the most significant aide to the moulding of a world champion. He was unearthed in New York City, and the quiet-spoken, always respectful McQuillar was then lured across the Atlantic. During his ring career he fought three World champions, at Lightweight. McQuillar agreed to come in and pass on his considerable knowledge in helping to shape, sharpen, and put extra polish on Eastwood's prized fighter.

BJ explained: "McQuillar, who stayed six weeks in Belfast, was the best money could buy at that time, as a boxing coach. I first saw him in New York in the famous Gleason's Gym. I met him during the time we took McGuigan to box in Chicago. We went into the gym, and I noticed McQuillar doing some coaching. He would get into the ring to prove a point - making moves, blocking, and so forth. It was fascinating to watch. I felt he would provide something more for us. He had a big impact and influence on the improvements. He was a special guy for us, just like Ken Buchanan." The steps Eastwood took of bringing in Buchanan and McQuillar held a spin-off benefit for Eddie Shaw. There are guys who can make the science of boxing look easy, but there are very few of them about. McQuillar was a special influence at that early period of McGuigan's progress. And out of that Eddie's coaching ability became better and better.

Eastwood's son Brian said: "McQuillar was a fascinating character. On top of an interesting boxing career he was also a personal friend of a very famous music man - jazz icon Miles Davis, a horn player. During his boxing time McQuillar beat three world champions yet rarely talked about those days of his young boxing life. He was a modest, humble man, and a vital part of the boxing education programme for McGuigan."

Born on August 2, 1935, at Lackawanna, New York, McQuillar boxed out of Fort Huron, Michigan, and at times his name appeared in the results as Bobby McQuillan. A smooth-moving lightweight, he had 43 bouts, winning 35 - with 15 knock-outs. He lost six and drew two. Bobby won his first seven contests before losing on a third-round knockout in Cleveland to the famous Ike Williams. He won the Michigan State Lightweight title, and on February 28, 1948, drew over ten rounds with another ring legend - Joe 'Bones' Brown, in the Pelican Stadium, New Orleans. In a return that May, and at the same venue, he out-pointed Brown over ten rounds. He also beat another fighter who won a world title, when scoring a ten rounds decision over Jimmy Carter in New Orleans. Unfortunately, his career ended abruptly. On September 29, 1948, he scored an eighth-round TKO win against Kid Dinamita in Chicago. Dinamita allegedly died of injuries sustained in the bout, and McQuillar retired following this tragedy.

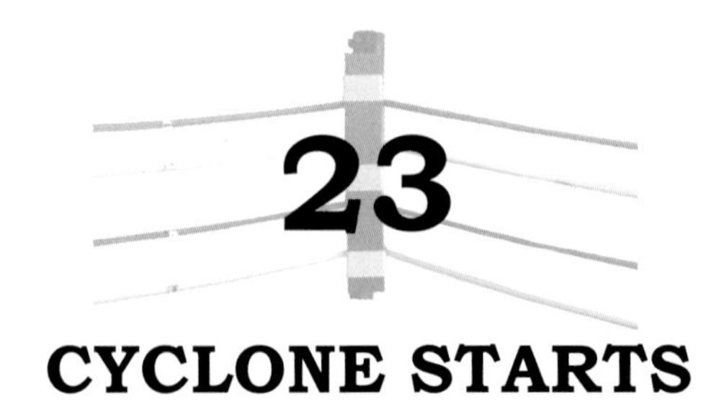

23

CYCLONE STARTS

THE PURSUIT of punching perfection and world honours for Barry McGuigan had an outdoor beginning in Dublin, yet excited manager Eastwood missed the first curtain call for the Cyclone, due to a previously booked family holiday. On May 10, 1981, the odyssey began in the centre of a soggy Dublin football pitch, at Dalymount Park, where the eager McGuigan was unleashed on hapless Manchester journeyman Selvin Bell.

The one-sided contest (rsf 2) was part of the undercard of an ill-fated European Lightweight title defence by Derry southpaw Charlie Nash. It was open-air anguish for Nash, crushed in seven rounds by heavy-hitting Italian Joey Gibilisco. It was obviously an evening of mixed emotions for Irish fight fans. Show promoter Philip McLaughlin headlined the bill with fellow Derryman Nash. Charlie, who once came close to dethroning WBC World Lightweight champion Jim Watt in Glasgow, was nearing the end of his ring journey. "I felt McGuigan would beat this guy, without any problems," Eastwood said.

McGuigan had good cause to remember his debut. During soft underfoot conditions, despite late summer, he had to use plastic bags over his boxing boots in order to walk across the football pitch to the ring. McGuigan was shaping up like Ireland's new Messiah with Mitts, but it was much too early to tell. Bell was no test. Next up was Gary Lucas at Wembley Arena. Nicaraguan Alexis Arguello boxed and beat Scotland's Jim Watt that same night for the WBC Lightweight belt.

Eastwood approached Jarvis Astaire, an old business associate who was one of the promoters, and asked him to put rookie McGuigan on the show. He was then invited to speak with Mickey Duff. It was one of the early contacts Eastwood made with Duff. The exercise eventually cost Eastwood money. Duff told him he already had too many fights on the bill, and could pay little. Eastwood was informed he'd have to pay for the opponent, and all his own expenses. "It cost me a good lot of money to get him a fight on that show. I think they allowed me £500 to cover everything. I paid four air fares, four hotel bills, up to the Thomas A'Beckett gym for training, and also money for our fighter. Whatever he got I made up the difference, but it was a big financial loser," claimed Eastwood. McGuigan beat Liverpool's Lucas on a fourth-round stoppage.

The best laid plans went completely awry next up when the young tiger suffered a shock to his system in his third outing. On a clear-sky August evening in 1981 McGuigan was left shocked and stunned in Byrne's adopted home in the England south coast town of Brighton, once voted the happiest seaside city in the United Kingdom. It turned out a night of sorrow, unexpected trauma, and tears for baffled Barry at the holiday resort where he dropped a disputed eight-round points decision. Eastwood had to produce all his powers of fatherly comfort and consolation for his stunned prospect.

BJ said: "The lead into the third McGuigan fight was when I said to Paddy Byrne it was costing a fortune to get our fellow on boxing shows so why don't we put on a bill of our own? Paddy said: 'Leave this to me'. Next thing is, he has a show going at this small hall, Brighton's Corn Exchange. Paddy was a very good organiser. He came back to me, and said: 'Look, tickets have been slow. Who would want to see a relatively unknown McGuigan boxing in Brighton?' I said: 'Go ahead, but keep the expenses down as much as possible'.

"Paddy replied: 'I've got this local guy, not a bad operator - Peter Eubank, who will give McGuigan a good workout.' However, the two-minute round stipulation by the British Boxing Board of Control did us in, because McGuigan was coming on strong near the end of every round. Anyway, we put that contest on to get our boy experience. Eubank was strong - a good operator in many ways. Ned (McCormick) and Eddie (Shaw) were there, and also the late Dermot McGuigan, Barry's brother. It was a learning experience for everybody."

Byrne accepted partial blame for McGuigan's first setback, and said: "I was obviously responsible for setting up the match that cost McGuigan his first defeat. I promoted the show. Peter Eubank lost something like five of his previous seven contests when I made the match. I was aware of McGuigan as an amateur, and knew he was going to be a bit special. Later on in his career you could see the way he could throw that left hook to the body. He was good, and even in those formative days I felt he would take care of Eubank. He had Eubank on the floor. I still have a letter I received from the British Boxing Board of Control telling me McGuigan would not be permitted to box six three-minute rounds. He would be allowed to box only in eight-two's, or six two's, against Eubank. Barney was not pleased."

The author was the sole Irish boxing journalist at ringside. Indeed, other than a local reporter I do not recall any of the so-termed boxing experts bothering to attend such an insignificant small show. This was to be the case for a number of McGuigan's early contests. I couldn't understand referee Roland Dakin's 78.5-78 summary in favour of Eubank. Afterwards, I remember an almost inconsolable McGuigan, in floods of tears, being comforted by his manager.

The other Irish fighter on the show, and making his professional debut under the Eastwood banner, was Belfast tough guy Frank 'Fra' McCullagh. The former Belfast Immaculata Club's Ulster amateur Light-heavyweight champion took a six-round decision against Chiswick-based Jamaica-born journeyman Glenroy Taylor. Referee for this contest, one that immediately followed the McGuigan-Eubank fight, was Jack Snipe. Busy cornermen for the two Eastwood boxers were McCormick and Shaw. All the way from Carrickfergus to attend the action was Eastwood's greyhound breeding associate and keen boxing fan Artie McGookin, who remained at Brighton after the fight-show to attend a local horse race meeting.

Eastwood insisted all the early outlay in the fine-tuning of McGuigan was well worthwhile. He also disclosed he set out ground rules that he did not take a percentage of McGuigan's purses throughout their alliance: "That is the way it went. I never took any money off him. Many managers take 25% of their boxer's purses. Some managers take more, like a third. I think McGuigan earned £500 in his hand for his opening few fights. If he had been a world champion he could not have been better treated, outside and inside." He maintained the early financial losses were part of a willing investment for the future of his fiery fighter. He stated McGuigan did not have to pay for the facilities, the training, nor for the sparring help such as Buchanan flying in and out, or Ken's hotel bill, and also the former World champion's pay-rate of £100 a day.

After the Brighton downer, it was an interesting examination for McGuigan. He met the very capable Renard. It was also Barry's first professional appearance in Belfast. The chin was tested in the Ulster Hall. "That was the start to the makings of McGuigan. Renard was a good test - unbeaten, and a strong fighter," BJ said, "McGuigan had one thing going for him in that fight - a good left jab, but he couldn't get the right hand over quickly enough. Eddie (Shaw) worked and worked on him to speed up the right-hand punch. He was not getting the right hand across. He was very raw then. Shaw also worked on perfecting the left hook to the body. McGuigan was a strong boy. It was Eddie who developed the special left hook down below. McGuigan was getting better all of the time. Eddie was bringing him along nicely."

Good quality sparring partners were imported, and this was beginning to pay dividends, proving very beneficial. Eastwood's decision to employ Buchanan, and later McQuillar, was all part of very serious stuff, and unheard of then in the grooming of an Irish-based professional boxer. In 1982, matchmaker Byrne brought in some quirky opposition from overseas, such as a greying Jose De La Sagra from Spain. He claimed he had to dye the fighter's hair. Then it was American Terry Pizarro, who caused some anxiety in that his weight was closer to that of a fast-tallking Flyweight. Byrne found out the New Yorker needed feeding up, that Pizarro was too light, and was also a mediocre fighter. Then it was the rematch against Manchester-born Eubank in the Ulster Hall.

"That was a good go," recalled Eastwood, "We had the contest against Ian Murray at Mayfair. Next in was Angel Oliver, and he was some angel. He also had to be dickied up before he was KO'd. We had Angel Licata in. He was hit early on the chin, and we followed that with a rematch against Lucas at Enniskillen. I took the fight in County Fermanagh because John Williamson, later to become head of the British Boxing Board of Control's Northern Ireland Area Council, was doing something down there. It was just as a favour to John, owner of the Clogher Valley Hotel."

Sadly, on June 14, 1982, the Cyclone's meteoric march ran into tragedy when he knocked out the brave but outclassed east African 'Young Ali' in the sixth round. In front of a bow-tied audience, in London's swish World Sporting Club, McGuigan entered with a 10-1 record. Nigerian Ali arrived with a traced ninth-round knock-out loss in his second fight, on March 8, 1981, to a Stix Macleod in Lagos. That was apparently his last contest before meeting McGuigan. The stricken Ali never regained consciousness. Eastwood said: "The unfortunate Young Ali was doing rightly. It was a very sad occasion, an awful tragedy. McGuigan also hurt his hand in that fight, and was attending a fellow in Navan to receive treatment on it for a couple of months after the Ali contest."

I remember the tragedy. I was merely a few feet away from the ring apron, within touching distance of where Young Ali crashed to the canvas. The fighter's eyes were blank long before he hit the deck. The ring fatality naturally affected McGuigan. He was deeply upset. The death of Young Ali again fuelled argument for the banning of boxing. Again, the so-termed Noble Art was described a 'barbaric sport'. Not for a first time was the morality of boxing severely questioned. The irony was the Ali incident helped to improve closer medical supervision of professional boxers imported to participate in contests in the United Kingdom. Stricter observance of medical tests, including the all-important CAT Scan, became obligatory, but all too late to avoid the Ali incident. It was a heartbreaking occasion. Ali was in a coma for five months before the life support respirator was switched off.

Understandably, McGuigan's immediate reaction was to declare he didn't want to box any more. Obviously, after a time of reflection, he continued, and three years later dedicated the world title win at Loftus Road to Young Ali. On October 5, 1982, Eastwood had his protégé back in the ring, against a rising fighter of Frank Warren's - 'Jumping' Jimmy Duncan. Born in Liverpool on October 21, 1956, Duncan arrived in Belfast with a 9-2 record, but retired in the fourth round. Eastwood remembered the Cyclone's comeback contest for another reason.

"Frank (Warren) and I fell out that night in Belfast. There was a mix-up over the money agreement. Paddy (Byrne) did the deal. Ernie Fossey, God rest him, was standing there too after the fight. The deal, as I recall, was they would get £1,000 in cash for expenses. I gave Frank the £1,000. He said that was not it. Paddy said Eastwood was right - that was the figure we agreed on. I lost my temper. I paid him the extra money, and said I would have nothing more to do with him. We met up in later years, shook hands, and all that is history."

Next in line for McGuigan was another critical contest on the way to a shot at the British title. He met Paul Huggins, who was going well, heading for the big time, it seemed. Eastwood Promotions won that fight for Belfast on a purse offer. It was a final eliminator for the British Featherweight Championship. Huggins was strong, a come to-fight lad. It was a good contest, while it lasted. "McGuigan had the best of him, stopping Huggins in the fifth round. Then, in early 1983, McGuigan looked a million dollars when beating Vernon Penprase for the vacant British Featherweight title," added Eastwood, "Funnily enough, that night I felt sorry for the kid from Plymouth. In May of that year it was down to Navan, County Meath, with McGuigan in against the tough Sammy Meck. It was KO 6 for our man. My son Stephen was the promoter for a Sunday afternoon show that really did not click. It was poorly attended, a bummer."

Always on the lookout to gain a fresh edge, Eastwood agreed to take his exciting prospect to the United States, and parade McGuigan's potential in front of Irish-American fight fans in Chicago. The trip was also a means towards an end, in trying to improve his punching phenomenon. American Lavon McGowan was the selected victim, in at the deep end against McGuigan in the DiVinci Manor, Chicago, on July 1983. The lanky fighter from Davenport, Iowa, who finished with a 3-7-1 record, was taken out in the opening round.

Also on the show, and stretching his unbeaten record to 17, was Hammersmith heavyweight Frank Bruno against Mike Jameson.

Californian Jameson, who was stopped in the second round by big Frank, was of Irish descent. He sported a shamrock emblem on his shorts. Born in June, 1954, he was the first fighter to take Mike Tyson past four rounds, losing in Atlantic City before the end of the fifth stanza as Tyson went to 17-0. Jameson, incidentally, had one contest in England, losing on points to Horace Notice in the Royal Albert Hall. He also had distance bouts with Randall 'Tex' Cobb and Michael Dokes. Future World Welterweight champion Lloyd 'Ragamuffin Man' Honeyghan from Bermondsey also featured in the Windy City bill. Fresh from winning the British Championship, Jamaica-born Honeyghan scored a tenth-round stoppage of Kevin Austin.

Eastwood said: "Our USA connection, to help find opponents there, was Robert Mittlemann. The trip to Chicago, and also calling in at New York, managed to get us introduced to a few important people in the fight game in the States. Frank Bruno was top of the show in Chicago. They were looking for a financial backer for the promotion. Mickey Duff contacted me to try and help find a sponsor in Ireland - because they had big ideas to beam the show back here, via Satellite. I said I might get a few grand for the small-hall bill in Chicago, but I wanted my man on the show. I fixed it up, and managed to get the Trustee Savings Bank to be the sponsor. Eddie Shaw and I headed out there with McGuigan, who had a great time meeting people, going to the John Collin's Gym, sparring. That trip made a difference. In Chicago, I met an Irish guy with relatives in County Clare, Bob Galloway. He was Chief of Police, and loved the boxing. He opened the doors to a lot of things in Chicago. He took us to this gym where out-of-work Mexican boxers were queuing up to spar, to make a few dollars."

BJ also took a curious interest in the rags-to-riches rise of the Chicago show's promoter, Cedric Kushner. The South African's arrival as a deck hand on a German freighter in the United States in 1971 led to promoting concerts, and in 1977 Kushner was part of the success story of chart toppers Fleetwood Mac. Enterprising Kushner switched his interest to boxing in 1981. His first fighters were middleweights Teddy Mann and John Collins. He later held promotional links with 'Sugar' Shane Mosely, flyweight Irene Pacheco, and heavyweight Hasim Rahman. After the show in Chicago the Irish party moved east to New York.

"There we met Mittleman, who later on managed Oscar De La Hoya. He marked our card. You had to go along and meet some of the influential folk in boxing. You can call all the people you have never met and talk as much as you like over the telephone, but it is not the same as meeting face to face," said Eastwood, who insisted that trip to New York and Chicago laid the groundwork to bigger things. While in New York, McGuigan trained in the famous Gleason's Gym. There, Eastwood met and signed up top coach McQuillar.

24 CITIZEN PAIN

MANY minefields had to be negotiated outside the ring before McGuigan reached what some fight folk consider the pinnacle of his punching career, the historic outdoor evening at Shepherds Bush in 1985. One early controversy that ignited some ripples of discontent in the Republic of Ireland was the Clones-based Cyclone's decision to apply for and take out British citizenship.

Commentators and writers south of Hackballscross, a County Louth hamlet on the Border that divides Northern Ireland from the Republic of Ireland, appeared puzzled why Barry should relinquish his birthright, and at this stage of the boxer's burgeoning professional career. Conveniently overlooked was the fact that before leaving the amateur ranks McGuigan represented Northern Ireland, and won gold in the 1978 Commonwealth Games at Edmonton. I believe the first fighter from outside the 'Six Counties' to box for Northern Ireland was Ballyshannon, County Donegal, horsetrader and powerful middleweight Paddy Doherty. For the McGuigan issue, Eastwood once again turned to using well-oiled wheels within wheels to secure the identity switch, and push his protégé on to another stepping-stone test, the winning of the British Featherweight Championship.

Eastwood said: "Firstly, the reason he fought for a British title was because it was felt it was the right way to go. It was the path to get him up there at that time, leading eventually to the world ratings. McGuigan was not going to be considered for a European title fight by just being a fellow who had ten or twelve wins. He had to win a British, or some other title. There was no Irish title about at the time. Secondly, he wanted to fight for the British title. He could see it as the way forward, the way ahead. It was not my problem. If he had not wanted to fight for the British title he would not have taken out British citizenship.

"The bid to get McGuigan into the WBA ratings started a long way back in his career. To achieve British citizenship I had, again, to do a lot of manoeuvring to get him that. It was not just a simple case of merely applying. I had to approach civil servants and politicians. I had letters to and fro, why and where. At the finish up, I am saying to Government officials it would be a great thing, with the problems in Northern Ireland, and all that. McGuigan was doing a good job, bringing people together. I think the word 'peace' had a good lot to do with it at the end of the day. I had to touch the forelock to a few people in high places."

Once the dust settled, McGuigan impressively set about mowing down opposition to reach a title fight, and in his 15th contest became the first Irish boxer since Billy 'Spider' Kelly to win the British Featherweight crown. It was Barry's first time to have a famous and prestigious Lonsdale Belt strapped around his waist. The show was truly on the road, yet from a facile victory against a game but outclassed Vernon Penprase of Plymouth. Penprase was down twice before the action at the Ulster Hall ended in the second round. The ever-improving McGuigan was in a different class.

Also, peace broke out on the streets of Northern Ireland when the Clones Cyclone was in ring action. Fight fans from both sides of the religious and political divide during that strife-torn period joined in harmony to cheer on the electrifying exploits of the Cyclone. Boxing, along with many other sports, rose above the hardships of an uneasy life in that troubled time. Obviously flags and emblems could easily cause offence, could create unnecessary tension in one camp or the other. An ingenious way of solving some of the side issues was the creation of a 'Peace Flag' to follow Ireland's favourite fighter of that era. Instrumental in setting up the idea was the late Belfast politician and boxing aficionado Paddy Devlin, whose proposal was carried to a conclusion by Eastwood's matchmaker Byrne.

The 'Peace Flag' became a symbol of the McGuigan time of plenty. It proved an appropriate path to take, and soon gained global recognition. Eastwood remembered the hows and whys of a very prudent idea: "We always had this problem with trying not to upset Catholics and Protestants. Flags and also National anthems were bad news.So, we decided we would do away with them. But, if we were going to have something like a European title fight or a British title fight we knew we had to come up with a special flag. I think the first time the 'Peace Flag' was used in a McGuigan contest was at the European title fight, when he won it against Valerio Nati at the King's Hall, on November 16, 1983. The late Joy Williams, Head of Sport at the BBC, Belfast, and other folk were saying we would have to do this or do that.

"Former politician Paddy Devlin, a great follower of boxing, said to me: 'Look, you want to have something neutral. Why don't you get a peace flag, or some sort of a symbol to that effect?' I talked it over with Paddy Byrne, that we should investigate the possibilities of getting a special flag with peace emblems on it in London. Byrne said: 'Leave this to me' - and off he went to visit different flag shops in London and Brighton to consider what a peace flag looked like. He got the flag. That was it. The other thing was, we also looked for an anthem to play before a big fight. The 'Londonderry Air' song, better known as 'Danny Boy', was the selection, and composer Phil Coulter did a special rendering for us of Danny Boy. I recall him suggesting we should have one with plenty of beat in it. That was that."

The flag issue did not entirely fade away during the early days. There was an 'incident' that could be termed a contradiction of the puncher's peace process before a bout in London's Royal Albert Hall. The hullabaloo outside the dressing rooms involved an Eastwood minder, Harry 'Red Dog' O'Neill, before McGuigan made a defence of the European Featherweight title. "What happened was," explained BJ, "We were ready to come out of the dressing room for one of those tuppence-halfpenny fights at Kensington. McGuigan knocked out Esteban Eguia. However, there was a last-minute hitch before fight-time, which caused a delay when we were ready to go to the ring. A fellow who worked for Mickey Duff was holding aloft the Union Jack flag. "Duff said: 'You are going with the Union Jack.'

“My man Harry O'Neill, a legendary ex-Antrim and Ulster Gaelic footballer, intervened: 'Hold on a minute. McGuigan doesn't fight under the Union Jack. He fights only under the Peace Flag. This is the flag here', says Harry, showing Duff the Peace Flag, and insisted the Union Jack flag was not going out with us. It was ironic peace should be placed aside for a few very hairy moments in the tunnel. A couple of London heavies argued otherwise, and Harry threatened to break somebody's jaw. It was tense in the tunnel as an infuriated 'Red Dog' declared he would wrap the Peace flagpole around somebody's neck! It brought a new meaning to the word 'peace'. We paraded out into the Albert Hall under the Flag of Peace, and that was the end of the Union Jack incident in London."

KING'S HALL REVIVAL

EASTWOOD'S boxing bandwagon began to move to a higher level when the purse offer for the European Featherweight belt was won to bring Italian Nati to Belfast. The phenomenal fight followers of McGuigan were rapidly outgrowing small-hall settings. It was time to move up the Lisburn Road to the fabled King's Hall, scene of so many gripping ring wars. Perhaps the most memorable event at the Balmoral venue was Rinty Monaghan's win of the World Flyweight crown in 1948, when stopping Scotland's Jackie Paterson in the seventh round.

The flamboyant Bob Gardiner, a bookmaker later to have a young Eastwood as a near business neighbour and rival in Carrickfergus, was the promoter of this historic first World title fight to be staged in a Belfast ring. Incidentally, a special blue plaque in memory of Rinty was unveiled at the King's Hall in 2007. The famous arena, built by the Royal Ulster Agricultural Society in the Balmoral complex and opened on May 29, 1934, housed many other unforgettable fight nights. The generally recognised first major bill was on November 20, 1935, in the Exhibition Centre and paraded Jimmy Warnock, a slick southpaw flyweight from Belfast's Shankill Road, against a stiff-punching French fighter Maurice Huguenin. The Parisian bantamweight, who had been in with Valentin Angelman and Panama Al Brown, gave our James an awkward time before the local hero took the honours over ten rounds.

Late in the second round fleet-footed Warnock was floored by a slining right hook. Referee Jack Curphey was about to go the full count. In front of 10,000 flabbergasted fans a wobbling Warnock rose at 'six', was in great distress - but saved by the bell before giving Huguenin a boxing lesson. The Promoter was Belfast bookmaker Jim 'Pickles' Rice, the matchmaker

Jim Edgar, and the MC and timekeeper Jack Hinds. Also on the bill were Belfast's Pat Marrinan, losing in the fifth round to former cowboy and Canadian Light-heavyweight champion Ed Wenstob, and Irish Bantamweight champion Jackie Quinn (Belfast), losing on points to Glasgow-born Canadian champion Jack 'Spider' Armstrong.

On March 12, 1936, Warnock scored a 12-round points decision over Scottish legend Benny Lynch. Promoter Edgar was unable to have the Scot's world title at stake. Apparently the British Boxing Board of Control would not sanction it, because of a pre-ordained elimination process. The World belt was also not on offer when Warnock repeated the dose in a rematch, this time over 15 rounds on June 2, 1937, and in front of 20,000 partisan Lynch fans in Glasgow Celtic Football Club's Parkhead Stadium. Warnock, who recovered from a first-round knock-down, later took part in a final eliminator, but was stopped in four rounds by a 19-year-old Goldbourne, Manchester, blacksmith with a dark piercing stare - Peter Kane.

The Belfast boxing boom of the post World War Two era of the late 1949's, and through the 1950's, included many highlight nights in the King's Hall. Local derby dust-ups included fiery wars involving all-action Belfast lightweight Gerry Smyth and Lisburn's Jim Keery. Smyth, always prone to eyebrow damage, won and lost inside a 17-week period against Keery, starting in September, 1948, and then losing on a TKO 3 on January 25, 1949. It was fabulous fight entertainment. On February 23, 1952, Smyth, who went to the well 64 times, first nicked the Northern Ireland Area Lightweight title on a 12-round points decision over fellow Belfast ring legend Mickey O'Neill. He also lost and won against Ricky McCullough for the Area title, and out-scored a previously unbeaten Paddy Graham in a Lightweight title defence on March 26, 1956. Three months later Smyth hung up the gloves, after losing in the ninth round to Roy Baird.

During that period the place was awash with top-notch boxers. There were also Irish fighters involved in parading their talents in shows galore in England and Scotland. After Rinty Monaghan's glorious but all too short reign as king of the wee world, the Irish fans searched for a replacement idol. The answer eventually arrived in the form of Derry's dapper and distinguished ringmaster Billy 'Spider' Kelly. He was the supreme shifty box-fighter, a classic defensive ring artiste, pure poetry in motion, a genius with gloves.

At times, his phenomenal artistry was misunderstood. Billy and his box of tricks were often badgered by over-fussy referees, especially for ducking too low. Kelly generally left his opponents punching air, chasing shadows. He was heading for the high ground in the world ratings, with talks in the pipeline about a possible shot at the top guys, Willie Pep or Sandy Saddler, when the roof started to cave in. Perceived dubious decisions against the young Spider stopped him in his tracks.

There was also the undignified ringside riot in Belfast's major arena when he lost his British Featherweight crown. Unfortunate disturbances followed the disbelief of the fans when Cambuslang-born Charlie Hill had his hands raised to take the title from Kelly. Chairs and other missiles were hurled at the ring by irate followers of Kelly. They felt their hero was a clear winner. Some officials had to seek protection underneath the ring apron. Promoter of that infamous occasion was George Connell, who was also well known as the proprietor of Top Hat productions run by Stanley Orr in Lisburn's Bow Street 'Ballroom of Romance'. Imported were world quality entertainers such as Sandy Shaw, Little Richard, Roy Orbinson, Acker Bilk, the Bee Gees, and fabled Irish showbands including the Miami, the Royal, and Dave Glover.

International boxing shows in the King's Hall were Connell's main focus, and in Billy Kelly he had an outstanding home-grown attraction. Spider, one of the biggest crowd pullers ever with his dazzling style, also lost the Empire title in dramatic circumstance when chilled by Nigeria's Hogan 'Kid' Bassey. Then there was the rise and fall of another Kelly, Belfast southpaw bantamweight John. He was the quiet man from the Ormeau Road area who took the British and European titles from Scotland's Peter Keenan. Sadly, Kelly suffered a stunning second-round loss to the powerful Robert Cohen in a European title fight.

The doors shut, and it seemed forever, on October 20, 1962, after the epic struggle between previous Irish amateur team colleagues and 1956 Olympic Bronze medallists, Gilroy and Caldwell. Promoted on many occasions by Jack Solomons, and managed by Jimmy McAree, hard-hitting southpaw Gilroy retained his British and Empire Bantamweight Championship belts, and then put away his gloves for good. Caldwell's cut eye problem robbed the fans of the full 15 rounds of electrifying toe-to-toe action. The famous fight, a joint promotion by Solomons and Connell, had a supporting cast that included Eddie Shaw stopping Sheffield lightweight Neil Hawcroft. Belfast slickster Jim 'Spike' McCormick lost over ten rounds to human whirlwind Boswell St Louis, a lightweight from Trinidad. Killough-born welter Paddy Graham lost in the second round to Belfast's Sammy Cowan. Also featured were Belfast flyweight Alex O'Neill, out-scoring Glasgow's Danny Lee over eight rounds, and ginger-haired bantamweight Peter Lavery losing in the fifth round to Ghana's Denis Adjei.

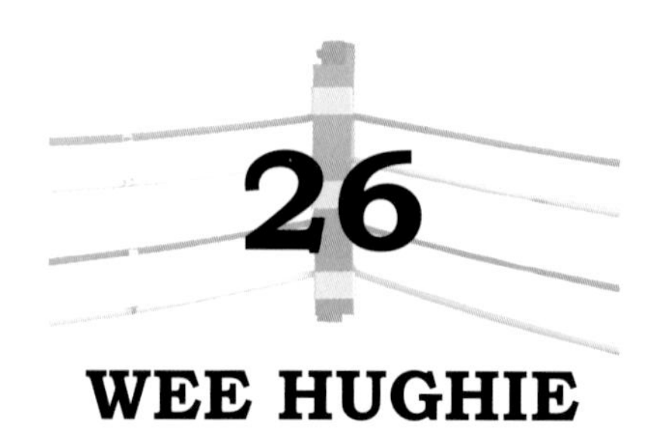

WEE HUGHIE

HUGH Russell was a vital early player in the Eastwood stable. He made history during his colourful ring career. The chirpy portsider, a Lonsdale Belt outright winner, scooped success in reverse order. First off, he won the British Bantamweight Championship, and then slimmed down to win the British Flyweight title. A bronze medallist at both the Commonwealth and Olympic Games, he retired after another blood-letting battle, scoring a 12th-round stoppage win at the King's Hall. Never short on bravery, the wee warrior, plagued by cut eyebrows, came from behind in sensational fashion to halt Scotland's Charlie Brown.

On February 23, 1985, Russell retained the British Flyweight Championship on the same show headlined by Barry McGuigan, when the Cyclone scored a seriously significant ten-rounds points win over former World Featherweight champion Juan LaPorte. On many occasions Hughie's contests ran in tandem to those of McGuigan. The win against Brown was Russell's 17th of a 19-bout career. Born on December 15, 1959, he began life at Carrick Hill in central Belfast, and later the family moved to live in Duncairn Parade, off the Antrim Road in north Belfast. Round the corner was the cosmopolitan Holy Family boxing club on the New Lodge Road. Coached by Gerry Storey, Russell followed in the footsteps of older brother Sean, who was a double winner of the Ulster Amateur Bantamweight title and later became a qualified professional referee and judge.

"Boxing was in the family, on my mother Eileen's side," explained Hugh, who was named after his father. "My uncles, Johnny and Jimmy Nolan, did a bit of amateur boxing. My older brother Seanie started in the nearby Holy Family gym, and it seemed the natural thing for me to do to follow him. My other brother Frankie had a few Juvenile fights. Brother Sean was the amateur Bantamweight champion at Ulster and Irish level. In 1978, he lost his Ulster title to a young Barry McGuigan. On the same night, in the Ulster Hall, I won the Ulster amateur Flyweight title from Jimmy Carson. Jimmy was the reigning champion for a few years. He would have been favourite to beat me, while our Sean was fancied to beat this young McGuigan guy. I think everybody tore up their betting dockets that night.

"After the 1980 Moscow Olympics, when I won a bronze medal, I had a couple of contests back home and then emigrated to Canada, and on my own. I was engaged to Kathy then, but wanted to see how a life in Alberta might work out. I went to Edmonton where I previously boxed in the 1978 Commonwealth Games, but was soon homesick and returned to Belfast. Incidentally, there was a whole controversy about me going to the Olympics in Moscow. Dave McAuley was the national Flyweight champion, yet not sent. When I came back we met, and I beat him. I fought Dave McAuley five times as an amateur, and won the lot.

"I first beat him at 4 stone in the old Down and Connor Juvenile Championships. When he turned professional, he joined Eastwood and we sparred in the Castle Street gym. Dave is a nice kid, and was also fortunate to be there and get chances to fight for World titles. Trying to make eight stone is not easy. It is very hard to get the weight off. There is not a lot left when you are boxing at flyweight. I should know. I was a flyweight as an amateur and gained most of my successes as a flyweight."

He outlined the need to box at bantamweight, when he turned professional, was down to a severe shortage of flyweight opponents. At that time there was little action in the British Flyweight division. It was very hard to get fights at 8 stone, and he needed work: "Obviously, to return home with an Olympic medal and then turn professional after a couple of hundred amateur bouts, the ordinary flyweights did not want to fight me. So, it meant I was meeting guys bigger - bantamweights. I did reasonably well," added Russell.

"After I lost the British Bantamweight title to Davy (Larmour) I went back to box in my natural division. It was the way things worked out. It is also easy to look back and say I probably should not have defended my British Bantamweight title so quickly after winning it. The first Larmour fight in the British eliminator was a hard one. I won the title on the 25th of January 1983 against John Feeney, and defended it on the second of

March, 1983, against Larmour. It was not a big lot of time out of the gym for me. Having said that, it was a decision taken by us all. We all agreed on the title defence. I was not forced to do anything. Boxers, in the end, make the decision. They put their legs through the ropes. I was light at bantamweight. We had a couple of contests set up down at flyweight, and then the chance came up to meet Kelvin Smart for the British title. It ended in the seventh round."

Russell's colourful paid career included the two ferocious fights with Larmour. He won the first at the Ulster Hall on October 5, 1982. The encounter was a gory eliminator for the British Bantamweight Championship. The intriguing contest was also for the vacant Northern Ireland area and the Irish Bantamweight Championships. After the 12-round points decision, Russell progressed to clinch the British title on January 21, 1983, at the Ulster Hall. John Feeney of Hartlepool was disqualified by England referee Sid Nathan in the 13th round - 'for blatant and excessive misuse of the head'.

Larmour then gained revenge when Russell put the title on the line. It was the bloodbath revisited in 1983, a significant milestone that marked the re-opening of Ireland's home of professional boxing, the King's Hall. Eastwood Promotions felt it was a good time to take a gamble, test the waters and move the fight shows up-market to the famous arena. It proved the correct decision, and it opened the door to a glittering array of magnificent international boxing productions.The great tradition was revived and upheld once again, starting on March 2, 1983. Russell and Larmour headlined the first show back there in 21 years. It was delightfully fitting an all-Belfast battle for the British Bantamweight Championship should be the contest to take up the baton from the Gilroy-Caldwell all-Belfast British Bantamweight war.

Fight interest in Northern Ireland was again reaching fever pitch, because of McGuigan's progress. It proved the right time to re-open the doors of the legendary arena. Promoter Stephen Eastwood's fight programme view then was: 'Big-time boxing has always been synonymous with the King's Hall, and it gives me great pleasure to re-unite them. Professional boxing in Belfast has certainly flourished during the past year, and tonight sees a new height reached in this surging revival.' The match between Little Red and the laid-back Larmour, a Shankill Road man then trained by former British Bantamweight champion Paddy Maguire of the Falls Road, was Russell's first and last defence of the British title. Ex-Commonwealth Games gold medallist Larmour produced a big finish through the 11th and 12th rounds, and had his hands raised by Harry Gibbs on a points summary of 118 to 116.5.

Also on the line was the Northern Ireland Area crown. Russell, who weighed 8st 3.5lbs, promptly indicated he was turning his attention to the Flyweight division. The historic bridge-building bill, to herald the return of international boxing to the arena beside the Balmoral Showgrounds and Balmoral Golf Club, also paraded a thundering Catchweight eight-rounder (inside 8st 13.5 lbs) between Liverpool's Keith Wallace and Pat Doherty of Croydon. Wallace pinched a 79.5-78 decision. Eddie Shaw made a sentimental pilgrimage back to the Mecca of Irish boxing as Russell's trainer. Eddie planned to be doubly employed, but McGuigan was unable to fight that night.

He had to withdraw from a proposed match with Plymouth's Vernon Penprase for the British Featherweight Championship, which had been vacated by Newport's Steve Simms. McGuigan, who was downed by a virus infection, had to wait a further five weeks before winning the title, in the Ulster Hall. He would soon make his special impact in the main arena, now that the big boxing buzz was back.

October 5, 1983, marked the start to another professional boxing season in Belfast, with McGuigan packing the Ulster Hall for his contest against Ruben Herrasme. The fight programme for the Wednesday night Smirnoff-backed programme cost 50 pence. The front cover legend declared 'International Boxing - Featuring the return of Barry and Little Red.' British Featherweight champion McGuigan, who blasted out beanpole American Lavon McGowan in the first round in Chicago on July 9, weighed 9st 1.5lbs. Promoter Stephen Eastwood welcomed Barry back, following the Cyclone's facile win in the Windy City. He also confirmed Hugh Russell was to embark upon the British Flyweight Championship trail. Also, there were the debuts of Dave 'Boy' McAuley and Gary 'Peppy' Muir - two very exciting prospects with knockout punches.

Steward in charge was Deryk Monteith, matchmaker/whip Paddy Byrne, M C - Danny Small, and timekeeper Dan McAllister. The 22-year-old McGuigan's 18th contest and tenth in Belfast was a scheduled ten-rounder against 24-year-old Herrasme from the Dominican Republic. Ruben, who weighed in at 9st 4lbs, arrived with an indifferent ring record of 20 wins and 24 defeats. He lasted merely 5 mins 58 seconds. Man in the middle was Cardiff's James Brimmell. Russell, 23, weighed 8st 2.5 lbs against Herrasme's fellow countryman Julio Guerrero, a 23-year-old with an 18-win, one draw and two defeat record. Brimmell gave 'Wee' Hughie a 79.5 to 76.5 points verdict. McAuley had to settle for a bantamweight debut draw over six two-minute rounds against Nigeria's John Mwainu. The 'Boy' conceded Mwainu almost four pounds on the scales. Referee was Barney Wilson.

Russell raced on to secure a unique place in British Championship history, as the first fighter to move down a division to win a second title. On the night of January 25, 1984, in the King's Hall where McGuigan survived an acid test against Charm Chiteule, 'Little Red' beat Kelvin Smart for the British Flyweight Championship on a seventh-round technical knockout. Smart was forced to retire because of distressing eye damage.

On November 13, 1984, and after suffering a fifth-round stoppage at the hands of Jose Torres in the King's Hall (4-4-1984), Russell made a successful first defence of the Flyweight title. He stopped Scotland's Danny Flynn in the eighth round in the Ulster Hall. Flynn hit the deck four times. Hugh made sure of outright ownership of the Lonsdale Belt from the farewell-to-arms affair against Brown. He became the second Irish fighter, after fellow southpaw Gilroy, to make a prestigious Lonsdale Belt his own property. After two months of soul searching Little Red officially announced his retirement from the ring.

Russell enjoyed his brush with fame, and said: "I was the second boxer in the Eastwood stable, McGuigan obviously the first. I always thought I had very good people around me. The Eastwoods - Barney, young Stephen. I had no problems with any of them. Hopefully they had no problems with me. It was a good era for professional boxing, very exciting. At the time I turned professional there was precious little happening in boxing in Northern Ireland, yet I felt with Barry McGuigan turning professional, and with Eastwood involved, things might take off. I believed there was the possibility of something exciting happening. It looked that way, as I felt Barney was the right person coming in to take the game forward. There was no talk of professional boxing in Belfast, until that stage. Eastwood put life back into the game.

"My last fight was against Charlie Brown, and I cut up in that fight at the King's Hall. I did suffer from cuts throughout my career, I must admit, but I was also fortunate enough in that respect as Barney had good men in the corner such as Paddy Byrne and Eddie Shaw. Byrne was probably one of the best cuts men in the world. The first of the two fights against Davy Larmour turned into a bit of a shock for English referee Mike Jacobs. He looked lovely coming into the ring, but not too hot leaving it. Neither was I, nor Davy. Mr Jacobs was covered in blood, his once-white shirt a mess, redder than my hair. It was a final eliminator for the British Bantamweight title Also at stake were the Northern Ireland and Irish Bantamweight titles. I was cut above and below both eyes. Larmour was cut above both eyes."

Eastwood remembered the blood letting: "That first night Hugh fought Davy was really something. I never saw as much blood spilled in a boxing match, until then. There was blood everywhere. The canvas was red with blood." Byrne, the man with the swab, cracked: "Wee Hugh Russell could have bled for Ireland. The biggest cut problems I ever experienced while working for Eastwood Promotions were with Hugh. A great little fighter, but he bled like a pig. Some of his fights were unbelievable, especially against Davy Larmour. The other big bleeder I worked with was Soren Sondergard, a Dane and a European champion."

Russell added: "I am on the British Board of Control's Northern Ireland Area Council, and I can say that situations such as I was involved with against Davy Larmour would not happen now. Fights like that would not be allowed to continue. Things have tightened up considerably on that side of boxing. I was very fortunate Paddy Byrne was able to handle the situation, although I was suffering from more severe cuts than Davy. His damage around the eyes probably looked a lot worse than mine, because the cuts were still bleeding. The rematch at the King's Hall later down the line was not so bloody, when Davy beat me for the British title. In my last contest, against Charlie Brown at the King's Hall, I was cut above the right eye, an old wound re-opened. That night I won the Lonsdale Belt outright, something I always wanted to do.

"It was also a time to quit the game. There was no movement at that stage of me getting a world title fight. The Championships then were the WBA and WBC. There was precious little chance of fighting for one, so I felt no point in hanging on. Even in Europe, the champion, an Italian (Franco Cherchi), appeared somewhat inactive. The British fight scene then was probably the liveliest in world boxing at that time. Still, I made up my mind to quit shortly after the Brown fight, because I was not going to get a chance to compete for a World title. I didn't think it was worthwhile getting back into the ring again, and taking the abuse you have to take to win fights when there would be nothing at stake."

Russell wisely increased interest in his hobby, amateur photography. He progressed nicely along the shutter-speed path. It all began with involvement in the Christian Brothers Past Pupils' course in Belfast. The pastime progressed to a more serious level when he joined the *Irish News* daily morning newspaper in Belfast, as a trainee press photographer under Brendan Murphy. It proved a good move, especially linking with boxing buff Murphy. "I felt this was my way forward," said Russell, "Photography was what I enjoyed doing, and the line I would try and take for the future. It was probably one of the biggest decisions I made in my life. Retiring from the ring was difficult, but eventually I took up a full-time job in press photography. It was brave move for me at that stage. When you are winning fights people think you are brilliant. I am glad I finished on a winning note. I lost my British Bantamweight title very quickly. The same people who came into my changing room the night I won the title from John Feeney were next door in Davy Larmour's dressing room.

"A year to the day after that disappointment I won the British Flyweight title, and the same people were back in my changing room. You learn from that. You have to watch you don't become carried away by success. In those days there were many tremendous shows in the Ulster Hall, and in the King's Hall. I felt very fortunate to be boxing in that era. Stuff like that, the atmosphere, it lifts you. There were great occasions, including the likes of Dave McAuley, who came into the Eastwood gym a very short time after me, and McGuigan. Dave was in some great fights, and probably did not get the recognition he deserved. Some of the McAuley battles were terrific, especially against Bassa and Blanco. I saw them. I was at ringside. He didn't win the Blanco one at the King's Hall, yet got the narrow decision. At that stage, I was outside the ropes taking photographs for the *Irish News* morning newspaper. I still kept close contact with the boys in the Eastwood gym."

EUROVISION

McGUIGAN'S delayed debut in the King's Hall was greeted with high enthusiasm and great expectation. The Cyclone was making his first meaningful move towards the big time. His apprenticeship was over. Conquering Europe was crucial, in order to gain a leg up to the fringes of world level. Eastwood brought the metaphorical mountain climb to Mohammad, but Valerio Nati would be no pushover - an opponent with a pedigree.

The Italian was an extremely experienced box-fighter, and the ideal stepping stone for McGuigan when they met on November 16, 1983, in a European Featherweight title bout. The home hero didn't disappoint. He won on a sixth-round stoppage. Referee Kurt Halbarch halted the action after 2 mins 33 secs of that round. This was the way forward to ultimate glory. So far, so good. Another hurdle conquered.

McGuigan's 'search and destroy' approach was beginning to send a message of menace out to the world stage. The winning of the European belt was the first significant rung on the ladder. The conflict against Nati was also in the first big international boxing show to be held in the King's Hall since the Gilroy-Caldwell epic of 1962. Stephen Eastwood promoted the bill, and the BBC screened it.

Eastwood Promotions won the rights to stage fight on a purse offer, and a massive crowd shoe-horned into the King's Hall. Irish fight fans sensed there was something very special stirring as they eased into the Cyclone's slipstream with the 'Here-we-Go' war cry. McGuigan's impressive victory against such a noted fighter as Nati was a career-defining occasion. The contests for the most exciting and best supported Irish fighter in years became tougher from then on, generally moving to a higher punching plane - apart from a couple of imposed and ridiculously one-sided European title defences.

However, Eastwood's best-laid plans almost came a cropper in the next hurdle. On January 25, 1984, the obstacle was the very dangerous Charm 'Shuffle' Chiteule from Zambia. The charm went out the window once the fighter went to work with his impressively confident operation inside the ropes. Eastwood referred to this acid test as a crossroads examination. Born on October 10, 1953, Chiteule, who finished with a record of 28 wins, five defeats and one draw, was attempting to get back to the mainstream. On February 2, 1982, he lost by TKO 10 to the fearsome Ghanaian Azumah Nelson at Lusaka, for the British Commonwealth Championship and also the African Featherweight title. Earlier, on May 4, 1980, he beat England's Dave Needham at Lusaka for the British Commonwealth Featherweight crown.

His King's Hall cracker with the Cyclone was listed a final eliminator for the very same Commonwealth Championship. It was to be Chiteule's penultimate ring outing, and ended when he was stopped in the tenth round, but not before dishing out jarring jabs and some roughhouse treatment on the home hero. As the absorbing action progressed the widespread frisson in the Hall was palpable. At times, it became no-holds-barred battle, with low blows, the lot. It was McGuigan's 20th contest, requiring raw courage and tremendous heart and guts to come out the other side with a 10th-round stoppage by referee Roland Dakin..

Eastwood remembered the milestone match-up: "That was very hard, but an important learning experience. It was only then I realised McGuigan had only one tactic, which was to go forward, and that he was not good when having to go back. His feet were all wrong. If he could back his opponent up he could murder him, but if not he had big problems. His footwork did improve from that fight with Chiteule. There was a lot of work done on that, improvement on his movement, more lateral movement needed. When he was going forward it was all right, but when somebody was jabbing him his head went back. Eddie (Shaw) got him to come in more from the crouch Chiteule retired from ring warfare in 1984 with a 28-5-1 record, and later became President of the Zambian Boxing Federation. Tragically, Chiteule, who was coached for a period in London by the late George Francis, died of Malaria in May 2008. He was 54.

April 4, 1984, was the next test for Barry, and against World-ranked Jose Caba of the Dominican Republic at King's Hall. It was another examination on the ladder to fame and fortune. Caba had a crack at a world title before that. He stayed at La Mon, but apparently had trouble in making the weight. The 12-rounder was billed an eliminator for the WBC World title, then held by Wilfredo Gomez. Incidentally, on the Saturday night before the McGuigan Caba contest, Gomez beat LaPorte, and was then ordered to defend within 60 days against Nelson.

For his 21st bout, McGuigan weighed 8st 12 and one quarter lbs. Helping Barry prepare for the Caba encounter was McQuillar. Sparring partners included Carmelo Negron and Ricky Young. Caba, represented by Mickey Duff and with 26 bouts (23 wins) under his belt, was ranked fourth. He came off a 15-round points loss in Italy to Pedroza for the WBA crown. His CV also included other name opponents such as Danny 'Red' Lopez, Jackie Beard and Jorge Garcia. Caba, who scaled 9 stone, folded after 2 mins 30 secs of the seventh round. Referee was Cardiff's James Brimmell.

The chief supporting bout featured Russell against a dangerous Mexican born, Arizona-based Jose Torres, once a knock-out winner against Charlie Magri. It turned out a disaster for 'Little Red'. He seemed to be getting into his stride in the fourth round, but was stopped by hard-hitting 24-year-old Torres of Tucson in the fifth. The bill also paraded Young Patsy Quinn (McAllister). He forced Dublin's P.J. Davitt into retirement at the end of the eighth round. It was an Irish Welterweight title eliminator. Busy Larne Bantam Roy Webb scored a 60-57.5 points win against Manchester's Mohammed Lovelock. Belfast's David Irving, who later became a prominent referee, notched a third-round stoppage win against Hull Light-welterweight John Murray.

McGuigan was off to London in early June, to defend the European title against Esteban Eguia in Kensington. It proved a total mismatch. The effete Eguia was taken out in the third round. Then, it was back to Belfast on June 30, 1984, when McGuigan met American Paul deVorce, who lasted into the fifth round. The next contest was on Saturday October 13, 1984, also in Belfast where Felipe Orozco was Ko'd in the second round. For this international bill in the King's Hall, promoter Stephen Eastwood highlighted the increasing interest shown by American television on McGuigan.

He commented in the show programme: 'We extend a hearty welcome to NBC, the American TV network, who come to not only show our own hero Barry McGuigan but also to capture the live atmosphere which professional boxing produces at the King's Hall. Jointly topping the bill is that most popular exponent of the fistic art, Cornelius Boza-Edwards, now boxing at lightweight and currently ranked at No. 6 by the WBC.' McGuigan's 23rd outing was against a Columbian with a pipe-cleaner frame. It was also the 23-year-old's first professional encounter against a lefty.

Miami-based Orozco, once a top junior featherweight, had a height advantage of four inches, but was cut down to size in the second round. Ugandan Boza-Edwards crushed Charlie 'Choo Choo' Brown of Upper Darby, Philadelphia, after 1.47 of the third round. The undercard included Dave 'Boy' McAuley, Rocky McGran and David Irving. McGuigan's preparations included spars against Boza-Edwards, a world-class southpaw, and Hugh Russell. On December 19, 1984, in the Ulster Hall, McGuigan met Clyde Ruan. With the European and British titles at stake McGuigan gave a really solid showing, and ended it with a knock-out in the 4th round. The best test was yet to come, against Juan LaPorte in the King's Hall on February 23, 1985, yet the dream of World honours might well have ended in the ashcan.

28

SHARK INFESTED WATERS

MAKING major moves that mattered, to achieve ultimate targets, Eastwood knew he needed to gain a foot inside the front door of the movers and shakers of world boxing in order to secure an edge for his fighters, starting with McGuigan's push for Featherweight honours. So, he had to touch gloves with some of the most influential people in the punch game.

He decided to row into shark-infested waters with the World Boxing Association. Eastwood's immediate target, once the Cyclone was beginning to blast holes through the British and European Featherweight scene, was to get on really friendly terms with the right fight people. His forward-planning meant he had to seek out the powerbrokers who pressed the buttons, those figures who held all the leverage in the fighter rankings. It wasn't easy, at first. Nothing is ever quite what it seems, not black and white.

Often in the grey areas you can witness and wonder why a fighter with a genuine claim to a world title fight is repeatedly overlooked. It is obvious you need the right connections in what can be close to an almost clandestine cloak and dagger business. With bucket-loads of big bucks washing around the overloaded Championships, you have to be totally naive about world boxing affairs not to appreciate there is the game within the game involving all of the so-termed alphabet organisations who offer 'World' belts.

Eastwood quickly caught on how to go with the flow, roll with the metaphoric punches, where to tap into the right oil well. He had to get close to some of the 'Mr Bigs' of boxing to unlock doors. This required nurturing WBA potentates, and especially the establishment of a close working understanding with one of the then WBA mandarins, Jose 'Pepe' Cordero of San Juan, Puerto Rico. You won't trace too much information about the late Pepe, sometimes known as Pappy, among the list of WBA officials.

BJ's carefully constructed strategy, to elevate McGuigan to a crack at a World title, meant he had to cosy up to Cordero, at that time arguably the most controversial influences among the gallery of global boxing manipulators. The WBA emerged from the old National Boxing Association that started life in 1921. It had limited jurisdiction then, when confined to parts of the United States. The name changed to WBA in 1962. In 1964, Panamanian Dr Elias Cordova became the first Latin-American to take a place on the WBA Executive Council, and ten years later was installed the Association's President. In 1977 he was replaced as President by Fernando Mandry Galindez of Venezuela. Then, it was Panama's Rodrigo Sanchez from 1979-'82, with Venezuela's Gilberto Mendoza from 1982 onwards.

Eastwood attended a WBA Convention in San Juan in 1982, and a year later at Margarito in Venezuela. There were further Conventions in Philadelphia, Miami, Reno and Costa Rico. He preferred the 'Pappy' not 'Pepe' nickname for heavyweight wheeler-dealer Cordero, who waddled away from the WBA during the 1988 annual conference in Venezuela to help set up yet another 'alphabet' ruling body. The World Boxing Organisation was formed, and paraded a badge that featured the high valued objectives in a logo: 'Dignity-Democracy-Honesty'. Five years earlier the International Boxing Federation emerged. The confusing state of World boxing became ever more acute. Apparently Cordero was part of a breakaway group from the WBA to set up the WBO with a base in Puerto Rico. First WBO President was Ramon Pina Acevedo of the Dominican Republic.

Long before that, the wily Pepe, also a fight manager from 1976, had a major background say in the moving of McGuigan into the chute as a World Championship contender. Eastwood quickly cottoned on to the singularly impressive power-broker influence of Cordero. "Pappy was the personality who had control of San Juan fighters. He was a big man in every sense. He travelled first class, and needed two seats in an aeroplane," added Eastwood, "Pappy was huge, weighing between 25 and

30 stone. He controlled a lot of fighters. I had to make contact with him. He was the person who opened up things when I was trying to make a few contacts. He also later approached me about Wilfredo Gomez fighting McGuigan. We got involved in that, and he also opened outlets for me to a few places. It was a scary job going to Puerto Rico to hold a first meeting with Cordero. It was like a scene from a film, like meeting a Godfather. I had a date to see him in San Juan.

"Pappy was some boy, something different. It was a fresh experience for me. I had an appointment with him, and was taken there by two big bodyguards who ushered me into a huge room where this giant of a man was sitting with his back to me. That must have been his style. He swung around, and sat in a seat opposite me. 'So, you are Eastwood from Ireland. What do you want done,' he enquired, 'Right. So, you want this boy McGuigan considered. Is he ready for a title fight yet?' I answered no, but told him shortly the boxer would be a legitimate contender. Says Pappy: 'As far as eventually fighting for the title your boy will have to box champion Eusebio Pedroza. That will prove to be very awkward, because Pedroza may now not want to come out of his country, Panama. Look, money will get him out. I will speak with Louis Spada, and also to Dr Cordova in Panama.' "

Eastwood added: "What Cordero decreed was the word. If he said that will be all right, it was. Your boxer can fight or he can't fight, or you are suspended, or look - you won't be fighting for this or that title. Pappy was an all-powerful man then in the WBA, as far as I was concerned. He'd say: 'Right - okay. If your man wins his next couple of contests we can do this or that.' He told me if I was thinking that way then McGuigan must be pretty good. He advised me to come back and see him after McGuigan did something worthwhile. He also told me there was a chance he could help get him into the top-ten rankings, in the meantime. That was how I got the foot in the World door."

That trip also offered Eastwood the opportunity to meet Gomez. The first of many key visits to San Juan was around the time Caba boxed in Belfast. Dipping into the deep end of the world pool, and swimming with thebarracudas of boxing, was the fast track to reach the summit for McGuigan and also for Eastwood's five other World champions. During his contacts with the folk who mattered most, in top WBA circles, he also met another influential man, Jimmy Binns, who later was the WBA supervisor for the McGuigan-Cabrera cracker in Dublin.

Eastwood said: "At that time Binns was a major lawyer in Philadelphia, a real big-timer with Irish connections. When he was the WBA supervisor at the RDS he was entertained by the Government down there, in Dublin. I became very friendly with him before that. He was a top operator. I remember going into his office in Philadelphia. He loved the Irish, and his Irish connection. I recall somebody coming in to see him when I was there. Binns had a clock. If someone came in to hold an official discussion it was either a 15-minute consultation, a half-hour meeting, or an hour. Whatever it was, he would put the clock on, and it was a very steep fee to talk to him. He represented the WBA, and appeared for them in many big court cases. Funnily enough, he kept a record of his WBA cases, just like a fighter. He used to send it out, stating: 'WBA versus so and so . . . KO second round.' According to his record he never lost a case for them."

After the Cyclone petered out, the years of negotiations in the Caribbean helped open doors in other areas. Eastwood, by then, knew how to 'kow-tow' with the suits who headed all the World Championship bodies. His first contact at World level was with the WBA. He then locked into the IBF through Dave 'Boy' McAuley beating Duke McKenzie. Later, Paul Hodkinson was the main link to WBC affairs, when Hoko eventually won the Featherweight title. To achieve that end Barney had to make contact with Jose Sulaiman, the controversial head of the WBC.

Eastwood added: "He (Sulaiman) wrote to me on one occasion. It is amazing how the grapevine works, surprising how things happen. Obviously he had been chatting with someone who had been friendly with me when I was in America. Mostly they were WBA folk, and then I had this note complimenting me. My name was fairly well known by then. As a result of the letter, I made it my business to go and see Sulaiman. I met him a couple of times, a very soft-spoken guy. He invited us, myself and the late Tony Baker, to a WBC Conference. I was also invited to Sulaiman's home in Mexico City, where the Mexicans treated him like a god. He was very helpful, within reason. I can also remember suggesting some move or other, to which he replied it would be going rather far. Anyhow, we managed to get 'Hoko' pushed in there. That was how the door opened to the WBC.

"As far as the WBO was concerned I called them the BO champions in the early days. Later on, Chris Eubank was great for the WBO, giving it better recognition - and then it was Steve Collins, and on to Joe Calzaghe. I was always very proud to say I had IBF, WBA and WBC champions, but no BO champions. We almost made it in WBO, though. Getting Ray Close in with Eubank for the Super-middleweight title was mainly because Close wanted it, if at all possible."

Eastwood conceded: "Yes, I was involved in a lot of things, a lot of tough deals. I have been around a lot of guys who have done it all, been at the top. They had World champions, and different things. You become smarter to the moves along the way, after meeting such people. I also learned early in my involvement with the fight game it is not what you are allowed to do but what you can get away with. I also learned ways and means to achieve things in the chess game from other boxing people like Tito Lectoure. Tito was great. I met other folk like him in boxing, all very knowledgeable guys, tops in their own fields, and people who also knew how to cut corners and make the right connections. I built up contacts. I had to. If you can touch for the right men you are in there. It is all about making contacts, and hoping they turn out to be the right ones to improve your fighters. At a later stage in our gym's progress a man who brought a lot of fighters here to Belfast was Robert Mittleman of New York.

"He later bought Oscar De La Hoya, who turned professional with him and had his first dozen fights for him. De La Hoya was doing all right, but Mittleman did not have the money. Apparently Robert had a bit of clout, but not sufficient finance, and allegedly was managing De La Hoya on a shoestring. I believe promoter Bob Arum came along. After promoting one of De La Hoya's contests. Bob said Oscar wanted to go with him. I think, at the finish up, Arum got the fighter out of his contract. I do believe Mittleman was apparently paid in the region of $1m. De La Hoya went from strength to strength, and on to also promoting in a big way in the States. He formed Golden Boy Promotions, and became a mega-fight promoter." Mittleman, a controversial figure during the early 21st Century in the American fight scene, became important to Eastwood's operation.

Eastwood also had a strong contact with Mickey Duff in London: "I also had a good record of my boxers against those handled by Duff, who was then the top man of the UK in World boxing. I got in former World Featherweight contender Caba to fight McGuigan, through his manager Duff. I think I had six of my fighters against six of Duff's. And, do you know something, he never got a win against any of my boxers. Caba was one. Former Commonwealth champion Chiteule, who gave McGuigan a lot of trouble, was another."

COMING OF AGE

FORMER WBC world champion Juan LaPorte was the chosen one to find out if Irish hero McGuigan was now adequately equipped to make the final push for global glory. The Puerto Rican was in a different class to anything the Cyclone encountered up to that memorable meeting. McGuigan recognised that fascinating fight as a career climb to a new and more demanding level of excellence.

Of all the McGuigan fights, I look back on this hurdle as his most accomplished performance. Obviously the higher-profile beating of Pedroza was exceptional, especially from a historical context yet requiring total focus, but the beating of LaPorte was the tops in my book. My writings in the News Letter, Belfast, suggested it was a moment-of-truth tussle. During countdown Eddie Shaw said: "The main job now is to get Barry into the right thinking, to fight the right fight."

I also revealed the growing outside interest in McGuigan's flourishing career with the news that CBS television of the United States was to beam the battle on their coast-to-coast network in America. I mentioned in previewing of the fight that Barry: "cannot afford to be reckless against such a class tradesman', and that LaPorte 'would provide a searching examination of McGuigan's true potential.' I also warned LaPorte was always capable of landing a big right-hander, should McGuigan become careless in his customary wade-in tactic.

The Cyclone, earning his largest purse - apparently a clear £50,000 with allegedly no deductions for expenses - manfully managed to twice survive the blurring hand speed and power of the switch-hitting New York-based fighter's right hook. LaPorte was coming off a narrow loss to Gomez, but the bout in Belfast was a significantly crucial clash for both boxers; one apparently on the slide, the other on the way up. It was a clash of classic quality that raised hairs on the back of necks, hypnotic stuff. The spell-bound fans could not take their eyes off the epic battle of wits. Everyone in the packed arena knew this was the final hurdle for the busy but ultra-careful McGuigan against a very experienced power puncher with an economic style.

LaPorte, loaded up with ring and street smarts, was also well aware this was a crossroads contest for both fighters. He was always patiently probing for openings to try and take out McGuigan. He knew he had little chance of walking out of Belfast with a points decision. The Cyclone needed to come up with high quality goods for this one. In this risk business gambles have to be taken, to make sure a boxer has all the tools, mentally and physically, to make it to the top. This was the biggest examination of McGuigan's blossoming career, and he was merely a whisker away from walking into mortal danger against the lethal-punching LaPorte. Harry Gibbs was the middleman.

The Cyclone hit the canvas running in the shop-window showdown. He produced an amazing work-rate. His punches to the body had an early effect on LaPorte. However, Barry was hurt momentarily by right-handers in the fifth and ninth rounds to leave Irish fans almost frozen with high anxiety levels amid the nail-biting tension. A sturdily built, balanced and precise puncher, LaPorte bombed Barry with two really good right-hand shots. McGuigan took them well.

Eastwood said: "Maybe it is bad that he took the punches so well, in a different sense. Up to that, McGuigan was generally well protected around the chin, maybe worried about getting hit on the chin. After LaPorte I felt he probably became a little careless. Writers were printing how well he takes a punch. It is a virtue for a boxer to be able to take a good punch, but not a virtue to take too many of them. The LaPorte performance, nonetheless, proved McGuigan could go that one step further and win a world title. Where we had doubts before, when you were not sure, this was the final test."

Convinced it was ripe time to go after the main prize BJ disclosed it was through Gil Clancy, a noted ringside television commentator on fights in the United States, and Howie Albert, that the deal was sealed to set up the test for Barry against their fighter LaPorte. Incidentally, New Jersey-born Albert, who ran a New York-based fight managership with Clancy and once handled the affairs of Emile Griffiths, George Foreman and Jerry Quarry, died aged 86 in January 2009. Following McGuigan's fabulously focussed display and hugely significant victory we began wild speculation the next pit-stop stop could be to display his skills and tenacity in the Big Apple, in a proposed CBS television spectacular in Madison Square Garden. It was reported 15 million viewers in the United States witnessed the tingling test against LaPorte. A shot at a World belt was now firmly in McGuigan's gunsights.

I reflected on the fight: 'After ten furious rounds of blistering action from the packed King's Hall it was evident the Clones Cyclone has the heart, strength, skill and the punch to contest the Big One.' I also added: 'McGuigan's magnetic drawing power in the USA could lead to a match against Rocky Lockridge for the WBA Junior Lightweight crown. US agent Mickey Duff apparently planned to have talks with Lockridge's manager Dan Duva on March 13.'

My more detailed report of the ring action heralded: 'Barry passes the acid test' - and stated McGuigan 'took the best shots LaPorte could fire to take a convincing 99-97 decision from London referee Harry Gibbs.' The 7,000 screaming fans went delirious with delight when the Cyclone's arm was automatically raised, following the Gibbs summary of six rounds to McGuigan, two to LaPorte, and two even. My writings included: 'Barry has never been up against such a high-calibre opponent during his previous 25 contests. McGuigan must have known from the early rounds he was in for a true searching examination of his worth, as the 25-year-old New York-based LaPorte proved why he has never been put on the deck, nor stopped, during an illustrious amateur and professional career.

'In a night to remember McGuigan survived two critical stages in an absorbing battle, during the fifth and ninth rounds when swarthy LaPorte flashed home deadly right hand punches. Always a little suspect to consuming right handers, Barry stood up to the short-lived withering fire from the flashing fists of this superbly conditioned tradesman.' I added: 'In a sensational tenth round LaPorte produced an early short burst. It was a last-ditch stand by the ex-champion who knew he had one hope, to win by knockout. LaPorte then soaked up a non-stop bombardment that varied from short hooks to the body to a long raking left jab from marvellous McGuigan. The Cyclone finished with a huge right to LaPorte's chin.'

LaPorte, who was later taken to hospital with a suspected perforated eardrum, said: "It was the first time in my career I was really hurt." The gifted gladiator, who had previously contested six World Championship fights in his 31-bout career, added: "McGuigan's right hand really hurt me in the final round. I have a damaged ear. I was dizzy. I think it is time to retire. McGuigan should be champion of the World. My, is he strong." Howie Albert, manager of LaPorte, added: "Barry is the best fighter they've ever had in Europe. He was more than we bargained for." I also had a word with referee Harry Gibbs, who contributed to the praise: "I have been in this game for some considerable time, and I have not seen anything like McGuigan in Britain. I thought he was something special after his early fight with Renard. He was knocked to the canvas by Renard, but no count. McGuigan came back at Renard with such fury it told me this kid is good. Barry took the best LaPorte could throw, and was immediately back in there. I felt LaPorte shot his bolt in the ninth round."

McGuigan said: "I proved I can go ten rounds at a good lick. I was sharp, and I can take a punch. I took his best, and was back in there." This extra-special occasion for Irish boxing earned an outstanding McGuigan the right to take the final step to stardom. Eastwood knew this was the moment. It was time to make the big push for a shot at a World title. Beating LaPorte, who later opened a boxing gym in the Bronx, New York, did not create the assumption the Cyclone was automatically going to win a World title. It was, nonetheless, a monumental result that suggested McGuigan had a fair chance of becoming a World champion. At that time Eastwood was a fully-fledged paid-up member of the WBA. He knew everything that was happening there, and where he might be able to make a meaningful move. After the outstanding success against LaPorte there were general demands of the when and where of a World title fight. The level of expectation in Ireland was sky high.

BJ, who agreed to the fight at 9st 4lbs to suit LaPorte and CBS requirements, said: "After beating LaPorte I won't keep him back from having a go at one of the big ones. Barry is ready. A world title fight in Belfast is the dream, but if we have to go to the States to get the Championship we will reluctantly go there." The acid test against LaPorte provided the career cornerstone contest for McGuigan. By November, 1984, with a progress chart of 22-1, he was firmly in the frame for a crack at a World title, and generally listed sixth in the WBA rankings. Ahead of him were Bernard Taylor (5), Nelson (4), LaPorte (3), WBC champion Gomez (2), and numero uno Pedroza. The pecking-order chopped and changed.

One time, Barry was behind Antonio Esparragoza (Venezuela), Angel Mayor (Venezuela), Taylor, Nelson, Jorge Lujan (Panama) and Pedroza. Incidentally, Bernardo Checa was in at number eight, one slot behind Mexico's Marcos Villasana. In the WBC ratings, McGuigan was placed behind Jackie Beard (USA), Villasana, Nelson, and champion Gomez. Checa was listed 13th. However, after McGuigan's fantastic win against LaPorte it required some tense and tough talking to set up the superfight against Pedroza.

Before the bartering began, there was another defence of the European Championship in London, a bout with mandatory challenger Farid Gallouse of France. Gallouse, I felt, should not be in the same ring as McGuigan. It proved just that, a meaningless match. Referee Felix Marti stopped the farcical fight after 1.20 of the second round. It was, nonetheless, the occasion that revealed where McGuigan would soon be climbing the mountain, as WBA Featherweight champion Pedroza was scheduled to be a spectator. It was to be the Panamanian legend's first in-the-flesh close look at the Irishman in action. It was also to be the fight before a delegation representing Eastwood Promotions would meet the champion later that night in a London hotel for the massive-money talks. Contract negotiations followed after McGuigan's awesome dismantling of a scandalously over-matched Gallouse.

Anxious Eastwood probably hoped for a similarly fast and efficient outcome to the big-money discussions with ring legend Pedroza's eccentric manager Santiago Del Rio. Help was needed in the form of a bi-lingual globe-trotter from County Antrim to conclude the big-bucks bartering. Gerry Donnelly unwittingly found himself pitched into the eye of a contract storm when Eastwood first came to grips with the fiery Del Rio. The date was March 26, 1985, and the venue a plush room in London's Holiday Inn, Marble Arch. Donnelly, a fluent Spanish speaker, was the agreed interpreter. Born in 1951, in the seaside resort of Ballycastle, the six-footer is part of the famous Donnelly hurling dynasty, while his American-born cousin Shaun became golf club professional at the Castle Hume complex outside Enniskillen, County Fermanagh.

He spent four years working in Spain, north of Cadiz on the Atlantic coast and about two and half hours drive from Gibraltar. He was a casino manager, setting up the first casino there in 1978. "After General Franco died things eased off a little bit in Spain. I was in London working as a computer programmer for the Royal Bank of Scotland. A friend of mine, Patrick McCaughan from Ballycastle, told me he knew boys who had been working for casinos in the Bahamas, playing golf, water skiing, and stuff like that. That was right up my street, I felt. I'll have some of that, if at all possible. What happened then was I went to Spain to get into the casino business. They brought out teams to help launch the casino. So, I learned the Spanish language during that period," said Donnelly, who returned to London.

Off and on, he was in the city for 15 years, including working for a spell in the advertising business. He was also employed by the Playboy Club casino, which was shut down in 1977. He moved from the England capitol in the late 1980's to live in Johannesburg. Donnelly, who sold a night-club in South Africa and switched to the property-building market, recalled the Pedroza visits to London. Delighted to be around for the big fight at Loftus Road, he enjoyed the landmark World title battle. It was a special time to be involved.

The euphoria leading up to the big fight, and the excitement during and after was special. He also had to help sort out some Panamanian tantrums before and during the fight contract talks. Poe-faced Pedroza was passive, and generally never uttered a word. However, in the heated high-stakes debate the veteran champion's manager Del Rio was a constant thorn in Eastwood's side. It developed into a fractious meeting with concern at times the title chance for The Cyclone might not take place. Neither edgy Eastwood nor the volatile Del Rio liked to back off in this clash of cultures, both refusing to give ground.

The big prize for McGuigan and his mentor was within touching distance. All the hard work was about to reach fruition, all the clamouring and climbing of the rungs of the Featherweight ladder to secure a shot at a major belt. Money matters, as always, can create sticking points. The Panamanian party perhaps felt this would be the champion's last trip to the well, after 19 worldwide defences. A big pay-off pension fund was the insurance target of the Pedroza camp. Nonetheless, with Donnelly deciphering the Del Rio's demands for the fabled champion Eastwood Promotions eventually managed to secure Pedroza's signature to defend his title in London later that summer. Donnelly was thrilled to be at the coalface for the contract talks, and also called in to perform a nursemaid job for Pedroza during fight-week before the action at Loftus Road.

"I was the interpreter during very difficult contract negotiations in the Holiday Inn. London promoter Mickey Duff was also there in the room, as was the boxer Pedroza. It was very hard work, very tough talking. Barney walked out at one stage, although he came back in again. At one point I felt the deal would never be completed. Del Rio was a very awkward customer. He pushed chairs around. Barney and Del Rio were both battling for their own corners, as it were." Eventually, everything was agreed. The big-money deal decided. Donnelly had no problems in understanding what Del Rio was asking for. There was a lot of shouting. A lot of cash was involved, but eventually they got the deal done.

"Before the contest, I looked after Pedroza as interpreter for four days in London. He had no English whatsoever, not even broken English. I took him out to a nightclub once, for a meal in the since defunct Trocadero,off Shaftsbury Avenue. I have to say the champion did not take a drink, when we had a corner in the casino cordoned off for a party of six. It lasted just over an hour. I knew Pedroza was tight at making the weight. He trained nicely, and did not eat that much. I was up in the gym every day. Whenever he needed anything I would be around to help. Pedroza was generally quiet. I spoke to him quite often, and I recall stuff he mentioned about trying to get into politics back in Panama. His second wife was with him in London. She stayed well out of the way, in the hotel."

Promoter Stephen Eastwood remembered the war of words: "Del Rio was mad, but very clever." He spent anxious hours sitting in another room situated below the one that held the contract talks. The night-time company included his brother Fintan and eminent Scotland-born sports journalist Hugh McIlvanney, a winner of the International Boxing 'Hall of Fame's' 1986 Nat Fleischer Memorial Award for Excellence in Boxing Journalism. Donnelly, who was a friend of Brian Eastwood and the other members of Bruno's Irish contingent , J.R. McKillop, Gerry Hanratty and Marius O'Reilly, relayed what was happening in the marathon talks. Del Rio and Pedroza - the champion looking considerably over the Featherweight limit - arrived in London on the eve of McGuigan's fight with Gallouse. The Central Americans apparently took the hump when not met by Eastwood at the airport.

Stephen said: "They expected Dad to be out at the airport to greet them. Instead, we were getting McGuigan prepared for his European title defence. The Panamanians did not attend. Of course, that was all part of the build-up to the contract talks. Dad had to go and try and calm them down. Del Rio was unbelievably difficult to deal with, but it all ended in a successful conclusion, somewhere between four and five in the morning. Gerry (Donnelly) was upstairs. I went there a few times to clarify some detail. We sat mainly downstairs with Hugh McIlvanney. We would get relays that the big fight was on. Then we'd get the opposite news - that it was a no go, until a bottle of champagne was ordered and popped to seal the deal. Everything was finalised, everything agreed. Pedroza and Del Rio got a king's ransom to come and fight in London."

Eastwood's memory of the tempestuous gathering was: "We had to take the fight against Gallouse, yet should not have been in the same ring as McGuigan. Then it was into those stormy talks with Del Rio. Pedroza and Del Rio didn't go to the Gallouse fight, and left the next morning. The arrangement was to hold the talks afterwards. We met before McGuigan's contest for preliminary talks, but they were not happy - and then they did a runner on us. They left us sitting. It was very messy. We had to chase them.

"Del Rio just disappeared. He was very temperamental. We were worried then could we put it together. They were annoyed, and I believe they were gong to just clear off. They had every intention at the time of leaving London, but they couldn't get a flight out of London that evening. We eventually collared them. Certainly all this was upping the ante. They wanted extra things, such as options sorted out, and were not happy with that - and wanted guarantees and bankers' assurances."

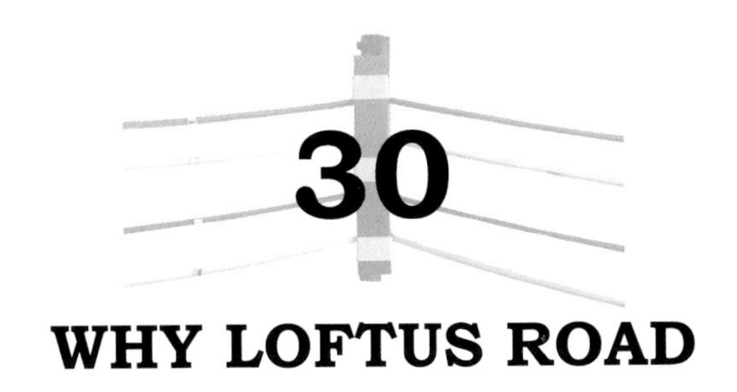

30 WHY LOFTUS ROAD

LONDON promoter Jarvis Astaire suggested to the Eastwood camp the Queen's Park Rangers FC ground would be an ideal outdoor summer's evening setting for McGuigan to take on the mighty Pedroza. BJ said renowned impresario Astaire mentioned the football ground at Loftus Road had an astro-turf covering, which would be ideal to handle seating arrangements and the weight of the ring. The venue was available for an outdoor promotion, but it proved to be a costly exercise.

Stephen Eastwood went to work on the demanding project, and all the implications: "People who don't know the game think you just walk in, stick up a ring, and lay out a few rows of seats There are so many things needed to be changed, rules to be adhered to such as fire restrictions, and so forth. Safety walls have to be built on the instructions of fire officers." Eastwood Promotions ran the show in association with Astaire, Mike Barrett and Mickey Duff. It was the most expensive boxing bill ever staged in England, up to that time.

Eastwood said: "We were into a couple of million pounds sterling to put on the show. Surprisingly, it made a little money, a small amount of profit. The show pulled in around 22,000 spectators. BBC television was involved. There was also television interest from North America, but the Panama and American TV monies were claimed by Pedroza." Stephen (Eastwood) confirmed the McGuigan-Pedroza contest was unquestionably the most expensive fight to be staged in the UK at that time. The artificial football pitch surface meant the promoter could lay the boards down on the ground without damaging it. "There was a terrific crowd, a fantastic night with London lit up. We had also arranged a laser show in the sky. It was meant to be the first of its kind in London. Jean Michel Jarrier did a great laser show in Paris. He was an orchestral musician. He did these super shows, with illuminated music, so to speak. I felt we should have a special laser show after the McGuigan fight.

"Just at the start of the fight the guy who ran the unique laser show was preparing for the possibility of using laser messages high up in the night sky, such as 'Congratulations Barry' - stuff like that. Barry had to win, of course, but half-way through the fight the technician handling the laser lights came to me to tell me the electric power was off. I was told by a certain individual the problem was insurmountable. As it turned out, somebody mischievously and deliberately pulled out the fuse from the electricity box. I believed it to be sabotage. We felt we knew who did it, but could never prove it. It was a shame. Still, it was a great night at Loftus Road. Despite that hiccup to annoy me, it was an exceptional occasion," he added.

Before the riveting action began there was taping trauma in the McGuigan dressing room. Short-fused Del Rio almost ruined the big occasion. The crafty Latin, probably fearing the end of the trail for the champion, tried to get a last-minute edge. It was an underhand trick, really, when he stormed into the Irishman's dressing room, obviously trying to unsettle the Cyclone. Eastwood blew his top on that Saturday morning, claiming 'no home protection' in the dressing room. Del Rio was not satisfied with the taping of Barry's fists.

"Mind you, it came close to blows with Del Rio. How dare he come in, and try to intimidate us, and with the supervisor at his shoulder," rasped Eastwood, "I said to the supervisor to get that lunatic (Del Rio) out of our dressing room or there would be really big trouble. I had enough of all the messing by that stage. My fighter was very upset, and just seconds before having to go out to enter the ring and contest the World Championship for a first time. It was scandalous. How that was allowed to happen I'll never know. And, I still say Pedroza was over nine stone at the weigh-in. There was a rumour Pedroza was locked in sauna before the weigh-in.

"Everything was done so quickly. I was very suspicious of the Panamanians. The Pedroza people were very awkward to work with. Of course, Pedroza successfully defended his title 19 times, and had many of his fights overseas. His camp knew how to deal with things at top level, and you find people like that difficult to work with. They have been around. They knew all the moves. Del Rio handled his man well, that's for sure. It was tough going for us, new ground. I lost verbal battles with Del Rio. He twice upended a table in my direction, deliberately during our early talks in attempting to clinch the title fight. He really went over the top in our dressing room. That was a bit much. Instead of losing just 99 rounds in the contract arguments I lost two more before the fight began, at the weigh-in and then the nasty hassle over the taping of McGuigan's hands. The WBA supervisor from Puerto Rico seemed to agree with Del Rio's demands. That was hard to swallow."

Eastwood didn't take the unseemly showdown with Del Rio lying down. Arguably not in the best possible taste, the Irish camp countered by conjuring up a stroke of Irish blarney by hiring a midget from a London circus to dress up as one of 'The Little People'. Rigged out in the traditional green and gold garb, and green bowler hat, the 'Leprechaun' made a surprise dart through the ropes and into the ring before the opening round. He shook his fist, and then fired some angel dust in the direction of Pedroza's corner, pretending to cast an Emerald Isle spell from the 'Wee Folk' on the bemused, if apparently impassive, defending champion Pedroza, and then skirted out of the ring. Matchmaker and cornerman Byrne was also busy both inside and outside the ring. On that late evening of high drama, gut-twisting tension, thrills and spills, he became involved in a curious cameo during the contest. It was all because of a strange sequence of events during the interval between some rounds.

Byrne was baffled by the perceived goings-on in Pedroza's corner: "I remember a very odd incident during the contest. I was in McGuigan's corner, but noticed what I felt were strange happenings in the other corner. I wondered what was going on. Something wasn't right, I felt. In the Panamanian's corner one of their men kept taking something out of a pocket and putting something in Pedroza's mouth between some rounds. They said it was an ice cube. I'd never seen that before. I went over to referee Stan Christodoulou during the fight to complain. I was suspicious. Everyone at the fight will remember me making a protest. Obviously Loftus Road was the high of the Barry McGuigan era."

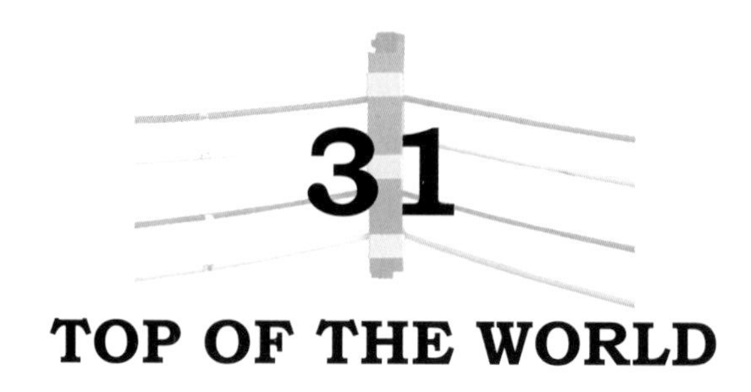

TOP OF THE WORLD

LOFTUS ROAD unwrapped what every Irish fight fan believed was an imperishable hero. The pinnacle of McGuigan's punching path to glory was unquestionably that balmy summer's evening on Saturday June 8, 1985. It was a night to remember. Ringside guests included top Northern Ireland sporting personalities Denis Taylor of World snooker fame and Olympic Games gold medallist Dame Mary Peters.

Before McGuigan and Pedroza entered the ring, news filtered down from Scotland that Ireland had yet another sporting hero. He was County Down's Bangor-born Walker Cup golfer Garth McGimpsey, winning the British Amateur Championship at Royal Dornock. There was a deafening racket around ringside when McGuigan emerged from his dressing room to face the sun going down. Soon it was twilight.

The ring lights were now switched on in the ring canopy. The partisan supporters went haywire with delight when a McGuigan right-hander toppled the proud Panamanian in the eighth round. That was the sure sign the Cyclone was in control of his own ring destiny, and would march on to take a clear decision. McGuigan boxed with patience and power. The younger, fresher fighter brought into play his previously sparingly used right hand to eventually discourage the champion.

Eastwood said: "I remember this guy Gerald Hayes, who came in from New Jersey to spar McGuigan before the world title fight. He kept urging McGuigan to 'throw a right - throw a right. You will beat Pedroza with the right'. Indeed, he was correct, as it was the right hand that caught Pedroza. God, Hayes could talk. He was good money well spent. I saw his fight with Pedroza, and he had Pedroza on the floor in a non-title fight in Panama City." Referee/judge for the 15-rounder was South Africa's

Stanley Christodoulou, making the thriller 148-138 for the dominant Cyclone. Danish judge Ove Ovessen had it 149-139, and completing the unanimous verdict was Venezuela's Fernando Viso with his 147-140 tally. WBA supervisor was Rafael Ramos Yordan.

Once McGuigan's arm was raised, and the belt tucked around his waist, it became sheer bedlam as faithful Irish fans hooted and hollered in typically boisterous celebration. Everyone at the ground seemed to be milling near the ropes, trying to slap Barry on the back or shake his hands. The new King of the Ring was whisked back to the sanctuary of the dressing-room. McGuigan, a dedicated athlete blessed with natural aggressive talent, a strong physique, and unwavering single-mindedness, and kingmaker Eastwood could now warmly reflect on a job well done.

They conquered their Everest in the unlikely surroundings of a football pitch. It had been, at times, a testing road to the top. Eastwood and McGuigan took time to enjoy a special moment, and indulge in a sharp intake of breath. There was an emotional scene in the QPR dressing-room. We were not to know this father-son embrace was also to be the beginning of the end of what appeared the perfect partnership.

I prefer to remember the good times. I was fortunate to winkle an exclusive first post-fight interview with Barry and his boss. It was a unique occasion, amid many moments of magic that intertwined among fact and folklore of the McGuigan era. Little did I know this very private and emotional meeting of souls, McGuigan and Eastwood, would never be again. Heavy shouldered security men were instructed by television officials not to let anyone, especially other media folk, enter the dressing-room area after the historic fight. The bow-tied bulkies did their best to keep me out, but had to step aside for the show extravaganza's promoter Stephen Eastwood. He invited me into a situation that was perhaps the last natural and instinctively united happy time experienced by the Cyclone and his Svengali.

Stephen said: "That was important for me to get O'Hara into the dressing room. You had been there from the start, and now you were not to be excluded. You were first in and saw the flood of emotion in that room, but sadly soon to be forgotten." It was an unforgettable experience to witness McGuigan and Eastwood reflecting on the wonderful journey, well away from all the hype and hassle, soaking up what happened inside that outdoor ring.

My exclusive report, in the Belfast News Letter and under the banner heading of 'He's the greatest', included: 'It was only then, McGuigan and the man who had faith in the magnificent fighting machine from County

Monaghan realised what really happened, the dream achieved. The wee man and his boss stared at each other in mutual admiration. 'Son,' says BJ, 'We've done it, we've done it. You are some kid. What a performance.' Barry nodded. Both men quietly embraced. McGuigan let a trickle of tears run down his face. It was akin to a proud father - successful son scene. And then Eastwood again broke the silence, and said: 'We are there now. Who would have believed a wee kid from Clones is now King of the World. You are the king. You will be champion of the World until you decide to retire.'

Barry replied: 'But boss, I still cannot believe it is over, that I am the champion. Pedroza had some class, but I still cannot feel the big feeling I anticipated I might if I won. I know it will all sink in after a few days time. What I feel now is the sense of enjoyment and pride in the result that the marvellous fans are experiencing. I feel so good physically and mentally that I could go another five or 10 rounds now, if required. I doubt if I have ever felt so strong and bouncing after a hard contest. I suppose I am still high on adrenaline - that's the super feeling at this moment.'

Almost an hour after the fight ended McGuigan, still in his boxing kit, managed to extricate himself from the media scrum and take a shower. During countdown to reaching the summit McGuigan applied himself with ruthless zeal to a training programme. At times, he had to be prized away from working out too much. His focus was awesome. He worked with the discipline of a Trappist monk. Long before meeting Pedroza, he unwittingly invented the catchphrase: 'Thank you very much, Mr Eastwood' - to be imitated in satirical song by Dublin comedy actor Dermot Morgan, later of 'Father Ted' television fame.

The new Irish superstar of sport then received tumultuous receptions during parades through the main thoroughfares of downtown Belfast and Dublin. Those were heady and very special times, and suitable reward for years of dedicated hard work. Irish fight fans enjoyed protracted celebrations after McGuigan's greatest triumph. Thousands of adoring fans from all walks of life and shades of opinion in Northern Ireland lined Belfast's city-centre streets to welcome home one of Ireland's biggest-ever sporting heroes. The euphoria of the win in London included open-top bus adulation in Dublin, with lots of backslapping, hordes of beaming faces. It seemed the feel-good fight factor would never end. The wicked-punching wizard clinically overpowered Pedroza. All high levels of expectation were fulfilled. But what next, we wondered. It was the best of times, with the public's insatiable appetite seeking ever more from the Cyclone.

PLANE SAILING

THE BEATING of the Central American icon Pedroza appeared just the beginning of a dizzy ride to total world domination. Barry was big box-office now, and in a mega manner. It was into a period beyond superlatives. McGuigan and Eastwood were flying high. Indeed, there were times, before and after the winning of the highest honour, when they were literally floating on the clouds.

During that pulsating period of unforgettable excitement the Eastwood fighters sometimes took off into the blue yonder, in a Piper Aztec six-seater private aeroplane that was 'parked' and primed at the ready at Newtownards Flying Club, around ten miles from Eastwood's home. The flying machine was often used to take trips to England to attend boxing shows. Eastwood purchased the 'plane during the early 1980's, and after the end of Dave Boy's reign he decided he had no further use for it.

He said: "The pilot was Commander Tony Tuke, a former helicopter pilot in the Royal Navy who lived at Newtownards. Tony worked for me, and did some other odd jobs for Eastwoods. The aeroplane was available to all my boxers, whenever needed. It had a reasonable range. We flew to places such as Paris and London. We flew to some horse race meetings in England, like Cheltenham. The 'plane was also used to go to Shannon in the south of Ireland, and down to St Angelo Airport in County Fermanagh. Many times we took off for the Farranfore airport in County Kerry to attend horse race meetings in the area - at Listowel, Killarney, and Tralee."

The Piper 'plane was all a part of the image, perhaps a message to world boxing that Eastwood had the good intentions to reach for the stars.

All the carefully sustained publicity, the precision planning and packaging, the creation of such a phenomenally successful and vibrant era for Irish boxing elevated McGuigan to the level of pop-idol status. Female fans were rapidly on the increase. The vision of boundless riches was turning towards reality, a boy from the sticks about to rule the boxing universe. There was growing speculation as to the worth of the new king.

Words and deeds were overtaken by what appeared a need to market the phenomenally determined fighter. McGuigan was a prized asset. An El Dorado of untold financial reward for the fighter could, according to speculators, be achieved on the western side of the Atlantic Ocean. Before then, it was domestic delight for the faithful fans, who could hardly contain themselves during this happiest of times. They were pleading for a McGuigan title defence as quickly as possible, the unbridled joy to continue. Soon there was the exciting news of a first defence of the title, and at the Holy Grail - in the King's Hall ring, the perfect setting for the homecoming of the hero. There was great delight when Eastwood Promotions confirmed that McGuigan was to make a defence against Bernard Taylor in the King's Hall, Belfast. As it turned out, it was to prove his last Championship contest, indeed his final fight, in the famed arena. The bout, set for Saturday, September 28, 1985, would round off an astonishing year in the history of Irish boxing.

The swashbuckling achievements of McGuigan sat alongside other notable happenings of 1985, which was also designated 'International Youth Year' by the United Nations. Mike Tyson made his professional debut in March, at Albany, New York. Sadly, May 29 heralded horror happenings in Heysel Stadium, Brussels, where 38 soccer spectators lost their lives during the European Cup final between Liverpool and Juventus. Born in 1985 were future sporting heroes such as Lewis Hamilton of Formula One racing; Portugal, Manchester United and Real Madrid soccer ace Christiano Ronaldo, and also England and Manchester United striker Wayne Rooney. Famous people who died in 1985 included film actors Sir Michael Redgrave, Edmond O'Brien, Rock Hudson, Yul Brynner, and also singer Ricky Nelson and band leader Nelson Riddle.

McGuigan's return to the big Belfast ring proved a tricky time during the early rounds against left-jabber Taylor. The 'B T Express' from the Volunteer State of Tennessee was unbeaten (32-0-1) until he ran into energetic McGuigan's body shots. He had been patiently waiting on the wings to secure a second crack at the WBA Featherweight crown, after holding Pedroza to a draw four years earlier - on August 14, 1982, in Charlotte, Tennessee. Taylor, 28, carried the vast experience of 17 years in top level combat into the King's Hall. He was managed by Ace Miller, who was also the pilot of WBA Heavyweight champion John Tate. Taylor was promoted in the USA by Bob Arum's 'Top Rank' organisation. He was a World Cup amateur gold medallist in 1976, but was denied the opportunity of participating in the 1980 0lympics in Moscow after US President Jimmy Carter withdrew the entire American team in protest at the Russian invasion of Afghanistan. Taylor assembled the staggering amateur record of 489 wins from 498 contests.

Eastwood said: "Taylor was the mandatory challenger to Pedroza, and had to be given step-aside money to allow us to progress and set up the McGuigan fight with Pedroza. Bob Arum was handling him, and he agreed to the delay. Taylor was a good clever boxer, but was done on the scales. Their man had him in our gym at 6.30 in the morning." McGuigan took some time to find the range, and get on the inside against the slick but generally negative counter-puncher. Referee for the mandatory match was Venezuela's Isidoro Rodriguez. A tortured Taylor decided by the end of the eighth round he had enough of McGuigan's discouraging body shots. Little did we realise then, after another night of 'Here We Go' chanting by the fanatical followers, it was to be the last of the Cyclone's glorious Belfast chapter in Irish prizefighting.

Riding along on the crest of a wave, the exuberant fight fans hoped the glory trail would never end. But, there were whisperings of negative vibes, the slowly simmering rumour of small ripples of discontent eating into the McGuigan-Eastwood relationship. Corrosion was apparently setting in, but what some folk felt was insidious interference did not surface until shortly before McGuigan's second defence.

Respected sports journalist Adam Coates, for many years the man with the caramel-coated voice of BBC's Radio Ulster Sport, spookily warned of the dangers lurking ahead after the Loftus Road breakthrough. In the countdown to McGuigan's first defence of the belt, the canny Scot from Aberdeen penned poignant words in the fight-show programme. He reckoned this was the beginning of a third and final phase of Barry's ring career. He declared: 'The demands on all his powers of alertness, guile and resolution will be as relentless as they were during the testing journey to the WBA Featherweight throne. Even more determined ambushers lurk along the trail.' And also with almost eerie insight, Adam added: 'There will be those not in boxing gloves who seek to profit. Faint but insistent voices will whisper in the corners of the champion's mind, 'Take it easy now, champ, no need to flog yourself any more.' So, into the heavily-mined path our champion now advances warily. Can he survive? 'Can he reign for as long as he would like? It is his stated intention to be champion for about two and half years. This was his calculation after he deposed Eusebio Pedroza at Loftus Road. That would probably entail about seven more successful title defences.'

The McGuigan-Taylor encounter also established the changing face of financial times. "Putting on major international boxing shows was becoming very expensive," argued Eastwood, "For that particular King's Hall bill, and the following one in Dublin, seat prices ranged from £160 to £30. That was some money for ringside seats then, in 1985 and '86. The top ringside seat for the Taylor fight was £150. It was very big money, but the fighters we were bringing in were hard to pay."

The King's Hall encounter bridged a very special nostalgic gap, another proud milestone in the history of universal boxing. It was the first World title joust in the famous fight arena in 36 years. On that previous occasion (September 30, 1949) Belfast's singing slugger John 'Rinty' Monaghan bowed out as the unbeaten undisputed World Flyweight champion. Rinty, born on August 21, 1920, in Belfast's 'Sailortown' dockland district, had to quit late in 1949, because he was suffering from breathing discomfort. The always chirpy champion decided to put the World, British, European and Commonwealth Championships on the line for a last time. He held onto the titles from a 15-rounds draw summary against England's Albert Edward Govier, better known as Terry Allen.

A professional since 14 years young, mercurial Monaghan put away the gloves to develop a cabaret and showband career. Also famed for his ring rendering of 'When Irish Eyes are Smiling' his prize-fight record was 43 wins (19 knock-outs), three draws, and eight defeats. By the by, in April 1950, Allen - the 'London Barrow Boy' - won the vacant title when beating Honore Pratesi in London, but lost the crown 98 days later to Dado Marino in Hawaii.

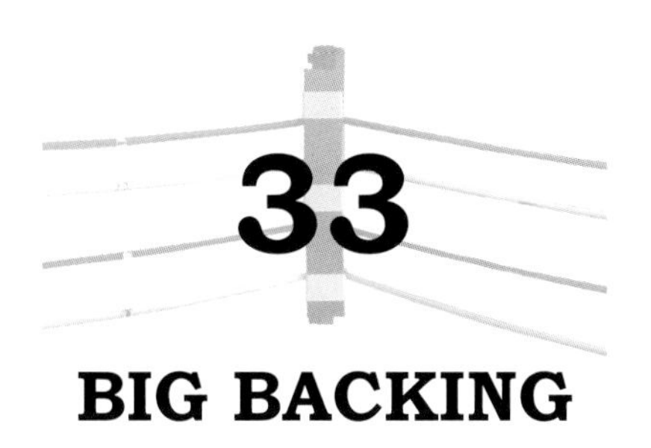

33

BIG BACKING

WHEN the McGuigan roadshow really reached top gear it required big bucks to stage the international promotions, and right in there among the nuts and bolts was a man of influence. Trevor McClintock, head of the Belfast wholesale drinks firm of Gilbey's at that time, helped to provide the significant major sponsorship support of Smirnoff vodka. This partnership proved highly productive. McClintock was an essential ally during the formative years of the great adventure.

McClintock contributed an immensely significant role the success story of the happy times of the Eastwood-McGuigan alliance. Like Stephen Eastwood, he stepped off the merry-go-round after Loftus Road. Gilbey's were in from the start, and through to the peak of winning the World title at Loftus Road. McClintock, who retired to live at St Andrew's in Scotland, was no stranger to up-front involvement in the vibrant sponsoring of sport in Northern Ireland.

He said: "Gilbey's did two years of boxing sponsorship before the McGuigan era. We supported the Ulster Amateur Boxing Championships, under the banner of J & B Whiskey. When Barry McGuigan quit the amateur ranks, to join BJ, we moved to sponsor professional boxing, through Eastwood Promotions. We said at the start, in 1981, the Smirnoff banner would sponsor Barry right through to his chance of winning the World title. After that, the Irish Permanent Building Society stepped in to take over the backing of Barry, and we moved away. We were not around when the fall-out happened, between Barry and BJ. We were out for a couple of years before Gilbey's came back with Smirnoff sponsorship for Dave 'Boy' McAuley fights."

McClintock, who was linked to the sale of the rare and very special 'Last Drop' whiskey, highlights McGuigan's win of the World title at Loftus Road as the pinnacle of excitement: "Obviously McGuigan's fight with Juan LaPorte was fabulous. I remember LaPorte landing one big punch late in the fight. It was fantastic. The occasion in London for the Pedroza fight was unbelievable. I was with the McGuigan corner, from the changing room to the ring. The one outstanding memory, from all the years of sponsorship involvement, I have is of the build-up moments leading to the fight. The American television producer had us timed from leaving the changing room to the ring, taking five seconds on to another mark inside the area, then ten seconds to get to another mark and so forth.

"It was to go like clockwork, the entrance of McGuigan to the ring. Instead, we ran into a wall of mad Irish supporters. It was chaotic at ringside, so much so we had to clamber across press seats and benches to reach the ropes and into McGuigan's corner. There was a similar delay after the McGuigan win. For a first time, it seemed, the American television company not only ran over their time limit they mapped out before the fight, but also after the fight. Other outstanding happenings were at the Friday evening weigh-ins, usually in the Belfast Europa Hotel. It was usually bedlam there, so many people milling around the scales to witness the weigh-ins. It was a very special time. It was terrific. There was very little else happening then. It was also an outstanding era for Gilbey's, helping to put the Smirnoff brand on the map."

Eastwood appreciated the support. This was a different time to that of his Sixties shows in the Ulster Hall. The boxers of the Eighties demanded very big money. Backing was needed, as the gate money was not enough to cover all the expenses. There were ever-increasing overheads: "Without sponsorship you were in grave danger of losing your tonsils. There were plenty of shows that didn't make a profit. There were many shows that proved a waste of time and money, as far as promoting was concerned. Ulster Hall shows were also becoming more difficult, when there was no TV money. The fights were just televised locally. It was quite a long time before the boxing shows attracted BBC television at international level."

BJ explained when a fighter came in from overseas for a major international bout, such as Valerio Nati for the European Featherweight Championship defence against McGuigan at the King's Hall, TV was present. In Nati's case, the fighter claimed the Italian TV loot along with his purse and sundry expenses: "Nati was well paid for that contest, because we won the purse offer for the Championship to be staged in Belfast in order to give McGuigan every edge possible. Later on, in other fights, if there was American television interest for American fighters involved they, the boxers, claimed a share of that money. It was not just as cut and dry, as simple as some people claimed, about how much money was made on boxing shows.

"Quite apart from paying other boxers on the undercard of promotions, there was the high cost of bringing in sparring partners, paying them, keeping them, keeping trainers. It is a big business if you have quite a number of fighters in your gym. It is like having a big stable of thoroughbred horses, you need winners. If you have the winners you have a chance. The huge show at Simmonscourt Hall, in Dublin's RDS complex, was OK from a promotional point of view. It was a tough second title defence for McGuigan, against Cabrera. We went to Dublin because it was then becoming very difficult for the Gilbey's Smirnoff support to continue backing shows at the King's Hall. The switch to Dublin was also due to financial support coming in from the Irish Permanent Building Society.

"There was now a large fight following for McGuigan in Dublin. It was also good for us to show him there for a second time in his professional career. The other thing was finance. It was good to run the World title show in Dublin because there was no V.A.T on purses, nor on ticket sales. Furthermore, any profit the show would make would not be taxed down there. We did all right out of that show."

Following the successful first defence of the WBA Featherweight title to close out a momentous year, the feel-good factor continued through January 1986 when McGuigan was named the WBA 'Fighter of the Year' for 1985. London boxing impresario and ex-professional fighter Mickey Duff accepted the award on McGuigan's behalf. The WBA 'Legend' selected for 1985 was former World Heavyweight champion Jersey Joe Walcott, and the official honoured was the referee of the McGuigan-Pedroza special, Stanley Christopolou. Incidentally, McGuigan was the first recipient of the British Boxing Board of Control's 'British Boxer of the Year' gong, in 1984, and understandably repeated the high achievement in 1985. His win against Pedroza was also recognised by the British Boxing Board of Control's 1985 'Contest of the Year'.

By now, the champion was into preparations for a voluntary defence of the Championship against Argentine's Fernando Sosa, scheduled for February 15, 1986. The Argentinean had 48 fights, with 42 wins (14 knockouts). Also in the media speculation was a hint McGuigan might soon take his flashing fists to the United States. Apart from winning, the Clones Cyclone needed to look good against Sosa to retain the interest and crucial support of US Television. Destination Dublin was to prove McGuigan's last title win. The ABC network was scheduled to beam the fight live to America. Sooner rather than later it was generally believed the champion would display his talents in the USA, but TV support would be necessary for such an undertaking. Eastwood travelled to Dublin in early January 1986 for a meeting with the sponsors, Irish Permanent Building Society. Eastwood Promotions were also locked in money talks with RTE Head of Television Sport, Tim O'Connor.

McGuigan's serious preparations for the match against Sosa were due to begin in Belfast on January 16. Due to check into the Bangor residence of Mrs Jean Anderson, he began early sparring and against Larne bantamweight Roy Webb. At that stage there was no indication Sosa, then Number 2 in the WBC rankings and Number 4 in the WBA ratings, was about to withdraw. His manager was the legendary Tito Lectoure, the fight mogul and owner of Lunar Park, Buenos Aires, and the mentor behind the career of Carlos Monzon. One of the greatest World Middleweight title holders of all time, Monzon retired in 1977 as undisputed champion.

Matchmaker Byrne and the Eastwood Organisation's General Manager Al Dillon took a trip to Dublin to look over possible facilities for Sosa to train in. On Monday January 20, McGuigan's camp met the media in the Eastwood gym. The place was chock-a-block with reporters and cameras, in from as far away as the USA and Switzerland, many doing documentaries. It was revealed the sparring partners signed up were Mexicans Yugo Antuiano and Joaquinacina Acuna, and also 19-year-old Manuel Mejia of Panama City, who was managed by Luis Spada. Eddie Shaw said McGuigan would complete 90 to 95 rounds of sparring by the time they wound up preparations in Dublin.

Significantly, McGuigan arrived in Dublin on the back of a deal with former professional golfer Roddy Carr of Dublin to be his merchandising agent. The *Irish Independent* reported Carr's recently formed Sports Organisation company CAMCORP also had a Fairway partnership with famous golfer Seve Ballesteros to promote the Spanish Open Golf

Championship. Tom Cryan's *Irish Independent* story of Friday February 1, 1986, stated: 'Roddy Carr, who had an unfortunate experience when he arranged closed circuit coverage at the National Stadium of McGuigan's defence against Bernard Taylor last year, flies into Belfast today to conclude a contract to act as merchandising agent for the world champion. My information is that ex-professional golfer Carr's job will be to sell McGuigan as an advertising medium in the business world.'

Carr, a member of the successful Great Britain and Ireland Walker Cup team against the United States in 1971, joined Mark McCormack's International Management Group (IMG). After spells in Cleveland, Ohio, and Hong Kong he left the Group a year earlier, and with older brother John set up CAMCORP, with offices in London and Dublin. A week before the big fight, Carr announced his sports marketing company agreed a deal to merchandise the Cyclone, and that his firm would be the champion's business adviser and agent, handling all commercial deals. Mentioned was the endorsements of a brand of potato crisp and a new line of soft drinks. During the launch Roddy stated the objective would be to align Barry with suitable clients "as a World champion who neither smokes nor drinks, he is a winning package for any product involving youth, energy, or being No 1."

Eastwood maintained: "I did not know, until the last minute, the Carr-McGuigan deal was done and dusted. I felt then the idea was probably to keep information from me for as long as possible. I think Roddy Carr was the first to come to me with the news. It didn't make any difference to me. Anyhow, I agreed to it, yet knowing I really had no option. At that time things were beginning to start rocking."

34

DISARRAY

ON JANUARY 31, 1986, the sock scene was thrown into confusion when Sosa withdrew. Apparently he damaged a finger during sparring with Ramon Dominguez. On Tuesday, February 4 it was disclosed Eastwood's agent Duff, who was in Tucson, Arizona, arranging the training preparations for his fighter John Mugabe to meet Marvin Hagler in a World Middleweight bout, was helping to find a replacement to meet McGuigan. Duff had 'connections' with the rugged Danilo Cabrera, the WBA's number 6 ranked from the Dominican Republic. The fearless 22-year-old, beaten twice then, showed confidence as the challenger. He was regarded a far heavier hitter than Sosa, scoring 17 short-route wins. Managed by Hector Rivera, he was in peak condition, in training to defend his Dominican Championship against Manuel Baptiste.

Eastwood's overall take on the upheaval in Dublin: "First of all, I had people searching all over for a replacement, working on all sorts of things. At the finish up, Mickey Duff said he had a control of this fighter Cabrero. For the right money we could get him to Dublin. Cabrera was a very late replacement, coming in at short notice." Cabrera's credentials to meet McGuigan were scrutinised not alone by the WBA but also by the giant US television network ABC, who transmitted the fight live across the Atlantic. ABC's Head of Sport, Bob Elger agreed, after watching tapes of Cabrera in action. The fighter was listed No 12 in the WBC ratings. McGuigan and Cabrera were scheduled to wind down their training schedules in a gym in the town of Swords, near Dublin Airport.

When promoter Brian Eastwood announced the fighter selected to meet Barry was to be Cabrera he stated: "Cabrera is one of the youngest fighters to meet McGuigan. He is a hungry, dangerous opponent." I ambled into

Dublin Airport on Monday, February 10, for the arrival of Cabrera, after his 18-hour journey. He missed the initial flight from Miami to New York because of a passport problem. The tiring trip took in Madrid and London. A weary, bleary Cabrera was still bouncy enough to declare: "I'm going to knock out this guy McGuigan." Known in his homeland as 'Kid Cuero Duro' - the hard one - he claimed a 107-bout amateur career, including 100 wins with 80 knock-outs. He had one brother and eight sisters, and once worked on a farm. He was earning his biggest purse, reputed to be $140,000. Apparently his previous best purse was $3,500.

Cabrera arrived in Dublin with stablemate Antonio Rivera, the 22-year-old WBA number 5 contender. Head trainer was Gregoria Benitez, father of famous triple World champion Wilfredo Benitez. Born on September 23, 1961, Cabrera was the Dominican Republic's Featherweight champion. He was climbing the World ratings. Like McGuigan, he worked out in the Fitness First health gym in Swords, County Dublin.

During countdown Eastwood was heard to declare: "If all goes well in Dublin, McGuigan's next Championship contest may be in Madison Square Garden." An American referee, Miami's Ed Eckert was appointed by the WBA. The judges named were Ed Levine (Miami), Louis Rodriguez (Venezuela) and Rogelia Perez (Panama). Fight Supervisor was Jimmy Binns of Philadelphia. The build-up to the abrasive battle was interesting. Cabrera looked relaxed during the Press Conference in Dublin. It was the first face-to-face meeting of the fighters. By contrast, a hint of unease surfaced in the McGuigan-Eastwood relationship when the champion first faced a battery of media questions. The Cyclone appeared edgy when an inquiry on money matters was raised. A Dublin news reporter had the temerity to speculate Eastwood Promotions could bank upwards of £700,000 on the venture. Eastwood described the suggestion as “a lot of rubbish.”

Times were changing, nonetheless. It used to be questions on how well Barry might fare in a fight, his condition, tactics needed, and could he win. Now it was a general media fixation with McGuigan's ever-increasing bank balance. Material achievements seemed to override the challenges inside the ring. The champion was asked if he was thinking about a possible defence in the United States, and all the big bucks likely to be earned there. He replied: 'No. I'm only concerned about Saturday night, right now.' The Cyclone, then regarded the highest earning professional boxer in UK history, made it clear he would not fight more than three times a year. Way back, on Wednesday, January 29, 1986, I penned confirmation by the 24-year-old WBA champion he would hang up the gloves when 27-years-of-age. His aim was to have just nine further fights, including the then proposed voluntary defence against the 27-year-old Sosa.

McGuigan predicted then: "My target is to quit the ring in three years time, and have three fights per year. My first target was to win the World Championship. Now I need something else, and I'd like to win the World Junior Lightweight Championship - maybe fight Gomez or Chavez. Gomez is the WBA champion, and Chavez is the WBC champion." It was also revealed McGuigan's match was to be beamed live coast-to-coast in the United States by the ABC television network. Importantly, the champion added: "I am still very keen to make it big in the United States. Some unkind things have been said and written by the American media. Some said LaPorte and Pedroza were over the hill. I want to change the American opinion of me."

The Cyclone's unexpectedly high level of discomfort in Dublin was an experience to suggest there was no compelling reason to risk taking him to the United States so soon after the physically and mentally demanding cruncher with Cabrera. It had been a thrilling trail to Loftus Road. The high ground was achieved in spectacular and convincing fashion, and along with it a sense of immortality. Beating Taylor in a first defence of the title was not easy, for a spell, yet neither was the test overly taxing or physically damaging for the new World 9-stone ruler. McGuigan fans anticipated another special show of raucous chanting and cheering in Dublin, but had to do endure some nail-biting moments.

It proved a frosty February night's work for the champion, before halting teak-tough Cabrera in the 14th round. A little bit of the old Cyclone sheen seemed to be missing for that first World title fight in Dublin in 63 years. This was into the trenches. The previously buoyant and bubbling McGuigan had to dig deep into man's basic survival instincts to overcome a painfully brutal battle of attrition. Crusty Cabrera appeared to have a reckless disregard for personal safety in a go-for-bust approach.

Ace cornerman Byrne had a busy time: "Cabrera, known as 'Old Boots' certainly proved to be as tough as old leather against McGuigan, who suffered a bad cut. They were going to stop the fight. The guy in the corner with Cabrera screamed at referee Eckert to do so. The fight continued, and Barry stopped him in the 14th round. Luckily, I patched up the McGuigan damage. It was a cold Saturday night outside the arena, but red-hot action inside the ring. I still have a press clipping declaring I saved McGuigan's boxing life as the defending champion, by solving the cut problem. Taylor was smart, but appeared to have no heart for the job. He was very elusive, a good jabber for a while, but Cabrera was different. It proved to be a difficult night for Barry."

The ending to McGuigan's Simmonscourt showdown, a brawl that included Cabrera taking an eighth-round hammering, arrived after 13.5 rounds. After 12 heated stanzas the varied points totals in favour of the champion were Perez 129-120, Rodriguez 129-122 and Levine 127-121. The champion needed six stitches in a left cheekbone wound. The rumour mill, nonetheless, was quickly at work suggesting he was likely to defend his title in May, with the probable venue New York or Las Vegas.

Eastwood claimed: "One of the reasons it was a rough night was because Cabrera backed McGuigan up. He put McGuigan on the back foot, and the champion couldn't get the feet right. The fight was stopped, and then it was started again. It was a very hard night's work for McGuigan. Cabrera was a rough character." After meeting McGuigan, in his next contest, Cabrera tried in vain for the WBC version. He was stopped in the tenth round, in Puerto Rico, by all-time great Azumah Nelson. He also lost a 12-round points decision in Tijuana to a rising Julio Cezar Chavez for the WBC Super-featherweight Championship. By the way, the undercard in Dublin featured Dave 'Boy' McAuley. The unbeaten 24-year-old was handed an eight-rounder before his proposed fight against Scotland's Charlie Brown in yet another British Flyweight Championship eliminator. He was matched and beat former British champion Kelvin Smart, who was dethroned by Hugh Russell.

Another unbeaten Larne fighter, 22-year-old bantamweight Roy Webb (10-0) was listed for an eight-rounder, and beat Mexico's Juan Castellanos. Webb, incidentally, was another prospect of high promise. He was looked after by Paddy Byrne and hooked inextricably to the Eastwood camp. Born on February 26, 1962, in Banbridge, the baby-faced fireball had an exemplary amateur record that included a Bantamweight silver medal from the 1982 Brisbane Commonwealth Games. Back home he won a hat-trick of Ulster Bantamweight titles - from 1980. Boxing out of Gerry Storey's Holy Family club in north Belfast, he also bagged the Irish Amateur Bantamweight crown of 1981 and the Ulster and Irish Featherweight titles of 1983. His late brother Kenny clinched two Ulster Featherweight titles, in 1977and '78.

"Roy was a very good kid," said Byrne, who arranged his paid debut in the King's Hall on January 25, 1984, when the headline action paraded McGuigan-Chiteule. Webb knocked out Swansea's Dai Williams in the second round. He remained in the slipstream of McGuigan exploits - shows featuring the Cyclone against Caba, DeVorce, Ruan, LaPorte, Galloise and a fifth-round stoppage of Danny Lee on the Loftus Road card. After halting Mexican Juan Castellanos in the third round at Simmonscourt, when backing the McGuigan-Cabrera action, his 11-fight unbeaten run ended in the Ulster Hall on April 22, 1986, when suffering an eight-round technical stoppage at the hands of Welsh fighter Peter Harris, who went on to win the British belt.

His second and last defeat of a 15-2-1 ring tally arrived two bouts later. Again it was an injury stoppage, in the seventh round to Birmingham's Rocky Lawlor in the Ulster Hall. On that January 17, 1986, bill Paul Hodkinson stopped Steve Sims. Webb, who became a successful car retailer in east Antrim and also an avid amateur golfer at his nearby Cairndhu Club, Larne, decided to quit the fight game despite scoring a second-round knock-out over Joe Donohoe of Walworth, London, in the Ulster Hall, on December 7, 1988. Topping that show was Crisanto Espana, beating Simon Eubank.

The drama in Dublin was another exciting fight-night experience for the faithful. The adoring fans loved the outcome, perhaps not fully aware of the enormity of the test nor that smouldering below the surface was a suspected level of unrest inside the Eastwood camp. On February 14, *Irish Independent's* Tom Cryan unwittingly also came close to one of the reasons why McGuigan and Eastwood would later part company: 'It is no secret,' he wrote, 'American television interests wanted a fight between McGuigan and Gomez, but it failed to materialise. If Cordero (Pepe) does turn up it will fuel speculation again about a New York bout later this year for the 9st 4lbs title.'

Is it possible the growing uncertainty behind the scenes, into which path the Cyclone should next take, was having a sub conscious effect on his performances. I summed up the Cyclone was over-anxious and over-eager against Cabrera, and that was one of the reasons he struggled. McGuigan, who was set to take a family holiday with wife Sandra and kids Blain and Daneka, said: "I'll be ready to fight again in May. I'll need a good eight weeks to allow the eye injuries to heal. I required six light stitches in the cut below the left eye. I'm okay, but Cabrera was some tough guy." He met the media in the foyer of the Berkeley Court Hotel.

I wrote: 'There was the clamour for more words from the man who had been through sheer hell.' The champion agreed he was not at his best against Cabrera, and added: "LaPorte was probably my hardest contest, but this guy was, by far, the most frustrating. He was very difficult to hit cleanly. What I realise now is that I still have a lot to learn. I have a lot of polishing up to do." McGuigan said referee Eckert accepted he should have spoken to Cabrera about his alleged wayward head and his thumb. The champion added the referee said he stopped the fight in the eighth round before the bell rang out, when Cabrera was half conscious and leaning on the champion's shoulder. The Cyclone thought the fight should have been over then.

Tom Cryan reported: 'McGuigan said the earliest possible time for his next defence is late May or June, when he is due to hold a mandatory defence against number one challenger Antonio Esparragoza of Venezuela, and that is likely to be in America. Besides Esparragoza, the other likely option for McGuigan is Antonio Rivera - the original choice after Sosa pulled out - or Sosa. The most likely dates for the contest are April 26 or June 14.' The landscape was beginning to change to a darker colouring in the Eastwood camp. Internal tensions were beginning to bubble. During post-Pedroza the mood slowly but inextricably changed away from the once happy-family relationship of McGuigan and Eastwood. Indeed, there may have been signs the gap was widening that we did not immediately pick up on, translate, or want to believe. Irish fight followers, myself included, hoped this amazing episode down the 'Yellow Brick Road' would go on for years, obviously appreciating the relatively short life of a prize-fighter.

Unknown to the outsider, it was seemingly becoming impossible to protect the new WBA king from the development of other influences. In no time at all it was all money talk, and with it an ever-widening gulf developing between Eastwood and his tiger. The mood was altering, just tilting a little bit at a time. Perhaps it was the price of fame, with the celebrity culture starting to kick in. Even the hardened hometown media men felt the wind of change. This was a sub-plot we did not anticipate. Early in the carefully choreographed rise of the Cyclone to World honours Eastwood quickly and cleverly cultivated a close understanding with the local press.

Many of the pure boxing writers around to help launch the unforgettable era were involved during Eastwood's first period of punch, when promoting in Belfast during the 1960's. Guided then by Mike Callahan, he learned the tricks of the trade, valuable lessons from that time on how to sell the product, and how to secure maximum media coverage from every outlet. The publicity machine, including the employment on a near full-time basis of affable Belfast sports photographer Alan McCullough, worked in close harmony with Irish journalists during the steady progress of the Cyclone. Soon the wider boxing world began to take notice of something special stirring in Belfast.

Eastwood explained: "The idea was to keep things in the forefront, and gain as much publicity as possible. The late Alan McCullough did the photographs for me, and sent the pictures to the papers. That happened almost on a daily basis, when we were coming up to a fight show. That kept it all going. Alan flooded the place with photographs. He was a nice fellow." There was a fairly comfortable, almost easy-going, relationship between the media regulars and the boxers in the Eastwood gym, also with the trainers, and with Eastwood. We felt part of the team. Maybe we unwittingly took access and availability for granted. Suddenly, things took an unexpected downturn during a period leading up to the McGuigan shot at the World title. Relationships became a shade strained when the seasoned Irish hacks, around from the birth of the boxing phenomenon from County Monaghan, were temporarily given the elbow.

McGuigan would not begin sparring in the Eastwood gym until all local fight reporters left the premises. By now, Barry began to experience the healthy benefits of contributing ghost-written column inches to a cross-Channel "popular" daily newspaper. This first came to light when my old Immaculata Club colleague Eddie Shaw invited me to step outside the gym; all in the best possible taste, I might add. Eddie asked me to leave. I recall being extremely stubborn at the time. I found it hard to accept I wasn't wanted in the gym. It was my first experience of being thrown out of any gym, having been involved in all aspects of boxing since single aged. It is hard to stomach being snubbed.

Other boxing writers meekly moved out of the gym, and down the steep stairway leading to Castle Street. Eastwood stayed at the back of his gym, out of things. Perhaps even then he was pondering on the rising reality of losing his grip on the Cyclone. I reluctantly agreed to Eddie's request. My good friend wanted to get on with his training programme for McGuigan. Still, the gym retained one writer from England, a new face. He had a dispensation to remain, and watch the Cyclone in full-throttle training.

It seemed hideously unfair to the rest of us. The old ways would never be the same again. Commercialism was rising rapidly to the surface. Fame has a price. Cheque-book journalism was swiftly moving in on all sports. That incident remains one of the few unpalatable images I have of the uniquely vibrant days of Barry McGuigan's career. I soon realised, and grudgingly accepted, it was a new way of life for any top sports person. I could not deny Barry his right to make the most from a growing reputation. Why shouldn't he play the fame game? After all, the prize-fighter's life is a relatively short one. But, I did object to the loathsome dictate of his new fringe employer, to decide regular boxing journalists would have limited access to McGuigan remarks.

We were to be curtailed to occasional group interview at open press days, conferences, weigh-ins, and post-fight gatherings. Fortunately, this little spell of aggravation faded. Still, bits and pieces outside the norm, and beyond my own naive belief in Corinthian values, began to chip away the good old days. Unknown to the adoring masses, the honeymoon period between Eastwood and the Cyclone was beginning to fray at the edges.

B.J. Eastwood and his boxing baubles

Poster for the Steve Collins-Reggie Johnson 12-rounder for the vacant WBA World Middleweight belt. The fight was held in the New Jersey on April 22, 1992. American Johnson took a disputed points decision. Referee Arthur Mercante deducted a point from both boxers in the fifth round for alleged low blows.

Racehorse Sandy Creek held by Alfie McLean after winning at Doncaster. Also celebrating the coup are former jockey Guy Hart and B J Eastwood.

B.J. and Frances with horse racing expert Cathal Curley.

Fight poster for Barry McGuigan's milestone match against Eusebio Pedroza.

The great Roberto Duran greets Eastwood.

Eastwood and son Brian welcome the great Sugar Ray Leonard to Belfast, before the 1985 McGuigan fight against Juan LaPorte at the King's Hall.

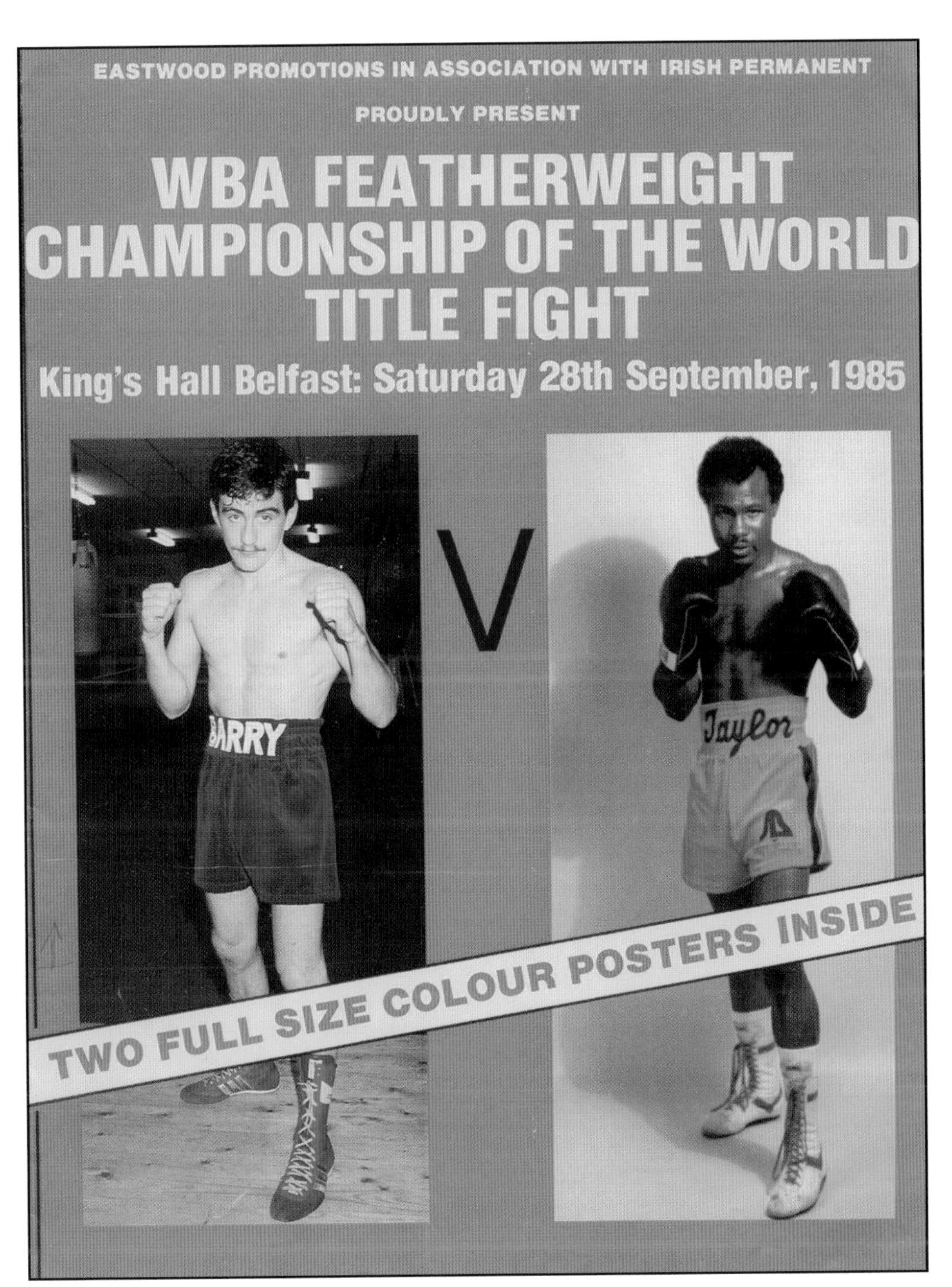

Poster of McGuigan's first defence of the WBA belt, against American Bernard Taylor. The contest, on September 28, 1985, in the King's Hall, proved to be the Cyclone's last fight in Belfast.

Fight promoter Brian 'Bruno' Eastwood enjoys the world-class company of famous Northern Ireland soccer stars Pat Jennings and George Best.

World Flyweight champion Dave McAuley and wife Wendy enjoy a social night out with B.J. and Frances Eastwood.

World Featherweight champion Barry McGuigan.

The People's Choice

in association with
EASTWOOD PROMOTIONS PRESENT

THE WBA WORLD FEATHERWEIGHT CHAMPIONSHIP

15 x 3 min Rounds at 9st 0lbs (Matchmaker: PADDY BYRNE)

Barry McGuigan V Danilo Cabrera

McGuigan's win at Loftus Road is depicted in the programme for his second defence of the WBA Championship, against Danilo Cabrera in Dublin. It was the Cyclone's last title fight victory.

A sombre foursome before McGuigan's first WBA title defence, and his last appearance in the King's Hall ring, Belfast. With the Clones Cyclone, before beating American Bernard Taylor in 1985, are Eddie Shaw, Paddy Byrne and Eastwood.

Dual British Flyweight and Bantamweight champion Hugh 'Little Red' Russell.

McGuigan misses with a left jab against Texan Steve Cruz early in the ill-fated 1986 final title defence held in Las Vegas.

Brian 'Bruno' Eastwood seen with former World Middleweight champion Alan Minter and London boxing promoter/agent/manager Mickey Duff.

American promoter Don King gets in on the act after Crisanto Espano wins the WBA World Welterweight belt.

Paul Hodkinson is belted up after winning the WBC Featherweight title.

Sam's the man - Belfast's Sam Storey en route to beating Croydon's Tony Burke, and become first winner of the British 12-stone Super-middleweight title.

May 1995 Trevor McClintock of Gilbeys (3rd left) and Eastwood aide Tony Baker (centre) with Eastwood-managed fighters Dave McAuley, John Lowey, Ray Close and Crisanto Espana seen during a charity function in Derry.

Eastwood watches Dave 'Boy' McAuley receive the 'Fight of the Year' trophy from Trevor McClintock of Gilbeys.

Eastwood, watched by his legal brief Paul Tweed, snubs the hand of friendship from Chris Eubank before 'Simply the Best' defended against Ray Close in Belfast..

World Flyweight champion Dave McAuley lands a playful left hook on famous England soccer winger, Sir Stanley Matthews

Eastwood stablemates Paul Hodkinson and Eamonn McAuley.

1991 WBA 'Manager of the Year' B. J. Eastwood is surrounded by happy campers and 'Champions All' - Dave McAuley (IBF Flyweight champion), Paul Hodkinson (WBC Featherweight champion), Crawford Ashley (British Light-heavyweight champion), Victor Cordoba (WBA Super-middleweight champion), Steve Collins (WBA Number One Middleweight contender) and Crisanto Espana (WBC International Welterweight champion)

Proud Eastwood celebrates his 1991 elevation to WBA `Manager of the Year' honour with three of his World champions - Dave McAuley, Victor Cordoba and Paul Hodkinson.

Eastwood's World Super-bantamweght champion Fabrice Benichou.

Some of the Eastwood boys in the company of London gangland celebrity Eddie Richardson (right) during a bow-tie, dinner-boxing show in London.

Ballymena's World Welterweight champion Eamonn Loughran with American challenger Tony Gannarelli, of Scotsdale, Arizona. Loughran won his 4th title defence in the sixth round in the Ulster Hall.

An image of the puncher's Peace Flag symbol, suggested for the McGuigan campaign by Belfast politician and boxing aficionado Paddy Devlin

Dave McAuley hams it up with Sir Henry Cooper.

The King's Hall, Belfast - legendary centre of Irish Professional Boxing

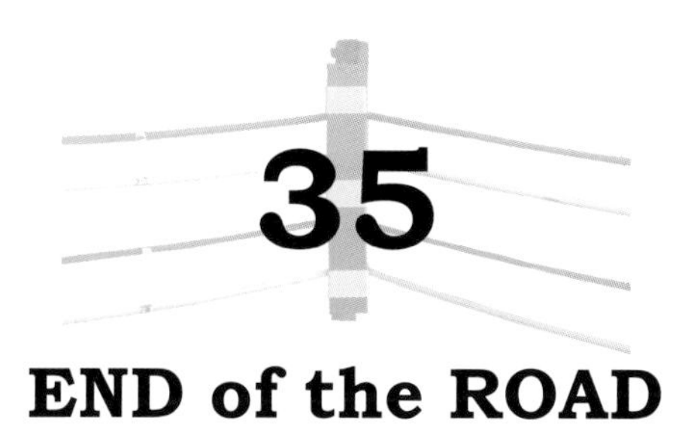

35

END of the ROAD

LOFTUS Road was the highest achievement for not only the Clones Cyclone but also for promoter Stephen Eastwood. The winning of the WBA Featherweight belt also marked the closure to rainbow's end in a variety of ways. Stephen was a key cog in the tunnel of vision, but in the lead into McGuigan's first defence of the title he decided he'd had enough of the fight game. He sometimes saw disturbing signs that life would never be the same again. How right he was. It wasn't long after Loftus Road that it all ended in extreme misery. Stephen disclosed after McGuigan won the WBA title he decided to abandon ship. He was not involved in the new lord of the ring's first defence of the title, against Taylor.

With tongue in cheek he said: "I was the first rat off the ship. I resigned as the promoter. I did not want to carry on doing it anymore. I was in from the start. There were so many different things to do, including going to the Boxing Board of Control on many occasions for different things. It was time to call it a day. There were many wonderful moments, of course. One of the best was the night we set up a bit of a special Irish welcome for the great Sugar Ray Leonard, when he came to Belfast for the McGuigan-LaPorte contest at the King's Hall. Sugar Ray enjoyed the deserved attention on the night before the fight. Around 30 people attended a special function held in his honour in The George Hotel at Clandeboye, Bangor, where Paul McDermott put it on for us.

"Once McGuigan won the World title, for my part I reckoned I had done what I wanted to do. I did not wish to continue. I looked around me and I saw people who were in this game a lifetime, the likes of Mickey Duff and Jarvis Astaire, and also a young Frank Warren was coming through.

I said to myself - I've just got to get off this ship, and quickly. Let me make it clear. It was not a bitter parting of the troops. Nothing like that. I still helped out from time to time. Young Bruno, my brother Brian, took it over. Dad also got a guy in he knew, named Al Dillon, who previously worked for Graham's the bookmakers. He came in to run the background side of things. I helped Al in some ways. In my period as promoter I had great people to assist me - like Ned McCourt, Charlie Gray, Harry O'Neill, Keeler McCullough, who was around the ringside customers with Harry, and Davy 'The Hat' Donnelly. There was also Paddy Mallon. Another great character at that time was the streetwise 'Cheeky' Charlie McKenna, selling the programmes.

"It was a good team, with the path eventually leading to that memorable evening on a football pitch in London. Winning the World title was a fabulous milestone. Other things still stick out in my mind. After the winning of the World title there was the greeting for the new champion in Belfast, and then I enjoyed being in the open-top bus going into O'Connell Street, Dublin. There was a crowd of 250,000 people in Dublin's main thoroughfare. A motorbike squad led us down in a cavalcade to the top of O'Connell Street, and then we got into the bus. As I looked over the side of the bus, I saw the authentic signpost saying 'Loftus Road, a quarter of a mile.' The sign was pulled out of the ground in London by a fan."

Stephen became aware of a change in the climate. The once warm McGuigan-Eastwood show of a father-son style relationship was apparently fragmenting. There were small signs of a growing unease creeping into the camp, leading up to the title defence against Taylor. Sadly, everything started to slip downhill after the high of Loftus Road. "I recall some sort of a problem in the training arrangements at that time, with Bangor landlady Jean Anderson in touch with my father," added Stephen, "Then he was told in no uncertain terms who was the World champion, and who would be calling the shots. That's the way I read it. That was the beginning of the end, I felt. Dad just could not believe the change that appeared to happen almost overnight. In my opinion, I believe my father then realised this was it. From his point of view this guy was now uncontrollable. Whatever we did to get him to become the champion of the world, to be successful, was not going to happen to us anymore. We realised then it was going to be different."

He preferred to remember the rewarding and enjoyable adventure to reach World Championship status. It was an exemplary, hugely exciting time. It was a thrill-a-minute, but now that the big prize had been achieved the sights were largely focussed on matters of finance. "For professional boxers it has to be this way, go after the big money at this high level. That is what they do for a living. I accept that," added Stephen, "but, the funny thing about our situation was remembering being there when my father said such this as: 'Barry, if you stay in the King's Hall you can fight there until you are eighty years old and you will never be beaten. It is smaller money, but you won't lose.'

"Okay, you could earn possibly three times the amount of money from one big fight in America. Unfortunately, one fight was all he was going to get. If he earned a third at the King's Hall for his first title defence he might have earned double that the next time. It might have taken two fights to earn what he possibly could have earned in the United States. By the third fight it would have beeneven bigger money, because the whole world would have been watching by then. The opponents coming here had so much going against them, when boxing McGuigan in the King's Hall. Sure, the hair stood up on the back of your head. However, it seemed he wanted to go quick, quick, quick at that stage."

He insisted it was right and proper Eastwood Promotions did not fold up the tent and fade away after the downer in Las Vegas: "After McGuigan's loss of the title the rest of the boxers in the Eastwood stable had as much right for things to carry on - Dave 'Boy', Hoko, Espana. Obviously, I was looking in from the outside, and fully condoned the decision that all the other boxers in the gym deserved not to be let down, or abandoned. The boxing game in Belfast never ever attained the same heights as that of the McGuigan rise to World honours. A blind man on a galloping kangaroo would recognise that. Still, we had some very exciting occasions involving fighters such as Hodkinson, Espana, Close and McAuley. It was my father's declared decision to retire from the fight game from the moment the very popular Dave Boy hung up his gloves."

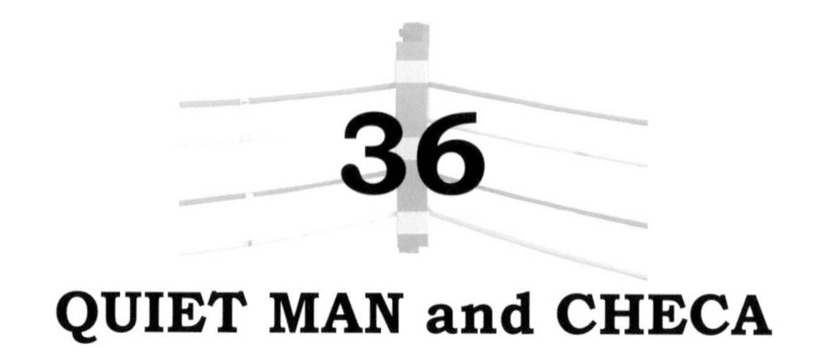

36

QUIET MAN and CHECA

LUIS SPADA, a mysterious, silent type from the Pampas, brought a significant degree of subtle influence to the Eastwood camp in the mid-1980's, and through to the early 1990's. He was deeply involved from the time of McGuigan's push for the World title. Based in Panama City, he was for a spell the manager of Roberto Duran. The Argentine-born boxing mogul was, I suspect, a master manipulator amid the heavy Latin leanings of the World Boxing Association on global fight affairs.

The shrewd Spada, later the WBA's 'Manager of the Year' for 1987, was a leading WBA enthusiast during countdown to the historic World Featherweight title fight at Loftus Road. Indeed, the Eastwood link with Spada lingered long after the shattering end to that golden era. The little man, who died in Panama during early 2009, ghosted around the perimeter of many major Eastwood promotions in Belfast. Known as 'Don Luis' in some quarters, his generally unrecognised rolling input to Irish boxing included the arrival in Belfast of class fighters such as Victor Cordoba. Before that, the lengthy service of former World Featherweight contender Checa began in the Eastwood gym.

The Central America connection continued right through from Spada securing the connections to Pedroza and on to Checa helping in coaching duties for Belfast fight trainer and manager John Breen. Checa, who started in amateur boxing with merely 16 fights as a Flyweight - but no international contests before turning professional, arrived in Belfast with a good punch pedigree despite not making it to the top.

Eastwood claimed: "Bernardo was badly managed in the early part of his career. I don't know what stage he joined Luis Spada, but by then Spada had two or three World champions under his wing. The big problem

Checa faced was that he was matched too often at weights he couldn't make. He was very experienced. He was a rated top-ten fighter, but they kept sticking him in at Super-bantamweight. He never could make the weight. His management team was just getting him into fights for a few quid, yet he was a very good boxer. He could tell you great stories, including one about his second fight, which I was at, against Antonio Esparragoza in 1986.

"He drew in a ten-rounder against Esparragoza in October, 1984, but he was well over the weight for the rematch. They made him sit in a car in Venezuela, a very hot country where the temperature could reach over 100, for six hours to lose the weight. He finished up suffering a second-round knock-out defeat. The reason he first came to Belfast was to spar with McGuigan prior to the Taylor fight. I remember McGuigan couldn't hit him at first, but we moved on from there.

"Checa also knew Gomez well, often helping with spar work. Late in Gomez's career Bernardo would arrive in San Juan from Panama on a Sunday to be all set to spar on the Monday, but when Monday came Gomez did not turn up in the gym. Bernardo would be told: 'Wilfredo is not training today. He doesn't feel too well.' Tuesday he is feeling a bit better, but is still not training. Wednesday he'd come in and train, but then say: 'Boys, the week is almost gone - so, no point in doing any more this week.' That was the first week's work over. Still, he rated Gomez a really good fighter. The first time he sparred, and was working well with him, he hit Gomez a good punch on the nose and hurt him.

"Gomez made him pay for it. Gomez gave him a hard time after that in the sparring. He reckoned Gomez was something special. Checa said Gomez used to blow up in weight because he lived it up, and yet he was an all-time great with 40 straight wins. Gomez had many World title fights and many knock-outs, but the high living eventually got to him - like it did Roberto Duran. Checa is a specialist boxing coach, in my view. He has supreme knowledge of boxing was important from the South American angle, and, above all, knows what he is talking about. He knows more about boxing than probably anybody I have ever met. He really is a genius as far as fight science is concerned."

In 1985, Checa came to Belfast for the first time, when still active as a boxer. He had his last fight in 1987, in the King's Hall. "I don't know if McGuigan learned anything from me," said Bernardo, "I could not speak English then, just Spanish and Portuguese. I did not show him anything. I just sparred. Eddie Shaw was there. I got on fine with Eddie. I get on well with everybody. Eddie was working to get the hook to the body. It is also my favourite shot for the orthodox boxer, the left hook to the body. Gomez was a very good body puncher. Pedroza was also a good body puncher."

He sparred with many World champions, including Gomez, Zapata, Pedroza, and also went to South Africa to help Brian Mitchell. He travelled to box in Venezuela, Puerto Rico, and sparred in the United States. Checa insisted he was not surprised by Pedroza's defeat at Loftus Road. He claimed the people of Panama were not shocked. They were expecting it at any time, he said. The general view in Panama was Pedroza was having trouble in making the weight. Checa conceded one of his heroes was well beaten by McGuigan. He thought the Cyclone would stop him.

"Pedroza was a completely different fighter to that of McGuigan, making 20 defences of his title. It was not a case of always defending his title in Panama, but he went everywhere - including trips to Japan and Italy. He was also defending his title against the best fighters around at that time. In my view, had McGuigan fought Pedroza a year earlier it would have been a different outcome. I firmly believe that. Before Pedroza boxed McGuigan, he defended in Panama in front of 15,000 in the National Gimnasio Nuevo. He boxed Jorge Lujan, a former World champion."

Lujan was the number one contender then. Apparently, it was a gruelling, strength-sapping fight for both of them. Pedroza was then having trouble in making the weight, yet won a unanimous points decision over 15 rounds. Checa revealed Pedroza ranks high in the list of all-time Panamanian fighters. Duran is first, Pedroza second and Zapata third. The top end of the list includes Ismael Laguna and 'Panama' Al Brown. Ranked 12th best featherweight in the world when McGuigan defeated Pedroza, Checa was a relative novice when he first sparred Pedroza. He had five professional fights at the time, all in Panama City. The sparring session was in the spacious Ignacio Maranon Gym, in the city centre. All the fighters trained in the same venue, and people who were taking time off work at their lunchtime break came in to watch the boxers train and spar. They looked in mainly to see Pedroza and Duran.

Checa added: "Up to 200 spectators would be in there at lunchtime. It was an amazing place, a hive of activity. I remember the first time I sparred with Pedroza. I looked down at the canvas. He looked down too, and I hit him one-two. I was cheeky. In the next round Pedroza threw the jab, and dropped his hands. I went in to throw a punch at what I thought was an easy target, and he caught me with an uppercut. He nailed me with the right, and cut my lip. That was a big lesson for me. He said to me: 'Respect the champ'. There is also a funny story regarding Pedroza's brilliant career. Before he became World champion he lost two fights in-a-row, and both by knock-out. That was when he was fighting at Bantam and Super-bantamweight. One day he came back to the gym and declared to everybody there, and very loud: 'I am coming back to the gym to try my best for the very last time. If I don't make it now boxing will be over for me. So, I try one more year.' He did, and became a true ring legend."

He recalled his first spar in the Eastwood gym against McGuigan, and noted right away he was facing a very strong fighter: "It was not one big punch that could hurt you but an accumulation. He had a problem in that he couldn't go back, nor cut the ring off from you, but Barry was extremely strong when he got you in a corner. I left for Panama before he defended against Taylor. My last fight was was in Belfast. I remember Mr Eastwood asking me over to spar again, and stay for another fight. I didn't want it any more, because frustration crept in by then. I did not wish to continue as a boxer. So, I decided to become a coach after my last fight, and returned home to Panama City."

With a 20-5-5 ring career chart he returned to his native City for seven and half years, before coming back to Northern Ireland and settling in Carrickfergus with wife Ruth, who is a nurse, and daughter Anna Michelle. He is a security official with Tesco. His coaching achievements involved him in 33 World Championship contests. He helped to train seven World champions - McAuley (IBF Flyweight), Hodkinson (WBC Featherweight), Cordoba (WBA Super-middleweight), Espana (WBA Welterweight), Fabrice Benichou (IBF Super-bantamweight), Orlando Soto (WBC Featherweight) and Roberto Duran (five times World champion). He also coached Sam Storey (British Super-middleweight) and Ray Close (European Super-middleweight).

He revealed he had a great grounding in the game. Pedro Avila was his coach. Avila, who died in 2009, was the trainer of Hilario Zapata and Bernardo Pinango, and also had spells coaching Gomez and Victor Calejas. He was rated one of the world's top trainers. Checa learned a lot from Avila, and brought it into his own coaching techniques. Having such a great mentor, along with all the experience of boxing top opponents and sparring against some of the world's greatest champions, enabled Checa to pass on the tips he picked up along the way to his fighters.

He stated: "This was great compensation after the disappointment of not reaching the top as a professional boxer, especially not getting the better of Esparragoza. We fought twice. I had the draw in Venezuela, when he was unbeaten. I stopped boxing at 24-years-old, and that is very early. Nowadays many guys are boxing until they are 40."

Overall, he sparred with 13 World champions during his career, and naturally picked up a lot of ring know-how along the way. He felt when he began in boxing he would become a World champion one day: "I believed I had the tools to do it, but destiny wasn't mine," claimed Checa.

The first fighter he looked after when he hung the gloves was Edgar Monserrat, a Panamanian super-flyweight who boxed three times for a World Championship. Monserrat met one of the Galaxy brothers, Khaosai from Thailand, and lost in a WBA Super-flyweight title fight in December, 1985, when stopped in the second round in Bangkok. He also lost in France, to Gilberto Roman in May, 1986, for the WBC belt, and then dropped out of the ratings. A southpaw, and nicknamed 'Bamby', he surprisingly beat Colombian Elvis Alvares, who was then in the top ten. "That win of July, 1987, put Edgar back in the ratings. He also moved up a weight and won the Panamanian Bantamweight title in May, 1988, but lost for WBA honours on November, 1988 - when stopped by Sung Kil Moon in Seoul. Edgar had 49 fights, with 30 wins, three draws, and 15 defeats."

During that coaching period in Panama he also brought a couple of fighters to Belfast. Thomas Arroya met Hodkinson in 1987. It was around that period when Eastwood invited Bernardo to stay and coach in Belfast. Checa told me how much he enjoyed his time in the Castle Street Gym. It was a good period for him. The McGuigan era was over then. Other fighters he coached in the Eastwood gym included Close for Ray's two controversial fights with Chris Eubank for the WBO Super-middleweight championship. Bernardo felt Close won the first bout, in Glasgow even though caught in the 11th round for a count. "The knockdown seemed to give the judges the excuse to let Eubank retain his belt," he said, "Ray was ahead by five points before the knock-down. The rematch in Belfast was also tense and tight, and again a good performance by Close." Also to benefit from Checa's coaching were Andy Holligan, Crawford Ashley, John Lowey, Nigel and Ritchie Wenton.

He added: "The Wenton brothers were very talented, but a little undisciplined, as was my younger brother Oscar. He was a Welterweight who could have been very good. Oscar stayed on to live and work in Belfast. You need dedication and good personal discipline to go along with natural ability in order to succeed in professional boxing." His favourite all-time fighter is fellow countryman Duran, who became a professional at 16, and was a World champion at 21. Duran inspired a posse of young Panamanian prospects to try and emulate him. A throwback to the old hard-rock style of box-fighting, he could do anything in any situation, including some moves outside the laws of the sport.

The one baffling blemish in five-time World champion Duran's amazing ring career was the puzzling 'No Mas' drama of 1980. 50,000 spectators watched in stunned silence in the New Orleans Superdome where he sensationally quit after 2:44 of the eighth round in a rematch with Sugar Ray Leonard. Checa would chat for hours on the merits of Duran, whom he trained during the ring legend's twilight days. He coached Duran for a contest against Hector Camacho, and for fights against Jorge Castro of Argentine. Checa's short time in the 45-year-old Duran's corner was also interestingly painful at times.

Always willing to don the gloves in sparring his ribcage took a real working over: "I sparred with Duran when I helped his training preparations for a contest with Camacho in Atlantic City. He ran out of sparring partners, so I stepped into the ring with him. He hit me everywhere, especially around the body. I had to quit after two rounds." Camacho won that June, 1996, match on a points decision. At stake was the obscure IBC Middleweight belt. Duran also lost on points to Castro in Buenos Aires on February, 1997, but four months later won the rematch on points in Panama. In August 1998, Duran suffered a stoppage when trying to win the WBA Middleweight belt from William Joppy in Las Vegas. It was coming towards the end of an amazing career for a ferocious box-brawler. He was once feared more than any fighter of his era.

Checa trained Duran for four fights, and insisted: "I rate Roberto my number one fighter. He was one of my boxing heroes. I agree Sugar Ray Robinson was wonderful, and Sugar Ray Leonard was very good. As a fan, I would say Muhammad Ali was the greatest, but as a professional I would not agree. Ali, for me a big guy who had great footwork and speedy hands, couldn't fight on the inside. He had to push the opponent away. He didn't throw a punch to the body, as punches all went to the head. Ali, in my opinion, was not the complete fighter, whereas Duran could box you, could fight you, and could cut you in two on the inside."

ONLY IN AMERICA

THE RUMOUR MILL was awash in early 1986 with predictions of McGuigan taking on Gomez, in a bid to become a two-title World champion. The faithful fans were behind their hero to go after legend status. The supporters of the Cyclone, then riding the crest of a wonderful wave of euphoria, couldn't get enough of arguably the most exciting and charismatic fighter to emerge from the Emerald Isle in many years.

It seemed McGuigan was going to follow the famous 19th Century warcry of USA journalist, reformer and Congressman Horace Greeley, to 'Go West young man' - and possibly meet Gomez in the States, in a WBA Junior Lightweight title fight. There was strong talk of backing by the USA television network ABC for such a mouth-watering showdown in Madison Square Garden. It was predicted one million dollars was on the table for Barry to box in New York before Christmas 1985, but allegedly the fight was vetoed because of 'domestic reasons'. Barry's wife Sandra was expecting a second baby.

Also in there was a mooted December, 1985, date in Egypt, of all places. This was the fanciful suggestion Gomez would defend in Cairo, with McGuigan to receive over a half-million sterling. When Gomez's manager Cordero arrived in Dublin to attend the McGuigan title defence against Cabrera, the media, myself included, jumped to the wrong conclusion the glamour match was a certainty to take place. What we did not realise was that the fight would never happen. Even two days after the McGuigan-Cabrera contest there was firm prediction of a Gomez-McGuigan collision. Cordero seemed to be dropping hints right, left and centre.

He said: "If the money is right Gomez will fight McGuigan anywhere. My own preference would be a New York fight some time in May." Pepe then intimated he would also be open to persuasion in a move up a weight class for his WBA Junior Featherweight champion Victor Calejas, to fight McGuigan in Belfast. Probably this was an unwitting hint the Gomez match was not to be. Still, there were recurring bouts of forecasting in the media about a fight for McGuigan against Gomez. All the while Eastwood had the Puerto Rican's signature on a contract, but kept the agreement hidden from the public.

BJ told me the press people never knew he had this contract, and said: "At that time I felt it probably would not have been good for me to reveal I had the contract. I suppose I was always hoping McGuigan would fight Gomez, and it would have looked bad if it became known McGuigan would not fight him. I still believe to this day the Gomez contest would have made an awful difference to him (McGuigan). Gomez was the real plum, and I could not see McGuigan turning it down. Look, we had what we first set out to achieve, the winning of the World Featherweight title at Loftus Road.

"I felt we needed a fresh direction. We struggled twice to defend it, against Taylor, and then against Cabrera. The contest in Dublin was to be a ticking-over fight, a good opportunity to show him there. We had to match him with somebody, firstly Sosa, and then the late replacement. If he had taken the fight against Gomez, he would obviously have been a two-title champion. A win against Gomez and who knows what doors could have opened for him."

Eastwood was at pains to point out why he went to such a lot of trouble during a trip to the Hispaniola region in October, 1985. He set up the golden opportunity for McGuigan. He felt this was the prudent path to take. It proved a waste of time, despite reaching an agreement in San Juan with the then WBA World Super-featherweight champion Gomez to defend his title against McGuigan. Time at the top was running out for Gomez, who first emerged as a fiery 5' 5" talent when winning the inaugural World Amateur Bantamweight Championship in Havana in 1974. He proved his potential by beating host nation hope Jorge Luis Romero in the final. Later that same year he turned professional, and clocked out with a 44-3-1 paid record.

The astute Eastwood engineered a deal he believed was right for McGuigan - to tackle the fading fighter, and at no risk to the County Monaghan man's WBA Featherweight belt. The Cyclone could have entered the history books as Ireland's double World champion, he claimed. The nuts and bolts of addendums to the contract suggest in early

March, 1986, Jose Cordero and Eastwood still harboured hope of setting up the contest.

Eastwood laid the intimate details on the line for the first time: "The deal I did was a great one. It was to be a temporary move up to the Super-featherweight division. McGuigan's WBA Featherweight title would not be at risk. Eastwood Promotions were prepared to give Gomez $775,000 to come to Ireland, or fight in New York, or wherever we could put on the biggest show. The contract agreement with Gomez was done in the presence of Pappy Cordero, then still one of the key men behind the WBA. Gomez agreed to defend his 9st 4lbs WBA title. He was coming very close to the end of his boxing days. It was coming fast on him. I managed to get Cordero and Gomez sign a contract, for Gomez to meet McGuigan, but McGuigan would not fight him."

Gomez started out as a bantamweight, then super-bantamweight, featherweight, and finally he became the World Super-featherweight champion late on in his career. Eastwood maintained the Puerto Rican multiple-champion's ring days were almost over. It was his opinion then that Gomez was, as they say so cruelly in the boxing game, just a 'dead man' walking. Gomez didn't have a fight in quite a while when Eastwood went out to see if he could hook him up in a defence against McGuigan. He remembered the meeting: "Cordero set up the talks. Gomez had a schoolteacher friend who acted as his interpreter. I stayed a few days in San Juan. Importantly, I also discovered Gomez was out of condition. He ballooned up to 14 stone, yet he was no bigger than Paul Hodkinson. I left with the contract in my pocket. Mickey Duff was with me in Puerto Rico when I secured the deal. I was saying to McGuigan this is a gift from Heaven, and if by the hand of God that he lost this fight then he would still have his Featherweight title.

"I told him if he won he could hold onto the 9st 4lbs title and give up the other - or vice versa. I felt it was business well done, but then all for nothing. McGuigan was about to make a second defence of the WBA Featherweight Championship in Dublin, against Sosa, the contest turning to a substitute fight against Cabrera in February, 1986. Cordero said he would come to Dublin. I don't think I let Cordero know the proposed big fight with Gomez was in serious doubt until after he arrived in Dublin. He came to the fight with Yvonne Glass, who was head of some television outlets in Latin America. I recall the cost of his seat was double. He took up two seats on a plane and at the fight, because of his enormous size.

"It cost close on £10,000 to bring the Cordero party to Dublin, and already we were about to lose a $50,000 dollar guarantee in the Gomez deal. Cordero witnessed McGuigan struggle in Dublin, yet still wanted to be involved - perhaps believing the fight with Gomez could still materialise. He said to me: 'Look, Wilfredo will defend his title anywhere against McGuigan'. He added the fight could be in Belfast, in Dublin, or also in London, or it could be in New York . . . whatever I wanted. But, McGuigan still did not want it."

Fight commentators came desperately close to the truth before and after the title fight with Cabrera. On the Monday morning issue of the *Irish Independent,* on February 17, 1986, the revered Reg Gutteridge, then *ITV's* Boxing Commentator, declared: 'A match to be made, before it is too late, is McGuigan challenging for the higher weight 9st 4lbs title against Wilfredo Gomez, a Puerto Rican great. I suspect Gomez, at 29, is carrying some lead in his legs. McGuigan, with nothing to lose, can win this one. To gather the mega bucks it must take place in America' Tom Cryan also revealed he held a chat with Cordero after the fight at Simmonscourt. Cryan suggested the time was ripe for McGuigan to parade his wares in America: "Jose 'Pepe' Cordero is the man who could hold the key to the Cyclone's future plans. He is manager of Wilfredo Gomez, the WBA's Super-featherweight champion, and also Victor Celejas, holder of WBA's Junior Featherweight title."

A highly interested spectator at the RDS, Cordero said he was impressed by McGuigan and added: "He makes mistakes, and there are some things he will have to learn - but he has a fighter's heart. He is good for boxing." Cryan added: 'American TV channels proposed a Gomez-McGuigan match in the States last December.' It was to be the next major move in the boxing calendar for the Cyclone, as far as Eastwood was concerned. Little did world boxing know such a deal fell into the dustbin despite patient purse negotiations by Eastwood Promotions.

38

SHIFTING AGENDA

THE IRISH fight scene was slowly simmering with the unthinkable speculation of a pending split between Eastwood and McGuigan. There was the anecdotal hint around the time of the defence against Taylor of McGuigan boxing in a hometown outdoor show, without Eastwood or Eastwood Promotions involved. The hoped-for setting, it was claimed, would be the amphitheatre of the Gaelic Athletic Association ground in the Cyclone's home town of Clones. There was an undercurrent of uncertainty in the air.

Eastwood agreed: "Things were changing. After Loftus Road he started to make a lot of decisions. We couldn't go on with the Gomez World title contest, couldn't put it together when he said no. He was going to America, but not to fight Gomez. I did not want him to box in America, but he did. He did not want to fight any place else but in America, after the title defence in Dublin. He had this thing about showing his face in the United States, and making so much money."

BJ knew of Roddy Carr's proposed input, and said: "It was reported at that time of Carr saying McGuigan would do well in America, and so forth. Remarks were coming out like 'the fighter is Irish, and is the only white World champion at the moment.' There was, I believe, advice given to McGuigan that he only had to turn up in America and he would be bombarded by millions of dollars worth of endorsements. It was in the papers before the fight against Cabrera, and it made things very awkward at a time I was doing all the homework on the possibility of a McGuigan-Gomez fight. McGuigan was still under contract, yet it left you in a hopeless position.

"On the Gomez fight situation I went to see him (McGuigan) for a talk, near Enniskillen. He was aware of the proposed fight with Gomez. I told him we got the deal done. But, the problem was, at that stage, he was beginning to listen to other people. Everybody seemed to be pulling against you. It was difficult. Before that, we could make decisions, and say to him: 'Look, here is the way we should go again. Here is what we have in mind, what we could try, here is the guy, the opponent we are fighting, what looks the best way to go,' Before the new developments, we could have said: 'That's it, it is done, the fight is on. This is who you are fighting.' But, from then on it was: 'Oh No'. Perhaps things were changing in the camp before Loftus Road, and I didn't see it, didn't notice. "Later on, I was informed there was something happening, overtures were allegedly being made to McGuigan around that period. One of the reasons why there was no publicity about a McGuigan-Gomez fight, but mere speculation in the media at the time, was because McGuigan said: 'No, no - I am not fighting him.' He said he would not fight Gomez for ten million dollars, even though the contest did not have to take place in America."

Eastwood retained the Gomez contact. The fading coloured sheets of legal jargon, for a defence against McGuigan, lie among his pile of boxing souvenirs. The parchment, including addendums, appeared a matter of great regret to Eastwood, testament to what might have been in all aspects of the beginning of the end of the once fabulous relationship he had with the Cyclone. "I buried the contract," said Eastwood, "Any talk then of McGuigan being seemingly afraid to fight Gomez would not have been good news. My signature is on the Gomez contract, signing it as manager on behalf of Eastwood Promotions. Legally that was still a binding contract. Pappy (Cordero) was a most disappointed man when McGuigan did not take it. Gomez and Cordero were bursting for the fight. I told McGuigan I spent quite some time out there, in San Juan, getting the contract for him. I told him Gomez was then over 14 stone. I said, 'Look, I was in touch with the WBA. They are not going to allow Gomez to fight a Championship contest after this. It is his last big payday, and you are not to lose your WBA Featherweight title."

Eastwood told me he also informed his champion that Gomez was spiralling into what is known cruelly in the boxing game as a 'shot fighter' - not the once great warrior he had been. He was at ringside to witness a classic in Puerto Rico, where chunky Gomez lost in the 13th round to Nelson. He watched on TV another thriller when Gomez met Lupe Pinter, who was coming up in weigh. It was one of the best fights ever. It was in

New Orleans, with Wilfredo winning by knockout in the 14th round. Gomez was at the peak of his powers then.

"My late son Fintan and also my son Stephen were at that fight. I was unable to make the trip. Around the time I was trying to seal a deal with Gomez, the WBA had a question mark over the once great fighter - as to whether he should be allowed to box again. He was completely out of condition, very much overweight, and had other personal problems. We finished up having to get a letter of clearance from the WBA, before anything could be signed." In later years there was an attempt to toss cold water on the proposed Gomez contest, claiming the contract may never have existed - and even if Eastwood had a deal it was argued the late USA promoter Dan Duva held options on Gomez, following a title win against American Rocky Lockridge.

Eastwood, who insisted the Puerto Rican fighter didn't give a damn where the contest to defend his title against McGuigan might take place, said: "During all the period of heavy negotiations with Cordero and Gomez the name of Duva was never mentioned. That was mentioned later, not by me nor Cordero, but it seemed to be an excuse. If there was an option, which we never heard of, it had nothing to do with Eastwood Promotions. That would have been between Cordero, who was getting $775,000 from us, and Duva to sort out. The fight would have been made, a contest already given WBA sanction. We had the TV people from Latin America involved - Yvonne Glass - and if there was the slightest problem she would not have wasted her time doing deals with us. I was also given an undertaking from WBA official Alberto Aleman this would be Gomez's last championship fight. The fight was subject to McGuigan agreeing to immediately relinquish one of the titles - if he beat Gomez."

Instead, Gomez lost his title to Alfredo Layne of Panama, when stopped in the ninth round. The irony of that outcome was not only the result but also the timing, on May 24, 1986, the month before McGuigan dropped his title in Las Vegas."It should have been Gomez against McGuigan, because I felt McGuigan would have knocked him out in a couple of rounds," claimed Eastwood, "Incidentally, there was a time early in that Gomez farewell title appearance when Layne was reluctant to get off his stool. Gomez put in a bit of an effort at the start of the contest, but was just standing there, merely a shadow of his old fighting self. Apparently, the cornermen had to slap Layne in the face, and then threw him out into the middle of the ring. He responded to stop Gomez. It was not to be for McGuigan. The other opportunity McGuigan could have got was to fight the boy from Ghana, Azumah Nelson."

BIG BUCKS

THE CONTENTIOUS contract with the Gomez camp featured a staggering fight fee of $775,000 for the Puerto Rican to defend against McGuigan. The agreement is dated the 27th day of October 1985, and states: "It is an agreement between Wilfredo Gomez of 907, Suite Popular, Center Santurce, Puerto Rico, who will engage in a Junior Lightweight boxing contest with B McGuigan, for the WBA title. Scheduled over 15 rounds, at 130 lbs weight. The date to be specified by the promoter, between the first of March 1986 and May 31st 1986."

An extra item in the contract was of both boxers agreeing not to engage in any other fight after February the first 1986 until this agreement has been completed. It is signed by Bernard J. Eastwood and Wilfredo Gomez. It is also signed and witnessed by Jose Cordero. It was also witnessed by M. Duff, and the parchment is stamped.

An Addendum, signed by all the aforementioned persons, and stamped, is: "This addendum signed today to be made part of the contract. Eastwood Promotions and Wilfredo Gomez, Clause 13. This clause will not apply after the 30th of November 1985. However, all parties should be bound to this agreement in this form. On November 8, 1985, the fighter will receive an advance of $50,000. In the event of the promoter not fulfilling the agreement, the above amount is non-refundable. Unless the fighter withdraws for any reason whatsoever the amount shall be refunded to the Promoter. The Promoter reserves all the rights made under this agreement. The Promoter agrees to establish an irrevocable letter of credit in favour of Wilfredo Gomez, not later than 21 days before the date of the bout - drawn from the bank of the Promoter's choosing, to a bank nominated by the boxer. Another Credit will be in the sum of $225,000, payable on production of newspaper of genuine circulation on the morning after the fight, stating that the fight had taken place."

That was the first part of the payment. The second part is another $225,000. There was also a Letter of Credit for $225,000 to be paid to Luis Spada, and to be held for the fighter. This amount to be paid in the form of a bank draft to the Bank of Panama. On the contract there is a payment stipulation of $275,000. Yvonne Glass of TV in Central America was part of the deal. Assigned to Puerto Rican television were the rights of Barry McGuigan's next three fights.

The Conditions were: "Barry McGuigan's next fight, in defence of his WBA Featherweight title scheduled to take place on January 25, 1986, in Dublin, his second bout - against Wilfredo Gomez, for the Junior Lightweight title, and Barry McGuigan's third World Championship fight, as yet undecided." There is an attached letter from Miss Glass to Eastwood Promotions, stating: "I am pleased to include approved papers granted by the World Boxing Association concerning the fight with Wilfredo Gomez and Barry McGuigan. Kindest regards and best wishes. 7th January 1986."

Eastwood added: "There is also a letter attached to the Contract from Alberto Aleman, Chairman of the WBA's Championship Committee. It was dated the fifth of January, 1986. It says: 'The WBA Championship Committee has approved on January the fourth 1986 the Championship fight of the Junior Lightweight division between Wilfredo Gomez and Barry McGuigan, contender." Another letter attached to the original contract was dated the third of March, 1986. It was an answer to a letter Barney Eastwood received as manager of McGuigan from the Chairman of the Championship Committee - Aleman. "He wrote to me stating if McGuigan wins the Junior title he would then have to give it up after 48 hours or give up the Featherweight title, one or the other," BJ said, "My answer was on the 3rd of March 1986: 'Dear Sir, This letter will confirm that in the event of Barry McGuigan winning the WBA Junior Lightweight title from Wilfredo Gomez he will immediately relinquish the title, and is prepared to make a mandatory defence of his WBA Featherweight title against the number one contender within 90 days of the Gomez fight'"

This was a time when media pre-occupation with money matters became a poignant pointer, I felt. A lot of people were now seemingly trying to cosy up to the new champion, who was a hot box-office attraction on the Irish side of the Atlantic. New frontiers were there to be conquered by the Cyclone. New faces were keen to get on board the bandwagon. Not too far down the trail, after beating Cabrera, awaited the cataclysmic conclusion in the Nevada desert, where the unthinkable became the unpalatable. The root of the growing problem seemed to be one of a possible cash cow waiting up ahead for the Cyclone.

Hours after the Cabrera contest the *Irish Independent* featured thought-provoking words by Belfast-born columnist Sam Smyth. Rummaging around in the money drawer it was claimed McGuigan made £300,000 from the bruising title defence. Smyth suggested Eastwood Promotions made a profit of £800,000 from the show. There was speculation of TV money from *RTE*, from *ABC*, and the estimated sponsorship backing of £130,000 from the Irish Permanent Building Society. McGuigan said after his gruelling experience in Dublin there was an 80% chance of boxing in America, either in Madison Square Garden or at Las Vegas.

"In hindsight, it seemed to be down to word and mind games at that stage, now that it is known the prospect of a fight against Gomez was already dead in the water at that time. I speculated in an article it could be 'all systems go in a bid to set up a two-million dollar clash with Gomez.' Years later, Eastwood contended: "McGuigan would have been hard to beat had he continued to defend his title in Ireland, especially in the King's Hall, Belfast. Why would you go to America?"

Still, after the showdown at Simmonscourt I reported Eastwood stating: 'We'll probably go to New York in late May, a fight before the World Cup soccer finals begin in Mexico. Barry also has endorsements to fulfil. Boxing Gomez is a prime-time bout, and all about money. Also to be considered is a mandatory title defence for Barry. There's no indication yet from the WBA, but we wouldn't mind a match with Antonio Esparragoza, the number one challenger from Venezuela. He's handled by Luis Spada, who was in Dublin. I may go to New York in a few week's time for talks with *ABC*. I'll probably do some business for Barry when I attend the Hagler-Mugabe World Middleweight fight in Las Vegas next month. The promoter has invited me and Herol Graham to be guests at the show.'

Beating Cabrera cleared the path for McGuigan to make a lucrative third defence of his belt, in the United States. Once Eastwood realised there was no way he could convince the champion to take up the option of a Super-featherweight title fight offer to meet Gomez he hopped on a plane and held talks in Las Vegas with promoter Bob Arum. A New York-born Harvard Law school educated former attorney who founded Top Rank Promotions, wily Arum was putting together a major mid-summer show in Las Vegas. It would be known as 'The Triple Hitters'.

Eastwood's take on that tricky time was: "McGuigan reported back to me after Simmonscourt that he had considered all things and that he definitely did not want to fight Gomez. The fight in Las Vegas came about after Roddy Carr arrived on the scene. There was a piece in the newspapers from Roddy declaring McGuigan would be a draw in the States, especially as an Irish world champion, and people would love him in America. Roddy Carr had a job to do. I could understand that. He talked of getting millions of dollars worth of endorsements for McGuigan in America. I could see things were then sort of out of my hands at that stage. I could see then this was the way McGuigan intended to go. It went on from there. That was it. We signed for the show. McGuigan was happy enough to go there. But, towards the end of the training programme he was having second thoughts. Things became difficult out there, in California. Eddie (Shaw) was close to the stage of saying: 'Here boys, I'm out of here, and off home to Belfast.' It was an awkward time."

Before that, the changing climate within the camp was manifesting itself in various ways. Material gain may well have unwittingly blunted some of the fighting edge. The boxer began, I felt, to lean towards becoming more of an entertainer, a celebrity. I always maintained, and once said so to McGuigan, that the prime of his prize-fighting really ended at Loftus Road. The Cyclone's professional career exploded onto the scene in a football field in north Dublin and the best of his boxing days as good as finished on a football pitch in west London.

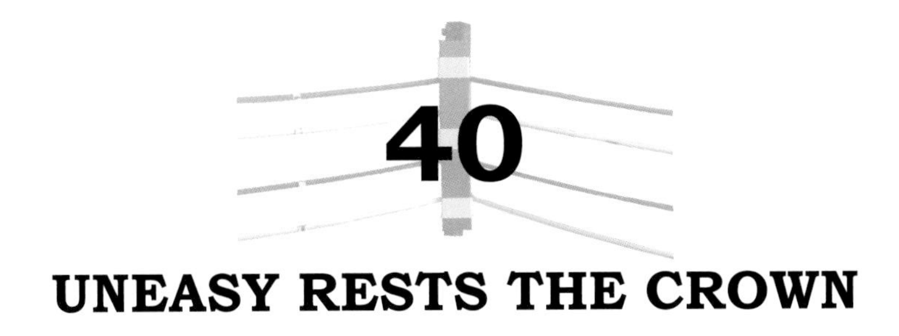

40

UNEASY RESTS THE CROWN

BEFORE the ill-fated fight in the Nevada desert the vibes were not overly healthy. The 25-year-old McGuigan seemed to voice a degree of disillusionment during countdown. Significantly, he never mentioned Eastwood nor anybody connected with his professional ring career to that point, but again said he would like to quit boxing by the age of 27. The champion declared, merely a few weeks before his third defence, he had leanings towards work outside the ropes as an inter-round commentator, and also voiced he was losing his interest as a boxer.

Perhaps the Cyclone had some sort of uneasy subconscious premonition when time was closing in on his match against Steve Cruz. He may have been having second thoughts when he remarked he might not have the fanatical support in Las Vegas he enjoyed in Ireland. He felt he was becoming "a bit sceptical" about having to fight in America, especially in Las Vegas.

Jack Magowan, the revered boxing writer for the *Belfast Telegraph* reported on May 1,1986, that the fight in Vegas would begin at 6 o'clock Nevada time, 2.00pm British time. Eastwood said McGuigan would have have nearly five weeks to get acclimatised, and would leave for Palm Springs, California, on May 20. It was estimated early in the proceedings McGuigan would earn at least £half-a-million for his 31st contest. Before leaving for America, McGuigan told Magowan: "My contest with Sosa in Las Vegas represents a new element in my career." Barry also revealed: "I plan to retire when I'm 28, and could have half-a-dozen good fights ahead of me. It's likely they'll all be in the States."

On Monday, May 26, Magowan reported McGuigan was tired, after taking part in five hard rounds of sparring, using four minutes in each round to copy Roberto Duran's schedule. Ironically at the same time Gomez was stopped in the nineth round in San Juan by rank outsider Layne of Panama. Three days later Sosa was yet again ruled out, this time because he suffered double vision. He had detached retina problems in both eyes, and required immediate surgery. Replacement speculation surrounded WBA's No 5 rated 22-year-old Antonio Rivera, a stablemate of Cabrera's, and also a relatively unknown Texan, Steve Cruz of Fort Worth. The *Irish Press*, Dublin, reported promoter Bob Arum saying:: "We believe Cruz would prove a very suitable opponent for Barry, and we favour him very much. The fact he is American, and a number of his professional fights have been seen on closed-circuit television in the US, is another reason why we feel he should be chosen."

Magowan stated: 'McGuigan, after tense discussion with BJ, agreed to meet Cruz.' Eastwood told Magowan: "The promoter gave us a choice of four opponents, but I know the man I would select. One look at Cruz on film, and Eddie Shaw and I both agreed this was the guy for Barry." Eastwood also conceded the champion was uneasy: "Barry is not happy about Sosa's withdrawal and change of opponent, but he knows he must fight somebody good. The kind of money he's getting simply demands it. Cruz is a good stand-up puncher, who'll come to fight. Had he been a runner I wouldn't have entertained him."

Sparring fodder had to be changed to simulate the style of the new opposition. Three boxers left, and four fresh faces came into the training camp at Palm Springs. It was a confusing time, as Eastwood recalled: "We were right back into the same problem we had in Dublin. It was a back-to-back headache, Sosa tossing a spanner in the works yet again. As soon as we heard the news of Sosa's problem we got a list of people, half-a-dozen possible opponents, and were free to pick whoever we wanted. We knew of their records. It took a few days for me to discover McGuigan was discussing with somebody else what he should do. Selecting a replacement for Sosa initially came down to a short-list of four names, as far as I recall, but it became very awkward in reaching a decision. At one stage McGuigan said he was thinking of going home. I told him he could if he wanted to. Eventually we settled on Cruz. Luis Spada was there, and said - 'Look, this guy you are going to fight is nothing.'

"There was also a fellow called Miguel Diaz in Las Vegas. You've seen him on television regularly working in the corners. He was originally from Argentina, and was in with all the big fighters. He did cuts and corner work. A very experienced guy, he took the fighters in our training camp out to run in the mornings - McGuigan, Duran, the whole lot of them. He said, in front of Spada, and I think McGuigan may have been there too, this fellow Cruz is nothing. Diaz said to Spada: 'If Cruz beats him you can have my house for nothing.'"

Before the shutters crashed down on the dream time, Bob Arum included the popular Irish fighter in a special countdown show that was given the full razzmatazz. Legal eagle Arum decided on a hard sell for the multi-million dollar dazzler by sending McGuigan, Hearns and Duran on a publicity junket throughout the United States. Paddy Byrne also went with BJ and McGuigan on the barnstorming tour of major American cities. A private jet, laid on by Arum, had the entourage calling in on ten cities to sell the 'Triple Hitters' show. Duran was not there at the start of the tour. The party included Fernando Sosa and his Buenos Aires manager Juan Carlos Lectoure, who shut down his Lunar Park Gym in 1987. That sad closure marked the end of a glory era in Argentine boxing that included such ring craftsmen as Carlos Monzon, Nicolo Locche, Victor Galindez and Juan Domingo Roldan.

Byrne said: "There were press conferences everywhere we went. It took around twelve days. Sometimes we did two cities on the same day. We were all over the bloody place on that trip. Everywhere we went there were cameras, television interviews, reporters. In some places there would be up to 30 photographers. There might be over 20 newspapers reporters as well. We'd go to a hotel in the afternoon. Next morning we'd be up at six or seven o'clock, and into one of the two private aeroplanes available to us which belonged to Caesar's Palace.

"The jets had huge chairs and sofas. The entourage would fly to Chicago, Texas, or wherever, to sell the show. We probably covered 20 States. Barry and Duran got on very well during that trip. We once went to a famous restaurant in New York, Victor's I think was the name and owned by a Cuban. Duran used to go there a lot. On the night we went there we were placed on a platform, where all the celebrities sat and pictures were then taken when Duran came in. He was an amazing character. You want to see Duran do his skipping routine. It was unbelievable."

There was a trial weigh-in during May. But, in the countdown to the show, turmoil set into the Eastwood camp at Palm Springs when Sosa withdrew. Sosa dropped his second bombshell inside four months on a proposed battle with Barry. Duran was in the training camp. Bomber Graham, then in the Eastwood stable and on the undercard, arrived from Sheffield to get acclimatised. McGuigan then ran into an ankle problem during a sparring session. Conflicting stories and varied viewpoints were now seeping from the California training camp.

Jack Magowan wrote on Monday, June 2: 'Barry McGuigan is treating an ankle injury suffered in training for his Las Vegas fight as nothing more than a mild aggravation. Barry stated he'd been to Los Angeles,to see America's top name in sports medicine, Doctor Anthony Daly, and he insists it's only a sprain, not even a bad sprain.' Jack wrote the damage was allegedly done by Mexican sparring help Francisco Zegura, with the champion's heel catching on the ring canvas. Other reports had the spar opponent as another Mexican Umberto Sosa.

Eastwood said: "He was hit on the chin by sparring partner Jeff Franklin, who was world class. He knocked McGuigan down. The ankle then went. Whatever way he fell he twisted the ankle, which went up." There was a frantic scramble to try and find a cure for the ankle damage. The tense Irish camp needed this setback like the proverbial hole in the head. McGuigan was helped in recovery by an American expert in charge of physio and sports injuries for the LA Lakers basketball team. BJ went to Dr Daly's Sports Medical Centre in Los Angeles. Dr Daly suggested McGuigan's ankle should be looked at by this expert on injuries. The damaged ankle wasn't broken. Eastwood was told what to do. Dr Daly also said there was Mike Shiminskey, one of the top men at treating such sporting injuries and in charge of player-injury problems with the L A Lakers basketball team.

"Shiminskey, who was from Portland, Oregon, wasn't too busy then with the Lakers, but was going to see his family. At first he said: No chance', but I made it worth his while to come to the training camp, to make sure the problem was sorted out," added Eastwood, "He did the strappings, putting the ankle in ice and so on - and did the exercises with McGuigan. This guy said no rest for the ankle, but work it every day for half-an-hour, and then put the ankle in ice for half-an-hour, and then work it again. He said he would have McGuigan sparring in three to four days. When it came the time I said give McGuigan more rest and treatment just to be sure. McGuigan had around seven days in all before we got him in sparring again. The physio fellow had McGuigan jumping after about five days."

As is the ways of boxing, Franklin was later bragging about what he had done to World Featherweight champion McGuigan. Franklin, born on September 30, 1962, stood 5' 7", and was a useful operator. He featured on the undercard of the McGuigan-Cruz contest, winning a four-rounder against Evelio Perez. A resident of Las Vegas, rakish and loquacious Franklin had a career record of thirty outings, winning 22 and losing five. His ring record included a draw over twelve rounds against Bernard Taylor, in an NABF Featherweight title fight in Las Vegas. He also scored points wins against Steve Cruz and Tracey Harrison Patterson.

"Franklin, a good fighter and rated, arrived back at training camp with two birds in tow. He wore a big Texas Stetson," recalled Eastwood, "A colourful kid, he had been away playing himself. He was on wages. After McGuigan did some sparring against other opponents we brought Franklin back. The fighter had been telling everyone, boasting how he knocked down the World champion in sparring. He got into the ring again, trying to knock him down again, but this time McGuigan worked him over. McGuigan also looked good in the process. Incidentally, the last I heard of Franklin he finished up a bellboy in one of the big Las Vegas hotels. He wrote to me. He also met me in Vegas the next time I was out there."

41

GLITTER GULCH

ON MONDAY, June 9, 1986, Jack Magowan printed his talk with Luis Spada, who said: "McGuigan came here looking ring rusty. Barry cannot afford long intervals between fights, which is why he took so long to tame Cabrera in Dublin four months ago. His attitude to the game, I fear, may have changed. It's time somebody warned Barry about the dangers of getting soft - soft in mind as well as body. He should be fighting as often as he did before winning the Championship, and that means six times a year, at least."

Magowan also remarked: 'The arrival last week of Sandra McGuigan and family seems to have sparked some tongue-wagging among the fight fraternity of Palm Springs.' On Thursday, June 12 McGuigan was due to appear on the famous Johnny Carson TV show in Los Angeles. Around that time there seemed a curious change in betting patterns for the fight. Did the insiders know all was not well at the Palm Springs camp, and perhaps McGuigan was becoming vulnerable. It was alleged one punter placed a $100,000 bet on Cruz to win and scoop half-a-million dollars. At one point Cruz was listed a 6 to 1 outsider, and McGuigan 1-7.

In the *Belfast Telegraph* issue of Thursday June 19, McGuigan, close to final preparations for his reputed £650,000 pay night, was reported as saying: "I boxed badly in my last fight because I lost patience and tried hard to satisfy the fans with a knock-out win. There will be no such impetuosity this time. I promise." It was also predicted McGuigan's next fight would be in Belfast or Dublin, and against Esparragoza. The champion declared: "I have my fans at home to think about. Vegas is a new and exciting territory for me, and so would New York if that's where my next American contest is being planned. Before that, I would like to go back to the King's Hall." On Friday, June 20, Eastwood disclosed McGuigan threatened to turn his back on the one million dollar pay-night in Las Vegas, and also it took over two days to reach a decision on replacement fighter Cruz.

Magowan wrote: 'And that clearly fuelled rumours all was not well in their highly successful manager-fighter relationship.' Eastwood insisted that: "Even though we have had some differences of opinion they're no more than that. It is true Barry worries a lot, and has this terrible fear of losing; of having his World title, plus everything else he owns and loves, suddenly taken away from him. The talk about a rift between us is absolute nonsense. This has been a difficult fight to get Barry ready for, what with that injury to his ankle and a mysterious pain in his ear, but he'll be all right on the night."

It was estimated the US Inland Revenue Authority would nab $250,000 of the champion's purse, but he would be able to claw some of it back through expenses incurred in the States. It was also claimed McGuigan was the highest paid fighter on the show, at one million dollars. Hearns was to get $900,000, Duran $100,000, and Cruz $70,000. The appointed referee was American Richard Steele from Las Vegas, who previously handled 30 world title fights including Hagler-Hearns and Pryor-Arguello. Ironically, the intriguing build-up to the big boxing bill was temporarily blown off the main sporting pages back in Belfast because of World Cup final news of Northern Ireland's soccer team in Guadalajara. But it quickly became headline news when Cruz caused the upset of '86.

THE RING Magazine selected the Cruz seismic scuttling of McGuigan the 'Fight of the Year' for 1986. Referee Steele contributed to one of a number of critical happenings in the contest when it was felt he harshly docked a point off McGuigan in the latter half of the fight. Crucial to the narrow points outcome was McGuigan going down in the final round. Las Vegas also proved to be the final fight frontier in the once robustly rewarding relationship between Eastwood and McGuigan. Rumour, mostly a mangler of the truth, began to circulate of unrest before the fighter and manager set off from the Emerald Isle for the title defence.

By the time preparations in a California training camp were well under way, with signed up local sparring help such as Jeff Franklin and Fresno fighter Larry Villareal, original opponent Sosa was out of the picture. The decision to set up the fight against Cruz delighted the Texan's wily manager Dave Gorman, who also handled the affairs of Don Curry and Gene Hatcher. He died in April, 2004, aged 61. Right in the mix was cuts ace Byrne, watching the beginning of the end in California, where it became a fraught fight plan. "We were in Palm Springs for six weeks before the Cruz fight," said Byrne, "We used to get up around five o'clock in the morning, Barney and all. It was so hot yet Eastwood would go out on the road with the other people. Often I would hear a door slam when we were getting up. It would be Duran coming in, from a party."

Unfortunately, the glamour bill, on June 23, 1986, plunged to a horror show for McGuigan. It was a case of tarnished glory, yet some ringside writers at the time listed the absorbing 15-rounder the best championship fight seen in the casino capitol of the world. I'm not so sure many fight folks would now subscribe to that generously high assessment. It is merely a faded memory of one of world boxing's great upsets, with the forever image of a distraught McGuigan jerkily stumbling backwards across the ring in the final round. Few fight fans will remember much about the undercard. Detroit's original 'Hitman' Hearns, born in Memphis, Tennessee, on October 10, 1958, stopped fellow American Mark Medal. Referee Davey Pearl halted the WBC Light-middleweight title bout, because of severe eyebrow damage sustained by former IBF champion Medal. Born in Manhattan, and living in New Jersey, this was to be Medal's penultimate bout.

Duran, now beefed up to the middleweight grade, lost a split decision over ten rounds to Marvin Hagler's half-brother Robbie Sims. The amazing Duran's career (103-16) lasted until July, 2001, when he lost in a Super-middleweight 12-rounder to Hector Camacho in Denver, Colorado. Before the action, McGuigan and Eastwood each received a special Caesar's Palace track suit.

Eastwood retained the flashy memento: "Jay Edson, who was the advance agent for Bob Arum's Top Rank who also spent time in Belfast to oversee the McGuigan-Taylor fight on behalf of Bob Arum, brought me the suit to my hotel room, and also a lovely car rug." Edson, once a noted fight referee, was then part of the Top Rank team. In 1990, the Boxing Writers' of America honoured him with the coveted James J Walker Award for long and meritorious service to boxing. Another prominent Arum operative was the colourful publicist Irving Rudd, who maintained a lengthy contact with Eastwood, and for many years after the Vegas upset.

"He was a very funny, lively wee guy," said Eastwood. Brooklyn born, in 1917, the irrepressible Rudd, a Damon Runyan-type character who was also a James J. Walker Award winner (1985), died in 2000. Before joining Arum, the livewire little man with the waspish wit was also a publicist in boxing for Don King and Mike Jacobs, and in baseball for the Brooklyn Dodgers. The Cruz McGuigan contest opened the closed-circuit telecast from an open-air car park, and in heat rising above 100 degrees. It was a match-up widely regarded a warm-up before the Cyclone's mandatory title defence against Esparragoza. Cruz, a plumber's assistant, was a former amateur Golden Gloves Bantamweight champion. McGuigan, repeatedly linked to a unification fight against the fearsome Azumah Nelson, was expected to canter through this one.

The Cyclone was installed the clear favourite, yet an accumulation of things conspired to turn his time-marking defence into a disaster of staggering proportions. Cool Cruz boxed liked never before. He appeared to have an answer to most things Barry did. Just when it seemed the champion's natural relentless style was taking command in the 10th round Cruz dropped him with a surprise left hook to the chin. Now treading treacle, McGuigan was cruelly docked a late point by referee Steele, following an alleged stray blow south of the border.

The champion's boxing world was splitting at the seams, yet he bravely battled back in rounds 13 and 14 to inspire the belief he could retain his title. But, Cruz knocked him down in the closing round to take all three scorecard summaries. Judges for that fateful fight were Angel Tovar 143-142, Medardo Villalobos 143-139, and Guy Jutras 142-141. Suffering from dehydration, and a headache, a weary McGuigan was taken to the Valley Hospital for a CAT Scan, and an overnight stop. Irving Rudd informed to the media shortly after the fight that McGuigan was going off to hospital for a check-up.

Rudd said: "He has a bad headache, and is in a state of exhaustion. The fighter has been examined by doctors, who have applied icepacks to his chest and head to help lower his temperature." The ringside doctors also recommended a Cat Scan. McGuigan came back from hospital to meet the Press at poolside in Caesar's Palace Hotel. Media reports include McGuigan confessing: "My legs were gone. My feet were in blisters from the eighth round, and I was totally dehydrated. I lost concentration in the second half of the contest. To lose a fight with victory within your grasp is a bitter pill to swallow."

Michael McGeary's fight summary in the *Irish News*, Belfast, included a front page report: 'Cruz took all McGuigan could throw at him.' McGuigan is quoted: 'I have no complaints. He deserved to win. My accuracy was a mile off. I'm not sure what I did wrong. You have your off nights. Unfortunately this was one of them.' He said he might try to regain his title, or move up to Junior Lightweight. It is fair to state neither fighter, Cruz nor McGuigan, was the same after this gruelling contest. McGuigan made a comeback two years later. Cruz lost the title in the first defence, and his ring career is regarded nothing higher than moderate. He retired in 1993. While 1985 was to prove McGuigan's apogee in the ring it was the swift crash in 1986, ironically a time declared 'International Year of Peace' by United Nations. 1986 is also remembered as the year Irish-born mare 'Dawn Run' won the Cheltenham Gold Cup.

On May 31, the FIFA's World Cup finals opened in Mexico, and a month later Argentina beat West Germany 3-2 for the title. On November 22,

Mike Tyson won his first World Heavyweight title by beating the ill-fated Trevor Berbick in Las Vegas. On December 8, future World Light-welterweight champion Amir Khan was born in Bolton. Prominent people who died in 1986 included musician Phil Lynott of 'Thin Lizzy', film actor/singer Gordon MacRae, film actress Lilli Palmer, film actors Cary Grant, Ray Milland, Broderick Crawford, Forrest Tucker, Scatman Crothers, and Sterling Hayden, film director Otto Preminger, Wallis Simpson - wife of the late Duke of Windsor - and jazz musician Benny Goodman.

TRAUMA TIME

THE TRIP to The Strip in mid-summer 1986 remained an excruciatingly unhappy memory for Eastwood. With a degree of understatement he said: "Things did not work out, obviously. I don't know where it all went wrong. The other guy was nothing, as they say in the trade. Yes, it was hot. There is no doubt about that. I cannot argue against the heat factor. It was hot for the other guy, too. We all knew McGuigan was going to be fighting on June 26 in Las Vegas. And it wasn't me that wanted to go to America for this title defence, in the first place.

"I wanted him to fight Gomez for the 9st 4lbs title. I felt he would knock Gomez out. That was the fight to take, but other people were at him. I believe they were saying: 'Go you to America, where you will get the big bucks. You are Irish'. I felt McGuigan) could see the big bucks out in America, the endorsements, and so on."

Not long after the Las Vegas horror show the fall-out between Eastwood and McGuigan was sickeningly sudden, and terminal. First off, it became a time of universal confusion from the moment the hand of Cruz was raised as the new WBA Featherweight champion of the World. Numbing despair followed the ruins of Las Vegas. Devoted followers of the wonder years had problems in accepting the cruel reality that boxing life in Ireland would never be the same again. Following the eclipse of the Cyclone it was painfully evident the good old days of a barnstorming Barry McGuigan and the ringmaster influence of B.J. Eastwood were close to becoming a memory.

All of a sudden, to the outside world, the cocoon of confidence that was nurtured by the McGuigan-Eastwood alliance was ruthlessly ripped away. Replacing what must be regarded as one of the greatest of Irish boxing achievements, until after Loftus Road, was naked animosity. World boxing was rocked to it's foundations. Initially it seemed the Eastwood-McGuigan partnership, so phenomenally successful for four years, might survive the setback. The big divide, suddenly expanding as wide as the Grand Canyon, surfaced soon after the traumatic trip to Nevada.

Heavyweight legal eagles donned the gloves in a series of high-powered and high-profile productions of High Court law suits. Few World boxing champions, exceptions include Heavyweights Gene Tunney and Rocky Marciano, are ever able to go through their careers in the pain game without having to stare into the cracked face of a mirror. The so-termed sporting side of the 'Noble Art' was shunted into a black corner for the Cyclone, and merely a few months after the harsh facts of this brutally demanding sport began to seep to the surface at Simmonscourt.

In Dublin, McGuigan had to endure the rougher side of life inside the ring against Cabrera. Not since the clash with Charm Chiteule did he really have to suck it and see. After all the years of dedication, hard work, and often effortless success inside the ropes, the Cyclone had to deal with an unexpectedly high level of anxiety. Perhaps there was some sort of message in that tightrope test against Cabrera. One fight later, ironically against a second successive late replacement for the injury-afflicted Sosa, dreams of attaining super-star status were left in tatters.

While it seemed inconceivable, even illogical at that time, the loss to Cruz was right to the heart of what boxing can be all about. By its very nature it has to be a cruel game. After rolling along on the crest of a wave came the crash. The unedifying aftermath was stupendously stark. When the reality of the situation set in the ever-resourceful Irish fight fans turned their focus on a fresh hero, Dave 'Boy' McAuley, and after that Steve Collins. The McGuigan roller-coaster would soon become a memory.

It is relatively easy to describe the good times of the Eastwood-McGuigan saga. The happy days were, without question, the most enjoyable of my career. This passage of Eastwood's life is a special story in itself, one of achievement, World acclaim for both manager and fighter, and then the awfulness of the acrimonious ending. To illustrate the Eastwood story I knew I'd have to try and recapture the gut-wrenching period of raw hate. A magnificent passage of Irish prize-fighting lay mutilated forever. What started out as a dream became a reality, and then plunged to a nightmare scenario. Picking up the pieces could not have been easy for either parties. Eastwood buried himself into planning the best way forward for his remaining band of talented boxers. Included were Hodkinson, McAuley, Espana, Cordova, Ray Close, the Wenton brothers, Sam Storey, Fabrice Benichou and John Lowey.

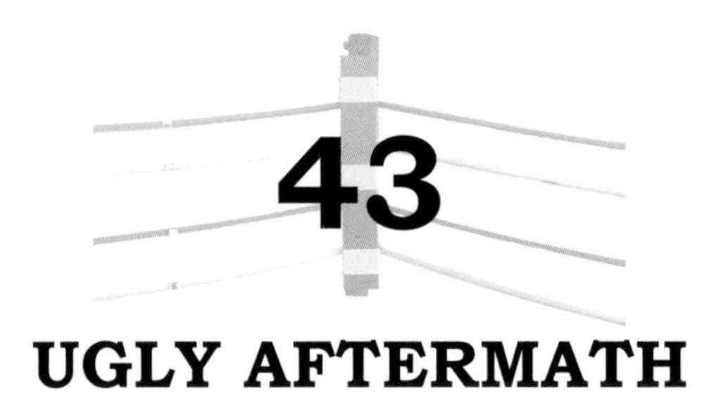

43

UGLY AFTERMATH

RECRIMINATIONS were instantly predictable after McGuigan's title tumble. The *Irish News* of Tuesday June 25, 1986, carried a front page story, headlined 'FURY AT BARRY'S TORRID DESERT ORDEAL'. The copy opened with: 'Barry McGuigan's native Clones was still reeling last night from the devastation of his World title defeat by Steve Cruz at Las Vegas'.

The story continued: 'There was bitter anger in the McGuigan household, and among the former World champ's hometown supporters, over the management procedure that led Barry to defend his crown in the torrid Nevada heat. Barry's mother Katie, who adhered to her rule never to watch her son box on TV, was in a near state of exhaustion early yesterday as she watched a video of the fight, and outspokenly hit out at the fact that Barry was forced to box in Las Vegas. It was complete mismanagement, to have staged the fight there,' she declared, adding, 'He would have been happy enough to box in New York or Chicago, which are not too hot for somebody from this environment as the heat beat him. It is definitely to do with the TV networks because they decide where the fights will be.'

Mrs McGuigan also revealed last night that Barry wanted to withdraw from the World title defence after the original challenger Fernando Sosa withdrew, and both he and other family members consistently opposed staging the fight in Las Vegas. Following an early morning phone call from Barry at his hospital bed in Las Vegas, Mrs McGuigan said: 'It was the heat that got him - it was inhuman.'

Martin Breheny, in the *Irish Press* issue of Wednesday June 25, 1986, also questioned the wisdom of the venue, the heat, the timing of the contest. However, he added his opinion that 'those who decry Eastwood's decision as madness must remember that McGuigan came within one round of victory on Monday night. Had he survived, the decision to box in Las Vegas would not be questioned. Once he was beaten, however, the knives were out for Eastwood. Such is the difference between success and failure.'

Breheny added: 'The timing, of course, was decided by Irish and British TV who wanted the fight on as early as possible on Tuesday morning. It has not taken long for the knockers to come to the surface.' It was also speculated: 'McGuigan might still be champion but for referee Richard Steele's order that a point be deducted for a low blow in the 12th round. That point cost McGuigan the fight.'

On the front page of the same *Irish Press* issue a report included: "Within an hour of being discharged from hospital in last Vegas last night, McGuigan made a direct attack on Mr Eastwood over decisions to put his Featherweight title on the line in Caesar's Palace on Monday night. 'It was the wrong place at the wrong time of year, at the wrong time of day. Had it been winter time, it might have been okay, or even if it was later in the evening when it got cooler. We have gone over this a thousand times. I didn't like it from the beginning. I didn't like the trip - it was too severe, too tiring, too far away from home, and it takes too long to acclimatise. You can't breathe, and my feet were blistering very badly during the fight. I slowed down dreadfully in the second half of the fight.'

It soon became clear there would be a smartingly painful parting of the ways between boxer and manager. In October, 1986, the war between McGuigan and Eastwood was under way. Paddy Byrne had a further say in the ugly aftermath to Las Vegas. A report stated he claimed he saw promoter Bob Arum and Denmark's boxing mogul Mogens Palle holding talks with McGuigan and the Cyclone's legal adviser in Las Vegas. Byrne was back in the Nevada hotspot to act as cuts man for Viking heavyweight Steffan Tangstad in a World title match against Michael Spinks. The once holy alliance of McGuigan and Eastwood was now heading over the cliff.

My own sentiments, printed on October 12, 1986, included: 'There was no higher point to climb for the McGuigan-Eastwood partnership than the night of open-air magic when the Cyclone out-gunned and out-smarted the great Panamanian Eusebio Pedroza.' I added my tuppence worth: 'With so much loot to be earned, outside influences hopped aboard the gravy train and destroyed the good times. Since Loftus Road there's been a rising tide of whingeing and cringing, ignited by people consumed by envy. My humble view is that neither McGuigan nor Eastwood quite realised a year ago the growing disturbing influences, now bitterly mischievous, may well have had the singularly crucial reason for the decline and fall of a golden era. It's all too late for tears. Yes, the wolves have taken over'.

The seeds of discontent in the Eastwood-McGuigan relationship were, apparently, sown not too long after the high of Loftus Road. As is generally the case, money matters became the root of the unrest. It was now into cash-registry territory. Once the target of World title honour was achieved the wonderful sporting saga suddenly started sinking to a dollar-driven nightmare.

Eastwood said: "Eastwood Promotions started to make money for a first time from the show at Loftus Road. It was reasonable money, but we were behind a substantial amount of cash going into that. The Bernard Taylor show at the King's Hall made some money. However, out of that promotion Bob Arum, the man behind Taylor, took most of the money, including the American TV cash. On top of that there was the 'stepaside' money paid to let us negotiate and set up the World title fight against Pedroza. The Dublin show involving Cabrera did well, made a good profit. I felt at that time other people now around him were saying: 'Without you there is no show. You are the man. Look what you could make. You could make it big in America'."

Sam Smyth of the *Irish Independent* discovered around this juncture that Eastwood received an official letter from McGuigan, wanting clear detail of all terms agreed for contests, all contract information, and so forth. The inference was clear. The growing period of uncomfortably strained dealings between boxer and manager was starting to move away from one of alleged 'deceptive unco-operation' to blunt animosity.

"They put me on notice then," declared an extremely frank Eastwood, "As I have stated I came back with a signed contract from Gomez, before the Dublin title defence. Things, however, were now so awkward, getting worse and worse, so I went to meet him (McGuigan) near Enniskillen to discuss a fight with Gomez. It was very much a wind of change, from a time when we were meeting nearly every day in the gym, and so on, to a situation when people were doing a runner on me. From being able to talk about fight plans, possible opponents, training plans - but now I am chasing him. That was why I went to meet him just outside Enniskillen, almost in his own backyard.

"I would have gone to Timbuktu to try and get that fight against Gomez, to make him a two-time World champion. Gomez agreeing to sign was the good news, yet I knew the sands were shifting. Look, in my view, that was the fight to take, against Gomez - a household name, and one of the greatest fighters the world has ever seen. Gomez was an ideal opponent. I was not happy about McGuigan, the way he performed in his previous fights - against Taylor, against Cabrera, and even against Pedroza.

"I am saying, where do we go from here? What do we do. He is sitting on top of the mountain now, as the World Featherweight champion. Gomez was the way to go, meeting a boxer who, as the say in the trade, is regarded a 'shot' fighter. In my opinion, it was a terrible mistake to turn down that fight. Gomez was sent from God for McGuigan, the greatest scalp at that time we could possibly get, the biggest name about. That was the jackpot match. We knew he (McGuigan) was a good wee fighter, great at going forward but couldn't go back. McGuigan, in my view, would have won it in two or three rounds, because Gomez was the perfect opponent for him at that time. Maybe after that he could have said he (McGuigan) was hanging up his gloves, and he would have gone down in history as a great Irish fighter who became a two-weight World champion.

"Frances (Mrs Eastwood) wanted me to jump off the train then. She definitely did, but I felt if I got off the train it was letting them take over. Maybe it would have been the right thing to do, just leave it all behind me, but I have never been a guy to walk away from anything. It would have been a different thing had McGuigan come to me, maybe with his wife and his father. Who knows. Perhaps they could have said they wanted to do their own thing. Maybe I could have said, go ahead - and I'd take a percentage, say 20%, but I knew the vultures were sitting on the wings, and about to take over the whole show. It just annoyed me.

"I did not wish to hand over to these people who had never run a boxing show, who never knew what it was like to be dealing with the people who run world boxing, to be up all night ringing boxing managers, promoters and officials in South America, in Latin America, in the United States, in Europe, when trying to make a match for somebody. It was, I felt, proved later when the options were bought on McGuigan. They decided they'd have to have a go at this guy Eastwood. They wanted rid of me. They could see themselves moving closer to getting into the chair, and complete control. They felt they were holding all the aces. They sent me several letters."

The opening move to the colossal crash was a tetchy meeting in the Dunadry Hotel, at leafy Templepatrick, County Antrim. Eastwood insisted he was reluctant to attend, but knew the pertinacious battery of requests was not going to subside. So, he decided to attend the showdown at Dunadry, but before going made a move of the unexpected. He called up leading London lawyer Oscar Beuselinck to deal with some letters, and then invited him to sit in at the meeting.

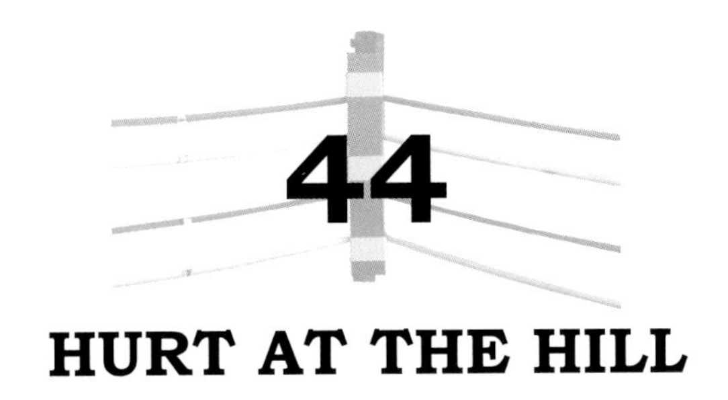

44

HURT AT THE HILL

FRANCES Eastwood couldn't disguise the hurt. Her eyes were a giveaway. I was pleasantly surprised this petite cornerstone behind her childhood sweetheart volunteered a small outpouring of her innermost thoughts on the very public break-up of B.J. and what she regarded as a once pampered puncher.

Throughout my many spells, over a two-and-a-half-year period, of interviewing her husband at The Hill, the lady of the house graciously materialised with the best china cups, tea or coffee, and chocolate biscuits. She did not appear too interested in the proceedings, all the talk about boxing, and retreated. In her engaging mannerism of weighing up people through unblinkered focus, as if searching through your thought processes, I pondered that she probably wondered if the proposed book project, detailed warts and all, on BJ's experiences in boxing, would be a worthwhile exercise. I could well understand why Frances Eastwood had more than her fill of the boxing game.

The severe mental scars of the Eastwood-McGuigan crash would never be healed. By raking over the coals I found the embers were still red hot. The short but also revealing chat I had almost became confessional of sorts, yet knowing the pain would never go away. Here was the wife and major steadying influence of her very public partner's success story in the bookmaking and property business, and in professional boxing, still afflicted by one of the most unhappy periods in Irish and World boxing history.

Despite achieving such a high degree of deserved privilege in a lifestyle befitting a millionaire, she retained old-fashioned values, never flaunting the self-achieved successes of her family, never discarding her roots, and never forgetting the hardships she and Barney once had to overcome. However, having been forced to endure such an unwelcome intruder as deep hurt from what she regarded inexplicable betrayal, Frances expressed a forthright view she, still to this day, cannot comprehend why people once seemingly loyal to the Eastwood family should turn on their friend and benefactor.

Close to a quarter-century failed to wash away and overcome the revulsion and anguish she felt all those years ago. The harrowing legal war of words between her husband and the Eastwood family's one-time house guest appeared to remain firmly lodged in a mental cabinet file of that traumatic time, when she witnessed the carnage caused by the High Court cases. It was a period that so cruelly and clinically consigned a segment of Eastwood family life to the ashcan.

She had good reason to wonder why the universally renowned partnership of her husband and McGuigan should end in a cockpit of hate. Frances first happily recalled the exuberance and high expectation when BJ signed on the burgeoning young boxer, and then laid out plans to try and conquer the world. There was that unique time-frame of fabulous achievement. She watched proudly on the wings, but always with reservation. The quietly firm influence behind the family business, she confessed she was never happy at her husband's second period of deep involvement in professional boxing. Still, it seemed all worthwhile when WBA Featherweight Championship status was achieved, but just as suddenly fame and fortune would create envy, unrest and the spiteful split.

Her face painted a picture of puzzlement and pain as she listened to grim-faced wig-adorned gentlemen in black robes laying bare the very soul of the Eastwood family. It was living through a nightmare then at the Belfast Courts, and even after all the years of water under such a dark and forbidding bridge this nasty passage of jurisprudence refuses to go away.

"I don't know why he (McGuigan) did what he did. I felt no matter what advice he got from other people, concerning Barney and the case he was taking against Barney, he should have known himself, in his own heart, what he was doing was not right," said Frances, who had a motherly input from the moment McGuigan began his professional career. She worried about, and fussed over, this young prospect, that he might be hurt in the ring.

At that time McGuigan became one of the family, and often stayed for spells in the early Eastwood residence at Gortnagreenen, outside Holywood, County Down. The birth of a future World champion began with the fighter living in the house, and having his own rooming quarter. This was a clear message of intent by B.J. Eastwood, no ordinary manager boxer alliance. This was particularly special, and Frances Eastwood recognised the intense enthusiasm BJ was devoting to the project. What may have set out to be a philanthropic pastime turned into an all-consuming adventure for her husband, who invested heavily in time and resources. In those days the Eastwood-McGuigan association was close to the heart of the lady of the house.

She played her part: "There was nobody treated as well as Barry McGuigan when he first came to our house. From Day One he was treated like God Almighty. He wanted for nothing, and even things he didn't want we got for him. He was absolutely ruined. It was an exciting time all right, from the start, but I suffered terribly from pressure. When he (McGuigan) was fighting, I worried he might suffer an injury. I even felt stress when he left the house in the morning to do his roadwork. Remember this was in the early 1980's. I didn't tell Barney then that I suffered awfully from the stress of it all. I suffered when McGuigan was fighting. Every time he (McGuigan) fought I was up to 'High Doh' hoping that he (McGuigan) would win."

Frances may well have experienced an unwitting premonition that things might not turn out well in the end. She was initially against her husband going back into the boxing arena, but always followed, supported, and backed his sporting instincts ever since BJ played Gaelic football. "I started going to Gaelic matches to watch him playing for Tyrone, and at 16-years-of-age when he won the All-Ireland Minor Football Championship medal. I took an interest then. My own sporting involvement was in hockey, camogie and then golf. I won a Northern Ireland Junior Schools' hockey medal when I was a student at Magherafelt High. I was not so good at the camogie, after playing so much hockey."

A talented amateur golfer, who once played to a nine-handicap at Carrickfergus Golf club, she kept a careful watching brief during BJ's promotional sortie into boxing during the 1960's. I had the feeling she was relieved when he walked away from it. Unsurprisingly, when the interest in McGuigan surfaced, and then the project took on a life of its own, Frances was concerned.

"I didn't really want him going back to the boxing," she insisted, "He (Barney) took a notion. We had enough of the boxing during the first period, in the 1960's. When Barney decided to become manager of Barry McGuigan I agree it was a great time for everybody, when things were going well. Barney put so much effort into it, but it had a sad ending." She also recalled when her instincts warned her that the outwardly happy partnership between her husband and the rising star of the ring was becoming fragile: "I knew things were changing, but didn't say anything. Long before McGuigan became World champion things were changing. I could sense things were not the same. McGuigan changed before winning the World title. Our son Stephen didn't like the way things were going, and retired as the promoter after Loftus Road."

45

HIGH STAKES

OSCAR Beuselinck seemed out of place, but certainly not out of his depth as Eastwood's nonetheless strange yet apt legal choice to sit through the opening bout of bitterness. One of London's outstanding libel lawyers of the 20th Century, he answered Eastwood's call. Not a person to easily, if at all, intimidate Beuselinck basically observed the proceedings. The father of singer/actor Paul Nicholas (born Paul Oscar Beuselinck) enjoyed a high-profile career that was on a parallel to the humble start of Eastwood. Both left school at 14. Both became self-made success stories.

Beuselinck, who died in December, 1997, and Eastwood were kindred spirits, of a sort. The son of a Belgian sea-cook and an English mother, he was reared in the slums of Hoxton, in the heart of London. He was blocked from securing a grammar school education because his father was not British. By chance, he saw messenger boys delivering case papers to Court chambers, managed a job as a tea boy, and eventually became an outside clerk for a music law firm. He was encouraged to take the exams and become a managing clerk, and then a solicitor. He developed into a leading legal light for Jewish clients in the Metropolis.

The stocky Beuselinck built up the London firm of Wright, Webb, Syrett after World War Two to be the leading show business legal practice. He also gained a high reputation in libel work. Like Eastwood, he thrived on living on the edge. From tea boy in 1933 he created a similarly styled success story to that of BJ. The professional boxing scene was hardly his game, but he knew how to read sign, and how to act once the gloves came off in litigation cases. Regarded a fearsome and abrasive negotiator, with an expert eye for the weaknesses in a case, he didn't pass much comment when Eastwood was as good as told by the phalanx of some of Northern Ireland's then brightest legal brains to cough up millions or else head for the High Court, and the high jump.

The astute Beuselinck's summation after the meeting of restless and agitated minds at Dunadry was to create a shift in emphasis, to do the unlikely. He noted McGuigan's 'silks' all came from the same closely-knit cloth, all top Catholic lawyers involved in the mainstream circuit in Northern Ireland. His opinion suggested Eastwood should hire local legal help, people on the ground who knew the full history of the famous boxing alliance that had turned sour, but also strongly advocated the selection of solicitors and barristers not remotely connected to any past working relationships with McGuigan's advisors.

"I was called to attend at Dunadry. That was my first meeting with them. They were calling me to account. Firstly, I was going to go along on my own. I did not want anyone here involved. My solicitor then was Desmond Dorris of Cookstown. I decided to call in Oscar Beuselinck, who did a few things for me in London. I talked Oscar into taking a flight over to nearby Belfast International Airport."

Eastwood felt he was now being painted a brown-shoed bookie villain, with recurring innuendo of all sorts of wrong doings, including an alleged heavy wager on Cruz to beat his own fighter. "The place was full of rumour after Las Vegas. I became the really big bad wolf. I was a bookmaker, a gambler, so it stood to reason lots of people would willingly believe the rumours, and think I had money on Cruz. There were lots of stories flying about, putting the blame on me. I asked around. Apparently there was big gambler from Texas who backed Cruz at 6 to 1."

All the bad vibes led into the meeting of minds at Dunadry. Eastwood considered it was a threatening environment. He felt the opposition approached the occasion with what appeared to him as excessive zeal, and added: "It was big stuff at the Hotel. I was told before this they were really going after me, claiming McGuigan was wrongfully looked after in Las Vegas. There was talk of wanting five million sterling. A big room was booked by them, and also two small rooms on each end. They arrived before me, and I was informed there was a number of police on duty,. I felt they were trying to intimidate me. It was two of us against a team of solicitors and barristers.

"They claimed he (McGuigan) said this and said that. All the while McGuigan stayed in their small room. I said: 'Bring him out. I'll talk to him.' They would not allow him to come out and talk to me, face to face. I said I had nothing to hide. Then I was told this was going to cost me a lot of money. One legal person told me we could do it the hard way or the easy way. He said it would take a good few million pounds to settle this. I said: 'Settle what?' They said he (McGuigan) feels an injustice has been done to him.

"I decided to leave, bade them 'Good Day', and they said it could be a very big case, would be bad publicity for me and my family. Oscar listened, and afterwards his view was he felt they brought me there to try and completely intimidate me. He also suggested I needed somebody on the ground in Northern Ireland who was not involved in any way with that whole circle of legal people, somebody completely detached from that crowd." Eastwood conceded his emotions were downcast then. He didn't want this sorry scenario, but sensed an unfettered frenzy to give him the bum's rush, and also try to shred his bank balance. McGuigan, he reluctantly and finally realised, was beyond his influence. The good old days were over, the fighter seeking a new and fresh direction to reach Eldorado. BJ's time was over. Now he felt cornered, but determined to fight this to the end. He decided it was time to circle the wagons.

Very soon Eastwood was to gain confirmation that he was also to feel he had inherited Julius Caesar's back. McGuigan's firm and unwavering intent to split was hard to take, and when the gloves came off in the High Court Eastwood was to notice that a well-known QC supposedly on his side was really in the enemy camp. It was now a case of 'Et Tu Brutus', but Eastwood quickly realised he was more fortunate than Caesar. He was still alive, and about to blaze back.

"After the meeting at the Dunadry, I discussed the situation with my good friend and business associate Alfie McLean. He suggested I first should hold a chat with a certain legal person who had been involved in my affairs for years. I did so, but during that meeting I was again told I couldn't win, and it was going to take a good few million to settle. I said that was the second time in a week I was told that. It was then I realised I was going to be attacked from all quarters.

"So, I decided to contact one man I could really trust, politician Paddy Devlin, and he came up with the view I needed to go to 'the other side of the house' and hire a non-Catholic barrister, just as Oscar Beuselinck suggested. Paddy mentioned the name of Robert McCartney, a man I never met but knew of. Paddy (Devlin) came back to me, and said Bob McCartney would take the case providing a solicitor who often worked for him is instructed. That was Paul Tweed, with Ben Stephens the junior barrister."

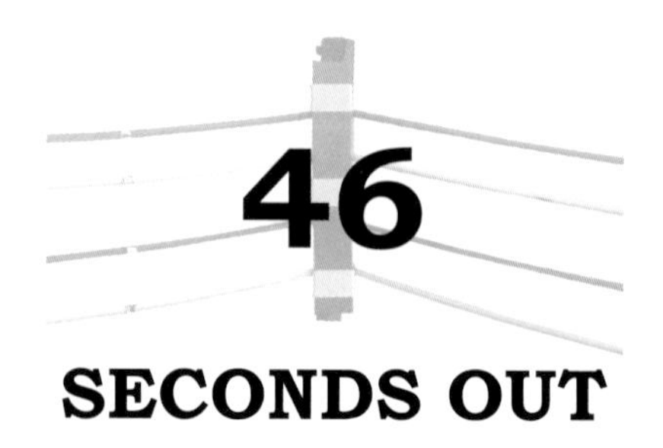

46

SECONDS OUT

EASTWOOD'S decision to choose a blue-coloured corner against the green on the other side of the Law Court seemed an outrageous gamble. When the metaphorical knuckle-dusters were donned the brilliant mind of Michael Lavery QC was the main man in Team McGuigan, and instructed by McGuigan's solicitor Eamonn McEvoy. They faced Team Eastwood's Robert 'Bob' McCartney, later of Unionist fame in the North Down hustings area, junior barrister Ben Stephens, and a young solicitor Paul Tweed, a rising light in the litigation world. It was now down to the ruthless combat in the electric atmosphere of Amphitheatre.

Many times during the unfortunate yet fascinating days of legal debate in the main libel case it seemed the bookmaker was sure to take the ten count. It was expected Eastwood would cough up loads of lolly. Still, as the days rolled by the balance began to slowly swing in favour of Eastwood. Bangor-reared Paul Tweed retained a computer-like recollection of the famous libel case. The senior partner of Johnsons Solicitors of Wellington Place, Belfast, however, insists all the rancour and the public glare of the Court Actions could have been avoided.

Born on June 6, 1955, in Belfast, he was a couple of years ahead of ex-Ryder Cup golfer and quirky golf analyst David Feherty at Bangor Grammar, and then graduated through Queen's University. He confessed to having no interest in boxing until called to join Bob McCartney in the ring of rancour. Tweed participated in League squash and tennis. He also ran marathons to keep fit, and was in the first Belfast and the first Newtownards marathons. He was convinced a well orchestrated 'ambush' was laid to try and intimidate Eastwood into submission at the Dunadry Hotel.

"It was well known who was involved in the autumn of 1986, and we were brought in during late 1986. The first case was in June 1987, and the last case in February 1992," said Tweed, "Barney always said he would pay a 'marker' that was never in dispute, but held back the money because they were suing him. After Dunadry, Paddy Devlin recommended Bob (McCartney), who in turn recommended my firm. Through this I created a lasting friendship with Barney. Some nights we sat to the early hours discussing what to do. We were working out strategy. Barney was very much of the old school, handshake on deals. He was superb at getting things arranged, doing a deal, but not so careful at getting the paperwork done in those days.

"After Las Vegas he started getting letters, hand-written letters, all written by McGuigan, but clearly words of lawyers used. I knew they were that, but by whom I don't know. I can only surmise. The first Case was the 'marker' for the quarter of a million pounds sterling to McGuigan. The minute they started litigation Barney held back that payment, one he promised to give McGuigan should the boxer lose to Cruz in Las Vegas. So, the first case was effectively a draw. It was what we regarded as a Mexican stand-off, the marker of £250,000 paid by Barney, and £200,000 for a two-fight option, making a total of £450, 000 to resolve the case."

It didn't end there for Tweed. There were other smaller libel actions to clear up, and also back to Court to claim Eastwood's rights on options over McGuigan's next two fights. "I heard he (McGuigan) is going to have his first fight since Las Vegas, and in London. He is to fight for Frank Warren. They thought it was all over then, that I'd let sleeping dogs lie and so forth, but I asked Paul (Tweed) about the options I was awarded from the first Court case," added Eastwood, "I paid for the options, and was determined to enforce them, or at least ensure nobody else could step in and take advantage. I said I suffered in many ways, all the bad publicity that I was to blame for everything. There comes a time in your life when you have to take a stand, so here we go again. I said privately they could buy the options from me.

"They offered 50 grand (£50,000). I would not consider it, saying they were not even in the ballpark. Next offer was 100 grand. I insisted on 200 grand, and certain things to be signed to make the clean breakaway. I also said I wanted the money lodged, or an irrevocable letter of credit, or an irrevocable banker's cheque for the full amount. Court was due to start in ten minutes. I went into the courtroom, the only person there, and then I heard through a message from outside that another 25 grand was added, to make it 175. I said no. I would rather hold onto the options on McGuigan's fights, and do without the money. It had to be 200 grand, I said. Court opened. Perhaps half-an-hour in, after discussing documents, a 15-minute break was sought from the judge. The next thing was an agreement to pay the 200 grand. We signed up. That was the end of the whole thing." Eastwood obviously meant the end of the old rip-roaring ring-of-confidence partnership, one that took on and shook the boxing world but now suffering the final fatal blow. Still, there was one more sickening saga to be played out.

47

THE BIG ISSUE

PAUL Tweed remembered how the 1992 libel case first came to his notice. Eastwood's faithful aide, the late Tony Baker was the bearer of bad tidings, that the legal battles were not over. "Tony Baker consulted me on behalf of Barney regarding allegations he found in a video brought out by *Channel 5* as a biography on McGuigan," said Tweed, "McGuigan claimed to have been injured before he went into the ring in Las Vegas. I immediately put both McGuigan and *Channel 5* on notice. It was into the legendary libel action against Barry McGuigan and *Channel 5*. McGuigan's allegations on the video were extremely provocative and unfounded. So we sued both, the *Channel 5* Production Company and McGuigan. The rest is legal history."

He also stated: "The big libel case could have been settled at the door of the Court for a payment of £20,000 to the Belfast's Royal Victoria Hospital Intensive Care Unit, where Barney's son Fintan died. We put that to them before the Case started. It was rejected." The whole scene turned nasty, according to Tweed; "The proceedings were absolute vitriol from the word go," he claimed.

"Yet, most definitely, the whole thing could have been avoided. I believe PolyGram/Channel 5 would have settled. Brian Walker represented them, and we have always had a very good relationship with him, but the McGuigan people would not talk. It was one of THE most vitriolic cases I was ever involved in. One of the judges made the comment the correspondence between myself and McEvoy was more defamatory than the actual subject allegations. There was a great bitterness there. It finished £450,000 plus costs - £850,000 in total, awarded to Barney. I believe the reason the jury ordered. £450,000 was because that was what it cost Barney in the initial pay-off of £250,000."

Tweed claimed a private detective followed him and Bob McCartney: "When Barney was giving evidence he could not talk to his lawyers during that period. He could not meet us during lunch. Bob and I went to lunch in a bar near the High Court, Bittles, and there was a private investigator we knew watching us, to try and see if there was one wrong move, any contact between us and Barney. That is how low things slumped. It became so personal. Another incident was when Barney's guard dogs found a couple of intruders in the grounds, at the time he was in the witness box himself. Rightly or wrongly, we assumed private investigators had been keeping a watch on Barney even at his own private home. The intruders were lucky to have escaped in one piece!"

Faith in the BJ camp was unwavering, despite a constant drip-feed of opinion in firm favour of a McGuigan victory. "We always believed we would win. Some people believed we would lose the case," added Tweed, "Bob and I used to walk along the coastal path at Cultra, in the early hours of the morning to work out strategies for the next day. Throughout the trial, and indeed during the run up to it, I was constantly reminded by people of McGuigan's popularity - and that a Belfast Jury would never find against him. In fact, the opposite turned out to be the case, with Barney being miles ahead of Barry in the popularity stakes, which was borne out by the Jury's finding. Barney remained resolutely confident throughout the Hearing, notwithstanding the pessimism emanating from the Bar Library and legal circles, generally.

"Throughout the case we believe a steady flow of information was fed to the press, information favourable to McGuigan, and this in turn resulted in fairly negative coverage so far as Barney was concerned - at least in the run up to the jury's award. In contrast, our approach had been to keep all 'lips zipped' in order to ensure that no one had any idea as to our thoughts, our concerns or more importantly our strategy. We had also heard a Bentley limousine had been lined up for what was supposed to have been McGuigan's triumphant departure after the case, in the mistaken belief that he was going to be the victor. In the event, he still left in the Bentley, but with a very sorry look on his face!

The four-way meeting of minds - Eastwood, McCartney, Tweed and Stephens - helped to formulate a successful battle plan. It was to prove an exciting, yet often exasperating time, on both body and soul. McCartney, then regarded at the top of his game, and Stephens, a man of meticulous attachment to minute legal detail and painstaking research, worked in tandem to impressive effect. McCartney, a deep thinker and an aggressive advocate who came from a working-class background like Eastwood, was able to relate exceptionally well to the Belfast jury.

Given that the spin was stacked against BJ, it proved a remarkable piece of skilled strategy. The Eastwood survival was also down to a determined BJ, whose gut instincts and driving force maintained a high level of optimism in his team of defenders. Tweed also did some of his own detective work leading into what became the biggest libel case, at that time, in the island of Ireland. The biggest in the UK then involved Elton John. Why the McGuigan camp scorned a deal before heading in front of the Court was obvious. There was firm conviction McGuigan would win.

"The reason they did that was because they thought they had a star witness in a Dr Johnson, a houseman in a hospital in the United States that treated McGuigan," added Tweed, "In Northern Ireland you don't have to give a witness list. The Doctor brought in from America was their first witness. We were ambushed. We couldn't believe it, because Barney and I covered five US cities inside a week. We saw Shiminsky, the physiotherapist, in Denver. Then we flew down to Las Vegas to meet boxer Jeff Franklin. He knocked McGuigan down in sparring. When he came back to the training camp to again spar with him, he hoped would be a repeat performance, only on this occasion he was given a hard time by McGuigan. Unfortunately, Franklin, having originally agreed to attend the Hearing in Belfast, then decided not to come, saying Belfast was too dangerous.

"However, we got the fight referee Richard Steele in Las Vegas, and he came to Belfast. Also fight judge Guy Jutras. They were top class, really credible. We also spoke to Bob Arum and Miguel Diaz. We came back from the States and I thought it was in the bag, yet I was baffled we couldn't find this Dr Johnson. That was why they were so confident. Then, one of Bob's first questions to Dr Johnson was: 'You know about boxing?' The Doctor said, yes. Bob then says: 'Tell me, which hand would a southpaw lead with?' It was a 50-50 answer, but he got it wrong.

"Ben Stephens, a great legal mind who worked superbly with Bob to make it an excellent team, flicked through the pages of the book on the libel to pick up on points. One of the classic lines in the Case, and quite poignant, I felt, was when Bob McCartney questioned McGuigan on a point. Bob said: 'When you were ill in hospital Barney and Frances called up with a flask of home-made vegetable soup for you. Do you not remember that?' The answer was: 'Ok big deal, they brought up some soup.' Bob slowly and deliberately turned away from McGuigan, faced the jury, and said: 'Will you give this man credit for nothing?' I could see a wee shift in the jury. It was a very important turn in the case, even if it sounds totally innocuous - yet showing he (McGuigan) wouldn't give Barney credit for anything."

Self-confessed workaholic Tweed thrives on the chase and the challenge, and built an international reputation from the McGuigan-Eastwood legal war: "It certainly got me noticed," he conceded, "That case was very helpful to me. The Eastwood case was a huge one for me, a tremendous experience, yet I knew nothing about boxing. I was not at any of the McGuigan fights. I hadn't the time, too busy working. I work an 18-hour day. At that time my career was going through the roof, including major insurance claims. Along came the Eastwood-McGuigan case, lasting five weeks. Barney is one of the most interesting guys I've met. He is epic company, absolutely, and that kept us going through the case. He has the most astute judgement. I call him golden gloves. He believes in living on the edge.

"Before Eastwood-McGuigan I was involved in the so-termed 'Cream Bun' libel case against the *Sunday World* newspaper in the mid-80's. That was a big one. After Eastwood cases things developed into defending in libel cases for Liam Neeson, then Britney Spears, Harrison Ford, Jennifer Lopez and Van Morrison. Eastwood was the biggest case up to then."

The Eastwood-McGuigan case developed into an amazingly absorbing legal battle. The world awaited with baited breath. The general consensus of opinion among the media covering the cut and thrust was one that leaned in favour of McGuigan emerging victorious.

Deric Henderson, Ireland Editor of the *Press Association,* said: "It was the most dramatic Court case I ever covered, and that includes cases such as the Shankill Butchers, the Gibraltar Inquests, and the Supergrass Trials. Nothing could compare with the drama that unfolded in the Belfast High Court in the hours leading up to the judgement. Before the jury found in favour of Barney Eastwood I had my story written, ready to file the copy over the telephone, so confident Barry McGuigan would win the case. There was me, before computer laptops came into being, waiting on the jury verdict, and with my story penned in my notebook.

"I think I had words such as 'Former World boxing champion Barry McGuigan delivered a knockout blow to his former manager Barney Eastwood at the High Court in Belfast. The jury awarded him . . . ' but left space for the damages to be revealed. I also remember standing in the foyer of the Courthouse, near Barney Eastwood, as we all awaited the call to go back into court for the verdict. I said to Barney that McGuigan looked like winning. He said to me: 'Would like to put a wager on that?'. I will never forget when the verdict was announced. I glanced round me to see McGuigan's head going back. He was in a bench behind me. I was in the body of the court. I glanced over my left shoulder, and saw Barry McGuigan's head falling back 180 degrees."

Born in Omagh in 1951, Henderson added: "It was the most dramatic finish to a court case in my 40 years of reporting. I wouldn't know a lightweight boxer from a heavyweight, but this High Court case was edge-of-the-seat drama. This one was absolutely sensational stuff."

Eastwood will always have those amazing moments etched in his head: "Leading up to the final day of the case.there was a whisper circulating the Law Courts that we were not doing very well, and it was felt the jury seemed to be leaning towards McGuigan. A few members of the media had picked up on this, and I believe it was clouding their judgement. The fact our team had been under strict orders to remain completely silent during the case may have given the opposition the view that we were not confident. However, nothing could have been further from the truth. Our legals had always been confident right throughout the case. All our homework had been done. Paul Tweed was consistently confident. His motto was - 'the battle must be won before it is fought.'

"The fact we were silent gave the opposition the impression we were not confident. Nothing was coming from our side. It was a case of 'Mum's the word'. I remember Paul Tweed saying to me: 'We are doing all right', but it must be silence from everyone. I said I was as silent as the grave. Our legals thought when McGuigan started to answer questions from Robert McCartney he did his best to look a little innocent schoolboy. By the time McCartney had finished with him he portrayed a completely different look. Around that time I believe I remarked to our team - and it was picked up by some members of the media - that McGuigan had the face of an angel and the mind of a fox. He didn't fool the jury."

Eastwood then disclosed what he considered two other crucial happenings generally overlooked during the twists and turns of the legal battle. These involved training camp notes taken by the late Eddie Shaw before the contest in Las Vegas, and a special medical brace used to help McGuigan overcome ankle damage at Palm Springs. The hand-written document and the brace were gathered up from a hotel room after the fight in Las Vegas by Eastwood security man Danny McAllen, a former policeman.

BJ added: "It was discovered, at a late stage, that the document we came across was in Eddie's writing, and midway through the case his widow, Mary Shaw confirmed that it was her late husband's handwriting. I think we had to ask special permission from the Judge to have this entered as evidence. Mary came down to the Court. She was called to the box to confirm it was Eddie's hand writing, and I believe it was also confirmed by a hand-writing expert. The document gave a record of the daily training programme for McGuigan at Palm Springs. It revealed the number of rounds sparred by McGuigan, and weights taken, during the days prior to having the ankle injury - and then the gap caused by the ankle injury. Then it showed the daily sparring after the restart, and the rounds involved and against whom right up to going from the training camp to the fight in Las Vegas."

On the issue of the medical brace he added: "Danny McAllen gave evidence, and had to withstand a battery of verbal punches because his story at first, of the special strapping, was not believed. The QC gave him a very hard time. It was suggested 'the court had only Danny's word for it'. This, in my view, was one of the high points in the case - when McAllen said he could prove it, because he had the brace with him. He bent down and came up with the item to show it to everyone. From being a pinnacle discussion, to try and make us look bad, all of a sudden it was made out it was not important he had it.

"These were some of the main reasons why we felt confident we would win the case. A couple of reporters gathered around me shortly before the decision was announced. Some asked - are you confident? I said there were reasons why I thought we would win. Our legal team felt McGuigan did not impress the jury. We had the soup situation, the Eddie Shaw notes on training, and the medical brace - all crucial parts of our strategy. I also added I had right on my side, and said McGuigan was the best looked-after, best catered-for fighter from this island.

"It also must be remembered the bookmakers in Belfast were offering McGuigan at odds against, something like 5 to 4. Also, there was a rumour a few large cash bets had been placed on McGuigan to win. All along they were saying McGuigan was a lovely wee boy, and that many people were on his side."

McGuigan would appear to have read the whole thing wrong from Day One, because the ordinary man in the street clearly had confidence in Eastwood. He was from here, worked and lived here, still lives here, had a great friendship with boxers and the public here, not only in Belfast but also throughout the country, from as far back as the 1960's. Any enquiries around his homeland confirm that this loyalty, friendship and respect remains to this day.

Eastwood said: "For that final court case, the bookmakers understood the situation, and got it right by making me the favourite and McGuigan odds against. It then came down to that final day in the court. I sat quietly when the Jury went out. The real climax was when the Jury came back in again, with the verdict. I'd never seen a courthouse so full of people. It was bunged. You could hear a pin dropping. It was like trying to squeeze 20,000 fans into the Ulster Hall. All of a sudden the result is given, and this enormous cheer went up.

"There was uproar in the Court. People got up and cheered, as if somebody knocked somebody out. It was massive. You would have thought it was a World title fight. Despite all that I don't know why I didn't get up from my seat. Even Frances got up. The only person who did not get up was me. I just sat there. I showed no emotion."

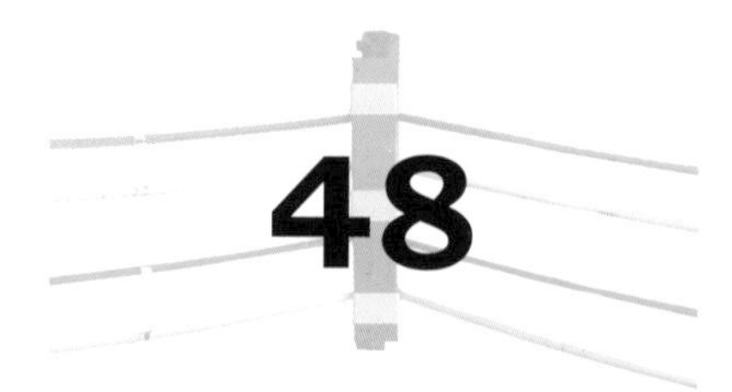

PICKING UP PIECES

FOLLOWING the end to the protracted draining legal wrangles, and the final curtain on McGuigan's fight career, the Cyclone continued to work on developing other interests. He eventually became a ubiquitous boxing analyst and showbiz personality. Eastwood and McGuigan have, no doubt, their own contrasting personal thoughts on why the unpalatable happened. The demons may well remain.

The heartbreak of Las Vegas heralded the blunt reality that the golden days were over. There would be no more: 'Thank you very much, Mr Eastwood' - and all those happy incidents and outstanding ring results. Gone for good were the spinetingling fight shows, fading to shadowy memory of a very special time. I suppose varied opinion on the end was permissible after the fall-out. Reams of so-called informed opinion from self-styled impeachable sources filled the newspapers, endless words voiced during radio and television interviews. It was of no consequence. There would be no patching up of differences. It was beyond the death rattle threshold. The fatal split between Eastwood and McGuigan had to play out a painstakingly lengthy and distressing course.

Eastwood reflected on the glory days: "Of course it was because of McGuigan I came back into boxing. He (McGuigan) was a great draw. The publicity generated was tremendous. Everybody liked him. It all fitted in. He just came on the scene at the right time. Not only because of his ability but also he had great charisma. He was also king of the gym, although there is no doubt I had far more respect from and more camaraderie with all the other fighters in the gym. They got on well with me, and never complained. He (McGuigan) was always travelling first class, while the other boxers were in tourist class."

Two decades after the earthquake-style crack in the crust of one of Irish boxing's greatest periods you could still smell a whiff of cordite. Eastwood emerged from being vilified to securing vindication, yet I felt it prudent to shadowbox around the edges of the remains. Time, it is said, is generally the great healer. In this case, not so. We still ponder why such a magnificently enjoyable chapter in boxing should come a cropper; why BJ and Barry hit the buffers in what was surely a tragedy of monumental proportions.

The rancour remained, following the battery of legal cases that finally completed the trainwreck of what had been a fascinating father-son relationship. The Eastwood-McGuigan days in the sun helped people rise above the gloomy times of the 'Troubles' in Northern Ireland. The high-profile break-up all but ended a golden time in Irish professional boxing. Eastwood, however, insisted the sadness and the ill-fated venture in Las Vegas could have been prevented, perhaps the split delayed. Until now, he was reluctant to talk about one of the greatest fall-outs in prizefighting since the 'Manassa Mauler', Irish-American Jack Dempsey, parted company with his manager Jack 'Doc' Kearns over alleged financial problems. That the Eastwood-McGuigan parting could have been avoided is of no significance today.

Eastwood claimed: "The dark days of the court cases I did not want to happen. For sure, it all could have been avoided. I did everything I could to try and prevent the court cases from happening. But they (McGuigan's legal advisers) bombarded me in every way with all sorts of things. I said it was a nonsense. They wouldn't stop. I said I would give them all the trouble they wanted. I continued to say this shouldn't be done and that shouldn't be done, and tried to get in touch with them several times. I later said, during a TV interview after the final big Court case, that he (McGuigan) had more advisers than the Queen had soldiers. The Court cases, everything, could have been avoided - the Gomez fight taken, and so forth - but before all that happened we have to be proud of what he achieved, and also after he retired from boxing, just are we are proud of Dave Boy."

Professional sports take a normal hold on most folk worldwide, should it be the magnetic attraction of golf, soccer, baseball, rugby, grid iron or boxing. The reason for this, I believe, is because of the many professional sporting personalities. I cannot help but think of exemplary athletes such as Muhammad Ali, Sugar Ray Robinson, Pele, George Best and Tiger Woods who displayed such a high level of ability that glorified their physical capabilities. Once the perceived shimmer of near invincibility slips from a top professional sportsperson, he or she becomes an ordinary mortal like the rest of us. Barry McGuigan seemed to be destined for the high altar, until his career unravelled with almost surgical swiftness. Still, what we retain forever from the McGuigan-Eastwood saga is the warm memory of the best days.

Eastwood seen with McGuigan and former World Lightweight champion Ken Buchanan before a sparring session.

Top Rank promoter Bob Arum meets Barry McGuigan, cuts ace Paddy Byrne and Eastwood.

Panamanian legend Roberto Duran greets McGuigan and Eastwood.

Old Cookstown neighbours meet in Belfast - the late Tony McAuley, a song writer, Irish traditonal musician and BBC TV *and* Radio Ulster *programme producer, with B.J. and Frances Eastwood.*

Early days in McGuigan's career - seen in a playful fight promotion shoot with Eastwood, Gilbey's show backer Trevor McClintock and promoter Stephen Eastwood (right).

Glory moment as McGuigan hugs Eastwood after winning the World title.

Former World champion Juan LaPorte with mentor Howie Albert before meeting McGuigan in a cross-roads contest in Belfast, 1985.

Panamanian legend Eusebio Pedroza.

McGuigan sqares off in defining test against Juan LaPorte.

McGuigan-Pedroza in toe to toe action.

Happy times for McGuigan and coach Eddie Shaw, after winning the British title.

10-6-85

He's the greatest

EMOTIONS ran high long into the night after Barry's breathtaking dismantling of Pedroza. And deep within the bowels of QPR's magnificent building there was a private and extremely touching scene involving McGuigan and manager Barney Eastwood.

It took some time for the dust to settle from the moment McGuigan's hand was raised aloft by South African referee Stan Christopoulous and the Cyclone was declared king of the world.

Leaving the ring proved a back-slapping obstacle race for the new champion and then he had to endure, still in his boxing kit, a lengthy Press conference in the QPR's players' lounge.

Almost one hour later, Barry had managed to take a well-deserved shower and a few beaming smiles into a mirror

Barry talks exclusively to the News Letter's Denis O'Hara in his dressing room after his victory

himself it was all for real.

Surrounded by security men and officials, Barry's private quarters were shut off from the ecstatic Press, public and well-meaning friends ... but I had the privilege of staying with the super hero ... an experience I won't ever forget.

McGuigan and the man who had faith in the magnificent fighting machine from Co Monaghan realised what had really happened ... the dream had been realised; they were now away from all the hype and hassle.

The wee man and the Boss stared at each other in mutual admiration.

"Son," says B J "we've done it ... we've done it ... you are some kid ... what a performance."

Barry nodded. Both men quietly embraced. McGuigan let a trickle of tears run down his face. It was a proud father-successful son scene.

And then B J said: "We are there now. Who would have believed that a wee kid from Clones is now king of the world. You are the king. You will be champion of the world until you decide to retire."

Barry replied: "But boss, I still cannot believe it is over ... that I'm the champion. Pedroza had some class but I still cannot feel the big feeling I anticipated I might if I won.

"Now that I've done it, it just seems, for the moment anyhow, like after another big fight

To Page 2

The author's special report of McGuigan's historic breakthrough at Loftus Road.

Dave 'Boy' McAuley checks up on his status in the Ring *Record book of 1986/'87.*

McGuigan sensationally drops Pedroza at Loftus Road.

Dave 'Boy' McAuley on his way to dethroning IBF Flyweight king Duke McKenzie.

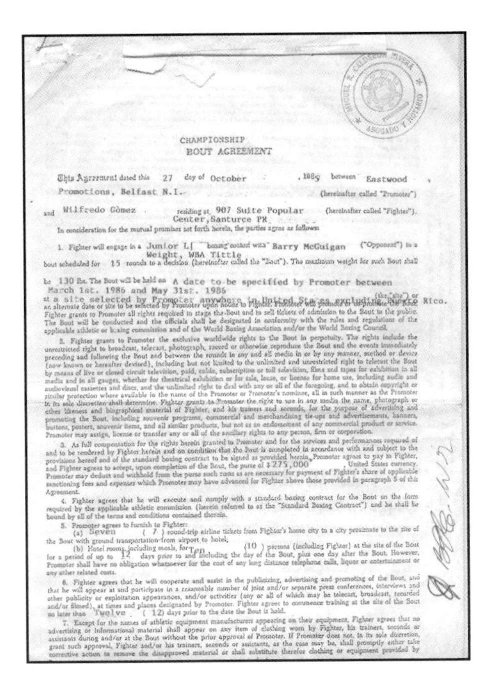

CHAMPIONSHIP
BOUT AGREEMENT

This Agreement dated this 27 day of October, 1985 between Eastwood Promotions, Belfast N.I. (hereinafter called "Promoter") and Wilfredo Gòmez residing at 907 Suite Popular Center, Santurce PR (hereinafter called "Fighter").

In consideration for the mutual promises set forth herein, the parties agree as follows:

1. Fighter will engage in a Junior L[Weight, WBA Tittle boxing contest with Barry McGuigan ("Opponent") in a bout scheduled for 15 rounds to a decision (hereinafter called the "Bout"). The maximum weight for such Bout shall be 130 lbs. The Bout will be held on A date to be specified by Promoter between March 1st. 1986 and May 31st. 1986 at a site selected by Promoter anywhere in United States excluding Puerto Rico. (the "site") or an alternate date or site to be selected by Promoter upon notice to Fighter. Promoter will promote or co-promote the Bout. Fighter grants to Promoter all rights required to stage the Bout and to sell tickets of admission to the Bout to the public. The Bout will be conducted and the officials shall be designated in conformity with the rules and regulations of the applicable athletic or boxing commission and of the World Boxing Association and/or the World Boxing Council.

2. Fighter grants to Promoter the exclusive worldwide rights to the Bout in perpetuity. The rights include the unrestricted right to broadcast, telecast, photograph, record or otherwise reproduce the Bout and the events immediately preceding and following the Bout and between the rounds in any and all media in or by any manner, method or device (now known or hereafter devised), including but not limited to the unlimited and unrestricted right to telecast the Bout by means of live or closed circuit television, paid, cable, subscription or toll television, films and tapes for exhibition in all media and in all gauges, whether for theatrical exhibition or for sale, lease, or license for home use, including audio and audiovisual cassettes and discs, and the unlimited right to deal with any or all of the foregoing, and to obtain copyright or similar protection where available in the name of the Promoter or Promoter's nominee, all in such manner as the Promoter in its sole discretion shall determine. Fighter grants to Promoter the right to use in any media the name, photograph or other likeness and biographical material of Fighter, and his trainers and seconds, for the purpose of advertising and promoting the Bout, including souvenir programs, commercial and merchandising tie-ups and advertisements, banners, buttons, posters, souvenir items, and all similar products, but not as an endorsement of any commercial product or service. Promoter may assign, license or transfer any or all of the ancillary rights to any person, firm or corporation.

3. As full compensation for the rights herein granted to Promoter and for the services and performances required of and to be rendered by Fighter herein and on condition that the Bout is completed in accordance with and subject to the provisions hereof and of the standard boxing contract to be signed as provided herein, Promoter agrees to pay to Fighter, and Fighter agrees to accept, upon completion of the Bout, the purse of $275,000, United States currency. Promoter may deduct and withhold from the purse such sums as are necessary for payment of Fighter's share of applicable sanctioning fees and expenses which Promoter may have advanced for Fighter above those provided in paragraph 5 of this Agreement.

4. Fighter agrees that he will execute and comply with a standard boxing contract for the Bout on the form required by the applicable athletic commission (herein referred to as the "Standard Boxing Contract") and he shall be bound by all of the terms and conditions contained therein.

5. Promoter agrees to furnish to Fighter:
(a) Seven (7) round-trip airline tickets from Fighter's home city to a city proximate to the site of the Bout with ground transportation from airport to hotel;
(b) Hotel rooms, including meals, for Ten (10) persons (including Fighter) at the site of the Bout for a period of up to 12 days prior to and including the day of the Bout, plus one day after the Bout. However, Promoter shall have no obligation whatsoever for the cost of any long distance telephone calls, liquor or entertainment or any other related costs.

6. Fighter agrees that he will cooperate and assist in the publicizing, advertising and promoting of the Bout, and that he will appear at and participate in a reasonable number of joint and/or separate press conferences, interviews and other publicity or exploitation appearances, and/or activities (any or all of which may be telecast, broadcast, recorded and/or filmed), at times and places designated by Promoter. Fighter agrees to commence training at the site of the Bout no later than Twelve (12) days prior to the date the Bout is held.

7. Except for the names of athletic equipment manufacturers appearing on their equipment, Fighter agrees that no advertising or informational material shall appear on any item of clothing worn by Fighter, his trainers, seconds or assistants during and/or at the Bout without the prior approval of Promoter. If Promoter does not, in its sole discretion, grant such approval, Fighter and/or his trainers, seconds or assistants, as the case may be, shall promptly either take corrective action to remove the disapproved material or shall substitute therefor clothing or equipment provided by

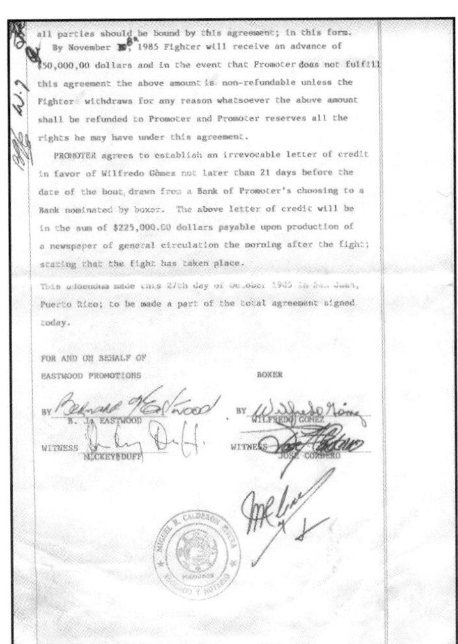

all parties should be bound by this agreement; in this form.

By November 15, 1985 Fighter will receive an advance of $50,000,00 dollars and in the event that Promoter does not fulfill this agreement the above amount is non-refundable unless the Fighter withdraws for any reason whatsoever the above amount shall be refunded to Promoter and Promoter reserves all the rights he may have under this agreement.

PROMOTER agrees to establish an irrevocable letter of credit in favor of Wilfredo Gòmez not later than 21 days before the date of the bout, drawn from a Bank of Promoter's choosing to a Bank nominated by boxer. The above letter of credit will be in the sum of $225,000.00 dollars payable upon production of a newspaper of general circulation the morning after the fight; stating that the fight has taken place.

This addendum made this 27th day of October 1985 in San Juan, Puerto Rico; to be made a part of the total agreement signed today.

FOR AND ON BEHALF OF
EASTWOOD PROMOTIONS

BY B. J. EASTWOOD

WITNESS MICKEY DUFF

BOXER

BY WILFREDO GOMEZ

WITNESS JOSE CORDERO

Top and bottom part of Gomez contract agreement.

Irish Independent

SPECIAL EDITION

WEATHER

Appeal KO leaves McGuigan facing £½m libel bill

McGuigan throws in towel

Re-launch

Terms

BBC in libel pay-out to Eastwood

MILLIONAIRE bookmaker Barney Eastwood was awarded libel damages today over remarks by Barry McGuigan – the boxer he guided to a world crown before their well-publicised split.

In the High Court in Belfast the BBC agreed to pay substantial damages to Mr Eastwood and also apologised to him.

The case arose out of a broadcast in May 1989 in the 'Sporting Greats' series when the former world champion was interviewed by Eamonn Holmes.

Ben Stephens, QC, said it was suggested in the programme that Mr Eastwood, who was Barry McGuigan's manager, had not prepared him properly for a world championship defence in 1986 when he lost his title to Steve Cruz.

"This allegation was entirely without foundation and reflected adversely on Mr Eastwood's professional integrity," said Mr Stephens.

He said the BBC regretted publishing the allegation, withdrew it unreservedly and wished to apologise publicly to Mr Eastwood.

"The BBC has agreed to pay Mr Eastwood a substantial sum by way of damages and to pay his legal costs."

Mr Stephens said Mr Eastwood accepted the BBC did not wish or intend to attack his reputation.

Henry Toner, QC, said the BBC wished to associate itself with the remarks by Mr Eastwood's counsel and to repeat their regret that the allegation was broadcast.

Outside the court Paul Tweed, a partner in law firm Johnsons, said: "Although Mr Eastwood was extremely disappointed the BBC should have seen fit to allow the broadcast in the first place, he is very satisfied with the outcome, including the categoric apology by the BBC.

"He hopes that this will finally see an end to a saga which had already been the subject of a clear and decisive jury verdict in our client's favour some time ago."

Mr Tweed was referring to the 1992 libel action when Mr Eastwood was awarded £450,000 against Mr McGuigan and Channel 5 Video Ltd over the boxer's remarks about his condition prior to the Cruz fight in Las Vegas.

Barney Eastwood: Damages for McGuigan remarks

JOHNSONS SOLICITORS

THE SUNDAY TRIBUNE

Bonar law
The clash of absolutes in the abortion debate. News

UMP collapse
Tatters, the beef industry in chaos. News

Limerick rugby
An eight page celebration of the best club rugby in Ireland. Pages 33 to 40

BARNEY V BARRY

Outright win: Legal punch-up ends with 450,000 award to manager

Eastwood lands libel KO

JOHNSONS

Sad conclusion to the Eastwood-McGuigan liason through libel case reports in the Irish Independent *and* Sunday Tribune.

Dave McAuley, sporting a bruised left eye from his upset win against Duke McKenzie in London, watches his boss B.J. Eastwood and coach Eddie Shaw hold aloft the IBF World Flyweight belt as they descend from Eastwood's private plane at Newtownards airport

British Board of Contol official Deryk Monteith presents the Board's 'Fight of the Year' gong to Dave 'Boy' McAuley in 1987. Included is coach Eddie Shaw and the Board's Medical officer Dr Pat McHugh.

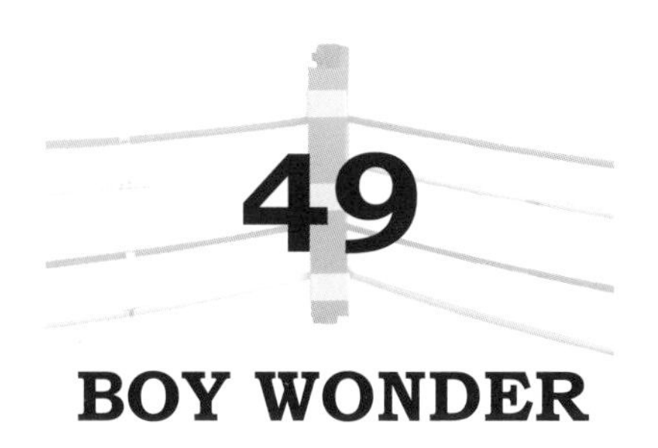

49

BOY WONDER

DAVE 'Boy' McAuley emerged from the shadow of Barry McGuigan to stamp his own distinctive brand of unpredictable mayhem. He was the Eastwood camp's lean, mean machine. Tall for a flyweight, at 5' 7", he generally held a height and reach advantage over opponents. Rising Phoenix-like from the ashes, despite such a depressing time caused by the shuddering demise of the Cyclone, McAuley stepped into the boxing breech. An underscored talent of one-punch ability, he picked up the baton to maintain the boxing buzz in Belfast.

The 'Boy' spectacularly defied the laws of gravity by repeatedly bouncing off the canvas to win fights in the most thrilling circumstances. Born on June 15, 1961, 17 miles from Belfast in Larne, County Antrim, he made his professional debut on October 5, 1983. A former top amateur light-flyweight and then flyweight champion, he had a relatively short career. But, boy was it spectacular and always interesting!

By his 13th fight he became the fourth Northern Ireland fighter to win the British Flyweight Championship. He followed in the footsteps of Hugh Russell, John Caldwell and Rinty Monaghan by knocking out Scotland's 'Wee' Joe Kelly in the ninth round in Glasgow on October 20, 1986. It has to be remembered by this time the Cyclone was sadly out of the Eastwood picture. In his 14th bout Dave became the new Irish idol, ironically through losing in one of the most sensationally brutal battles seen in the King's Hall ring. Eastwood felt his heavy hitter had a chance against one of the world's best small scrappers of that era, Colombia's Fidel Bassa. BJ was almost right.

The brave 'Boy' somehow survived a torrid first round, including an eight-count and a cut on his right eyebrow. The unbeaten Bassa seemed bemused that the new British king was still upright and coming back. The

South American looked shocked when shipping a huge left hook in the second round. He then resorted to dangerous use of his head and was lectured by Chicago referee Nate Morgan. It became tales of the unexpected as McAuley grew in confidence, mainly through shots to the body, and helped to make it an amazing slugfest. He staggered Bassa with a left hook in the fifth, and then had the champion down from the same punch in the sixth stanza, but bafflingly no count was given by the referee.

In the seventh round it was Bassa's turn to sustain facial damage, a gash on his right eyebrow. Again he was ticked off for alleged head-butting. In the next round McAuley suffered a cut below his left eye, and also nose damage, but came within a whisker of winning in a phenomenal ninth round. He twice dumped the champion to the canvas. With the fans feverishly urging him on through the pain barrier, and adding chants of 'Here we go' the first move was off the ropes with a snappy left hook counter - and after Bassa surfaced from the boards he nailed him with a right uppercut. Bassa gained unsteady legs, and held on like a leech over the closing thirty pulsating seconds to deny McAuley another clean shot. This survival action was to save his title.

Sadly, the 'Boy' did not get another chance and suffered a 13th-round knock-out on April 25, 1987. Referee Morgan tolled out the fateful 'ten' after 1.45. Not of great consolation to the fighting Irishman was the fact the 25-year-old McAuley was ahead on all three cards before a mixture of exhaustion when Bassa's power ended the argument. Judge Harmodo Cedeno's tally was 115-112, Ove Ovesen 114-112, and York vanNixon 114-112. By losing with such bravery during a white-knuckle brawl, in what was also the last 15-rounder for this Championship belt, the part-time chef from the Antrim Coast became an overnight family favourite. The cracking contest was recognised by the British Boxing Board of Control for the 1987 'British Contest of the Year' honour. Amazingly, it was the fight to ignite McAuley's career, and regarded in some quarters the best contest in the world that year.

Other Eastwood fighters on that super show were Sam Storey, Roy Webb, Alan McCullough (older brother of ex-WBC Bantamweight champion Wayne McCullough), Bernardo Checa, Paul Hodkinson, and Belfast's heavy-handed former ABA Lightweight champion Eamonn McAuley, a grandnephew of Rinty Monaghan. It was an unexpected elevation for Dave Boy, to be trading leather with Bassa; to materialise from relative obscurity to gain a crack at a World title. To be blunt, he had no right to be in the same ring as the chunky South American, as he was nowhere near the top ten in the World rankings. Afterall, he slimmed from bantamweight to plunder the British Flyweight championship from

Kelly yet one fight later he was involved in the mesmeric match with Bassa. How did that happen?

Eastwood pulled a few strings, and conceded: "From a World level aspect Dave was really inexperienced. I had to speak with a few of 'my pals' in South America. Dave's big chance inadvertently came out of the fact I attended the Bassa title win against the defending champion Hilario Zapata on February 13, 1987, in Barranquilla, Colombia. "I have never seen a fight like this, tremendous. The contest was outdoors, in the Country Club Tennis Stadium. Zapata was boxing the lugs off Bassa for a while. Then Bassa came back into the fight. On one occasion he backed Zapata into a corner when some guy on the edge of the ring apron stuck his hand under the ropes and pulled Zapata's feet from under him. Zapata went down. The referee didn't notice the hand incident, and gave Zapata a count. What a carry on! Zapata lost his title on a unanimous decision."

After the fight Eastwood held a chat with Bassa's managerial team and suggested a handy job for the new champion would be in Belfast against McAuley. "Deep down I felt McAuley would have a puncher's chance," claimed Eastwood, "it was an expensive fight. When you bring in the champion of the World you have to pay them well. They look at their options, and it always ends up all about money."

After the unlucky 13th-round, and first loss of his career, there were new horizons awaiting the brave one. The fight fans wanted more of McAuley. Unfortunately, the title rematch against Bassa did not live up to expectations. In his 16th outing, on Saturday March 28, 1988, the 'Boy' lost a relatively tame and totally forgettable cat and mouse 12-rounder in the King's Hall. The judges this time had their respective sums all in favour of Bassa. Judge Lou Moret made it 114-113, Samuel Conde 115-113, and Mike Glienna 116-112. The bill also featured the rare Belfast appearance of Belfast's Oldpark-reared Terry Magee. Included were Roy Webb and Andy Holligan.

Next time out, McAuley shocked world boxing by pinching the IBF Flyweight version over twelve rounds, taking the title from multiple World champion Duke McKenzie in London. It was an amazing outcome. Dapper Duke was one of the most recognised and busy fighters of the late 1980's and early 1990's. The little Londoner became a triple World champion - at Flyweight, Bantamweight and Super-bantamweight. Croydon-born McKenzie lost to Welshman Steve Robinson in a bid to win a World Featherweight belt. The youngest of five brothers, including ex-British and Commonwealth Light-welterweight champion Clinton, he finished with a 39-7 record.

Slap bang in the middle of his career he bumped into Dave Boy. McKenzie won the vacant British Flyweight belt against Danny Flynn in his 11th outing, the European title from Charlie Magri in his 14th contest, and the IBF World Flyweight belt in his 21st contest. On October 5, 1988, he halted southpaw champion Rolando Bohol of the Philippines at Wembley, and defended successfully against California southpaw Tony DeLuca in the Royal Albert Hall. Unbeaten in 23 bouts, McKenzie had to endure the shock of losing to McAuley, a fighter whose World ambitions seemed somewhat vague after twice losing to Bassa. Still, 'The Boy' upset the applecart by outsmarting McKenzie. It was something of an accident when Dave was handed the career-defining crack at the Duke.

Eastwood explained how the opportunity came out of the blue. Mickey Duff managed McKenzie, and probably thought Dave Boy couldn't upset the odds: "Duff rang me twenty days before the contest with a problem, to tell me somebody due in from overseas to fight McKenzie for the World Flyweight title in London had withdrawn. Mickey asked if I had anybody over in Belfast, who could help out by stepping in as a late replacement. He knew full well the only eligible fighter I had at the weight was Dave Boy. Obviously McAuley was the man for the job, but I said I wouldn't put Dave in at such short notice."

BJ confessed he played mind games with Duff, because Dave Boy was really in good shape at that time. He knew he would have his fighter ready. The bartering continued. Duff dithered, claiming he could not give much money to McAuley. Eastwood turned down the initial fight offer: "Soon we started to again talk money. Whatever the first purse offer was I was holding out for more. By now, Mickey was probably thinking this was an easy job for his fighter. He finally agreed terms, perhaps believing McAuley would not be really ready. Mickey perhaps also felt Dave Boy had little ambition after the two defeats against Bassa, merely taking the fight at three week's notice. He got a surprise."

McAuley remembered the intrigue that led to his third opportunity to win a World crown for a first time. He switched focus from trying to get his hands around the WBA belt to boxing for the IBF title. On June 7, 1989, he hit the jackpot despite being out of the ring for 15 months since that second fight against Bassa. He was a massive underdog against McKenzie. "But," claimed McAuley, "We hoodwinked Mickey Duff, Duke's manager/promoter, into thinking I was a soft touch. We let it out I was merely keen to bank a few pounds, that I wasn't training properly, and so on. I had an idea I could beat McKenzie. I studied tapes of some of his fights, and came to the conclusion he was the classic bully in the ring. Everything had to go for him inside the ropes. By that, I mean he had to get things his own way. He didn't like being pushed back. We went to London ten days before the fight at Wembley Arena. Nobody came near me. The media folk in London were not interested in me. I was Dave Who?

"I was a 5-to-1 rank outsider, a hick from the sticks, and given no chance. I was happy with that situation because I was under no pressure. I attended press conferences, including some in the famous Thomas A'Beckett gym. I was hardly noticed. I may have been asked one or two silly questions. It was all about Duke McKenzie, which was fine. He was 23 and Zero on his record going into the contest. I knew from the first round I was going to beat McKenzie. I suspect he also knew. I caught him with a cracking left hook to the body in that first round. I can remember it well. He was hurt. I could hear him gasp.

"I knew from then on the fight was mine, and I won nearly every round after that. Once, however, I picked up a cut above an eye. I could hear McKenzie's manager Duff yelling to the referee: 'His eye is cut, stop the fight.' I went on to take a unanimous decision." Former American Heavyweight Randy Neumann was the referee. The judging summaries were: Chris Wollesen 115-113, Berne Friedkin 117-110, and Mike Glienna 115-113. McAuley's breakthrough to the big league also earned him the British Boxing Board of Control's highest award as the 1991 'British Boxer of the Year'.

"After the contest there was a press conference in my dressing room," recalled McAuley, "McKenzie was the next big thing at that time. He was about to hit the top stuff in America, apparently. His fight against me attracted some American boxing writers. I got up midway through the press conference, and went round to Duke's dressing room. The only people in there were Duke and his brother Clinton. It was a big gunk for him to lose his title. I fully understood that. It was no big surprise to me their dressing room was almost empty. When you are a winner in the boxing game everybody wants to clap you on the back, can't do enough for you, keen to do something for you - open doors, carry bags. It's the same old story. Once you lose, nobody sticks around, as your so-called new friends melt away like snow off a ditch. I was left alone after I lost that first World title fight against Bassa. I knew how Duke felt that night. Once you lose in boxing no-one wants to know you."

The Boy's win of the World belt was superb. Not only did he provide magnificently thrilling and entertaining contests but also temporarily extended a disillusioned Eastwood's interest in professional boxing. The big banger also proved a delightfully refreshing outlet for the fans, taking the fight focus away from the the legal morass of the McGuigan-Eastwood break-up.

McAuley, a punching paradox, delayed the inevitability of Barney closing down the Castle Street gym, and proudly stated: "During my ring career I became the most successful post-War professional prize-fighter in Irish history, with five winning World title defences. Barney Eastwood made me. I also maintain he made Barry McGuigan, Hugh Russell, Crisanto Espana, Paul Hodkinson, Ray Close and Toby Cordoba. He also had a say in the making of Steve Collins and Eamonn Loughran, who started as a professional in the Castle Street gym. Also, there was Sam Storey. Barney ran the most successful gym in Europe at that time, and one of the top three professional gyms in the world. He steered six World champions through his gym, along with European and British champions. There is no doubt about it, he made Irish professional boxing in my time.

"I could not comment on what happened in Irish boxing before Barney Eastwood came on the fight scene. But, I do know he had a really big influence during a certain period on the boxing game in Ireland, and that stretched as far as England, to the Continent of Europe, and to America. He was a very big player in world boxing during the Eighties, and through a part of the Nineties, and once said to me: 'McAuley, when you retire I will' - and he did. It goes to show, without his involvement boxing died for a very long time in Northern Ireland.

"He was the biggest thing to hit professional boxing here, as far as I am concerned. Everybody in the fight game here benefited from the fact Barney Eastwood was behind it - the whole lot. If it wasn't for Barney you may never have heard of Barry McGuigan, nor of me. We might have boxed professionally, probably in England. But, in my opinion we would never have been looked after the same way, nor had the same successes. Regardless if you like or loathe Barney Eastwood he made superstars out of some of his fighters. It is there in black and white what he achieved in boxing, and for boxers. He is arguably the best thing that ever happened to Irish fighting. Certainly, boxing in Northern Ireland had a very good run for twelve special years."

Overlooked by the Irish Amateur Boxing Association for a place in the Irish team at the 1980 Moscow Olympics, a dispirited McAuley, who had legendary southpaw Olympic Games bronze medallist and Commonwealth Games gold winner Jim McCourt as his coach in the Belfast St Agnes Club, decided to turn professional. He approached Eastwood, and joined the stable in the slipstream of Barry McGuigan and Hugh Russell.

The 'Boy' recalled: "I won All-Ireland Junior and Senior Amateur titles under Jim McCourt, and made the international team. Jim was a good coach. I turned professional under him, but then I suggested we go downtown to the Eastwood gym, where there were professionals and I could get in some top sparring." However, McCourt would not go to the Eastwood gym with McAuley. Instead, Dave's uncle Jim O'Neill, his mother Marion's brother, went with him to strike a deal with Eastwood. Out of the ring for some time, there was hard work to be done before he made his debut as a professional fighter. His first introduction to sparring in the Eastwood Gym was against McGuigan. "I sparred three rounds, and he put me down," recalled McAuley, "He apologised to me after every big punch. Barry hit me with two great head shots, and one powerful body punch. He was very strong."

McAuley also sparred with the overseas help brought in for McGuigan, people like Puerto Rico's Carmelo Negron, who was based in Illinois. Negron stood just under 5' 2". His 33-bout career had 24 wins, and 23 of those by knockout. That sort of quality sparring helped to bring McAuley to an acceptable level of sharpness. The 'Boy' made an undistinguished start on October 5, 1983, in a draw over six rounds in the Ulster Hall against Manchester-based journeyman John Mwaimu. It almost proved the end before the beginning.

He explained: "I made a statement to my family if I lost my first fight it would be my last, that I would instantly quit boxing, pack it in for good. It was a close call, and that draw just kept me in there. Maybe I should have taken the hint then and quit, but that draw kept me hanging in. I later outpointed Mwaimu in my sixth fight, at the King's Hall on October 13, 1984." McAuley scored a 59-57.5 win then, with the mathematics by referee Barney Wilson.

The bantamweight match was on the undercard of McGuigan blasting skinny South American Felipe Orozco in two rounds. McAuley chinned eight opponents in his 18 wins. However, he also became familiar with the shape and heat strength of the lights above the rings. Dave spent many anxious moments staring up at them, from a horizontal position, yet suffered merely one stoppage defeat. He was a bit of a 'canvas-back' at times, and made no secret of the fact he was dumped on the seat of his pants 22 times in 23 contests. The statistic is an astonishing anomaly.

"I had a cauliflower arse," cracked the witty McAuley, whose place in World boxing has been understated. His three defeats were in World title tests against Colombians Fidel Bassa (2) and Rodolfo Blanco. Game as badger, and a boxing reporter's dream, Dave used to declare before contests he would 'batter' opponents into submission. Quite often he did, but had to endure some hairy moments of high anxiety. He often left his fans open-mouthed and wondering if the wiry one would survive. Who can forget the first blood-curdling confrontations with Bassa and Blanco?

The first fight against Bassa, named the British 'Contest of the Year', and then a 12-rounder IBF title defence against Blanco rank as two of the most thrilling brawls ever witnessed in the King's Hall arena. Not unlike Billy Conn's famous first tilt at the World Heavyweight title against Joe Louis, the 'Boy' was within touching distance of causing a major upset against the fearsome Bassa. It remains a case of what might have been. Three rounds to go he was in front.

McAuley said: "People still argue I would have been the WBA champion had it been a 12-rounder. I don't subscribe to that theory. If it had been a 12-rounder that contest would have been fought differently, on his behalf and on mine. I was ahead on the judges cards after 12 rounds, but circumstances would have been different in a shorter fight. The whole pace of the contest would have been different. I had three rounds to go, a long time in a tough contest. I was down in the first round. He was down twice in the ninth round. It was a real big occasion for me. Imagine me boxing for a World title in my 14th contest.

"That must be some sort of a record. Don't forget, the guy who beat me took the WBA Flyweight title from one of the all time greats of boxing, Hilario Zapata, who had 21 defences of his title. The first contest against Bassa and the first against Blanco were the two toughest fights of my career. The rematch with Bassa was a big letdown. It didn't sparkle. There was no repeat brawl. Each of us knew one mistake could result in being knocked out. I was beaten, no excuses, although some folk thought I deserved a draw."

After winning the IBF version, McAuley ran into another Columbian tough nut, Blanco. The 'Boy' concedes he was more than fortunate not only to avoid a knock-out loss but to also retain the title on a disputed decision, on September 15, 1990. Fortunately for McAuley, referee Waldemar Schmidt seemed to be, like the fans, hypnotised by the furious action. The 'Boy' twice hit the deck in the second round. How he stayed afloat is probably down to the quick thinking of his cornermen. Bernardo Checa seemed to spin between the ropes a precious second before the bell sounded and drag the confused, almost limp, fighter back to his stool.

Anyone who has ever consumed heavy concussive thumps like that to the whiskers knows the complete scenario appears to slip to slow motion. The brain is scrambled. The mind records noise and instructions arriving from a distance, in echo-like waves as if coming from the bottom of an empty oil drum. Amazingly, McAuley survived a serious crisis. The cornermen kept cool, yet worked like fury during the sixty seconds respite and then pushed their hero back into the firing line. McAuley consumed flash knockdowns in the 3rd and 11th rounds. But he was not in real trouble during those trips to the canvas. The turning point to save the title in arguable circumstance was Dave's sensational switch and swivel of the hips and shoulders to a southpaw attack and floor Blanco in the ninth round.

On the final bell my ringside sums suggested the Boy's bravery in bombing back from the brink would certainly influence the three judges. I believed McAuley could keep his title on a draw verdict. Quite often the history of World Championship boxing outcomes, never mind the undercard hometowners, make you squirm. Even McAuley looked sheepishly down at his bootlaces, relieved when awarded the unanimous decision. Judge Frank Brinette was closest to reality with his 113-111 tally. Judge Knud Jenson made it 117-113, while former World Middleweight contender Attilio 'Rocky' Castellani was exceedingly generous when awarding the fight to the champion on a five-round margin of 115-110.

Castellani was a very welcome guest to Belfast, adding lustre to the the occasion. Born in Luzerne, Pennsylvania, on May 26, 1926, the former US Marine had an impressive ring track record of 65-14-4, boxing during what some fight folk classed the golden era of the Middleweights. He lost over 15 rounds in San Francisco in a 1954 World Middleweight Championship contest against Hawaii's Carl 'Bobo' Olson. His opponents during a 13-year career also included magical Middleweight names such as Sugar Ray Robinson (even dropping the great one early in a losing bout), Joey Giardello, Billy Graham, Kid Gavilan, Johnny Bratton, Tony Janiro and Gene Fullmer. Castellani, who had his first six fights under the 'nom-de-guerre' of Rocky Wargo, died aged 82 in August 2008. Rocky must have been highly impressed by McAuley's magnificent display of sheer guts. The Irishman, fighting by instinct, was a sight to behold.

McAuley has little recollection of what happened in that second round: "Blanco had me down twice within a minute. I didn't know where I was, not a clue at the time if I was in the King's Hall or in the old King's Arms Hotel back in Larne. I was fortunate in my career to be blessed with a quick recovery rate. See, when I'm hit, and before I go down, just as my ass hits the canvas, I am alert. I have to admit, however, I was rightly scrambled that night against Blanco. He missed the boat. I did the switch that turned the fight, went from orthodox to southpaw, and nailed him. I put him down.

"His defence was so tight I couldn't get through before that with good punches, left hooks nor orthodox right-hand punches. I couldn't get to him, until then. My right-hand shots normally did not go in straight, nor my left hands. They went in around the side. A jab was no use, not enough power. I was also trying too hard to get a good clean crack at him. So, I just suddenly switched. Bang, and down he went. Respected TV boxing commentator Harry Carpenter said it was one of the best moves he ever witnessed in the ring. At the end, the points result could have gone either way. I was given the verdict, yet had the decision gone against me it would not have been an outrage. Blanco deserved a draw, and that would have been fine." Locally-based supporting fighters on that memorable production were Noel Magee, Close, Espana, Ritchie Wenton and Lowey.

BREAKTHROUGH

WINNING the IBF title made up for the twin disappointments against Bassa. The Boy, voted the 1991 British 'Boxer of the Year', enjoyed some rich reward, including an eye-catching defence against South Africa's intriguing tiny tearaway, 'Baby' Jake Matlala, who, like McKenzie, also won three World titles. Not too far down the trail, however, McAuley was to experience that empty feeling. The end of his ring road was in Spain, 1992, when losing the title in his sixth defence through a disputed points defeat in a rematch with Blanco in Bilbao.

"The gloves were put away after the trip to Spain. I was 32 at the time. Who knows what I might have done had the decision in Bilbao been different," reflected the 'Boy'. "My title loss obviously cost me a lot of money, deprived me of more big fights and further title defences, or whatever. Before Bilbao, I was offered three World title bouts. Had I managed to retain my title, there was the opportunity to go to Las Vegas and fight Michael Carbajal.

"He was the World Light-flyweight champion. There had been serious discussions of one million dollars on the table for me to go there. It was a big-bucks contest in the pipeline, but I was denied the golden opportunity. Whether I would have taken up that offer remains forever a mystery. My ambition was to retire the undefeated World Flyweight champion. But, that decision in Bilbao ruined the plans. My personal target was to make one more defence after boxing Blanco, and quit."

McAuley confessed he was coming to the end, anyway. He sustained many injuries. He attended physio session three days a week when preparing for the last of his two World title defences: "I didn't have all that many fights but I had many, many hard contests in my 23-bout career. I took part in no less than nine World Championship fights - one World title eliminator, and one British Championship contest."

One of the influences on his career was Panamanian icon Zapata, who was brought in by Eastwood to help McAuley prepare for the first defence of the WBA Flyweight belt against southpaw Dodie Penalosa of the Philippines. Legendary southpaw Zapata participated in two-dozen World Championship contests, mostly over 15 rounds. The bouts ranged from Light-flyweight to Flyweight. He also boxed most of his Championship tests outside of his native Panama. He was prepared to punch-for-pay anywhere on the planet. He featured five times in South Korea, also five in Japan, three in Venezuela, and two in the United States.

He won the WBA title at the second attempt, beating Alonzo Gonzales for the vacant Championship. Zapata also paraded his instinctive skills in Colombia against McAuley's future foe Bassa at Barranquilla, but lost a 15-round points decision and the WBA Flyweight title on February, 1987. Born on August 19, 1958, the Panama City fighter apparently gained early inspiration to become a professional boxer. When 12 years of age his legendary fellow countryman Roberto Duran gave him the present of a set of boxing gloves. He turned professional in 1977, and finished with a record of 43 wins (15 knockouts), 10 defeats and one draw.

McAuley said: "Zapata was brilliant for me. Even though he was retired when he came to Belfast he was still a very slick fighter." The battling 'Boy' has not been forgotten. He enjoys chin-wagging about the old days. It makes a change to stop and smell the flowers, not the smelling salts. It is an ever-lengthening gap since his farewell fight to be out of the hot news, yet still to be constantly remembered.

Coach Checa held McAuley in the highest esteem: "Dave Boy was a hard worker, and a hard hitter. The first fight I was involved with Dave was helping in his corner when he won the World title from Duke McKenzie. Eddie Shaw was in charge then. Before his big chance in London, McAuley was inactive for 15 months. He had everything against him. It is possible the McKenzie camp felt Dave 'Boy' would be a soft touch. It was good night. He won it easy."

Checa was also in McAuley's corner when the Boy went back to London in November, 1988, to defend against Dodie Penalosa, a fighter who had been around at the top level for some time and was very experienced. Bernardo rated the first McAuley-Blanco fight in the King's Hall as 'unbelievable'. He had a crucial influence in helping the Boy survive moments of gut-churning crisis: "I remember jumping into the ring to pick McAuley up and bring him back to the corner. He was down twice. He came back from a desperate situation to put Blanco down, yet was fortunate to get the decision, I have to admit. Dave brought a lot of excitement and entertainment.

"When he fought Blanco for a second time he deserved to win what was a poor fight in Bilbao. Both boxers were conscious of what happened in the first fight, and tried not be put down, especially Blanco. He didn't deserve to take the title because of that. He did not try hard enough. Dave Boy did not deserve to lose his title. I was in the corner for all of Dave's World Championship fights, right to the end. He had six defences, five of those successful. He deserved better recognition for that. For ability and excitement value I'd give him eight out of ten. From a technical aspect, he initially had the dangerous habit of leaving his head unprotected, because he was too upright. We worked on that, and he improved a lot. We brought Zapata in from Panama to spar with Dave before the title defence against Penalosa. Zapata, even though retired, was special. He dropped Dave in their first spar. Zapata had 24 world title fights. Twice he was Junior Flyweight champion and once the Flyweight champion of the World."

McAuley lives in a well-appointed bungalow on a hill overlooking the sleepy seaside hamlet of Drain's Bay, outside Larne, County Antrim. When not pulling pints of beer in his family-owned Halfway House Hotel hostelry, further north up Antrim's scenic Coast Road route, he works in boxing as a ringside analyst. Nearby is one member of the then Eastwood boxing backroom team who kept close tabs on McAuley's career - Michael 'Flop' Abram, a kindred sprit of Dave McAuley, coming from the same part the world in County Antrim. Carnlough-born Abram joined the Eastwood Organisation in February, 1987. Brian Eastwood involved him in the boxing promotions, and he took a special interest in Dave Boy's progress.

"I arrived at Eastwoods around the same time as Dave Boy," he said, "We brought over Espana and Cordoba from South and Central America. Sam Storey became the first British Super-middleweight champion during my time there." He was appointed General Manager. Bruno was the promoter after his brother Stephen stepped down in the wake of McGuigan's win at Loftus Road in 1985. Al Dillon also came in at the start with Abram, left for a spell and came back on the scene later on. Abram added: "It was a very interesting time. I remember driving boxers to the gym and back from the Bangor guest house of Jean Anderson. I met Espana, Cordoba and Arroya. When Al Dillon left I was thrown into the deep end. When a fight show was set up I did a plan of the seating. Bruno (Eastwood) worked with the TV people. At times I was involved in helping with the setting up of camera placings in the arena. I also looked after all the stewards and bouncers. I was responsible for all the ticket-money returns, and often did liaison with McAuley."

He was with Dave for all his big fights, including the World title win in London where he placed a 'good-sized' bet on him: "You could have managed a price of 7 to 2 at ringside. The late Eddie Shaw and I took that ringside wager for McAuley to win. It was the first big bet I really ever had on Dave. I thought for a moment he had lost the fight, but really McAuley won quite well. I think maybe my nerves were bad, because of the heavy gamble. I knew McAuley was bouncing going into that fight, yet was not expected to win. I gave him a big chance of becoming World champion. Bruno was great. He was the high-powered guy. He had great faith in McAuley becoming the champion. I generally stayed with Dave two or three nights before a big contest. I tried to psyche Dave the whole time. Had he been psyched enough for the WBA title re-match against Bassa he would have won it."

'Flop' felt McAuley didn't believe he could win the return title bout. Because he fought as well as he did in the first Bassa World Championship contest, despite losing, he gained everybody's admiration: "He also shot up the World rankings. Barney was able to get the return fight when Bassa stayed at Greenan Lodge Hotel, later known as the Balmoral Hotel, on Black's Road, Belfast. On the night before the return fight there were guys in the next room to Bassa, playing music - partying and drinking all night. It had no adverse effect on the Colombian."

Abram retained a close connection with the McAuley family, especially with the Boy's father Donald in Carnlough: "He was also a total gentleman. I never saw anything as dignified as the night Dave Boy lost to Bassa, in the first fight. His father was so proud of the young man, yet never at any time tried to get any limelight for himself. I found Donald to be very unassuming, very modest. Dave Boy became a superstar overnight, even though he lost. Donald, a big man of some 6'1" tall, would not have any talk about boxing back home. Even when Dave won the World title you would not have known Donald was Dave Boy's father."

His take on the end of the Boy's ring career, the loss of the title in disputed circumstances to Blanco: "I thought he won in Bilbao. I felt he was done over like a kipper. I was involved in the running of the show." While Dave Boy remained the tops with Flop, Abram held a special affection for World Welterweight champion Espana: "I remember the day Claws won the World title. Taylor, his opponent, looked like a smaller version of Mike Tyson. I recall coming out of the weigh-in that morning in London with Bruno when he introduced me to Nigel Benn, who said he had a friend who had been in the same training camp as Taylor.

"Benn said the sparring partner for Taylor rocked the American a few times, put him on his knees. So, Bruno looked at me and said he felt Taylor may well have had a fight too many. Taylor was coming off a very hard contest against Cesar Chavez. Referee Richard Steele stopped the fight with a few seconds to go, when Taylor was apparently ahead on points. Obviously Chavez won. Bruno felt that fight was too much for Taylor. Also, I believed Crisanto was just so much on top of his game. I had a few quid on Claws to win the title. I backed Crisanto to win inside the distance. The odds for that were 7 to 2. I didn't have any sweat at all about Espana winning the Championship. I just knew. I really felt Crisanto didn't concern himself he was in a World Championship contest for a first time. It was just another fight for him, and he knocked Taylor out."

McAuley's retirement, of course, was the end of the track for Eastwood, who said: "It was the shutdown of another era. Boxing in Ireland seems to go through cycles. In the old days you could pick out some fighters such as Jim 'Spider' Kelly, Tommy Armour, Jimmy Warnock, Bunty Doran, and then the world success of Rinty Monaghan. We had the Kellys - John and Billy to follow. We got over that spell, and then into the Gilroy and Caldwell era. We got over that, and into another quiet period. We had some interesting domestic action involving boxers such as Jim McCann, Seanie McCaffrey, Peter Sharpe, Henry Turkington, Young John McCormick. They were in small shows for me, and then we went again into a vibrant area through McGuigan, and on to our other World champions."

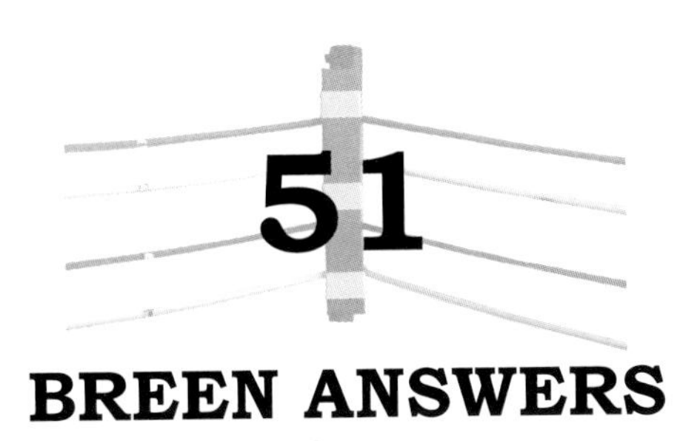

51

BREEN ANSWERS

JOHN Breen became part of the Eastwood gym coaching staff in 1990. He was invited to join a seriously ailing Eddie Shaw and Bernardo Checa. He was an amateur and professional middleweight tutored by Shaw and Ned McCormick during his formative fight days. Breen started in boxing at 15-years-of-age, in 1965, in the old Belfast Immaculata Youth Club gym when it was housed in a derelict warehouse off Durham Street.

Born on July 31, 1950, Breen boxed 27 times as a professional, losing 18 bouts. From Scotch Street, in the lower Falls, he made his debut in the Ulster Hall on March 5, 1975, outpointing Carl McCarthy over six rounds. John lost his next fight, a points setback against the rugged English fighter Tony Sibson in Brighton. "I turned professional with local ex-professional fighter Gerry Hassett, who came from the Kashmir Road area of Belfast and eventually settled in Downpatrick, County Down," added Breen, who left Hassett after two contests to join London's former British Featherweight champion Al Phillips. Belfast lightweight Paddy Graham was also with Phillips.

Breen moved because he was offered merely £50 to meet Henry Turkington. Ned McCormick advised him to turn it down. John explained he was told if he didn't take the fight against The Turk he would be handed back the contract. He retrieved the contract, signed with 'Aldgate Tiger' Phillips, but also remained involved with Shaw and McCormick. Later he met Pat Brogan in Manchester, Tony Sibson, again at Dudley, and went the distance in Belfast against the fearsome Turkington brothers, Henry and Willie. He finished his ring career under Phillips and went into coaching amateurs in his Immaculata club, including Fra McCullough, who was about to turn professional.

He also coached former Commonwealth Games Welterweight silver medallist Kenny Beattie, who was preparing to turn professional under Mike Callahan.

Southpaw Beattie, later a supervisor at the Grove Baths, Belfast, was waiting for a debut fight, but time dragged on. Tired of the delay, Kenny changed his mind and stayed amateur.Breen's early grooming as an active boxer helped him progress in later life to become one of Ireland's top professional trainers and managers. Fighters under his charge included Eamonn Magee, Neil Sinclair, Paul McCloskey, Kevin O'Hara, Stephen Haughian, Jim Rock and Marty Rogan.

Breen said: "The Immaculata Club during the old gym days was a fascinating place. It was a terrific learning experience. There was always something important happening, including great young prospects emerging every year. In my early days the top young amateur fighters included Andrew McCormick and Paddy Moore. Ned McCormick, Andrew's father, was the boss of bosses. He was chief trainer of boxers such as Jim McCourt, Spike McCormack, Peter Sharpe, Barney Wilson, Alex McGavock, Terry Hanna, Paddy Maguire, Jim McAuley and many many others at that time. Fitness trainer was Jimmy McGivern, along with Vinty McGurk.

"Ned came from Massereene Street in the lower Falls. He was my first trainer. Even when Eddie (Shaw) looked after me as a professional, Ned was still my main trainer. There was only one Ned McCormick. The same sentiment is for Eddie (Shaw), a lovely man. Incidentally, the first professional Eddie coached was lightweight Paddy Graham." He also remembered the inimitable and incorrigible Spike McCormack and some amateurs, including myself, occasionally slipping away early from the training programme for a quick pint of Guinness in a snug of Joe Gorman's pub on the corner of Elizabeth and Albert Streets.

John added: "Eddie (Shaw) was with Ned when McGuigan trained in the new Immaculata gym at Farcett Walk, Divis Tower. Ned then left the Eastwood coaching programme. At that time I was out of boxing, running my security business." He recalled joining the Eastwood coaching staff under very sad circumstances: "Fra McCullagh rang to say Barney Eastwood wanted to hold a talk with me. I contacted Barney, who invited me down to the gym on the following Monday. I was informed Eddie was not too well, and Barney wanted to know if I would give Eddie a helping hand. He told me the money wouldn't be too good, at the start. I felt it would be a privilege to join the stable."

Checa was also helping with the coaching, brought back from Panama to help after fitness trainer Paul McCullagh left. When Breen walked into the gym to start his new job the boxers in training included McAuley, Hodkinson, the Wenton brothers - Ritchie and Nigel, Cordoba, Espana, Crawford Ashley, Noel Magee, Ray Close and John Lowey. It was hard work, looking after all the World-class fighters at the one time. McGuigan was long gone. It was 1990. Breen was working in the gym about twelve months when tragedy struck. Eddie Shaw died.

Breen added: "That was an awful blow to boxing, and more especially to Eddie's family. I was there until the gym shut down. It really ended with McAuley's loss of the IBF title to Blanco. The 'Boy', Barney's last champion, was unfortunate in Bilbao. I was there. I felt he won the fight, or at the very least deserved to come out with a draw - although I thought he stole the first fight against Blanco in Belfast. A draw was the best McAuley deserved from that amazing contest in the King's Hall, and the worst he deserved was a draw in Spain.

"In the ring, before the decision was announced in Bilbao, McAuley was so sure he won he said to Blanco he would give him another fight. That was the best McAuley boxed in a long time, so controlled, and one of the few fights he did not got down in. Dave Boy did not get the recognition he deserved. After Bilbao there were still a few boys hanging around the gym such as Close, Lowey, Eamonn Magee - who signed professional under Mike Callahan - and Dublin's Jim Rock."

Eastwood planned to pull down the shutters on the Castle Street gym, and with it all the golden memories, but allowed Breen to stay for as long as he needed the time to find premises and set up a new gym. In 1998, he opened the Breen Gym after a chat with Belfast bar owner Tony Diver, who had an empty storeroom above his Monaco pub in the city centre. Breen worked hard to keep professional boxing afloat in Northern Ireland, ever since Eastwood pulled down the curtain.

"Barney kept professional boxing going for years. His contribution to Irish boxing was immense, fantastic," he insisted, "I learned the coaching game through training in the Immaculata gym and then working in the Eastwood gym. Checa also coached in my gym for a long time. I brought him back in from Panama mainly to coach Neil Sinclair. I had two champions at the time - Eamonn Magee and Sinclair. Bernardo stayed with me for 18 months."

SUPER SCOUSER

PAUL Hodkinson was a sawn-off, in-your-face fighter from Kirby, Liverpool. The lion-hearted former ABA (1986) Featherweight champion had to go through hell and high water before adding a second World Featherweight belt to the Eastwood list of high honours. Born in Liverpool, on September 14, 1965, he stood 5' 4"- and was the WBC Featherweight champion from November 13, 1991 to April 28, 1993.

A flinty fighter of unquestionable courage, he had a 22-3-1 record, and was a professional from 1986 to 1994. Nicknamed 'Hoko', he gave a very good imitation of perpetual motion during a contest - a human windmill in the mould of the great American Henry Armstrong. Often overly courageous because of his lack of stature, reach disadvantage, and the obvious need to get to close grips with a quarry to be effective, Paul quickly became a very popular performer in front of the knowledgeable Irish fight followers.

His modus operandi of cluster punching was probably best suited to telephone-booth battles. He became an honorary Irish fighter, and tried his level best to fill the void left by McGuigan's departure from the scene. An approach was made to Eastwood, to take the fireball under his wing. "A fellow in Liverpool rang me to say there was a kid in Kirby he was involved with who was thinking of turning professional," recalled Eastwood, "Two or three people were after his signature, he said. I said, every week I was offered boys to manage. That was true at that time. I said to this guy I would like to see the young prospect first, before I would commit myself."

Eastwood offered the boy full attention and top training facilities. Hoko arrived to look over the facility at Castle Street. McGuigan was in training in the gym at that period, and Hoko sparred with him a couple of times. "Paul was small but a very able guy, a good all-action fighter," declared BJ, "He had a great heart, and was a nice lad. He was very good at what he did, and was well mannered. Everything was right about him. He could handle himself. He messed about in our gym for about a month, and then he went home. I told him to think things over. Then I received a 'phone call from him, saying he wanted to turn pro, and that he wanted me to be his manager."

On July 19, 1986, Hodkinson made his debut, at Wembley, and was also taken to Panama City in July, 1987. It was an opportunity to get him a fight, as boxing shows in Belfast were few and far between at that time. Luis Spada set up a contest against Panamanian Thomas Arguelles. It finished a draw over eight rounds. On October 29, 1986, Hoko made his first Belfast ring appearance in his fourth fight, stopping Craig Windsor during the second round in the Ulster Hall. Halting Steve Simms on January 17, 1987, was a leap forward. On January 27, 1988, he stopped Dublin's Ritchie Foster in the third round, and did the same to Peter Harris, in the 12th round at Port Talbot, Wales, on May 18, 1988, to win the British Featherweight Championship. On April 12, 1989, he plundered the vacant European title against Raymond Armand, on a second-round stoppage at the Ulster Hall. The onwards and upwards march became more demanding.

Eastwood recalled a stormy time in a step-up fight that almost went wrong in Manchester. "Paul was boxing in the big Hall at the G-Mex against Mexican Eduardo Montoya in a final World Championship eliminator. I sent the late Tony Baker to go and see the fighter after he arrived at the last minute from Mexico. Montoya came in the night prior to the weigh-in because of travel delays. British Boxing Board of Control officials gave us permission to use him despite the circumstances. Tony (Baker) went down to the Mexican and his minder with our scales to have a check weigh-in. I think Montoya was closer to 9st 10lbs than 9 stone. Tony came back with the bad news the fighter was loads over the limit. Problems we had, and problems we certainly did not need.

"We considered making the fight at a higher weight. Tony went back, however, and the trainer told him the fighter was taking tablets and he would be okay on the scales. I said I didn't believe in miracles. So, we got the scales down early in the morning for a check. I was out of bed at six o'clock. We went to the Mexican's room, and the boxer amazingly was merely half-a-pound over the limit with three hours to go."

Eduardo 'Fili' Montoya, born on November 20, 1960, finished with a 16-7-1 record. On September 9, 1989, the Mexican Featherweight champion had a crack at the WBA Featherweight title, losing on a fifth-round stoppage to Antonio Esparragoza at Baja, California. The fight with Hoko was his last chance of making it to another title shot, and almost did. The records show Montoya weighed in at 125.5 lbs. Hodkinson went straight at his opponent, as usual, backed him onto the ropes in the second round, and the Mexican stood there with one foot out.

Eastwood said: "He had not done a thing since the fight began. Suddenly, Montoya moved his head back, slipped a punch from Paul, and hit Hoko right on the button, knocking him head over heels. I was flabbergasted, as I thought it was over. But, Paul got up and held on in our corner. The bell rang five seconds later to end the round. We put water over Paul on the stool. He kept asking who won the fight. I was in two minds about putting him out out again. By right, I should not have sent Paul back into the fight. We felt if Paul hits Montoya he will stop the Mexican. He did just that. What a great little fighter. Paul came back to the corner, a big winner, yet kept asking who won. I realised something was wrong, took him out the back door and straight to a hospital. He was kept in overnight, suffering from a touch of concussion."

Hodkinson qualified for a rattle at the World belt, but ran into a really brutal brick wall in 1990. Disaster struck in the little warrior's 19th bout, and in the G-Mex Centre, Manchester. On June 2, he lost on an eighth-round stoppage to Mexican tough guy Marcos Villasana (49-7-3). The vacant WBC crown was at stake. Referee Arthur Mercante, the 1988 recipient of the International Boxing Hall of Fame's James J. Walker Award for long and meritorious service to boxing, stopped it at 2.58. Hoko suffered serious eyebrow injury setbacks.

Eastwood added: "After that we managed to cure the eye problem. I got special stuff for his eyes. Funnily enough, people in the boxing game have been ringing me now and then wanting to know the secret of our cure for Hoko's eyes. He never had any problems after that." Coach Checa said: "Hoko was small for the Featherweight grade. He had good combination punches, was busy and had plenty of heart. He was well ahead on points against Villasana when he had to be pulled out of the action. Thankfully, before the rematch, a secret solution was found to overcome his eyebrow problems."

Hodkinson returned to the ring that October, at Wembley, for a defence of European title. He stopped Guy Bellehigue. A rejuvenated Hoko was now ready for the return against the hefty-hooking Villasana, and took ample revenge at Maysfield Leisure Centre, Belfast, on November 13, 1991. He scored a unanimous points win for WBC title. Referee was Vince Delgado. On April 25, 1992, he easily won on a third-round TKO against McGuigan's nemesis Steve Cruz, also at Maysfield. It was his first title defence. Irish fight fans were curious to have another look at reputation wrecker Cruz, the former US National 1981 Golden Gloves amateur Bantamweight champion.

It was an eerie occasion, with referee Rolando Barrovecchio halting the action after 65 seconds of round three. Eastwood gained some satisfaction from repairing part of the torment and after-shock of the McGuigan defeat in Las Vegas. This marked the end of the Texas 'Super Kid'. It was his fourth last fight. Cruz turned professional in the Will Rogers Coliseum, Fort Worth, on October, 1981. Born on November 2, 1963, he finished with a 37 (ko 19)-8 record. Winning the title from McGuigan was the unexpected high. He quickly lost the crown, on March 6, 1987, to Esparragoza in the 12th round, and in front of his home city fans. He later lost on points to Jorge Paez, in a bid to take the IBF belt, on August 6, 1989.

Cruz dipped below the radar, while Hodkinson's career was soaring. On September 12, 1992, the 'Gulliver with Gloves' went to Blaqnac, near Toulouse, France, for his second WBC defence. Hoko took a TKO decision after 1.35 of the 10th round against Fabrice Benichou. Fabrice, who became another of Eastwood's World champions, made it a tough time for Paul before it ended. Two judges were in favour of Hoko when the fight was stopped, while one judge made it even. On February 3, 1993, there was the third defence against Ricardo Cepeda at Earls Court, London, where Paul scored a TKO 4 result. There was also some speculation of a unification fight with Colin McMillan of Hackney, London, the first British holder of the WBO belt. It didn't come to pass, with both fighters losing their respective championships to different opposition.

In a fateful fourth WBC defence, on the 28th of April, 1993, Hoko lost by a seventh-round stoppage to Mexico's Gregorio Vargas in Dublin's National Stadium. Referee Arthur Mercante halted it after 2.27. Eastwood tried to dissuade his gallant warrior of meeting Vargas, and insisted: "The defence against Vargas in Dublin was a mistake, I feel. I wanted Paul to give up his title, and not take this mandatory defence of the

Championship. I had a notion he was on the slip at that time. I looked at things in a different way then from some other folk, in that there were a few easier fights out there for Paul."

He told Hoko that defending against Vargas would be a very tricky test. Vargas was an extremely dangerous opponent. He explained the whole thing to the proud fighter, who replied: 'BJ, are you expecting me to give up my Championship, just hand the title in?' Eastwood said: 'Yes'. He wanted his brilliant battler to take a couple of relatively easy fights in England, and then match him for a World title again.

Financially, the boss felt, Hoko would be much better off, and added: "We were told to fight Vargas. The Vargas people had been waiting for a long time to meet Paul for the title. I felt Paul should move elsewhere. It made good business sense to do that, and also in my fighter's best interests. But, Paul said to me: 'BJ, the only way I am giving up my title is that somebody will have to beat me for it.' He is very proud man. I could understand that. I still said I was not too happy about it. I stated in the media at the time that it would be a very, very difficult fight, and I would prefer Paul to go in another direction in the meantime. But, having said that, I emphasised it was his choice to fight Vargas. Paul had every chance, but I believed it would be extremely difficult. How do you tell the fighter that."

BJ became a close associate of the iconic American middleman, Mercante, a fitness fanatic and a boxing referee since 1957, kept in touch with Eastwood ever since handling two of Hoko's world title fights. Hoko's next fight, on March 12, 1994, proved to be his last. He suffered a TKO loss to Steve Robinson in the Cardiff Ice Rink. It was a typically gallant but futile bid to try and win the WBO belt. He was pulled out of the firing line by referee Dave Parris of England after 1.40 of the 12th round. The furious action was deemed by the British Boxing Board of Control the 'British Contest of the Year'. He believed Hoko had a hope against Robinson. The opportunity was there to become a World champion again. Robinson was okay in Barney's book, but Paul had a chance against the strong, dogged Welshman. It didn't work out.

Eastwood reflected: "The trainers, including John Breen, felt Hoko was still jumping out of his skin, yet I had the feeling there wasn't the old sparkle. The fight against Vargas took a lot out of him." Of his 26 contests, Hoko participated in seven World title fights, four Europeans, and three British championship contests. He was elevated to the Scouser 'Hall of Fame' list that includes John Conteh and Nel Tarleton.

53

BRUNO

BRIAN Eastwood, eldest son of the family, was generally at the heart of all that was going down during the halcyon McGuigan era, and beyond. The fight game was in his blood. Affectionately known as Bruno, he was weaned on boxing during his schoolboy days at Carrickfergus. Happy times were recalled. He used to box when he was eight, nine and ten. At first he sparred a lot with brother Peter in the family garage.

He was born upstairs, over the Corner Bar in Carrickfergus. Billy Anthony ran a boxing club in Carrickfergus, and this was where Bruno and his brothers were taken to learn the rudiments of the sweet science. Anthony was a former professional pugilist in the Welterweight division, and using the 'nom de guerre' of Billy Corbett. He had a ring record of 29 contests, with 18 wins. Born in Carrickfergus, on September 9, 1932, he met useful opposition such as Eddie Phillips, Gerry Hassett, and Dundalk-born Irish Middleweight champion Cliff Garvey.

Bruno said: "Dad got me into the boxing to learn to look after myself. I remember a hard bully in Primary school, bigger than me. Everybody feared him. After six months in the boxing club I built up sufficient courage and cheek to have a go at the bully, and managed to give him a beating. A week later, the bully joined the boxing club to learn how to box. We became friends. We had great amateur shows in Carrickfergus Town Hall, and also in nearby Larne. Dad also used to take me on a Wednesday night into Belfast. I was brought to the De LaSalle gym on the Glen Road, Belfast, which was run by big Sam Hayes. He used to arrange sparring sessions, matching two boys together of approximately the same height and weight.

"We would do three rounds. It was rough enough, yet a good learning process. A few weeks there and you soon got your confidence. I also continued to train in Carrickfergus where there would be up to 16 boxers any night working out in the gym. The premises then were in the Minorca area, beside the old brickworks at the top of Davis Street. Later on, I was incarcerated for five years, a student boarder in St.Malachy's College, at the bottom end of Belfast's Antrim Road. There was no boxing there. My sporting interests changed to following the College's MacRory Cup Gaelic football team."

The player St Malachy's College students looked up to then was Martin O'Neill from Kilrea, who was later to gain fame in soccer with Nottingham Forest's European Cup-winning side. He was also in the Northern Ireland team that contested the 1982 World Cup finals in Spain, and became the international team captain. A natural born leader, O'Neill later managed a number of clubs including Wycombe Wanderers, Leicester City, Glasgow Celtic and Aston Villa. The St. Malachy's team, with O'Neill the skipper and a brilliant playmaker, was involved in one of the best ever All-Ireland Colleges' football finals for the Hogan Cup at Croke Park, Dublin. The Ulster champions were beaten by a late goal.

Bruno moved away from College days to join the family's bookmaking enterprise, and then into the boxing scene. He took up the promoter baton from brother Stephen for the McGuigan-Taylor and McGuigan-Cabrero title defences. It was a seamless take over of the reins. He not only enjoyed the roller-coaster ride of the Cyclone days but also held a special interest in a South American import who thrilled the Irish fans with his chilling power. Blessed with basic raw strength, Crisanto Espana was carefully channelled into a fearsome fighting machine, at Welterweight. The Venezuelan held a special place in the heart and mind of Bruno, who was also intrigued by the stunning exploits of Dave 'Boy' McAuley. The era of the Eastwood gym in Castle Street wasn't just about one fighter. It quickly grew away from that mindset, argued Bruno. There was a stable of boxers to cater for.

There was an infrastructure established, and one to be maintained. Eastwoods didn't merely promote one boxer. A group of highly talented fighters came with the territory as Bruno explained: "We needed other boxers to make the shows. I was involved with everything - the logistics, keeping the thing going, putting together fight-show programmes, promotions, press conferences, and so forth." Boxing, like all sports, creates diverse opinion - and Bruno was never short of a few: "It is always subjective, the merits of a fighter. The greatest fighter Dad ever had in his stable, in my humble view, was Espana. Claws was just an enigma. The other fighters in the stable then could not keep up with him during the morning roadwork. Of course, he'd been a top marathon runner in Venezuela. Toby Cordoba from Panama wasn't bad either, a tough guy. But, I recall the day in the gym when I first saw Crisanto knocking him onto the ropes when using 16-ounce gloves, and not wearing headgear. That was enough to tell me how exceptionally powerful Espana was."

However, he readily accepts the rise of McGuigan brought about the evolvement of such a successful Eastwood stable of fighters: "Dave Boy did us proud, and deserves more recognition - absolutely. In my own mind, anyway, I take some credit for Dave Boy's success when he won the World title. The one thing about Dave was, he always respected my opinion on different boxers, different fights. I kept telling him he was a certainty to win the World title fight against Duke McKenzie in London. Everybody rated McKenzie a sure-fire winner, to retain the Championship. I didn't think that way. I reckoned McKenzie didn't have the power to bother Dave Boy. If the 'Boy' could get the jab going and shock McKenzie with the strength of his left lead he'd be the new champion."

Bruno believed if the Duke could be prevented from coming in on top of him McAuley was an absolute certainty. He claimed once Dave Boy was able to hurt McKenzie with one big shot that would be his way to success. McAuley, he argued, needed an awful lot of convincing, but eventually he did believe. He also insisted that for excitement and high-octane drama you could not better the 'Boy's' phenomenal first fights with Bassa and Blanco. "Dave Boy looked like he was completely gone in the second round against Blanco. Then he came back, switched, and hit Blanco with a surprise right hook. What a night!"

Once McAuley settled into the gym regime as a new professional he quickly began to parade punching power during sparring sessions. Dave was born with that natural special hitting power to take out an opponent. Bruno's belief was that once a fighter felt the jolting McAuley one-shot he realised the 'Boy' could really punch, and then became wary of being knocked out. Bruno, with that quizzing close-range and unwavering straight look into your face, to test for instant reaction, added: "The man my father brought in from Panama to help with the sparring for McAuley - the great Zapata - was an important move in Dave Boy's career. What a record Zapata had in World Championship boxing, and in that era competing in 15-round bouts more than anybody else."

54

POSITIVE PASSAGE

BRUNO Eastwood was totally immersed in all the trauma, drama, the unparalleled excitement of World achievement and eventual tragedy of the McGuigan campaign. He compared the wonder years to the thrill of riding a surfboard at the top of a giant wave. "It was an exceptional passage in Irish sport. We were all blinded at a time by the excitement, the possibilities of winning a World title, lots of emotion, and the phenomenal fans behind the whole thing," recalled Bruno, who could chin-wag about boxing all day long.

He hardly missed a punch thrown from the moment the ambitious McGuigan project was launched by his father. "It was great. I loved it. The motivation behind McGuigan, and his aspiration to win a World title, was such a driving force, a positive thing, that it carried the whole bandwagon straight through to Loftus Road. Along that amazing journey he did take a really hard hit from LaPorte. He came within a hair's breath of suffering a knockout in that fight. When he became World champion all those positive early things changed to a different nature, in my view. It was a negative propulsion on the basis he was afraid of losing the title, afraid of what he would lose in financial terms, of status and so forth. Before the winning of the WBA title at Loftus Road it was a positive wave that pushed him forward."

Bruno recalled the anticipation in the Eastwood household when his father made such a fuss of moving back to the fight game as a manager, and signing Commonwealth Games gold medallist McGuigan. "As a member of the Eastwood family I can candidly state Dad ate, drank, and slept the Barry McGuigan project from the moment he signed up the fighter. Dad is one of those guys if he wants a thing badly enough he will go to all ends to achieve his target. He wanted it well done, to go after a World title, and this he did. My brothers agree with me that McGuigan, for a time, was Dad's favourite son. It was as simple as that in those early days. But, when people got between that arrangement it soon began to sour."

He claimed his father was interpreting that change as a case of McGuigan biting the hand that was feeding him, after BJ did everything possible for the fighter. He believed McGuigan listened to fireside opinion from people who knew nothing about boxing. Was the split inevitable, no matter the outcome in Las Vegas against Cruz? "McGuigan was allowing people to get between him and Dad. Simple as that," insisted candid Bruno, "Maybe once the World title was achieved it was believed my father became obsolete, not needed anymore. The fighter was at a new level after Loftus Road, and commanding a lot more money. What killed McGuigan's advisors, in my opinion, was that Dad was getting all the promotional rights. I suspect they felt McGuigan could promote himself, and then he would get that too. Dad did not go into family business expansion at that time, but went in search of a World boxing champion. He was seeking out a dream, as he always loved boxing from way back when he was a very young man."

He added his father's ambition was obviously achieved at Loftus Road, but then his pride was hurt even though he had completed his original objective. "He didn't want McGuigan to leave him," insisted Bruno, "You have to remember too, the boxing world is not full of angels. You have to deal with a variety of people to get the job done, which Dad did to get McGuigan to the world title. For $200,000, Dad could have had Azumah Nelson in that ring at Loftus Road. Instead, the McGuigan-Pedroza bout held the greater appeal, yet it became the costliest fight to be staged in England since Cassius Clay boxed there."

At the time it was reputed to be a world record purse for any World Featherweight Championship contest. Included was a payout to Pedroza which I believe was in the region of £1.2 million (sterling). "When everybody was in the one team, and the one family, it was a unique and very special time," claimed Bruno, "McGuigan was head of the gym. When he marched into the gym in Castle Street he was the man, and in Dad's mind McGuigan was certainly 'The Man'."

Before the Pedroza fight, Eastwood fitted up an outdoor ring in what was then Bruno's back garden at Broom Cottage, outside Holywood, County Down. It was to get a feel of what it might be like when boxing outdoors at Loftus Road. The ring was the full 24-feet square, erected by Ned McCourt on a plinth, to give the effect of climbing up into the ring. It was just a perfect World Championship ring. Eastwood remembered the great outdoors exercise, before the big fight against Pedroza. He felt McGuigan was working really poorly in the gym before that.

BJ said: "It can happen to boxers, possibly beginning to go over the top in training. He just was not finding it, and was sluggish. I said we have to do something to lift him, to try and freshen him up. So, we put up a full-sized ring in the open air, to simulate the conditions we would meet at Loftus Road. McGuigan had his first professional contest in open air in Dublin. A few pressmen were there at what was to be the last sparring session before meeting Pedroza." Arranged for McGuigan's workout were three different spar helpers. Eastwood also made a pact with the timekeeper, on a hand stopwatch, to make the rounds two and a half minutes long. According to him the first sparring partner did two rounds. The second fighter stepped in and was caught by a body punch. The third sparring guy also went the same way. It was a confidence booster, and seemed to pump up McGuigan ahead of the big test.

Bruno returned to the sudden dip in relationships, the downside of the McGuigan time: "After Loftus Road we had the first World title defence against Taylor at the King's Hall, and then down to Dublin. Things were changing. We knew that. Before the Cabrera contest in Dublin, it was all set up for McGuigan to box Gomez for the WBA Super-featherweight title, and the opportunity to become a double World champion. When McGuigan turned down the fight, Panamanian manager Luis Spada and Dad bought the rights of the Gomez defence. The next guy was Alfredo Layne of Panama, who was generally regarded a mediocre boxer, and one not really equipped to cope at that level of world boxing. Yet Layne went in and stopped Gomez.

"Spada and Dad owned the rights on Layne, and subsequently on the South African guy Brian Mitchell, who beat Layne for the WBA Super-featherweight belt. In other words, while McGuigan did not take advantage of that opportunity against Gomez, who was not even a shadow of his former self, Dad certainly did. I think that proved the point. It is my contention that even after he won the World Featherweight Championship

McGuigan did not think he was as great a fighter as everybody else thought he was. Way back, he was exposed a bit against Chiteule, and then there was the fight against LaPorte.

"The negative thing manifested itself in that he would arrive seven weeks before a fight to get ready for a contest. You only peak at certain times. He arrived to start training when it was felt he was already 99% fit. He was going over the top. One thing about McGuigan that you cannot take away from him is that he was an insatiable trainer. He trained, trained, and often over-trained. In my view, he felt he had to be stronger and faster, but all those things were, at times, counter-productive. His big punch was the left hook to the body.

"McGuigan's road to the top was exciting. There were many important aspects along the way. For example, Buchanan was a great influence. We had the best in to help, including the very important influence of American McQuillar. Gaining benefits from all this was Eddie Shaw. One of Eddie's great assets was he did not take the huff, always seeking to improve his own knowledge of coaching. Imagine in other sport when a specialist coach is brought in the head coach inevitably would walk out in anger.

"Nine times out of ten the bringing in of a Buchanan or a McQuillar would be resented. Not so in the case of Eddie. Who is the trainer here, he could well have asked? Eddie was always a learner. He wanted to improve himself, and would not allow any pettiness to get in the way of achieving the objective of making McGuigan a World champion. That was tremendous. That sort of training formula would not have worked with anyone else but Eddie Shaw. He was as disappointed as the rest of us when things turned sour.

"Fights became more problematical when McGuigan boxed at top level. One thing overrides everything else. Styles make fights. A can beat B, and B can beat C. It doesn't mean A will beat C, because there could be different styles. A good example was the McGuigan fight in Dublin, where Cabrera gave him plenty of trouble."

He felt the deep sadness of McGuigan losing the World title. He knew it was the end of a glittering and unique era. The question he continued to ask himself since then was why did McGuigan not wish to clear his record and look for a rematch? Eastwoods, he argued, could have imported Cruz to the King's Hall, to Dublin, to the Royal Albert Hall, or to Wembley "Every time he was offered a return with Cruz he turned it down," claimed Bruno, "That all happened within the space of an hour at the High Court, during the time when the Case on the Options was going on. We had to provide opponents in the options, and one was obviously Steve Cruz. So, our legal team put it to his legal team we would arrange a rematch with Cruz, to give McGuigan the opportunity to get his revenge. They talked to Barry about it, came back and said no - as he (McGuigan) was moving up to 9st 4lbs.

"Then we said that was okay as Cruz would fight McGuigan at Catchweights or at 9st 4. His legal team discussed this new offer with McGuigan, and came back to our legal team to again say no. It was a fight everyone wanted to see. Everybody wanted to know why it didn't happen. It was perhaps one of those situations, just like Buchanan was apparently not all that interested in getting into the ring again with Duran, his nemesis. In life, it is reckoned every man has his price. But fear of losing the speculated astronomical figures McGuigan could earn, after he became a World champion, did him in the end. I was in California to attend the training camp in 1986. I wasn't on the earlier whistle-stop tour to promote the bill in Las Vegas, but I went to Palm Springs at least a month leading up to the fight in Las Vegas."

Bruno, who jetted into camp with a new addition to the Eastwood stable, featherweight Hodkinson, added: "I felt McGuigan wondered what Hoko was doing there, and was maybe a bit uneasy, but Dad wanted Hoko out there. It was like young Arsenal soccer teenager Theo Walcott going to the World Cup with England, and not kicking a ball. Hodkinson was still an amateur then, but was soon to turn professional. I was around the Palm Springs camp. But, all that followed is a very unhappy memory. I have to say, McGuigan has done well for himself in recent years. He also did a good job in his boxing career . . . up to and including the winning of the World title."

55

SPECIAL CLAWS

BARRY McGuigan's barnstorming march to World title honours and the overlapping excitement provided by Dave 'Boy' McAuley were cornerstones to the unparalleled buzz ignited by the Eastwood influence. At one stage the gym was awash with champions of varying degrees of achievement, and also young punching prospects keen to reach the top. The Castle Street sweat centre rocked to the sound bites of skipping ropes clicking on the wooden floor, fighters working on the pads or the speed ball, and amid the various training disciplines there was always the blaring music from a Ghetto Blaster.

You could hear amid all the almost manic happenings head coach Shaw barking out orders as he supervised ferociously competitive sparring sessions. Also, there was the cosmopolitan mixture of boxers who drifted in from from all parts of the globe. You could listen to the feverish jabberings of diverse dialects that stretched from Liverpool to Panama, to the United States, to Venezuela, not to mention the distinctive 'I'm gona batter him' Antrim Coast mutterings of a Dave Boy when coping with the back-breaking torture of being stretched on a bench to tighten stomach muscles. The puncher's parade then included Checa, Hodkinson, Close, Espana, Lowey, Loughran, Storey, Cordoba, Collins and the mercurial McAuley.

There was also the little and large show of wee Hoko and the gangling Espana, whose vicious punching made the raw boned Venezuelan an instant hit. He was a tough guy with a soft heart. He arrived in Belfast with an unbeaten 5-0 record. His older brother Ernesto was a prominent fight figure in Latin America, after winning the WBA World Lightweight belt. He succeeded Roberto Duran to the Championship. Born at La Flor on November 7, 1954, Ernesto was tall at 5'11" for the Lightweight division. Ten years after turning professional, in Caracas, Ernesto retired in August 1988 with a 36-8 record. He captured the vacant WBA crown on June 16, 1979 by knocking out Claude Noel of Trinidad and Tobago in the 13th round, at Hato Rey, Puerto Rico. Two years later Noel, a former British Commonwealth champion, would take the title.

Meantime, Ernesto made a successful title defence in Chicago, where he when beat local fighter Johnny Lira. In his next contest, on March 2, 1980, and when managed by the imposing WBA figure Jose 'Pepe' Cordero he lost the Championship to American Hilmer Kenty in the Joe Louis Arena, Detroit. He had Kenty down in the first round, but was stopped in the ninth. He also failed in a title rematch, when halted in the fourth round in San Juan. Espana also lost in two further efforts to try and recapture the WBA Lightweight crown. He went down to Arturo Frias in Los Angeles, and to the colourful Ray 'Boom Boom' Mancini at Warren, Ohio.

His barrel-chested younger brother Crisanto was better known in the home country as a quality marathon runner. Born on October 25, 1964, Crisanta was blessed with a great engine, long arms, and awesome natural power. Standing 5'10" he had his first five contests in Central America, four in his native Venezuela and one in Panama City.

Eastwood warmly recalled the first meeting in sweltering Caracas with the hit-man known as 'Claws': "I was in Venezuela, attending a WBA meeting, when this guy introduced himself. He said he was Ernesto Espana, a former World champion, and told me he had a younger brother who was twice as talented as he was, if given a really good chance. He mentioned Crisanto's name, and wanted me take him under my wing in Belfast. I said I would think about it, and for Crisanto to get in touch. Before I left the Hotel this bony looking guy arrived at my side. He was carrying a plastic shopping bag in his hand - with all his worldly belongings in it. He looked awkward, uncomfortable, but with a wide grin introduced himself.

"In very poor English he explains he is Crisanto Espana, and is ready right there and then to go with me to Belfast. I said 'Hold on. Things have to be arranged.' I was impressed, nonetheless. He looked very strong, obviously a fighter with possibilities. I said to him to go back to his home, and that we would send for him. We needed time to sort out the airline ticket to Belfast and accommodation in Northern Ireland. That is what I did, and, as they say - the rest is history. That was how it all started. Claws was some fighter."

Claws proved a hugely popular attraction during his time in Belfast. He mowed down a string of opponents. On February 12, 1991, his first major test was against durable veteran Luis Santana. He won the 12-round decision for the stepping-stone WBC International title at Maysfield Leisure Centre, Belfast. On June 11, 1992, the open-faced fighter with the toothy grin secured an easy TKO first-round decision against Kevin Whaley on the undercard of Dave Boy's World Flyweight title defence against Blanco in the Sports Pavilion, Bilbao.

The always affable Espana quickly moved into the big-time. On October 31, 1992, Eastwood lured noted American box-fighter Meldrick 'The Kid' Taylor of Philadelphia to defend his WBA Welterweight crown at Earl's Court, London. Taylor, who beat James 'Buddy' McGirt for the IBF Junior Welterweight title in 1988, went down to a disputed final-round stoppage to WBC Light-welterweight champion Julio Cesar Chavez in 1990, in Las Vegas. Rated the 'Fight of the Decade', Taylor lost to Chavez with two seconds remaining. It appeared Taylor, the 1982 Golden Gloves Bantamweight champion, was coasting until running into a hail of leather.

Taylor moved up to 10st 7lbs, and decisioned Aaron Davis for the WBA version in January 19, 1991. Later on, he failed to win the Junior Middleweight title against WBC's Terry Norris. Meldrick's showdown with Espana turned into a Halloween crackerjack. Switch-hitting Claws proved too strong, and halted 1984 Olympic Games Featherweight champion Taylor (29-2-1) after 2.11 of round eight. Referee was England's John Coyle. Coach Checa was closer than most to the supreme talent. Feeling the punching power first-hand was all part of his job. He liked to step through the ropes and don the gloves to get across instructions to his charges. Sometimes it became hot and heavy, especially against Espana.

Not only did he work the pads as trainer but also sparred, and said: "Crisanto was very popular with the Irish fans. He was, in my opinion, the best fighter in the Eastwood gym then. He had long arms, and was very powerful. He had a big chest, and great stamina. Claws was a very big puncher, and had a great record with just the one loss. A lot of things happened that went against Crisanto in the World title defence against Quartey. He was caught by a combination, and with a following right hand putting him down."

For that last title fight Espana wore out twelve sparring partners, because he was knocking them over so often in the gym. Never more than 10 stone 9lbs out of the gym he hit like a top Middleweight. Espana, named the 1993 British Boxing Board of Control's 'Overseas Boxer of the Year', made successful title defences against Rodolfo Aquilar at the Ulster Hall, and against Donovan Boucher at Old Trafford. Lurking around the corner was the heavy-handed Ike 'Bazooka' Quartey of Ghana, the mandatory challenger.

Quartey (25-0 then) took the Championship in mid-summer 1994, in the Marcel Cerdan Stadium at Levanois, Paris. He stopped Espana in the eleventh round. It was Crisanto's 30th contest, and first and only defeat. It was also the end of the glory road. He retired with a 31-1 record, including 25 stoppage wins. Apparently suffering from a suspected retina problem in one eye, he returned to his homeland after outpointing Paul Wesley of England on March 18, 1995, at Millstreet, Cork.

56

STOREY BOOKED

SOUTHPAW SAM Storey, a former Ulster and Irish amateur champion and international, was another special fighter and history maker for the Eastwood stable. Born in Belfast on August 9, 1963, he was the inaugural winner of the British Super-middleweight Championship. In September 1989, he beat Tony Burke of England on a 12-rounds decision in Belfast. The trailblazer successfully defended (Tko 9) against fellow Belfast fighter Noel Magee, and then lost the title in October 1990 to England's James Cook. English referee Mickey Vann halted the brutal battle in the 10th round at Maysfield, Belfast.

On August 27, 1994, the six-footer also failed in a gallant World title attempt when losing to WBO champion Chris Eubank in seven rounds at Cardiff. Always a pleasant and philosophical man, Sam bounced back to recapture the British title. In April, 1995 he defeated Ali Forbes at York Hall, London. After losing to Yorkshire's Henry Wharton, in a European and Commonwealth double title bout at Halifax, his final outing was on April 4, 1997. He lost a British title bout against David Starie at York Hall. Storey ended with a 25-6 record. He enjoyed carving out a special niche with that double British Super-middleweight achievement to secure outright ownership of the coveted Lonsdale Belt.

From Belfast's Antrim Road district, Sam couldn't help becoming involved in boxing. His father Gerry, later to be the Ireland and Northern Ireland team coach, was a trainer in the Holy Family Club situated in north Belfast's New Lodge Road. The old gym, with Jim 'Boxer' Hall one of the early prominent trainers, was a few yards from where Belfast's prince of sock and song John 'Rinty' Monaghan trained in his manager Frank

McAlorum's gym on his way to becoming the undisputed and unbeaten World Flyweight champion. There was a big boxing history and tradition in the area.

A scrawny Storey loafed around the Holy Family gym when a primary school student. Always curious about the fight game, he recalled: "I've been told I was taken to the gym when merely months old. My father Gerry was a trainer there. Our family house was about three hundred yards away from the Gym. I was born and bred in the New Lodge Road, in north Belfast and not far from the old 'Patrickville' gym, which was also on the same Road. It became a natural thing to do, to mosey into the gym, not only me but also my brothers Martin and Gerry. We joined the Holy Family gym, and got involved in boxing. We all took part in the training. I first boxed Championships in the Ulster Juveniles, winning the 4st 7lbs title. Bobby McAllister, son of a great Belfast professional Patsy Quinn (Gerry McAllister) was also coaching in the gym with my father."

Storey quickly graduated through the boxing grades, plundering titles from Juvenile to Ulster Junior - and on to the Ulster Senior Light-middleweight crowns in 1984 and '85. He was the national Light-middleweight champion when representing Ireland in the 1984 Olympic Games in Los Angeles, where he went out in the second series. A year later he was the Irish Amateur Middleweight champion. Sam turned to the paid game in 1985. His record features nine professional Championship contests, including one for a World belt.

He had the perfect grounding to do well, and said: "In the gym in my early days there were many top boxers such as Gerry Hamill - a Commonwealth Games Lightweight gold medallist - the Russell brothers - Hughie and Sean - Jimmy Carson, Sammy Vernon, Patsy Reid and John Matthews. I picked up bits and pieces of boxing skills from everyone. I always enjoyed watching Matthews. For a big fellow he was very nimble, had great footwork. I am not naturally left-handed, but became a southpaw because we had some very successful southpaws in the gym when I was a kid, including Sammy Vernon.

"I cannot really remember, but that is the way I started to box. I tried to turn around a couple of times to be an orthodox boxer, but it never worked out. I always felt uncomfortable. I probably tried to copy other fighters in the gym who were southpaws. Vernon was the best at that time. He turned pro with Burt McCarthy of London, but later maintained he entered professional boxing too early. He was 18, and a cracking amateur, but went to London to try and further his professional career."

Sam won every amateur title possible, right through from Ulster and Irish Juveniles, Ulster and Irish Juniors, and Ulster and Irish Seniors. He went to St. Malachy's Primary School at the bottom of the New Lodge Road, and then moved up to the Holy Family Primary School. Next it was to St. Patrick's Secondary School on the Antrim Road. "Harry Enright, who was Irish national boxing team coach before my father, was a schoolteacher there, at St. Patrick's - the Secondary School better known locally as Bearnageeha. After that, I moved on to the Christian Brothers School at Hightown, Glengormley. I boxed in the Europeans, Olympics, and once in the Commonwealth Federation Championships. After all that, I felt it was time to make a move away from the amateurs. Boxing was in my blood, and rather than look for a job or a trade I turned professional in December, 1985."

He had very good reason not to forget his baptism in the paid ranks. He met and defeated a middleweight from Brighton named Nigel Shingles, and ironically the fight was two weeks after the Belfast boy managed to clear up a painful medical setback from a bout of shingles. Lisburn referee Bob McMillan stopped the contest on 1.56 of the sixth round after Shingles hit the deck. The bout was a part of a Belfast bill headlined by a totally forgettable messy middleweight scrap involving Herol 'Bomber' Graham and slip-and-slide American Sanderline Williams. Master of defence, Graham was in the Eastwood camp then, after BJ purchased his contract from Brendan Ingle. Nottingham-born Graham, who later outclassed Ernie Rabotte in 104 seconds on the undercard of the Cruz-McGuigan match in Las Vegas, made an undistinguished first appearance in the Ulster Hall against wily Williams of Cleveland, Ohio.

Eminent London referee Harry Gibbs, unlike the frustrated fans, had to stay awake long enough to produce a 99-97 summary in favour of Graham. Williams, the 1982 US Golden Gloves Light-middleweight champion, was a very skilful ring mechanic who later lost close decisions to Iran Barkley, Frank Tate and Nigel Benn. Shifty Sanderline also participated in an odd-ball battle for the vacant NABA Middleweight crown against Baltimore-born Ron Essett in Cleveland on October 18, 1988. After the stipulated twelve rounds the fight was declared a draw. The boxers were invited to take part in a unique shoot-out, an extra round. Essett won the title on a split decision in what must be the lone 13-rounder to decide a Championship belt.

Back to Sam's story. The eager prospect was backed by Alfie McLean, a leading Northern Ireland bookmaker and a business associate of B.J. Eastwood. The tall, quiet McLean was Storey's manager at the start. He died in 2006. Sam said: "Alfie was a true gentleman, and very good to me when I switched to professional boxing. I was linked to Eastwood Promotions through Alfie McLean, and for my first couple of paid fights Bobby McAllister was my trainer and in my corner. Alfie looked after the business end of things."

Later, he was coached by Eddie Shaw, and on to his first British title. Before the historic Championship success, his first belt win was in April, 1987 when he beat Rocky McGran. Referee Sid Nathan gave Storey the points verdict over the ten rounds for the vacant Northern Ireland and Irish Middleweight titles in the King's Hall. That fight was on the undercard to Dave Boy's famous first battle with Bassa. Sam changed quickly into street clothes after his fight to get a seat near ringside and watch the crackerjack contest. Storey remained unbeaten until defending the Irish title in Boston Gardens against Steve Collins, on March 18, 1988. That was also his last contest in the 11st 6lbs division. He held a decision over Steve while an amateur, in the Irish Championships, but this time the tables were turned by the high-energy Dubliner.

"Steve had the edge on me because he was in full-time training in Boston, under the Petronelli brothers. He had the best of sparring against such top Americans as Robbie Sims and Marvin Hagler, while my preparations in Belfast did not go well for that one. I had a sparring partner who let me down, and then I suffered an eyebrow cut during sparring in Boston. On the morning of the fight I was in a sauna to make the weight. To be blunt, I did not expect to be able to go the ten rounds, but managed it. Steve was on the ball that night. Later down the line I sparred with Steve in the Eastwood gym. Further on, after he became World champion I won the British Super-middleweight Championship for a second time. After Steve's second win against Eubank in Cork, I was standing beside Eubank when Steve said he would defend against me. But it never happened."

Sam's disappointing trip to the States was soon forgotten when he moved up a grade, from 160 to 168 lbs. On December 7, 1988, he topped an Eastwood Promotion for the first time, clinching a sixth-round win against Darren Hobson of Leeds in the Ulster Hall. Hobson retired after this match-up with an 11-2 record. His other loss was to Nigel Benn. Two outings later Sam secured a special place in British boxing history as the first holder of the newly installed Super-middleweight division. He was paired against Croydon's Tony Burke for the belt on September 19, 1989, and in the Ulster Hall. He took the 12-rounds decision.

He rightly remained very proud of that extra-special exclusive achievement, something that cannot not be matched by anyone else. He was now comfortable in the 12-stone grade. It was a good move for him, as he seemed at ease with the extra couple of pounds. His first defence against the ever-willing Noel Magee in the Ulster Hall, on November, 1989, was a very interesting parochial punch-up between two north Belfast boys. Lots of friends and family from both sides attended the fight. Sam won on a ninth-round stoppage.

Sadly, in his second defence Sam consumed too many murderous right uppercuts from 6' 2" Jamaican-born James Cook of Peckham to lose the title at Maysfield after 1.14 of the tenth round. Ironically, Cook quickly vacated the crown to knock out France's Pierre-Frank Winterstein in the 12th-round in Paris for the European title. Sam's loss was a shattering setback Alfie McLean decided to step down as his manager. "Alfie felt that was as far as he could take me. He did well for me, and then I went my own way, became my own manager," he recalled, "The defence against Cook was a fight I should not have been involved in at that time, because two weeks before the contest I badly damaged an arm. I was unable to put a glove on for sparring, just doing skipping and shadow boxing. It was most unfortunate, yet I felt I was becoming stronger going into the tenth round. Then he landed those right upper-cuts."

Sam also lost his next fight, in Germany, yet it was an experience he never forgot. He accepted sparring work, and was away from home for three weeks to help Henry Maske, a 1988 Seoul Olympic Games Middleweight gold medallist for the then East Germany. Maske, who moved into the top bracket as a professional light-heavyweight, was a 6' 5" southpaw. He was preparing to fight an Italian southpaw, the Uganda-born Yawe Davis, who later won the EBU title. That was why Storey was brought into a training camp in Germany. Maske, who then lived in Frankfurt, scored his tenth straight result, a points win against Davis. Shortly after that, Henry beat Charles Williams for the IBF belt, and made ten defences before losing the World title to Virgil Hill in November, 1996.

Storey met Ali Saida in Berlin, on the Maske's show. It was all part of a money-sparring-fight deal. It was an eight-rounder against a Tunisian-born fighter living in Stuttgart. In the seventh round he had Saida on the deck. "It was one fight I won by the proverbial mile, but lost on a split decision," claimed Sam, "That about crowned one of the worst experiences of my life, the end of three frustrating weeks in the middle of nowhere. After training and sparring I was left completely on my own in a bed-sit for the three weeks. The training camp was beside a tiny village in the back of beyond, somewhere near the Polish border. It was a bleak time for me. Talk about a Spartan training regime! However, also in the camp was an up and coming heavyweight guy named Axel Schulz, who later fought George Foreman."

He sparred Schulz, who was also on that Berlin bill and knocked out Bradford's Steve Garber. Back home again he told his dad that fight folk should watch out for the emerging Schulz. "In 1995, I felt Schultz should have been given the decision against Foreman in an IBF World Heavyweight title fight in the MGM Grand, Las Vegas," added Storey, who built up a head of steam during an encouraging string of wins. Included was a third-round stoppage of England veteran Nigel Rafferty in Maysfield in April, 1992, who later paid him the highest complement in a *Boxing News* interview. Rafferty stated Sam was the only top British boxer of that time to stop him. The list included 'Bomber' Graham and heavy-hitting Errol Christie. One of the great survivors, he declared Storey the best opponent of his long career.

Sam enjoyed a good run of wins. After beating Fidel Castro Smith in the King's Hall at about ten to one in the morning, on the undercard of the WBO Super-middleweight title rematch between Chris Eubank and Ray Close, an offer to fight Eubank for his world belt landed in his lap. "My father was in close contact with Eubank's promoter Barry Hearn, because he trained some of Hearn's fighters.The World title bout was set for August 27, 1994. As the contest progressed against in Cardiff my confidence grew. John Breen was my coach then, and we had a plan for twelve rounds. We decided to let Eubank do his own thing for six rounds, and then go after him, mix it up. We felt Eubank would blow up in the second part of the fight. In the first round, I must admit, he was very strong in the clinches. I was prepared for that, but come the fourth round he was like putty - and blowing heavily, and in between rounds his cornermen were pouring water over his head..

"I was doing really well for five rounds, and felt I could win the title. It was then I believed it could be my night. He caught me with five or six punches in the fifth round. I hit him with right hook, and he backed up. The fifth round was mine, but in the sixth round he caught me with an absolute gem. I went down, but as I did my left leg went behind me. The ankle was damaged, but I got up and saw it out to the end of the round. He landed a couple of great punches in the seventh, including a right hander from the back of the hall that I never saw coming, and referee Dave Parris stopped it after sixty seconds."

After the Eubank disappointment he left trainer Breen. His father came into the corner. He secured another title fight, and on April 27, 1995, beat Ali Forbes on points in York Hall to regain the British Championship. Storey became the second fighter to do that, after Cook, in the Super-middleweight division. Beating Forbes earned him outright ownership of a Lonsdale Belt. He didn't defend the Championship. Instead, he gave it up to go after Leeds-born Henry Wharton on November 11, 1996, in Halifax. The fight was for the Yorkshire hero's European and Commonwealth titles.

Sam insisted: "My target was to win the European, and chase another crack at the World title. Unfortunately that plan didn't work out. It was a bit like the Eubank fight. I was doing well at the start. The opening three rounds against Wharton were the easiest I encountered since turning professional. But, Henry always had that very dangerous left hook, even though I was catching him easily with my right jab." Things began to turn pear-shaped for Storey towards the end of the third. Blood started seeping down his face from a cut on his left eyebrow. His worried father Gerry wanted to stop it. Sam wanted to see it through, and then Wharton unloaded his trademark left hook early in the fourth, and that was that. On April 8, 1997, he had his last contest. It was again for the British Super-middleweight belt. He tried to regain it for a second time, but lost to David Starie in York Hall, Bethnal Green.

Storey, who later moved to live in Spain, reflected on a roller-coaster career: "I regret the losses to Eubank and Wharton, because they were fights I was confident of winning. John Breen had me in perfect condition for the Eubank fight. My dad had me in great shape for the fight with Ali Forbes, and then for the big one with Wharton. Call it bad luck, if you will, but didn't get any breaks in those two contests against Eubank and Wharton."

PUNCHING PREACHER

RAY CLOSE always seemed too gentle a big man to be in a ring trying to hammer the daylights out of opponents. The six-footer with the high-pitched voice from east Belfast was a contradiction. He punched for pay out of the Eastwood stable, came within a whisker of winning the WBO World Super-middleweight belt and was also, at times, a lay preacher in Belfast. Close was the 'nearly man' of the Eastwood outfit, grossly unlucky not to win a World belt. Before turning professional he dominated the Ulster and Irish Amateur Middleweight scene, with back-to-back titles in 1987 and '88. He boxed out of the Ledley Hall Youth Club.

Born on January 20, 1969, he came from the Mount Merrion Crescent district of south east Belfast. His early sporting interests were in soccer and rugby, and during his second year at Knockbreda High School he participated in judo. He turned to boxing, and was coached by Herbie Young. From age 14 up to age 19, before he turned professional, he was unbeaten in Ulster and All-Ireland amateur boxing contests. He won two Ulster Senior titles and the corresponding Irish Middleweight Championships of 1986 and '87.

Close said: "My dream then was to box in the 1988 Olympic Games in Seoul, but I was overlooked. I was hoping to get to Korea, do well, and start in the professional game. It didn't happen. Ireland selectors didn't pick a middleweight in the team for Seoul. They sent Irish Light-middleweight champion Kieran Joyce of the Cork Sunnyside club, who seemingly was tight at his weight and instead boxed middleweight. While an amateur, and doing well, my eventual aim was to turn professional.

Not being sent to Seoul made up my mind, so I joined the Barney Eastwood stable. I was not long there before Eddie Shaw sadly left the gym. He was then very ill. Eddie was in my corner for my first three fights."

It was to prove an interesting path for Ray, starting on October 19, 1988, with a second-round stoppage of Steve Foster in the Ulster Hall. Referee Barney Wilson halted the action after 109 seconds. Not long after it became known how devout Close was in his private life. "I still go to pray at the Church of the Latter Day Saints. I didn't learn to be a preacher. We have one preacher in our church, but sometimes I would be invited to get up and talk in the Church."

Coaches Checa and Breen guided Ray to the European Super-middleweight Championship. It was the highlight of his ring career, although failing in his first attempt against holder Frank Nicotra in Seine-et-Marne, France, on July 3, 1992. He was dropped in the eighth round. When he regained his pins referee Walter Schall stopped the fight. On December 18, 1992, he gained a quick opportunity to get back into contention in a fight with Jean Roger Tsidjo at Oise, France. He won the eight-rounder on points, and it earned him a chance to again fight for the European title. Second time around he beat Italy's Vincenzo Nardiello at Lombardio, Switzerland, on March 17, 1993.

Close, who stopped him in the tenth round, said: "He was cut and taking quite a lot of leather at the time. The referee stepped in, gave him a standing count, allowed a bit more boxing, and then stopped it. That great win led almost right away to a shot at WBO World champion Eubank in Glasgow." Eastwood said: "Ray is a nice fellow, and was a very good boxer. The Eubank people made the approach, probably thinking Close, then the new European champion, would be an easy touch. In the first of two WBO contests Close would have taken the decision, instead of a draw against Eubank in Glasgow, but for the knockdown suffered in the 11th round. I think the next time they met, in the return in Belfast, it was also very close. Eubank was given the decision.

"For the Close-Eubank fight in the King's Hall we had Don King in from the United States. I think he was instrumental in getting in US TV for the fight and was also working with Frank Warren. He came to visit us at The Hill. I first met King during WBC Conventions and at a Steve Collins-Reggie Johnson World Middleweight contest in New Jersey. He was a friend of the promoter, who didn't come up with the irrevocable letter of credit 48 hours before the fight..Now it was weigh-in time, and my man (Collins) was on the scales.

"So, King stepped in and said this guy was good enough. King talked and talked - but I would not budge until the money was shown. I found King a hard man to do business with, but OK. He would say, sign the contract and then we'll discuss business. That was his style. He was involved somehow when Espana beat Taylor for the World title in London, and was there when his son managed Canadian boxer Donovan Boucher in a fight against Crisanto. King was one of many promoters I met and worked with - including Astaire, Arum, Duff, Kushner, the Acari brothers and Germany's Wilfred Sauerland."

Close relinquished the European title in order to engage hostilities with the enigmatic Eubank. He remained aggrieved after having to share the spoils over twelve rounds in the Scottish Exhibition Centre. On May 15, 1993, the former Northern Ireland and Irish Super-middleweight king unwittingly handed the fickle judges an escape hatch when he sustained that damaging knock-down in the 11th round. That gave Eubank a 10-8 round when the champion was staring down the barrel of defeat. Roy Francis made it 115-115. Dave Parris had it 116-113 in favour of Close, but Torben Hansen amazingly summarised it 116-112 in favour of Eubank.

After the routine fourth-round stoppage win of Ray Domenge in the King's Hall, Belfast, on October 16, 1993, the rematch against Eubank was set for the King's Hall, on May 21, 1994. Again, England's Pat Thomas was the middleman. This time Eubank was awarded a disputed split decision. There were no knock-downs. Roy Francis' summary was in favour of Close by three rounds, 117-114. Clark Samartino had it 115-114 for the champion, and there were gasps of disbelief when Eugene Glenn bafflingly totalled it 118 to 112 in favour of Eubank. The quality back-up bouts included Julio Cesar Vasquez halting Ahmed Dottue. Also in action were Ray Kane, Sam Storey, Danny Juma and Olympic gold medallist Michael Carruth.

Ray reflected: "In the first fight against Eubank the knock-down didn't help my cause. However, I felt I still did enough to win the fight. It was interesting that England judge Roy Francis made his score even, and that meant the draw to favour Eubank keeping his title. Remarkably, in the return Roy Francis gave me the fight by three points. I believe I beat Eubank easier and cleaner in Belfast than I did in Glasgow. But both decisions didn't go my way, and that's history." That night there was a bid to try and unsettle Eubank before the start to the fight. A midget dressed up like a Leprechaun popped between the ropes and threw stardust on the back of Eubank, yet it didn't seem to faze the champion. "Eubank wasn't a great boxer in my opinion,"claimed Close, "But he did have a very solid chin. That stuck by him in a good career. Looking back, it's all about what might have been, and I suppose I lived up to my name - close."

Sadly, it proved to be Ray's last ring appearance under British Board jurisdiction. There was a problem with a brain scan, and no chance of a third meeting with Eubank. He did not receive further medical clearance to fight in the United Kingdom. Eastwood said: "It was a huge bodyblow to Ray. After that setback I recommended Steve Collins to the WBO, to replace Close against Eubank."

Shattered Close maintained a dignified domestic calm when stripped of his British Boxing Board of Control licence in 1995, but fought on with an Irish Boxing Union licence and was accepted in America, in Illinois. After leaving the Eastwood stable, Ray was managed for contests in the Chicago area by County Galway-born folk, Mike Joyce and the brothers Martin and Oliver McGarry. He finished with a five-fight winning streak. On June 7, 1997, he packed it all in after a fifth-round stoppage of Larry Willis at Hawthorne Park, Cicero. He closed with a career chart of 25 wins, 3 defeats, and one draw. With a bit of fairness falling in his favour things could have been been much better. A winner of the European title he has every right to ponder on one incident in the past and wonder why he was not awarded a World title decision against the enigmatic Chris Eubank.

Living in Bangor, County Down, with wife Linda, three sons and one daughter Sarah he became a security officer at the George Best Belfast City Airport. He also religiously adhered to his Mormon beliefs. "I still do a bit of training to keep in trim, but leave the punching to my daughter Sarah," said Ray, "She took an interest in boxing after coming across an old press photograph of her sitting on my knee, in 1993, on the ring apron when I was training in the Eastwood gym. She was about nine-weeks-old then." In her first season she became the 2007 Underage All-Ireland girl's 56 kilo champion and was trained by Sandy Rice in the Abbey Boxing Club, Bangor. Sarah, 15 in April, 2008, when a student at Priory College, Holywood, went once a month to Dublin to train and spar with other IABA squad members.

Ray's oldest is William, who was 22 on the 18th of January, 2010, and heavily into soccer. He has no interest in boxing. He was then the goalkeeper for Bangor Rangers. Benjamin, 20 in May, 2009, took to music. He plays the piano and was also a singer in the Ulster Youth Choir. The youngest of the Close clan is Joshua, who was 14 in August, 2009. He was a midfield soccer prospect with the Bangor Rangers' Under-14 team. "I still take an interest in what is happening in boxing," added Close, "I don't get into the coaching side of boxing, but go down to the Abbey Club and train a bit. I used to spar some, but not any more. There comes a time to put away the gloves."

His old Ledley Hall Club amateur buddy John Lowey, a former Ulster and Irish Amateur Bantamweight champion and ex international, also had to emigrate and ply his trade in the United States. He passed through the portals of the Castle Street gym. The slick counterpuncher seemed to be heading for stardom after reeling off 13 straight wins under the Eastwood banner. But, like Close, his career went into tailspin when his British licence was withdrawn because of Scan irregularities. Nonetheless, Lowey also resurrected his career in Chicago, and won the low-key IBO World Super-bantamweight belt by stopping Juan Cardona in the fifth round on April 20, 1994. Lowey lost the title in a first defence when halted by Kennedy McKinney in the eighth round in Chicago, on October 2, 1995.

He also made a brave bid to win the WBC Super-bantamweight title, but was stopped by Mexican great Erik Morales in Tijuana, on December 12, 1997. Lowey returned to his Newtownards home, helped out with sparring work against Belfast's former World Flyweight contender Damaen Kelly, and later joined his ex-coach John Breen in the Belfast city centre gym.

58

TOBY and the CIRCUS CONNECTION

PANAMANIAN Victor 'Toby' Cordoba was a rugged southpaw with a patchy record when he arrived in the Eastwood 'League of Nations' gym. Born on December 31, 1973 at Punta, Panama, the 6' 1" hard man turned professional in 1981. He had 18 bouts, including the winning of the Panamanian Middleweight Championship, before joining the Eastwood camp. During his stay he notched a 5-1 record. On May 23, 1990, he had his last Belfast bout, an eight-round points decision against Frank Rhodes in the King's Hall. He then landed the golden opportunity to win a World title, although Eastwood's patience was pushed to the limit in trying to negotiate a French deal. On April 5, 1991, crusty Cordoba won the WBA Super-middleweight title from Chistophe Tiozzo of France, in Marseilles.

He made a successful defence against Vincento Nardiello, before losing the belt on a split decision to American Michael Nunn in Las Vegas - on September 11, 1992. The iconic Mills Lane was the referee. On January 30, 1993, Toby also lost narrowly on points in a rematch with Nunn in Memphis. He moved up a weight division, but failed in his bid to win the WBO Light-heavyweight belt against Leonardo Aguilar. He closed his career in 1999 with a 26-7-3 record.

Eastwood's sixth World champion was the much travelled Fabrice Benichou. Born in Madrid on April 5, 1966, he was a strange mixture . . . a French citizen, yet generally residing in Luxembourg. Benichou made sporadic sparring appearances in the compact Castle Street gym. He had a 66-bout record, winning 46 times and losing 18. The 5' 3" box-fighter was a European Bantamweight champion before coming to Belfast.

BJ said: "He was an amazing character, and a proper little gentleman.

He was a circus boy, born in a circus. He could speak eight languages, and a little Hebrew. When I was negotiating with people from Panama, from France, or wherever from all over the world who were ringing through to the gym, he could speak to any of them for me. It didn't matter what language they were using at the other end of the 'phone. I asked him how many languages he could handle. He told me, so I asked him then what the hell he was doing in boxing? The father arrived here along with a French man, asking me to if I would look after Fabrice. I did that, and we won the World title. He won a few fights while in our stable."

On March 10, 1989, under the Eastwood banner, battling Benichou bagged the IBF Super-bantamweight title on a 12-round split decision against Venezuelan southpaw Jose Sanabria. Coach Checa, who worked in his corner at Limoges when he won the IBF belt, disclosed Benichou boxed in Panama during the beginning and at the end of his career. "He was in Panama City as a young prospect, learning to be a professional boxer, and worked out in the same gym as me. I sparred him way back then." After two defences Benichou lost the World crown to Welcome Ncita, on March 10, 1990, and in Tel Aviv. He tried to win the WBA belt, but was on the weak side of a split decision to Luis Mendoza on October 18, 1990, at Bercy, France.

Seven months later, he won the European Featherweight title in a bout with England's John Davison at Brest, France. He made three successful defences of the crown. On March 14, 1992, he also made a game but vain bid to try and win the IBF Featherweight Championship against Mexico's Manuel Medina at Antibes, France. The ever-active 'Have Gloves Will Travel' Benichou continued in high-profile punch-ups. On September 12, 1992, he was stopped in ten rounds by an Eastwood stablemate Paul Hodkinson, in a WBC Featherweight title fight at Blagnas, France. He lost on a majority verdict to Maurizio Stecca for the European Featherweight Championship, and failed in a European Super-bantamweight title matchup against Spencer Oliver. Also in there, during the twilight phase of his career, was a points loss to Wayne McCullough at The Point Depot, Dublin, on November 12, 1994. Not long after Benichou became World champion he parted company with the Castle Street gym, once Eastwood's coaching staff suggested a rest was needed for the tiny terrier.

Eastwood explained: "His father said he wanted to put him in with so and so, but I suggested Fabrice should take a three or four month break from boxing. I felt the fellow needed a rest after coming off a terribly hard fight. The father insisted the opposite should happen. He would have had Fabrice fighting every other week. At the finish up, I said to Fabrice that what his father wanted him to do I was opposed to the proposals. I told Fabrice he could do with a good long rest to get himself well again. I also said there were good fights out there for him. He was champion at the time. He said: 'Yeah'. He agreed with me, but said he had to do what the family asked of him. His father kept insisting, so I told him to take Fabrice and train him. Occasionally I get a Christmas Card from Fabrice."

Benichou was part of a strong French connection Eastwood Promotions enjoyed with the Acaries brothers, Michel and Louis. The Paris-based pair had a lengthy pedigree in professional boxing. Louis came close to winning both the IBF and European Light-middleweight Championships. In his last outing, Louis lost on points, on June 1, 1985, to Carlos Santos for the IBF belt at the noted Parc des Princes football and rugby arena in Paris. He also tried in vain to win the European Middleweight crown, dropping a 12-rounds decision to England's Tony Sibson. Born in Alger, Algeria, he had a 45-bout career, winning 39 times.

59

CELTIC TIGER

EASTWOOD's thriving stable had a proxy influence on Dubliner Steve Collins' spectacular rise to World stardom. A natural-born fighting machine he arrived on the Belfast scene after leaving America, were he started his professional career with the Petronelli brothers in Boston.

Craggy Collins, who was never halted during his colourful 39-bout career, holds happy memories of that short period in Belfast: "I loved my time in the Eastwood Gym. It was a great gym where I had World-class sparring partners in Victor Cordoba and Crisanto Espana, both soon to become World champions. They were tough men. I was 20 months up there. I got on well with Barney, but I felt the world was changing in boxing when I decided to move on. I joined Barry Hearn." Eastwood kept an affectionately close watch on the career of Collins, and said: "Steve was a very strong guy."

The Celtic Warrior, born in the Dublin suburb of Cabra on July 21, 1964, was the Irish amateur Middleweight champion of 1986 when representing the John McCormick St Savour's Club. He turned professional and boxed 19 times in the United States before heading home in November, 1990. During his spell in America he took the Irish Middleweight belt off his old amateur adversary Sam Storey. It was his eighth contest, plundering a ten-rounds decision in Boston. In the process he reaped revenge for a loss in the Irish amateurs. A professional since October, 1986, swashbuckling Steve stormed to 36 wins from 39 contests. An enormously popular puncher with an outgoing personality, he retired as undefeated WBO Super middleweight champion.

Fighting came second nature to the always enthusiastic and confident Collins: "I started in boxing because it was in the family. My dad, Pascal, and his brother Terry boxed as amateurs. My mother's brother Jack O'Rourke was a former Irish Amateur Middleweight and Heavyweight champion. He beat Danny McAlinden, who later won the Irish Amateur Heavyweight title in 1967 before turning professional."

O'Rourke bagged the first of four Irish amateur crowns in 1963, the Middleweight honours while with the Dublin Guinness Club. He grew into the Heavyweight grade, winning in 1965 while still with the Guinness club, the 1966 title with Port of Dublin, and the 1971 Championship with British Railways. Collins had his first fight at eight years of age in the Corinthians club. The trainer was Maxie McCullough, the hugely respected Corinthians 1947 and '49 Irish Amateur Lightweight titleholder and also the 1949 European champion from the finals in Oslo.

Collins moved to the Arbour Hill club. Mickey Coffey and Mick Sutton were the trainers. Steve's brothers Roddy and Pascal followed him wherever he went, moving on to the Phoenix Club. P.J. Davitt, the former Irish Amateur Light- welterweight winner of 1979 and later a professional, and the great Peter Glennon - the 1939 Irish Amateur Featherweight champion, trained him there. Later, he moved on to be coached by former British professional champions, the brothers 'Young' John and Pat McCormick, in the St Saviour's Club. His prime target was to be a professional boxer, promising himself one day he would be a World champion.

He went to Brockton, Massachusetts, to be with Marvin Hagler and be trained and managed by the Petronelli brothers. Collins moved again to link with Floyd Patterson, and was trained for a short spell by the former World Heavyweight champion in New York City. Steve didn't have a contest under Patterson. While in the United States he lost to Mike McCallum for the Middleweight Championship. The 12-round setback against Jamaica-born 'Body Snatcher' McCallum was for the WBA belt, and held in Boston in February, 1990. Incidentally. it was McCallum who denied Belfast amateur southpaw Kenny Beattie from winning the 1978 Commonwealth Games Welterweight gold medal. They met in the Edmonton final.

Fighting American Kenny Snow was Collins' first outing under the Eastwood banner. Checa was in charge of the training. Again the Dubliner lost in a bid for top World Middleweight honours. His second attempt was against American southpaw Reggie Johnson on April 28, 1992, when he dropped a split decision for the vacant WBA crown in East Rutherford, New Jersey. Following the loss to the awkward Johnston he also made an unsuccessful bid to win the European Middleweight Championship. He was on the wrong end of a disputed 12-rounds decision in Italy against Zaire-born Italian Sumbu Kalambay, his third and last defeat.

"I was robbed in the fight with Johnson, and again in my next contest against Kalambay," claimed crusty Collins: "I had a fight after that, winning against Johnny Melfah, before leaving Eastwood. I felt Barney had lost the power in boxing politics." The Collins departure to Barry Hearn led to clinching the low-key WBO version of the World Middleweight Championship. In May, 1994, super-strong Steve, never lost for a word, halted England's Chris Pyatt in Sheffield. Then it was the move up a grade, and on to recognised World honours as a Super-middleweight kingpin in March, 1995, taking the WBO crown from Chris Eubank at Millstreet, Cork. British Boxing Board of Control officers selected the showdown the 1995 'British Contest of the Year'. He went to Hollywood, California, to be coached by Freddie Roach, who was his trainer until the end of the boxing career.

Stand-out scrapper Steve, whose general demeanour suggested he would be perfectly at home fighting in a phone booth, also bypassed Dave McAuley's Irish record of the most successful World title defences with seven safe results. Not unlike McAuley, who had five wins, Collins was also in the thick of very entertaining trench warfare, especially two high-voltage punch-ups against Eubanks and two rip-roaring battles against Nigel Benn. The six-footer won his last 15 contests, including the eight WBO title fights, but decided to retire after the third-round TKO title defence win on July 5, 1997 against Kansas fireman Craig Cummings in the Kelvin Hall, Glasgow. Collins was dropped in the first round, and for a third time in his career, but came back to give Cummings a hammering.

Steve was then linked to a defence against Joe Calzaghe, yet apparently was more interested in a big-money unification bout against WBC champion Roy Jones Jnr. However, he decided to retire. His younger brother Pascal also boxed professionally out of Massachusetts, and then became a boxing promoter. Another brother, Roddy did amateur boxing for a spell, but was best known as a soccer player of distinction. He had player and managerial stints with clubs such as Bohemians, Crusaders, Carlisle United, Bangor, Shamrock Rovers and Cork City.

"Brother Roddy is the best dressed man in Ireland," cracked Collins, "When he was playing in the Irish League I went to watch him in action. I was staying in the Jean Anderson guest house at Bangor. I was boxing out of the Eastwood gym. Roddy went out of soccer management for a spell, but stayed in football as a TV soccer match analyst. He also gave up running a crew of plasterers and bricklayers in the building trade around Dublin." Steve became a television fight analyst, also entered showbiz, and landed the bit part of a club doorman in the 1998 film 'Lock, Stock, and Two Smoking Barrels'. In 2010 Steve and brother Pascal opened a boxing gym in Dublin.

60

FLAMIN' EAMONN

BALLYMENA battler Eamonn Loughran was a rookie welterweight in the Eastwood camp. He took a different route to World recognition than another illustrious member of the Ballymena All Saints club. Liam Neeson was a former Ulster Amateur Youth Heavyweight champion, who put away the gloves to concentrate on achieving a glittering stage and film career.

"I never saw Liam box. He was long gone from the gym when I started. I met him a couple of occasions when he called into the club, including the time he came over from America to officially open up the new club premises in the early 1980's," said broad-shouldered Loughran. Before he really set out to reach the top he had to endure an embarrassing slap on the wrists from the British Boxing Board of Control. A World Junior Amateur Light-welterweight silver medallist in Havana (1987), he signed up to the Eastwood stable at 17-years-of-age.

On December 7, 1987, Loughran unwittingly made a little bit of local history. His paid debut proved to be illegal. He defeated Adam Muir of Greenock on a fourth-round disqualification in the Ulster Hall. Born on June 5, 1970, he was found to be five months below the British Boxing Board of Control's starting age limit of 18. Perhaps, in hindsight, he had no Senior Amateur experience worth noting and was a mite immature in making the switch to the paid ranks. However, after his late father Ned Loughran held talks with Eastwood the eager youngster decided to take the plunge.

He made his official paid debut a few days after his 18th birthday, when stopping Welsh light-middleweight Tony Britland in the opening round in Sheffield City Hall. His third outing without a vest was in Panama City, where he was held to a four-round draw by local middleweight Antonio Campbell on June 25, 1988, in the famous Gimnasio Nuevo venue. His first legitimate appearance in a Belfast ring was his next outing, on October 19, 1988, in the Ulster Hall. Referee Barney Wilson handed Eamonn a 60-56.5 result against Jamaica-born Stan King.

Eamonn remembered the career moves: "Willie Agnew was head coach of the All Saints Club in Ballymena when I joined. Willie did not do a lot of coaching with me. It was mainly Tony McAvoy and Martin Ward. Tony was retired from amateur boxing. Active boxers then in the club included Harry McKeown, Tommy O'Neill, Maurice Dempster, Francis McNally and Jimmy Meeke." Rock-hard Loughran, given total backing by his father and his uncle Seamus Loughran, instantly dominated Underage Championships. He won seven Juvenile titles, every honour possible at Ulster and Irish level, and was unbeaten for up to six years.

Eamonn's eye-catching progress led to representing Ireland in the World Junior Championships in Cuba. "I boxed in merely a few Senior Amateur fights because I turned professional after returning from Cuba," added the likeable Loughran, who finished with a 30-bout career that featured 26 wins, one draw, and one no-contest. After nine bouts he left the Eastwood management by mutual agreement and joined Barry Hearn Matchroom Promotions, but he looked on the time in Eastwood's Castle Street gym as a crucial learning experience. "I was there for a couple of years. The Eastwood Gym was very busy. Eddie (Shaw) was ill then, and becoming weaker and weaker. Still, he did a lot for me, and often had me in the ring for sparring with Espana. Eddie would urge me to try and nail Espana to see what would happen. I used to get the upper hand of Espana, who was tall, lanky but seemed to suit me. He was probably a better fighter than me, and would have beaten me in a real contest, but I did get to him from time to time during the sparring sessions.

"That was part of Eddie's strategy, to build my confidence. He would shout: 'Keep that going Eamonn.' It was all part of building me up for my fights. When you have somebody behind you poking and prodding all the time, as Eddie did, it helped to improve confidence. Checa was also there, and great for me. Once the sparring sessions were over Bernardo would come over and work with me on the pads. He showed me all the moves. Technically he was very good. I enjoyed my time there. It was a great learning experience.

"One of the main memories I have is going there to train alongside four fighters who were or were just about to be World Champions: McAuley, Hodkinson, Espana and Cordoba. Also working out in the gym then were British and European champions. I was a small fish in that big pool of fighters. Then when I went to Hearns gym I was trained by Freddie King. To be quite honest, when I left Eastwood I did most of the training on my own. I remembered the teachings of Eddie (Shaw), Bernardo (Checa) and also an Irish amateur team coach from Cuba, Nicholas Hernandez.

"Once you were taught by the likes of those top coaches somebody else is not going to show you anything new. I trained under the Cuban guy Hernandez for the World Juniors. Checa was something different. I was fortunate in that I had two of the best ever overseas coaches to hit the island of Ireland. I also had Eddie Shaw, a fantastic man."

Eastwood said: "Eamonn was a very strong fighter with plenty of heart. Bernardo spent the best part of two years with him, coaching him. Eamonn's father Ned then came in to see me, and said his son was unhappy. I said that was unfortunate, and I would let him go." Loughran's move to train in London meant fighting many times in England. He also boxed in Germany and in Spain. After an unbeaten run of 17 contests he suffered the first of two career defeats, when disqualified in the fifth round against Nigerian Tony Ekubia in Bury, on March 10, 1992. The useful Ekubia later became British and Commonwealth Light-welterweight champion.

Eamonn quickly recovered from the frustrating setback, and three fights later hit an unexpected jackpot. His first major move under Hearn was to stop Canada's Donovan Boucher. On November 24, 1992, he beat the odds and Boucher to clinch the Commonwealth Welterweight Championship in the Doncaster Dome. "Winning my first title was one of the biggest memories, when beating Boucher. He was a top-ranked World fighter then. Before I met him he had wins over Kirkland Laing, Mickey Hughes and Gary Jacobs." It was suggested to Loughran before the action if he managed to survive ten rounds against Boucher he would be doing well, and it would be a good experience for him. Few people gave Eamonn a chance. The referee was Adrian Morgan, who stopped the contest in the third round after Loughran nailed Boucher with a left hook, and put his opponent out through the ropes.

He made one defence of the title, beating Michael Benjamin of Guyana. Then it was the leap up the ladder to go into a fight for the vacant WBO

Championship. On Saturday October 16, 1993, he notched a unanimous decision against lanky Lorenzo Smith of Chicago in the King's Hall, Belfast. There were also wins on that show for Noel Magee, Ray Close and Ray Kane. At the same venue on Saturday January 22, 1994, in his first WBO title defence, he scored a successful 12-round decision against Italy's Alessandro Duran.

On the undercard were Steve Collins, Mark Delaney, Eamonn McAuley and Bernard McComiskey. Incidentally, Duran, son of former European Light-middleweight and Middleweight champion Juan Carlos Duran, made his professional debut in Chicago's DiVinci Manor on July 7, 1983. It was the same fight show that featured McGuigan knocking out McGowan in one round. Duran, born in Ferrara and a brother of ex-WBC Cruiserweight champion Massimiliano Duran, later won the obscure WBU Welterweight crown. In December, 1994, Loughran had to settle for a technical draw outcome in the G-Mex Centre, Manchester, following fourth-round injuries sustained in an accidental head-butt incident with southpaw former champion Manning Galloway of Columbus, Ohio.

On Saturday May 27, 1995, Loughran was involved in a non event against Angel Beltre of the Dominican Republic. The title defence in Belfast's King's Hall was declared a no-contest. Referee Roberto Ramirez called a halt after 2.23 of the third round following a clash of heads. Both fighters were badly cut. Loughran was ahead on points. Next up was a sixth-round technical stoppage of American Tony Ganarelli, who was dropped in the sixth round of the WBO belt defence in the Ulster Hall on August 26, 1995. Eamonn's rematch in a voluntary defence with former Los Angeles Olympic Games fighter Beltre resulted in a 12-round points decision in the Ulster Hall on October 7, 1995. It was to prove his last win, and his penultimate fight.

On April 13, 1996, he lost the WBO title in shattering circumstances. Shell-shocked Loughran was rescued by England referee Roy Francis in 51 seconds - stopped by leading contender Jose Luis Bueno, a 22-year-old from Durango, Mexico, in the Everton Park Centre, Liverpool. He was caught cold by a thudding right hander. He never recovered, and took two further trips to the canvas. Devastated Loughran needed time to consider his career, but never came back.

He explained the reason: "I took a year out, and then went to Jersey, in the Channel Islands, to train for two weeks with Stevie Collins. At that time my son was born. I realised the desire and the drive was not there anymore. I sparred with Steve (Collins) when he was preparing for a title fight against Nigel Benn. But, after that I didn't want to continue in boxing, nor more sparring. My enthusiasm wasn't there before my last fight, and even with a year away, a good break and rest, the hunger to continue in boxing was gone. There was no more fight in me. Maybe it was because I was into boxing at such a young age and that I turned professional so young."

Before he retired for good, he fleetingly contemplated a rematch against Bueno. He was also linked to a contest against Ireland's Barcelona Olympic gold medallist Michael Carruth, but stayed outside the ropes to concentrate on a healthy property enterprise. Carruth tried to bring the WBO laurels back to Ireland in September 1997, but lost in Aachen, Germany, to Romania's Michael Loewe. Another Irish fighter also failed to recover Loughran's belt. Commonwealth Games gold medallist Neil Sinclair of Monkstown, County Antrim, was stopped in December, 2000, in Sheffield by defending champion Daniel Santos, a Puerto Rican southpaw. Heavy-handed Sinclair, lacking sufficient experience despite dropping Santos in the first round, recovered from the setback to make a Lonsdale belt his own property as British Welterweight champion.

61

BOSS of BOSSES

DELIGHTED Eastwood was king of the heap when voted the World Boxing Association's 'Manager of the Year' for 1991. It was a richly deserved accolade, the first high honour for an Irish manager. All the years of devoted involvement in the unstinting support of amateur boxing, professional boxing, promoting small-hall boxing shows in the 1960's, and guiding six fighters to World belts secured suitable recognition.

The same year he was honoured, the 'Legend' selected was American Joey Giardello, a former World Middleweight champion who died in 2008. The top boxer award went to Kaosai Galaxy of Thailand. The glowing tribute in a glossy programme to celebrate all the awards, held during 1992, stated: 'Barney Eastwood collects fine paintings, rare clocks, object d'arts, and also, since 1985, World boxing champions. Barry McGuigan was his first. He won the WBA Featherweight title in 1985. A great year for Eastwood, but 1991 was even greater. He began with one World champion and closed it with three. Dave McAuley held onto his IBF Flyweight crown, as Paul Hodkinson took the WBC Featherweight title, and Victor Cordoba became WBA Super-middleweight king.'

There was also a published potted background history about Eastwood's rise from publican to bookmaker, to property speculator, to boxing promoter and to boxing manager. The occasion was, however, tinged with sadness. The Eastwood biography in the WBA awards' programme stated: 'Tragedies have cast shadows on his life in recent times. Fintan, a much loved son, died suddenly. Eddie Shaw, his superb trainer and coach, contracted terminal cancer.'

The programme also featured an advertisement from the Eastwood gym. It stated: 'Best Wishes to W.B.A. President Gilberto Mendoza . . .

from B.J. Eastwood and Victor Cordoba, W.B.A. World Super-middleweight champion.' The legend also trumpeted: 'Europe's Most Talented Gym' - Trainers: Bernardo Checa (Top Panamanian coach); John Breen (Belfast).' The advertisement also listed 16 boxers in the Eastwood Stable, headed then by World champions Cordoba and McAuley. Other leading lights included Crisanto Espana, number two at that time in the WBA Welterweight ratings, Steve Collins, ranked number one WBA Middleweight contender, European Featherweight champion Paul Hodkinson - then the number four in the WBA rankings, and British Middleweight champion Herol Graham, who was listed 10th in the WBA ratings. Also named in the Eastwood group were Panama's Francisco Arroya - the IBF Inter-continental Bantamweight champion, British Light-heavyweight champion Crawford Ashley, John Lowey, Ritchie Wenton, Nigel Wenton, Noel Magee, Joe Egan, Ray Close, Sam Storey and Oscar Checa.

The top manager trophy, presented by Jimmy Binns, was one of the proudest moments of Eastwood's influence in World boxing affairs. He retained many mementoes of the great occasions. The house on The Hill holds a Pandora's Box brimming with boxing memorabilia. The nostalgia attached hold special interest only to Eastwood and anyone with an enthusiastic hands-on knowledge of some of Ireland's most vibrant periods in professional boxing.

Eastwood's office-cum-trophy room has all sorts of treasures from the punching past, including most of the sets of gloves used by his famous World champions. Draped on the walls are gloves of all description, including some looking the worse for the wear and with obvious signs of having soaked up blood during battle. "Every glove in this place means something to me," insisted BJ, "Most of the gloves belonged to fights involving Crisanto, Dave Boy, McGuigan. They are mementoes of a special time gone past. Unfortunately, some people borrowed a couple of pair of gloves and never returned them. They were World title gloves. All gloves gathered down the years were the result of me just lifting them after the fights."

The ghostly gloves chronicle in many respects Eastwood's lifelong affection for boxing. He proudly brought down the mitt mementoes from their places of worship to read the names of the fighters involved, and the dates of the contests. Included were the gloves used by Jim Watt and Charlie Nash in their WBC Lightweight title fight held in Glasgow's Kelvin Arena on March 14, 1980. Referee was Sid Nathan. Watt, making a second defence, touched down in the first round. Nash, then with a 21-1 record and the European champion, sustained a gruesome gash following a clash of heads.

"I went to Glasgow to watch the fight, and managed to get my hands on the gloves afterwards. That was quite a contest, while it lasted," Eastwood recalled. Derry stylist Nash made three trips to the canvas in the fourth round before the controversial argument ended after 2.10. The judges summaries before the stoppage were - referee Nathan 29-28, James Brimmell 28-28, and John Coyle 29-28 all in favour of Watt. The Scot finished with a 38-8 record, retiring after losing the belt to Nicaraguan Alexis Arguello in his fifth defence, and also his first outside of Scotland. He was outpointed on June 20, 1981, in the Empire Pool, Wembley. Referee was Arthur Mercante.

Another set of gloves at The Hill was 'rescued' after a European Light-heavyweight title fight on March 5, 1995, in Marseilles. In the action was Belfast's Noel Magee against Fabrice Tiozzo, who won on a fourth-round stoppage. The always game Magee earlier lost in the eighth round to the then unbeaten Dariusz Michalczewski for the vacant IBF Inter-Continental Light-heavyweight title in Aachen on October 16, 1993. Eastwood had other gloves worn by Magee, when the fighter lost in September 28, 1992, to Maurice Core in Manchester, for the vacant British Light-heavyweight title. He also lost to fellow Belfast boxer Sam Storey, in a British Super-middleweight title bout in the Ulster Hall on November 29, 1989.

Persistent Magee hit the jackpot at Basildon, England, on May 9, 1995, when halting London's Garry Delaney for the British Commonwealth Light-heavyweight crown. Four months later he lost the title to Nicky Piper in Cardiff Arms Park. The 6' 1" brother of fellow prizefighters Terry and Eamonn Magee, was born on December 16, 1965, and finished with a 27-8-2 record. He retired after losing to fellow Oldpark-bred fighter Darren Corbett in an Irish Cruiserweight title fight in the Ulster Hall on April 29, 1997.

Gloves plundered from big-fight shows included those used in a February 28, 1991, European Light-heavyweight title between Eastwood fighter Crawford Ashley and Graciano Rocchigiani, with the German taking a points decision. Long haired Ashley (Gary Crawford) stood 6' 3", and took on the best at world level. He finished with a 33-10-1 record. He won the British title, but again had to endure heartbreak on September 23, 1992, when trying to take the EBU crown. He came out of Lombardi, Italy, with a draw against Yawe Davis. Big Ashley also had two unsuccessful cracks at World honours. He lost to Michael Nunn in Memphis (TKO 6) on April 23, 1993. After taking the vacant Commonwealth crown, on a points decision against Nicky Piper in Cardiff, he went to Nevada on April Fool's Day, 1995, only to lose to Virgil Hill for the WBA belt. Eventually, on March 1, 1997, he made it third-time-lucky in Europe, scoring a third-round knock-out over Roberto Perez at Everton Sports Centre, Liverpool. He bowed out on March 3, 1999, after losing (TKO 8) the British, Commonwealth and European belts to Clinton Woods in Manchester.

Eastwood was reminded of his short tenure as boss of Bomber Graham through the gloves used in Sheffield City Hall on June 8, 1988. Graham stopped James Cook in the fifth-round for the British Middleweight title vacated by Tony Sibson. Also hanging around were the gloves used on August 2, 1994, by Eubank in a WBO Super-middleweight title defence against Storey in Cardiff. BJ also 'liberated' gloves worn by Steve Collins, when the Dubliner lost to American Reggie Johnston for the WBA Middleweight Championship in New Jersey on April 27, 1992. The gloves used in the May 21, 1994, WBO Super middleweight fight between Chris Eubank and Ray Close also take a place of honour. One of the prized possessions are the gloves used on October 31, 1992, in the Earls Court Exhibition Centre where Espana halted Meldrick Taylor in the eighth round to become WBA Welterweight champion.

The boxing memorabilia also included a well-thumbed book that listed some of the names of boxers under Eastwood's control during the halcyon days of the Gym. Lodged with the British Boxing Board of Control on the 23rd of March, 1984, and registered to Eastwood, were Barry McGuigan, Frank McCullagh, Young Patsy Quinn, P.J. Davitt, Damien Fryers, Seamus McGuinness, Peppy Muir, David Irving, Mick Queally, Rocky McGran, Dave McAuley, Herol Graham, Eamonn McAuley, Paul Hodkinson, Roy Webb, Andy Holligan, Francis Harding, Nigel Wenton and John Lowey.

These were some of the fighters Eastwood controlled between 1984 and up to 1992. Incidentally, Holligan later became a British champion. He was the 1987 ABA Light-welterweight champion, and made his pro debut with the Eastwood camp in October, 1987. Holligan had seven fights out of the Belfast gym. He moved on, won the British Light-welterweight title, and also lost in the fifth round in a bid to win the WBC title. In December, 1993, he went down to the great Julio Cesar Chavez, in Pueblo, Mexico.

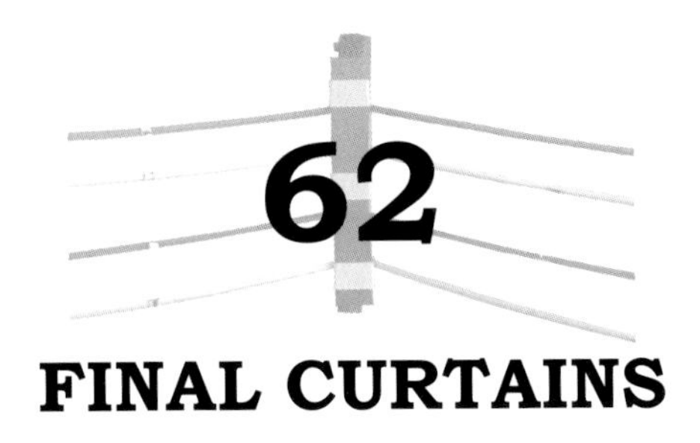

FINAL CURTAINS

RUEFUL reflection on a significantly telling contribution to Irish and World boxing moved Eastwood to the burning soul searcher of why did the McGuigan story go so horribly wrong? Did Eastwood assume too much? Was he unaware of a change in circumstance, of attitudes and interferences? Why did he not step off the wobbling merry-go-round like son Stephen did, after achieving the initial target? Perhaps Frances and he, and the supporting family, felt they invested too much of their lives into the McGuigan project to let go without a battle.

Eastwood conceded: "I have to confess I was very protective of McGuigan during the early period of his career. There is no doubt about it. I suppose I did that because I was trying to look to the future, to guide him towards a World title. We got there. That was the goal. Maybe I should have walked away then, like my son Stephen did after Loftus Road, but we had other fighters to think about."

Even before the drama of Loftus Road, the last high hurdle for McGuigan I care to remember, there were ever-shifting trends. The public wanted more and more of the Cyclone. The insatiable media wanted more of what was perceived a sure-fire winner. You had that gut feeling McGuigan was going all the way to the top. Success created a growing band of boxing experts. Barry's barnstorming soon catapulted him into the matinee idol category. Spectacular ring achievements were insular early on, but not for long. The 'Peace' idea, the early titles, and suddenly it was no longer an Irish phenomenon.

Eastwood added: "He won the British title, and then the European title, and my problems really began from there on. I could feel there was a bit of a change happening. He always had a few advisors, maybe half-a-dozen during the early days. That was OK, but after he won Europe the number of advisors multiplied. It was still workable, nonetheless. Then he had his Pedroza fight. He was World champion, and after that things altered. More and more people were giving advice, but significantly this time with a couple of key people holding influence."

BJ felt the shadowy aides could see big money everywhere, a bonanza in prospect: "I suspected they must have been saying among themselves: 'Jeez, this is a goldmine, McGuigan could be the biggest thing of all time in Irish sport'. I believed they were sure McGuigan was going to earn multi-millions, and also felt Eastwood was going to get a huge slice of it. I had a feeling they did not wish that to happen. probably saying:'There's no need for Eastwood to get any of it. Blah, blah, blah . . . and this wee lad from Clones needs to be protected from the likes of Eastwood.' I felt that was the reason for the beginning of the whole downfall."

Nonetheless, Eastwood looks back with pride: "What has always been overlooked was that I did not take up boxing management as a job. It was a hobby. It was a great investment in the first place, and a very exciting time while it lasted. Let me be blunt. I would not have signed up McGuigan in the first place, would not have gone to all the trouble, all the planning, building our own gym, if I didn't think he had the ability to go to the top. I had faith in him, that he could do it. Mind you, we only discovered his capabilities along the way. Every sportsman is the same.

"We had to be patient. We got to know the possibilities as we went along, and we matched him against opponents in such a way that we generally had that vital extra edge. He also had great charisma, that showbusiness thing about him. He probably inherited that from his father Pat, who was in show business as a top Irish singer and a Eurovision Song representative for Ireland. McGuigan had all that. It was a good time, and great for the public. It was during a period when people were crying out for something to lift things, brighten life, someone they could support in sport.

"I learned from the 1960's how to work with the media. It was an exciting era for the press when McGuigan came along. Supporters and reporters from all over Ireland came to see him. Sports journalists and news feature writers came regularly up from Dublin, from Cork, from

County Kerry, from all over the place, all wanting to know more and more of what was happening. The Irish media couldn't get enough of him. The publicity McGuigan generated and received during the early stages in Ireland was absolutely tremendous. People kept wanting to know what was next for the fighter. There was a high level of expectation, and so it got bigger and bigger, with media people coming in from England, Scotland - and then from the win against Valerio Nati there was increased interest from Europe."

The magical McGuigan hayride continued to snowball, to reach out to the TV moguls in America, and most importantly provided enlightment to everyone in Northern Ireland during a period of drudgery and depression. Winning the World belt made big news, brought massive, almost overnight, riches but almost as rapidly plunged to frightening freefall.

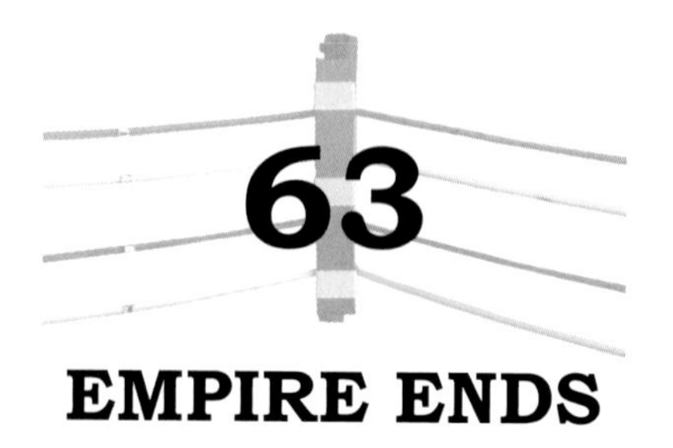

EMPIRE ENDS

FEBRUARY, 2008, proved a sentimental milestone for the Eastwood family. Over half-a-century of building a bookmaking empire in Northern Ireland was wiped away at stroke of a pen. It was obviously a painful wrench, although well cushioned by a cheque for £135 million from Ladbrokes. Still, the deal to part with the 55-chain of shops almost came unhinged at the eleventh hour.

Eastwood confessed he began to have second thoughts. "The sale of the shops was hard work," he said, "We had more than one party after us to buy the business. Even on the evening I signed the contract I still wasn't a seller at five o'clock late that afternoon. We were negotiating for quite a while. I told the purchaser then: 'If you want to buy the business here is the position'. There are certain things that would be important to me."

He revealed he included crucial provisos before sealing the deal: "At the finish-up there were three deal-breakers, three things in the transaction that had to be agreed. I insisted unless the three things were done according to my instructions I would not sign. One was to keep on the staff. The purchasers said they were not going to do this or that. On the day before the deal was agreed I said I would not travel up to Belfast to sign. I informed my solicitor to tell the people concerned if they were still interested to ring me between five and six o'clock. If they told my solicitor they agreed to the three items I would go into the city and sign. If they didn't agree I would feel free to walk away, no deal.

"By ten past six the next evening, a Wednesday, I had no communication at all. I said to myself then: 'Well - that's that'. I was just as pleased. I was beginning to feel it was not going to be all that simple to end the family's 54 years in the bookmaking business. The next thing was the phone rang. My solicitor asked me to come up to Belfast. He told me the purchasers had capitulated, and agreed in full. I went up to the city centre, and they said they thought we would be signing the deal about half past seven. We didn't sign until around a quarter to twelve. At one point I had a notion of going home. There were some other problems, some other solicitors - a real serious meeting. I suppose they didn't realise I had been in a few deal-breakers before in my lifetime, especially in sealing deals in boxing. At that late stage of the proceedings I would have been nearly as pleased had it not gone through. I have been thinking about it since, but it is done now, and that is that."

For this biography I was pleasantly surprised B.J. Eastwood initially agreed to let me try and scrape away the surface and come to a basic understanding of what makes this single-minded man tick. The journey he took me on was an absorbing adventure. I could equate with most of the links to sporting events, especially the great boxing occasions. I first wanted to dig beneath the skin, peel away the layers of protection he created after the McGuigan legal heartbreak, and find out why he bothered to spend a good chunk of his life, and also that of Frances, so closely associated with boxing. He bankrolled many amateur shows, always a generous backer to many boxing clubs and GAA clubs - and their money-raising promotions.

From his very earliest days, on the streets of Cookstown, there emerged the core conclusion to his successes. Eastwood never rested. The sharp mind remained ever active, forever working out moves. Once he relentlessly stalked and captured a prey or target, in his own quietly efficient way, this man with a logical and calculating mind, and natural-born gambling instincts, quickly moved on to the next objective.

Even after the horror of the bust-up with McGuigan, BJ, wife Frances, and family moved on to enlarge and modernize the bookmaking empire. In tandem was a property portfolio that mushroomed beyond all expectations. Despite the wrench of moving firstly away from the boxing, and then the bookmaking scene, there is no way I could envisage Eastwood idling at The Hill. He was created for the hustle and bustle of the market place, trading, bartering, the quick decisions. He's a restless soul in that respect, always on the prowl for a rewarding deal.

That is where he continued to be, the insatiable appetite always spurred on by the chase. My belief is he has never been a person who could sit on his hands, rest on his laurels, nor accept second best. Eastwood, a fighter from his days in short pants, has to be at the coalface.

He began as a wheeler-dealer. He stayed that way, and always provided wise council when keeping a weather eye on the progress of the family's enterprises. He signed off by conceding he continues to try and gain an edge in business deals. He remained an avid follower of the happenings in boxing affairs, and also his beloved Tyrone Gaelic football team.

After the sale of the bookmaking business, he said: "The dust never settles. I have loads of things to be doing. You move on. You look forward. It is never great to look back. There is no point in looking back with regrets. However, I have a regret from my wife's point of view. I probably never realised at the time how punishing the whole boxing thing was for Frances. An old country saying is that when you put your hand on the plough you should never look back. I suppose everybody looks back, takes a glimpse into the past. Then you look forward again. Occasionally I have looked back. It is natural. I saw a lot of things that didn't please me. I didn't run the boxing to get a living. It is something in my blood. I did not do it for money, but I also didn't do it to be a fool, to lose money, to give money away."

The author found the exercise on the life and always exciting times of B.J. Eastwood a fascinating journey. Having been index-linked to a good part of Eastwood's boxing forays, ever since the mid-1960 era, I was there in person, and able to avoid falling into the age-old trap that seems to afflict so many biographers of boxing personalities - of using reckless assumptions, innuendo, invented conversations, and the endless splurge of recycled errors.

This tale of 'Hooked on the Jab' is designed to give as accurate an insight as possible to the facets that make up the man of many parts, B.J. Eastwood, and his no small contribution to Irish and World professional boxing.

EASTWOOD'S SIX PACK

SIX of the best headed the Eastwood list of honours in professional boxing. Here are the career details of the six fighters he guided to World Championship success.

BARRY 'Clones Cyclone' McGUIGAN

Born February 28, 1961, at Clones, County Monaghan, Republic of Ireland
Career tally 32-3

RING RECORD

May 31 1989	Jim McDonnell	L	TKO 4
	G-Mex Centre, Manchester, England.		
Dec 1 1988	Julio Cesar Miranda	W	TKO 8
	Pickett's Lock Stadium, London.		
June 25 1988	Francisco Tomas Da Cruz	W	TKO 4
	Luton Town FC ground, Luton, England.		
Apl 20 1988	Nicky Perez	W	KO 4
	Alexandra Pavilion, London.		
June 23 1986	Steve Cruz	L	Pts 15
	Caesar's Palace, Las Vegas. USA.		
	WBA World Featherweight title.		
Feb 15 1986	Danilo Cabrera	W	TKO 14
	Simmonscourt RDS Arena, Dublin.		
	WBA World Featherweight title.		
Sept 28 1985	Bernard Taylor	W	TKO Ret 8
	King's Hall, Belfast.		
	WBA World Featherweight title.		
Jun 8 1985	Eusebio Pedroza	W	Pts 15
	Loftus Road Stadium, London.		
	WBA World Featherweight title.		

March 26 1985	Farid Gallouse Wembley Arena, London. European Featherweight title.	W	TKO 2
Feb 23 1985	Juan LaPorte King's Hall, Belfast.	W	Pts 10
Dec 19 1984	Clyde Ruan Ulster Hall, Belfast. European and British Featherweight titles.	W	KO 4
Oct 13 1984	Felipe Orozco King's Hall, Belfast.	W	KO 2
June 30 1984	Paul DeVorce King's Hall, Belfast.	W	TKO 5
June 5 1984	Esteban Eguia Royal Albert Hall, London, European Featherweight title.	W	TKO 3
Apl 4 1984	Jose Caba King's Hall, Belfast.	W	TKO 7
Jan 25 1984	Charm Chiteule King's Hall, Belfast.	W	TKO 10
Nov 16 1983	Valerio Nati King's Hall, Belfast. European Featherweight title.	W	KO 6
Oct 5 1983	Ruben Herasme Ulster Hall, Belfast.	W	KO 2
July 9 1983	Lavon McGowan DiVinci Manor Hotel, Chicago.	W	KO 1
May 22 1983	Sammy Meck Navan Exhibition Centre, Navan, County Meath. Republic of Ireland.	W	Rtd 6
April 12 1983	Vernon Penprase Ulster Hall, Belfast. Vacant British Featherweight title.	W	TKO 2
Nov 9 1982	Paul Huggins Ulster Hall, Belfast. Final Eliminator for British Featherweight title.	W	TKO 5
Oct 5 1982	Jimmy Duncan Ulster Hall, Belfast.	W	Rtd 4
June 14 1982	Young Ali WSC Mayfair, London. Young Ali died after 5 months in a coma.	W	KO 6
Apl 22 1982	Gary Lucas Lakeland Forum, Enniskillen, County Fermanagh.	W	KO 1

March 23 1982	Angelo Licata Ulster Hall, Belfast.	W	TKO 2
Feb 23 1982	Angel Oliver Ulster Hall, Belfast.	W	TKO 3
Feb 8 1982	Ian Murray WSC Mayfair, London.	W	TKO 3
Jan 27 1982	Jose Luis De La Sagra Ulster Hall, Belfast.	W	Pts 8
Dec 8 1981	Peter Eubank Ulster Hall, Belfast.	W	TKO 8
Oct 26 1981	Terry Pizzaro Ulster Hall, Belfast.	W	TKO 4
Sept 22 1981	Jean Marc Renard Ulster Hall, Belfast.	W	Pts 8
Aug 3 1981	Peter Eubank Corn Exchange Hall, Brighton, England.	L	Pts 8
Jun 20 1981	Gary Lucas Wembley Empire Pool, London.	W	TKO 4
May 10 1981	Selvin Bell Dalymount Park Dublin.	W	TKO 2

DAVE 'Boy' McAULEY

Born June 15, 1961. Larne, County Antrim, Northern Ireland.
Career tally 18-3-2.

RING RECORD.

June 11 1992	Rodolfo Blanco Sports Pavilion Bilbao, Spain. IBF World Flyweight title.	L	Pts 12
Sept 7 1991	Jacob 'Baby Jake' Matlala Maysfield Centre, Belfast. IBF World Flyweight title.	W	KO 10
May 11 1991	Pedro Jose Feliciano Maysfield Centre, Belfast. IBF World Flyweight title.	W	Pts 12
Sept 15 1990	Rodolfo Blanco King's Hall, Belfast. IBF World Flyweight title.	W	Pts 12
March 17 1990	Louis Curtis King's Hall, Belfast. IBF World Flyweight title.	W	Pts 12
Nov 8 1989	Dodie 'Boy' Penalosa. Wembley Grand Hall, London. IBF World Flyweight title.	W	Pts 12
June 7 1989	Duke McKenzie Wembley Arena, London. IBF World Flyweight title.	W	Pts 12
March 26 1988	Fidel Bassa. King's Hall, Belfast. WBA World Flyweight title.	L	Pts 12
Dec 7 1987	Roy Thompson Ulster Hall, Belfast.	W	Pts 10
April 25 1987	Fidel Bassa King's Hall, Belfast WBA World Flyweight title.	L	TKO 13
Oct 20 1986	'Wee' Joe Kelly Glasgow, Scotland. For vacant British Flyweight title.	W	TKO 9
Apl 22 1986	Charlie Brown King's Hall, Belfast.	W	TKO 1
Feb 15 1986	Kelvin Smart Simmonscourt RDS Arena, Dublin	W	DQ 6 (low blow)

June 8 1985	Bobby McDermott	W	TKO 10
	Loftus Road Stadium, London.		
	Eliminator for British Bantamweight Title.		
Feb 23 1985	Johnny Mack	W	TKO 1
	King's Hall, Belfast.		
Dec 10 1984	Graham 'Kid' Clarke	W	TKO 4
	Ulster Hall, Belfast.		
Nov 13 1984	Dave George	W	TKO 6
	Ulster Hall, Belfast.		
Oct 13 1984	John Mwaimu	W	Pts 6
	King's Hall, Belfast.		
Sept 17 1984	Roy Williams	W	Pts 6
	Brighton, England		
Feb 27 1984	Kenny Walsh	D	6
	Albany Hotel, Birmingham, England.		
Jan 25 1984	Ian Colbeck	W	Pts 6
	King's Hall, Belfast.		
Nov 16 1983	Dave Smith	W	KO 1
	King's Hall, Belfast.		
Oct 5 1983	John Mwaimu	D	6
	Ulster Hall, Belfast.		

PAUL 'HOKO' HODKINSON

Born September 14, 1965, Kirkby, Liverpool, England
Career tally 22-3-1

RING RECORD

March 12 1994	Steve Robinson	L	TKO 12
	Cardiff Ice Rnk, Wales.		
	WBO World Featherweight title.		
Apl 4 1993	Gregorio Vargas	L	TKO 7
	National Stadium, Dublin.		
	WBC Featherweight title.		
Feb 3 1993	Ricardo Cepeda	W	TKO 4
	Earls Court Arena, London		
	WBC Featherweight title.		
Sept 12 1992	Fabrice Benichou	W	TKO 10
	Blagnac, Haute-Garonne, France.		
	WBC Featherweight title.		
Apl 25 1992	Steve Cruz	W	TKO 3
	Maysfield Centre, Belfast.		
	WBC Featherweight title.		
Nov 13 1991	Marcos Villasana	W	Pts 12
	Maysfield Centre, Belfast.		
	WBC World Featherweight title.		
Oct 31 1990	Guy Bellehigue	W	KO 3
	Wembley Grand Hall, London.		
	European Featherweight title.		
June 2 1990	Marcos Villasana	L	TKO 8
	G-Mex Centre, Manchester, England.		
	WBC Vacant World Featherweight title.		
March 28 1990	Eduardo Montoya.	W	TKO 3
	G-Mex Centre, Manchester, England.		
Dec 13 1989	Farid Benredjeb	W	TKO 8
	Kirkby Centre, Liverpool, England.		
	European Featherweight title.		
Sept 6 1989	Peter Harris	W	TKO 9
	Port Talbot, Wales.		
	European and British Featherweight titles.		
Apl 12 1989	Raymond Armand	W	TKO 2
	Ulster Hall, Belfast.		
	Vacant European Featherweight title.		
Jan 18 1989	Johnny Carter	W	TKO 1
	Royal Albert Hall, London		

Dec 14 1988	Kevin Taylor Kirkby Centre, Liverpool, England. British Featherweight title.	W	TKO 2
May 18 1988	Peter Harris Port Talbot, Wales. British Featherweight title.	W	TKO 12
Jan 27 1988	Richie Foster Ulster Hall, Belfast.	W	TKO 3
Dec 7 1987	Marcos Smith Ulster Hall, Belfast.	W	TKO 7
Oct 19 1987	Tomas Arguelles Ulster Hall, Belfast.	W	KO 6
July 31 1987	Tomas Arguelles Panama City.	D	8
Apl 25 1987	Russell Jones King's Hall, Belfast.	W	TKO 6
Feb 26 1987	Kamel Djadda York Hall, London.	W	TKO 4
Jan 17 1987	Steve Sims Ulster Hall, Belfast.	W	KO 5
Oct 29 1986	Craig Windsor Ulster Hall, Belfast.	W	KO 2
Sept 29 1986	Les Remikie Mayfair, London.	W	TKO 4
Sept 17 1986	Phil Lashley Royal Albert Hall, London.	W	TKO 2
July 19 1986	Mark Champney Wembley Stadium, London.	W	KO 2

CRISANTO 'Claws' ESPANA

Born October 25, 1964, Venezuela
Career tally 31-1

RING RECORD

March 18 1995	Paul Wesley	W	Pts 6
	Millstreet, Cork.		
June 4 1994	Ike Quartey	L	TKO 11
	Palais Marcel Cerdan, Hauts-de-Seine, France.		
	WBA World Welterweight title.		
Oct 9 1993	Donovan Boucher	W	KO 10
	Old Trafford Stadium, Manchester, England.		
	WBA World Welterweight title.		
May 5 1993	Rodolfo Aguilar	W	Pts 12
	Ulster Hall, Belfast.		
	WBA World Welterweight title.		
Oct 31 1992	Meldrick Taylor	W	TKO 8
	Earls Court, London.		
	WBA World Welterweight title.		
July 3 1992	David Taylor	W	TKO 7
	Seine-et-Marne, France.		
June 11 1992	Kevin Whaley	W	TKO 1
	Sports Pavilion, Bilbao, Spain.		
Nov 12 1991	Hector Hugo Vilte	W	TKO 7
	Maysfield Centre, Belfast.		
	WBC International Welterweight title.		
Sept 7 1991	Newton Barnett	W	TKO 4
	Maysfield Centre, Belfast.		
May 30 1991	Larry McCall	W	TKO 4
	Sports Palace, Madrid, Spain.		
Feb 12 1991	Luis Santana	W	Pts 12
	Maysfied Centre, Belfast.		
	Vacant WBC International title.		
Oct 30 1990	Luis Mora	W	TKO 7
	Maysfield Centre, Belfast.		
Sept 15 1990	Felix Dubray	W	KO 4
	King's Hall, Belfast.		
May 23 1990	Francisco Bobadilla Frasqueri	W	TKO 4
	King's Hall, Belfast.		
March 28 1990	Jorge Hernandez	W	TKO 1
	G-Mex Centre, Manchester, England.		

Feb 21 1990	Delfino Marin	W	TKO 6
	Ulster Hall, Belfast.		
Dec 13 1989	Lloyd Christie	W	TKO 3
	(Retd) Sports Centre Kirkby, Liverpool, England.		
Nov 29 1989	Mario Moreno	W	Disq 1
	Ulster Hall, Belfast.		
Oct 31 1989	Carlos Zambrano	W	TKO 2
	Ulster Hall, Belfast.		
May 10 1989	Del Bryan	W	Pts 8
	Royal Albert Hall, London.		
April 12 1989	Antonio Campbell	W	TKO 2
	Ulster Hall, Belfast.		
March 8 1989	Judas Clottey	W	TKO 2
	Ulster Hall, Belfast.		
Feb 20 1989	Mike Essett	W	TKO 2
	Mayfair, London.		
Jan 25 1989	Billy Buchanan	W	TKO 3
	Ulster Hall, Belfast.		
Dec 14 1988	Gary Pemberton	W	KO 1
	Sports Centre Kirkby, Liverpool.		
Dec 7 1988	Simon Eubank	W	TKO 1
	Ulster Hall, Belfast.		
Oct 19 1988	DavePierre	W	Pts 6
	Ulster Hall, Belfast.		
Feb 21 1987	Rolando Ruiz	W	KO 1
	Panama City.		
Sept 7 1985	Edgar Rodriguez	W	TKO 3
	Caracas, Venezuela		
Oct 10 1984	Jorge Medina	W	TKO 1
	Isla Margarita, Venezuela.		
July 13 1984	Jose Campos	W	TKO 3
	Carupano, Venezuela		
Mar 30 1984	Elias Gonzalez	W	TKO 1
	Ciudad Bolivar, Venezuela.		

VICTOR 'Toby' CORDOBA

Born March 15, 1962, Punta Alegre, Panama
Career Tally 22-6-3

RING RECORD

July 30 1999	Eduardo Rodriguez Panama City.	W	TKO 4
June 17 1996	Leonardo Aguilar Inglewood, California. WBO NABO Light-heavyweight title.	L	TKO 4
Dec 17 1994	Tim Hillie Quito, Ecuador.	W	Pts 8
Nov 30 1993	Lumbala Tshibamba Marseille, France.	L	P 8
June 3 1993	Tony Booth Marseille, France.	W	Pts 8
Jan 30 1993	Michael Nunn Memphis, Tennessee. WBA World Super-middleweight title.	P	Pts 12
Sept 12 1992	Michael Nunn Las Vegas. USA WBA World Super-middleweight title.	L	Pts 12
Dec 13 1991	Vincenzo Nardiello Bercy, France. WBA World Super-middleweight title.	W	TKO 11
April 5 1991	Christophe Tiozzo Marseille, France. WBA World Super-middleweight title.	W	TKO 9
Nov 23 1990	Elvis Parks Marigot, Guadeloupe.	W	TKO 1
July 20 1990	Jean Noel Camara Arles, France.	W	TKO 2
May 23 1990	Frank Rhodes King's Hall, Belfast.	W	Pts 8
Nov 29 1989	Jose Carlos Da Silva Ulster Hall, Belfast.	W	Pts 8
Oct 31 1989	Blaine Logsdon Ulster Hall, Belfast.	W	TKO 2
Sept 19 1989	Abner Blackstock Ulster Hall, Belfast.	L	Disq 2
April 12 1989	Randy Smith Ulster Hall, Belfast.	W	Pts 8

March 8 1989	Anthony Logan Ulster Hall, Belfast.	W	TKO 1
Dec 19 1987	Tomas Polo-Ruiz San Andres, Colombia.	W	TKO 3
Oct 23 1987	Horacio Perez San Andres, Colombia.	W	KO 2
Sept 26 1987	Sigfrido Colorado Panama City.	W	TKO 2
Aug 30 1987	Jario Tovar San Andres, Colombia.	W	KO 7
Apl 10 1987	Dunio Mercado San Andres, Colombia.	W	KO 7
Aug 30 1985	Nestor Flores Panama City. Panamanian and WBA Fedelatin Middleweight titles.	W	KO 3
July 14 1985	Andre Mongelema Monte Carlo, Monaco.	W	Pts 8
March 30 1985	Ramon Matamba Panama City.	W	KO 3
Dec 28 1984	Jorge Montenegro Panama City.	W	KO 2
Nov 18 1984	Felix Rivas Panama City.	W	TKO 3
Oct 16 1982	Felix Rivas Panama City.	D	4
July 7 1982	Nestor Flores Panama City.	L	KO 3
March 5 1982	Felix Rivas Panama City.	D	4
May 30 1981	Felix Rivas Colon City, Panama.	D	4

FABRICE BENICHOU

Born April 5,1966, Madrid. French National. Luxembourg based.
Career tally 46-18-2

RING RECORD

Sept 30 2006	Jorge Samudio David, Panama. WBC Latino Featherweight title.	L	TKO 4
Dec 3 2005	Eduardo Julio Las Tablas, Panama.	W	TKO 4
Jan 31 1998	Spencer Oliver Pickett's Lock, London. European Super-bantamweight title.	L	TKO 4
Nov 29 1997	Martin Krastev Berck-sur-Mer, France.	W	TKO 8
Oct 11 1997	Valentin Dumitru Aubagne, France.	W	TKO 7
Apl 19 1997	Demir Nanev Aubagne, France.	W	TKO 6
Mar 29 1997	Luis Moreno Nord, France.	W	Pts 8
Mar 15 1997	Esteban Perez Quinones Moselle, France.	W	Pts 8
Nov 30 1996	Juan Estupinan Moselle, France.	W	Pts 8
Sept 28 1996	Peter Buckley London, England.	W	Pts 8
Mar 23 1996	Antoine Garcia Nord, France.	W	TKO 5
Feb 17 1996	Mehdi Labdouni Calais, France.	D	10
Apl 29 1995	Arlindo De Abreu Nord, France. French Featherweight title.	L	Pts 10
March 4 1995	Billy Hardy Aisne, France.	D	10
Jan 28 1995	Arlindo De Abreu Allauch, France.	W	Pts 10
Nov 12 1994	Wayne McCullough The Point Depot, Dublin. Republic of Ireland.	L	Pts 10

Sept 30 1994	Lee Cargle Combs, France.	W	Pts 8
Mar 18 1994	Esteban Perez Quinones Beausoleil, France.	W	Pts 8
June 3 1993	Stephane Haccoun Marseille, France.	L	Pts 10
Apl 15 1993	Roy Muniz Nord, France.	W	KO 2
Dec 18 1992	Maurizo Stecca Oise, France. European Featherweight title.	L	Pts 12
Sept 12 1992	Paul Hodkinson Blagnac, France. WBC World Featherweight title.	L	TKO 10
May 29 1992	John Davison Moselle, France. European Featherweight title.	W	Pts 12
Mar 14 1992	Manuel Medina Antibes, France. IBF World Featherweight title.	L	Pts 12
Nov 15 1991	Vincenzo Limatola Gard, France. European Featherweight title.	W	TKO 10
Aug 9 1991	Salvatore Bottigieri Juna-les-Pins, France. European Featherweight title.	W	TKO 8
May 25 1991	John Davison Brest, France. Vacant European Featherweight title.	W	Pts 12
Apl 1 1991	Jorge Alberto Pompe Monte Carlo, Monaco.	W	Pts 8
Feb 16 1991	Darryl Jones Deauville, France.	W	KO 1
Feb 2 1991	Ben Baez Manche, France.	W	TKO 7
Oct 18 1990	Luis Enrique Mendoza Bercy, France. WBA World Super-bantamweight title.	L	Pts 12
Aug 17 1990	Amos Cowart Nice, France.	W	KO 2
Mar 10 1990	Welcome Ncita Tel Aviv, Israel. IBF Super-bantamweight title.	L	Pts 12

Oct 7 1989	Ramon Cruz	W	Pts 12
	Bordeaux, France.		
	IBF Super-bantamweight title.		
June 10 1989	Frans Badenhorst	W	TKO 5
	Lazio, Italy.		
	IBF Super-bantamweight title.		
Mar 10 1989	Jose Sanabria	W	Pts 12
	Limoges, France.		
	IBF Super-bantamweight title.		
Jan 20 1989	Jose Gallegos	W	Pts 8
	Limoges, France.		
Dec 9 1988	Isidoro Medina	W	KO 2
	Aveyron, France.		
Nov 21 1988	Miguel Pequeno	W	Pts 8
	Forges, France.		
Nov 7 1988	Raymond Armand	L	Pts 8
	Paris, France.		
Sept 26 1988	Jose Sanabria	L	TKO 10
	Eure-et-Loir, France.		
	IBF Super-bantamweight title.		
June 24 1988	Alberto Contreras	W	TKO 3
	Las Vegas, USA.		
June 6 1988	Efren Chavez	W	Pts 8
	Las Vegas, Nevada.		
Apl 13 1988	Vincenzo Belcastro	L	KO 3
	Liguria, Italy.		
	European Bantamweight title.		
Jan 30 1988	Thierry Jacob	W	KO 9
	Calais, France.		
	Vacant European Bantamweight title.		
Nov 21 1987	Sonny Long	W	Pts 8
	Bercy, France.		
Oct 5 1987	Vncente Fernandez	W	Rtd 1
	Paris, France.		
Jul 6 1987	Haidar Nourredine	L	TKO 3
	Differdange, Luxembourg.		
Jun 23 1987	Shane Sylvester	W	Pts 8
	Paris, France.		
Apl 27 1987	James Tolliver	W	KO 1
	Paris, France.		
Mar 14 1987	Jean Paul Guillard	W	TKO 3
	Paris, France.		
Feb 13 1987	Moussa Sangare	L	TKO 6
	Rhone, France.		

Feb 6 1987	Rocky Lawlor Antibes, France.	W	KO 1
Jan 31 1987	Kelvin Smart Montpellier, France.	W	TKO 1
Nov 28 1986	Jose Otero Toulon, France.	W	Pts 8
Nov 3 1986	Juan Ramon Muriel Paris, France.	W	Pts 8
Sept 15 1986	Fernando Beltran Paris, France.	L	Pts 8
July 4 1986	Jalleleine Mastouri Lombardia, Italy.	W	Pts 6
May 9 1986	Abdulac Diane Sassari, Sardinia.	W	TKO 4
Feb 8 1986	Jesse Williams Miami Beach, Florida.	W	TKO 7
Nov 16 1985	Humberto Moreno Panama City.	W	TKO 3
July 19 1985	Gerardo Rodriguez Colon City, Panama.	W	Pts 4
June 15 1985	Ernesto Ford Panama City.	L	Pts 6
Oct 5 1984	Jose Chacon Barinas, Venezuela.	L	Pts 6
Aug 7 1984	Corrado Infanti Fallonica, Italy.	W	Pts 6
July 19 1984	Claudio Tanda Pistoia, Italy.	W	Pts 6

FIN